SHARON
Massachusetts
•
A History

Sharon American Revolution Bicentennial Committee
Sharon, Massachusetts

BLUE MUSTANG
P R E S S
Boston, Massachusetts

Sharon's Town Seal

Sharon's Town Seal was originated by Solomon Talbot in 1893. In his letter to the Selectmen he wrote: "I propose to place upon the Corporate Seal . . . the following devices; first, copies of natural scenery in the town viewed from a distance; secondly, emblems of incidents in the history of the town that shall characterize the individuality of the town as you would describe it in words."

In the left quarter of the shield is the outline of Moose Hill, the second highest point of land between Boston and Providence. The farm buildings shown typify the homesteads of farmers who tilled the rich lands between Moose Hill and the lake. In the field of the shield is beautiful Lake Massapoag, an Indian name meaning "Great Waters." In the right quarter is shown the gun house of the Sharon Artillery Company. This was the organization which elected Elijah Billings as Captain in 1781, and used the old gun house for an armory for nearly 50 years.

For the crest of the seal, Mr. Talbot chose two cannons crossed upon a pile of cannonballs to commemorate the industry established before the Revolutionary War by Edmund Quincy and Col. Richard Gridley, who cast the first cannon made in America to be used in that conflict.

To complete the description of the seal, a belt buckled and knotted at the base surrounds the shield bearing the words "2nd Precinct, 1740," the year of ecclesiastical separation from Stoughton, and "Sharon 1765" to record the political separation when it was incorporated as a district from part of Stoughton.

For the 1976 Edition:

© Copyright — Sharon American Revolution Bicentennial Committee 1976

Design and Layout by Joseph F. Mahoney

LIBRARY OF CONGRESS
CATALOG CARD NO.: 76 - 46882

For the 2005 Edition:
© 2005 by Sharon Historical Society.

ISBN: 0-9759737-3-8
PUBLISHED BY BLUE MUSTANG PRESS
www.bluemustangpress.com
Boston, Massachusetts
Printed in the United States of America

SHARON
Massachusetts
•
A History

Foreword to the 2005 Edition

The Sharon Historical Society is proud to present a reprinting of the Bicentennial book, *Sharon Massachusetts, A History*. This popular and unique volume was written by a number of individuals who volunteered as part of the National Bicentennial celebration of 1976 to write chapters on areas of interest and expertise.

The result is a volume that has been immensely popular, but went out of print immediately after 1976. A number of the authors have since moved or passed away. Their recollections, stories and research are preserved in this book and are now available again.
The so-called "Red Book" has been a favorite resource for those interested in Sharon's history. Forty-five chapters cover subjects from the "First Americans" to town government, religious institutions, schools, recreation, conservation, transportation and cultural groups of the 1970s. The history and lore of the town is collected in this volume by the lively contributions of these volunteer authors.

The Society has always recognized the value of this book. When we were approached by Blue Mustang Press to reprint it, we seized the opportunity. We are excited that we can share this book with today's readers of Sharon history.

The Bicentennial Committee's publication of the original book in 1976 re-kindled interest in local history. Under the leadership of a group including Chandler Jones, Karl Gelpke, Herb and Marilyn Gagnon, Katharine Cartwright, Karen Goober, Gordon Hughes and Barbara and Michael Riccards, the Sharon Historical Society was re-born in 1981. The original Society existed from 1903-1923. The notes and artifacts from that organization were the beginnings of the present day Society's collection.

Since 1981 the Society has grown in membership, run a capital campaign, obtained a 99 year lease from the town and constructed the present museum. Located on the site of the former High Street School, it opened to the public in 1999. We have catalogued thousands of artifacts, photos, letters, diaries, books and other material on Sharon history and feature additions. periodic public exhibits. We receive new items for the collection weekly and welcome further. The Society runs quarterly informational and social events, publishes an informative newsletter and maintains a website at www.sharonhistoricalsociety.org. Members of the Society work with the Sharon Public Schools on local history education.

It is the mission of the Society to educate, preserve and promote the history of Sharon. We hope this volume will find a wide readership. We hope, as well, that it will, as it did in its first incarnation, spark a wider interest in Sharon and its history.

The Sharon Historical Society
Sharon, Massachusetts
November 2005

CONTENTS

FOREWORD

This history of our town has been written and published by its citizens for the Sharon American Revolution Bicentennial Committee as part of our celebration of the two hundredth anniversary of the birth of the nation. Each chapter is identified as to its author. As in all enterprises, the book could not have been completed without the support and endeavors of many whose names do not appear as chapter authors. These people have supplied us with information, research, recollections and materials. Their help has been invaluable. Notable among them:

Robert W. Alence
Rachel Baker
Rev. Osmond J. Billings
Frank Chase
Arthur Collins
Eleanor Connors
Everett Downing
Suzanne Gray
Dr. Walter Griffin
William B. Keating

John L. Keeling
Louise P. Leavitt
Florence Gannett Moody
William Morgan
Hazel D. Morse
Henry L. Munson
Lawrence Peck
Carl Smith
Philip Stolar
Otis Tolman

Staff of the Sharon Public Library

The Sharon American Revolution Bicentennial Committee was appointed by the selectmen and was charged with developing and carrying out activities to commemorate the event. Members of the Committee are:

Chandler W. Jones, Chairman
Sydney S. Morgan, Vice-chairman
Dorothy Porter, Secretary
John T. Connors, Jr.
Karl A. Gelpke
Doris A. Gladstone

Gordon L. Hawes
Robert Levy
Dwight R. Pelton
Walter L. Reeve
Harold Schneiderman

The Friends of Sharon American Revolution Bicentennial Committee were organized to help raise additional funds in support of the bicentennial program. Members of the Friends are:

i

John Herburger,	Chairman
John Urann,	Treasurer
Mary Colaneri,	Secretary
Phyllis Brookfield, Laurie Durocher	
Lois Dole, Marilyn Goldberg	

The program of activities has been as follows:

June 28, 1973 — First meeting of the Sharon American Revolution Bicentennial Committee.

June 13, 1974 — Board of Selectmen reactivated the Sharon Militia Company.

November 12, 1974 — Presentation of "Sons of Liberty" at Junior and Senior High School.

April 14, 1975 — Opened Annual Town Meeting in colonial dress and read excerpts from minutes of 200 years ago. Assisted by the militia.

June 1975 — Bicycle tour of Easton on the 7th and Walpole on the 8th.

July 5, 1975 — Participated in the Independence day parade with the militia.

August 16-17, 1975 — Two day country fair.

October 18, 1975 — Sponsored the Deborah Sampson Bicentennial Women's Road Race with Sharon Road Runners Club.

December 1975 — Board of Selectmen proclaimed December 14 through December 20, 1975 as "Deborah Sampson Week". The week included wreath-laying ceremonies at her grave, full day arts festival, presentation of the play written and directed by William Appell and narrated by Pauline Moody, "She Was There", and the entertainment marathon.

March 1976 — An historical tour map of Sharon was distributed to every home in town.

April 12, 1976 — Opened Annual Town Meeting in colonial dress and read proclamation, adopted by the Great and General Court of the Colony of Massachusetts Bay, and read at town meeting 200 years ago. Assisted by the militia.

May 1976 — Signed the Wagon Train scroll, a "Pledge of Rededication" and delivered to Wagon Train for journey to Valley Forge.

June 1976 — Youth Council fire hydrant painting contest.

June 12, 1976 — Observance of National Flag Week at town office building.

July 4, 1976 — Participated in nationwide communicy bell-ringing at 2 PM, the moment in history in 1776 when the Liberty Bell proclaimed the signing of the Declaration of Independence. Participated in the parade with the militia.

August 1976 — Official opening of Old Post Road Park.

August 21-22, 1976 — Two day country fair.

September 18, 1976 — Bicentennial Ball.

November 15, 1976 — Publication of hard-bound volume. *Sharon, Massachusetts — A History*

The Bicentennial Committee undertook two projects with matching funds supplied by the Commonwealth: (1) The placing of plaques on houses of historic significance showing the date of construction and the original or best known owner and the installation of descriptive signs at sites of historic interest (2) The construction of a small park and picnic area adjacent to the Old Post Road and called "Old Post Road Park".

An historic tour map of Sharon was published with the help of the "Friends" and matching funds made available by the Norfolk County Development and Tourist Council.

The "Friends" with the Committee had two medals struck to commemorate Sharon's bicentennial. One medal honoring Deborah Sampson-Patriot, Woman Soldier of the Revolution with her portrait and the other showing a cannon with the words, Stoughtonham — Sharon, Where First Cannon Used In Revolution Were Cast.

In addition to these events, The Fortnightly Club of Sharon, Inc. produced a beautiful quilt illustrated in this volume and described as follows:

Designed by Louise D. Wentworth and executed by talented Club members, the quilt depicts in fine needlework the history of the Town. The project was initiated and planned by Marjorie Dunn, and carried forward by Marianne Glazier and Elizabeth Newcomb. Proceeds from the sale of tickets established a permanent Bicentennial Scholarship Fund for the youth of Sharon.

Marjorie Dunn, Edwina Andrews, Marianne Glazer, Elizabeth Newcomb, Louise D. Wentworth

Long-time residents will recognize the Old Town Hall (1883-1964) in the square done by Nikki Erkelens Surr; the East School House (the third in this location near Bay Road since 1766) by Isabelle Burlingame; Sharon Square (showing the old watering trough and Pettee's first store) by

Marianne Glazier and Laura Blickensderfer; and the Old Railroad Station by Marianne Glazier.

Landmarks and old homes illustrated are the Morse House (built in 1805 by Aaron Fisher with bricks brought as ballast from England and transported by oxcart from Taunton to Sharon) by Laura Blickensderfer; Cobb's Tavern (1740 in East Sharon. Here Jonathan Cobb opened the Town's first post office in 1819) by Ruth Preus. Hewins House (built in 1785 by the Hewins family) by Edwina Andrews; Savel House (erected ca 1730 — has seven fireplaces and a space in which to hide from the Indians) by Kate Foley; Unitarian Church (the third meeting house in this location) by Nancy Hays; Lake Massapoag by Katharine Cartwright; Pumping Station (earliest was 1838; present one 1896) by Laura Moore.

Other quilt squares show Revere Bells (the one in the Unitarian Church was cast by "Paul Revere & Son" in 1811; the one in the Congregational Church, in 1833 by "Revere Boston") by Emma Callahan; Town Seal (designed by Solomon Talbot) by Edwina Andrews; Deborah Sampson (soldier, lecturer, forerunner of Women's Lib.) by Laura Blickensderfer; Mann's Mill (1856) by Lillian Crossman; Revolutionary Cannon (cast at Stoughtonham Furnace on Gavin's Pond) by Elizabeth Cilley; Audubon Birds (representing the Audubon Society's first Massachusetts Sanctuary which is in Sharon) by Miriam Roselund; Sharon Industries (including shoe making, manufacturing of cutlery, and bottling of bitters) by Laura Moore; and Dr. Griffin's Car Climbing Moose Hill (a 1903 Franklin) by Emma Callahan.

Sharon is fortunate to have citizens whose talent and willingness combined to produce this volume. Material is included which illuminates its earliest years, and other which narrates the activities of its people and its government in recent times.

KARL A. GELPKE,
Chairman of History Book Committee
and Coordinating Editor

September 13, 1976

PROLOGUE

By Sidney F. Morgan

Sharon, "A better place to live because it is naturally beautiful," has evolved in two hundred years from a farming community, to a thriving industrial center, and finally to the suburban residential town that it is today.

Located eighteen miles south of Boston, capital of the state, and ten miles from Dedham, the county seat, it is bounded on the north by Norwood and Canton; on the east by Stoughton; on the southeast and south by Easton, Mansfield, and Foxborough; and on the west by Walpole.

Occupying the height of land between Boston and Providence, the town covers 24.31 square miles. Access is provided by two exits from Route I95, a limited access interstate highway, and by Route 1, both roads running in a north-south direction. Route 27 traverses the town from east to west. Train service to Boston and Providence is provided by Conrail.

Topography

The surface of Sharon is diversified and uneven and increases in height from the level of Traphole Brook on the northwest to an elevation of 302 feet above sea level at Post Office Square. Moose Hill, (Elev. -534') in the westerly portion, is the second highest point of land between the waters of Massachusetts and Narragansett Bays. Rattlesnake Hill (Elev. -430') on the east, Cow Hill and Bearfoot Hill on the south complete the highlands which almost ring the town.

Nestled in between these hills is Lake Massapoag, a spring fed lake covering approximately 400 acres, which is Sharon's greatest natural asset.

Geologically, Sharon is located in an area marked physically by glacial drumlins and kames, and by the beds of the original streams that flowed from the glaciers that at one time covered this part of the state. The land varies between two extremes, from rocky hilltops composed of Gloucester Stony Loam, with bedrock at or near the surface, to the glacial stream beds in which the course of centuries has built up substantial deposits of muck and peat, often to a depth of many feet.

Gloucester Stony Loam is composed on glacial drift derived mainly from granite and gneiss, with stone fragments and boulders up to several feet in diameter scattered on the surface and through the soil. The glacial deposit is shallow with bedrock cropping out in numerous places. The bedrock is syenite, which is like a granite except lacking the quartz component.

The richness of the soil in the ancient stream beds attracted the early settlers who farmed the land.

Services

Water today is obtained from five wells driven to an average depth of 65 feet, pumped to standpipes at the higher elevations to obtain pressure, and delivered by gravity to metered users.

Electricity is provided by the Boston Edison Company since Sharon is within their franchise area. Distribution throughout the town is 13,200 volts and is almost all overhead construction with pole mounted transformers providing the lower use voltage to the householder.

Dial telephone service is provided by the New England Telephone and Telegraph Company from an automated, unattended central station located on High Street. Distribution to subscribers is on joint use poles with the electric utility.

Newer developments in town have been designed with direct buried cables and pad mounted transformers to present a more pleasing appearance with increased reliability to the home owner.

Mail deliveries are made once a day from the Post Office located on South Main Street.

Government

With a 1975 population of 13,512, Sharon is still able to govern itself by means of an open town meeting. Administration is carried on by a board of three selectmen elected for three year terms. Day to day operation is by a full time executive secretary.

A twelve member Warrant Committee, elected at and by the town meeting, supervises the fiscal affairs of the town, investigating and making recommendations for action by the town on articles entered in the annual warrant.

Three elected Assessors evaluate the property in the town and set the tax rate based on the amount of money voted at town meeting. The 1975 tax rate was $51.00 per $1,000 property valuation. Total taxable property in town is valued at $134,788,930. In addition, untaxed property, that belonging to charitable organizations, the town, etc. is valued at $20,687,130.

The Municipal Office Building on South Main Street serves as the center for town government with offices for the Executive Secretary; the Treasurer/-Collector; the Town Accountant/Clerk; the Public Works Department; the Board of Assessors; and the Veterans' Agent. Meeting rooms are provided for the other established boards and committees such as the Planning Board; the Board of Appeals; Civil Defense; Conservation Commission; the Housing Authority; and the Personnel Board. Police and Fire Departments are located in a joint use building adjacent to the Municipal Office Building.

School Department administration is conducted from a converted school now serving as offices located on School Street.

The Recreation Department is located in the Sharon Community Center off Massapoag Avenue at the southerly end of the lake.

Civil History

The town of Dorchester originally included Milton, Canton, Stoughton, Sharon, Foxborough, and a part of Dedham.

All that part of Dorchester "beyond the Blue Hills" was set off from Dorchester in 1726 under the name of Stoughton after William Stoughton, one of the Dorchester Company, who was the lieutenant-governor appointed by the crown. This included Canton, which was the first parish; Sharon, the second parish; and Stoughton itself, which was the third parish.

Sharon progressed from a "Second Precinct" of Stoughton, to the District of Stoughtonham, to the town of Sharon over a period of forty-three years in the mid part of the 18th century.

The first settler in the area built a tavern called the "Wainman's Ordinary" about 1657 on the Old Post Road southwest of Wolomolopoag Pond. This area was called Pole Plain at the time, and was a midway stop for travellers from Boston to Providence. By 1661 there were about thirty families living in the vicinity. Ebenezer Billing's Tavern later located southeast of Wayman's Ordinary served the 18th century traveller in the same way. In addition it provided a community center for the people who had settled in the Pole Plain. Most had left Dorchester because of the high taxation necessitated by King Philip's War.

In 1740 the inhabitants of the area petitioned the governor to be set off as a separate town or precinct because it was too far to go to the nearest church at Canton Corner. The Colonial laws required support of and attendance at public worship on Sunday.

Their petition:

To His Excellency, Jonathan Belcher, Esq., Captain-General and Governor-in-Chief in and over His Majestie's Province of the Massachusetts Bay, in New England, and the Honorable, His Majestie's Council and House of Representatives of the General Court assembled at Boston, on the eighth day of June, 1739.

The petition of John Hixson and Benjamin Johnson, committee to prefer a petition to this court in behalf of the subscribers, inhabitants of the Southerly part of Stoughton, humbly sheweth:

Whereas, by the Providence of the all-disposing God, our lots are fallen to us at so great a distance from the Public worship of God, in the North part of the said town, that your petitioners cannot ever, without great difficulty, attend the public worship of God; Wherefore we have petitioned the town once and again, to be eased of the great difficulties we now labor under, but have been by them rejected, notwithstanding the great length of way which some of your petitioners live from the public worship in the North Part, about eight or nine miles; and in consideration of our great duty to attend the public worship of God, not only ourselves, but by our families and children, which, by the blessing of God, are greatly increased; Therefore, your petitioners have of late petitioned this Honorable Court to be set off a separate Town or Precinct, but this Honorable Court did not see cause to grant the petition. The reason, as we humbly conceive, was the answers to the petition, which were wrong and erroneous.

Therefore, your petitioners humbly pray that this Honorable Court, to see with your own eyes, by sending a committee to view the circumstances, at the charge and cost of the petitioners; that this Honorable Court may be rightly informed, and see the unjust proceedings of the Honorable respondents, and their fallacious answers to our former petitions; and as your petitioners are obliged by conscience and law to attend the worship of God, they have, by a free contribution, maintained preaching among themselves for a considerable time. Notwithstanding they have paid their proportional part to the North Part, where they can have but little or none advantage.

We would beg leave to inform this Honorable Court that since we have had preaching among us, it has encouraged some well minded persons to come and settle within the limits herein petitioned, and, if it should please the Honorable Court to grant our petition, it would be a great encouragement to a great many more, if your petitioners were in a capacity to have the ordinances of God administered among them; and your petitioners having had some experience, by their having maintained preaching among themselves, they look on themselves as able to maintain the worship of God.

Your petitioners, therefore, humbly pray this Honorable Court that they would please to send a committee to view our circumstances, that so your petitioners may be put into a capacity that they may have the ordinances of our Saviour settled among them, in a regular order, by setting them off as district, and separate town or princinct, viz.

(Here are given the bounds of the towns of Sharon and Foxboro.)

We humbly beg leave here to say, that what we now offer in respect to our being set off, is in sincerity for the promoting of the worship of God and religion in its purity among us.

Wherefore, we pray your Excellency and Honors would be please to hear our request, and grant our petition, and as we in duty bound, shall ever pray.

Benjamin Estey	Joshua Johnson
Timothy Tolman	Josiah Perry
Isaac Cummings	Eliakim Perry
John Smith	John Noyes
William Colwell	Eleazer Hawes
Samuel Cumings	Job Swift
William Richards	Jacob Estey
Samuel Estey	Daniel Richards
Samuel Dwelley	Joshua Whittemore
Nathaniel Coney	Ebenezer Hewins
Pelatiah Whittemore	Edward Belcher
Eleazer Puffer	Jeremiah Belcher
Joseph Ingraham	Matthew Hobbs
Samuel Lovel	Clifford Belcher
Matthias Puffer	Ephraim Payson

Abraham Chandler	Samuel Bird
Ebenezer Estey	Thomas Randall
William Webb	Thomas Rogers
Mayhew Tupper	Ebenezer Capen
Stephen Holland	William Wood
Benjamin Perry	Nathan Clark.

The respondents to this petition say:

The petitioners have used a great deal of craft in the course they have pursued, inasmuch as the town now owes the minister about eighty pounds, and the town has just laid out nearly one hundred pounds, in building a road for the petitioners to go to meeting, and now, not satisfied, they have built a church near their own doors, and ask to be set off as a Town, or Precinct.

The committee to whom the subject was referred came upon the premises, examined the circumstances, and reported the prayer of the petitioners ought to be granted.

The report was accepted, and the Second Precinct was set off and received the signature of Governor Belcher, July 2, 1740.

The words parish and precinct are used interchangeably in the old records because church and state were considered one. Thus by becoming the "Second Precinct" of Stoughton, the residents had achieved ecclesiastical separation, but were still bound politically to their mother town.

By 1765, the residents of the Second Precinct, having increased in number and in wealth, again ambitiously tried to become a town. Their petition to the General Court did not accomplish everything that they had hoped. They were granted the status of District, by the name of Stoughtonham on June 21, 1765. While this had the effect of separating them politically, they still had to share their representation to the General Court with Stoughton.

AN ACT FOR INCORPORATING THE SECOND PRECINCT, IN THE TOWN OF STOUGHTON, IN THE COUNTY OF SUFFOLK, AS IT NOW IS, INTO A DISTRICT BY THE NAME OF STOUGHTONHAM.

WHEREAS the inhabitants of the second precinct in Stoughton labour under great difficulties by reason of their distance from the place where the town-meetings are held in the said town,—

Be it therefore enacted by the Governor, Council and House of Representatives,

[SECT. 1.] That the second precinct in the town of Stoughton, by the same bounds and limits which the said second precinct now have, be and hereby are incorporated into a separate district by the name of Stoughtonham; and that the inhabitants thereof be vested with all the powers, privileges and immunities which the inhabitants of any town within this province do or by law ought to enjoy, excepting only the privilege of sending a representative to the general assembly; and that the inhabitants of said district shall have liberty, from time to time, to join with the town of Stoughton in the choice of a representative or representatives, which representatives may be chosen indifferently from said town or district, the pay or allowance of such representatives to be borne by the said town and district, according to their respective proportions of the province tax; and that the town of Stoughton, as often as they shall call a meeting for the choice of representatives, shall, from time to time, give seasonable notice to the clerk of the said district of Stoughtonham, for the time being, of the time and place for holding said meeting, to the end that the said district may join therein; and the clerk of said district shall set up, in some publick place in said district, a notification thereof accordingly.

Provided, nevertheless, —

And be it further enacted,

[SECT. 2.] That the said district shall pay their proportion of all such province, county and town taxes already granted to be raised in the town of Stoughton, and shall also bear their proportionable part of supporting the poor of the town of Stoughton that are at this time relieved by said town: *provided,* that the district of Stoughtonham shall not be liable to maintain any persons within the same who have been legally warned out of the town of Stoughton, but, by virtue of said warning, shall have the same privilege of removing such persons as the town of Stoughton could have in case they had remained therein.

And be it further enacted,

[SECT. 3.] That the town of Stoughton shall pay to the said district of Stoughtonham, yearly, and every year, their proportionable part of the income of all the money that is appropriated to the use of the school in Stoughton, and also their proportionable part of said Stoughton's part of the yearly profits and incomes of two farms that were appropriated by the town of Dorchester to the use of the school, one of which is now annexed to the town of Dedham, commonly called White's Farm, the other is now annexed to the town of Wrentham, and commonly called Hewes's Farm; all of which incomes and profits the said district of Stoughtonham shall be intitled to, and receive of the town of Stoughton, yearly, and every year, in the same proportion as they now pay their part of the province tax in said town. And be it further enacted,

[SECT. 4.] That Joseph Hewins, Esq., be and hereby is impowered to issue a warrant, directed to some principal inhabitant in said district, requiring him to warn all the inhabitants in said district, qualified to vote in town affairs, to meet, at such time, and place within said district, as he shall think proper, to chuse all such officers as towns, by law, are intitled to chuse.   [*Passed June* 21.]

It was ten years later (August 31, 1775) that an act of the Great and General Court elevated all districts in Massachusetts into towns.

[AN*] ACT DECLARATORY OF THE RIGHT OF CERTAIN TOWNS AND DISTRICTS IN THE COLONY OF THE [MASSACHUSETTS*] BAY, IN NEW ENGLAND, TO

ELECT AND DEPUTE A REPRESENTATIVE, OR REPRE-
SENTATIVES, TO SERVE FOR AND [REPRESENT TH*]EM
IN ANY GREAT AND GENERAL COURT OR ASSEMBLY
AT ANY TIME TO BE HELD AND KEPT FOR THE SERV-
ICE OF THE SAID COLONY.

WHEREAS there are divers acts or laws heretofore made and
passed by former general courts or assemblies of this colony, for
the incorporation of towns and districts, which, against common
right, and in derogation of the rights granted to the inhabitants of
this colony by the charter, contain an exception of the right and
priviledge of chusing and sending a representative to the great and
general court or assembly, —

Be it therefore e[nac*]ted [and dec*]lared by the Council and
House of Representatives in General Court assembled, and by the
authority [of the same,*]

[SECT. 1.] [Tha]t* henceforth every such exception contained
in any act or law heretofore made and passed by any [general*]
court or assembly of this colony, for the erecting or incorporating
any town or district, shall be held and taken to be altogether null
and void; and that every town and district in this colony, consisting of the number of thirty or more freeholders and other inhabitants, qualified by charter to vote in the election of a representative[s], shall henceforth be held and taken to have full right,
power and privilege to elect and depute one or more persons, being
freeholders and resident in such town or district, to serve for and
represent them in any great and general court or assembly
hereafter to be held and kept for this colony, according to the
limitations in an act or law of the general assembly [entitled "An
Act *] for ascertaining the number and regulating the house of
representatives;" any exception of that [right and *] priviledge
contained or expressed in the respective acts or laws, for the incorporation of such town or district notwithstanding.

And be it further enacted and declared by the authority
aforesaid,

[SECT. 3.] That every corporate body in this colony which in the
act for the incorporation thereof is said and declared to be made a
district, and has, by such act, granted to it, or is declared to be
vested with, the rights, powers, priviledges or immunities of a
town, with the exception of above mention[e]d of chusing and
sending a representative to the great and general court or assembly, [shall hence *] forth be, and shall be holden, taken and intended to be, a town to all intents [and purposes *] whatsoever.
[Passed August 23.

On March 11, 1776, the town voted that the selectmen shall petition to
have the name of the town altered to Washington, in honor of George
Washington. This petition was not granted because a town in the Berkshires
had beaten them to the name.

Finally, on February 25, 1783, an act of the legislature gave them the name
of Sharon.

AN ACT FOR DISCONTINUING THE NAME OF A TOWN IN THE COUNTY OF *SUFFOLK*, INCORPORATED BY THE NAME OF *STOUGHTONHAM*, AND CALLING THE SAME *SHARON*.

Be it enacted by the Senate and House of Representatives in General Court assembled, and by the Authority of the same, That the said Town of *Stoughtonham,* shall no longer bear that Name, but henceforth shall be called and known by the Name of *Sharon;* the aforesaid incorporating Act notwithstanding. And all Officers in said Town shall hold and exercise their respective Offices in the same Manner as they would have done had not the Name of said Town been altered.

February 25, 1783.

And Sharon we have been ever since.

Separation of church and state did not occur until 1822. The theological differences between the Trinitarian and Unitarian philosophies caused a separation in the church, which in turn caused confusion and strife in the civil ranks. Which was now the true state church? The legislature solved the problem by issuing an order that the towns choose their officers independently. Since then, the town and church have been distinct and separate organizations.

SHARON
Massachusetts

A History

King Philip's Rock - by Tradition This Great Leader of His People Met with His Sachems Here

Photo by: C. W. Jones

INDIANS, FIRST AMERICANS IN SHARON

By Mary D. Wade

CHAPTER 1

The native Americans whose territory included the present town of Sharon gave the state of Massachusetts its name. The Massachusetts Indians, along with the Abnaki, Narragansett and Wampanoag tribes, occupied New England when the white settlers first came. These tribes had as a common denominator the Algonquin language.

The word *massachusetts* has been translated in two ways. In the Algonquin language, where adjectives are combined with nouns into one word, the name can be broken down into "Massa" (large), "Wadchu" (hill) and "eset" (place).[1] In the pronunciation of the "place-of-the-great-hill" one syllable is lost. Many persons believe this interpretation refers to the Great Blue Hill in Canton. Certainly the Blue Hills are on every map of early New England, beginning with that of John Smith, which called them the Cheviot Hills.

Another translation breaks the word down as "Mos" (arrow) "Wachusett" (hill-place). This reference is believed to be an arrow-shaped hill close to Squantum on the Neponset River, a place where the sachem of the Massachusetts Indians had his home when the English arrived.[2] Another early map printed in William Wood's *New England's Prospect* in 1633 shows the "Naponsett River" with "Chicatobot sagamore" living close by. The town of Dorchester is also shown.

Chicataubut ruled a territory of some 800 square miles around Massachusetts Bay. It extended southward to Wampanoag territory (just south of Sharon), westward to the Narragansetts (Rhode Island) and northward to the Abnaki (Maine).

Chicataubut consented to the settlement of Dorchester. The original town, first established in 1630, had as its southern boundary the top of Blue Hill. However, in 1637 the court gave to Dorchester all the unallotted land from Blue Hill to a point near the Plymouth Colony line and westward to the grant made to Dedham. This territory included Sharon, Foxborough, Stoughton, and Canton.

The 40,000 acres lying "beyond the Blew Hills" was called the Dorchester New Grant after 1707. It first came into possession of the English in 1666, when the Massachusetts Indians deeded to them all the land beyond the Blue Hills to the "utmost extent thereof." They reserved for themselves Punkapog Plantation.[3]

Some confusion about the date of the deeds for this land comes from the fact that the General Court confirmed these deeds in 1720, and many deeds bear that date although the original transactions may have been in the century preceding.

The Massachusetts' undisputed territory extended as far south as Massapoag Pond here in Sharon. However, the ownership of the land between the lake and the Plymouth Colony line was not clear. Josias Wampatuck, Chicataubut's son, had had a controversy with the Wampanoags about it. The land became the subject of a meeting between Metacom, sachem of the Wampanoags, and Squamaug, acting sachem of the Massachusetts after Josias Wampatuck's death. Metacom is known better by the name King Philip, given to him by the English at the request of his father Ousemequin, or Massasoit.

Philip was a shrewd, able leader of his people and had become very concerned over the growing number of white settlers. He had observed that it was the English custom to pay the Indians for the land they took. The settlers had been very careful to try to obtain full title in their purchases. Not only were deeds signed by the Indian chief, but also by the person occupying the land at the present time.

This was because the Massachusetts Colony had a policy of making grants for new towns subject to any Indian claim. Persons buying property were advised to purchase the title from any Indian claiming the land. This policy was formulated to keep good relations between the two groups and to avoid charges of taking away Indian hunting grounds.

Philip, seeing that the settlers were taking more and more land from his people, used the purchase policy to his advantage where he could. One example occurred in Wrentham, where in 1662 he sold six square miles to the settlers. Seven years later he again claimed ownership of part of that land and asked for payment. He had enough of a case that he was paid the second time.[4]

A year later in 1670 he asked Dorchester for payment of the area south of Lake Massapoag. Squamaug, acting for the Massachusetts Indians, felt that the Wampanoags had no claim to the territory and wrote a letter of complaint to Captain Hopestill Foster, selectman for Dorchester.

Philip then asked for a meeting; consequently Captain Foster arranged for one to take place in the disputed territory in what is now Foxborough, at "Captain Hudson's farm at Wading River."[5]

On a map made in 1716 the Hudson house was shown as the only one in present-day Foxborough limits. His nearest neighbor to the north was Capt. Ebenezer Billings, whose tavern was on the Old Post Road at the Sharon-Foxborough line.[6] The Hudson house was burned in 1719 by Indians, fifty years after Philip and Squamaug's meeting there.

The outcome of the meeting at Hudson's farm was that the boundary was set at the Plymouth Colony line, which today marks the southern boundary of Norfolk County. In Sharon it is the line between our town and Mansfield.

It seems odd that a white man's boundary would be chosen to mark an ancient Indian territorial ground. Several reasons may be given. For one thing it was to the advantage of the Dorchester men that the boundary be set so that they did not again have to pay for the land. Also, it seems natural that Plymouth Colony, on the northern edge of Wampanoag territory, would have bought land to the end of that tribe's jurisdiction.

The traditional view of the Indian leading a nomadic life was not true in New England. There seemed to be a fairly well-established territory for a tribe. Within this area there was a place of summer residence and a winter residence.

The fact that the Indians did not stay in one place led the early settlers to believe that these "camps" were abandoned. Such was not the case. In accordance with the need for food and with the change of seasons, the Indians moved from place to place.

The spring was spent close to the fields where they grew maize, the staple of their diet. The summer was spent at the seashore gathering various forms of seafood. The fall called for a few weeks spent hunting, and the winter was spent at an interior valley.

Chicataubut, the Massachusetts' grand sachem, had a warm weather home called Squantum at the mouth of the Neponset River on Dorchester Neck in what is now South Boston. The tribe he lived with were called the Neponset Indians. His planting fields were close by, and he sometimes resided at Wessagusett (now Weymouth) and a place called Titicut (Bridgewater — Taunton, although that is much farther south than his other territory). Winter quarters for the Neponset Indians were at Milton Lower Falls where the salt and fresh waters meet on the Neponset River. The Indians called this place Unquety.[7]

It would be easy to assume that the handful of Pilgrims and the rather sizeable Puritan groups were surrounded by hordes of Indians, but such was not the case. At the time of the settlers' arrival, the area was not well populated.

An estimate of 25,000 Indians has been given for the year 1600, but the epidemic of 1616-17 had devastated the ones of the Massachusetts Bay area.[8] Although the Abnaki and the Narragansetts and to a great extent the Wampanoags in southeastern Massachusetts and Cape Cod had escaped the plague, it reduced the Pennacooks to such an estate they were no longer a force for the white settlers to be concerned about.

The Massachusetts Indians have been numbered as 3000 in 1615. By 1630, their wars with the Abnaki and the severe epidemic depleted them to a mere 500 persons.[9]

The nature of the disease has been the subject of speculation. Daniel Gookin, who had many opportunities to observe the native Americans, actually talked with Indians who witnessed the sickness. "I have discoursed with some old Indians, that were then youths; who say, that the bodies all over were exceeding yellow, describing it by a yellow garment they showed me, both before they died, and afterwards."[10]

The most likely explanation for the jaundice coloring would seem to be hepatitis. This disease of the liver causes a yellow color in its victims. One major source of hepatitis is contaminated shellfish. Since shellfish were a staple of the Indians' diet, especially in the summer, it would be interesting to know whether the disease first came at that time of the year, but the information is not available to us.

Although the Indians Gookin conversed with were Pawkunnawkutts (and he says the year was 1612-13), he states that the same disease struck the Massachusetts.

Into the vacuum created by the decrease of native population moved the English, whom the Massachusetts tribe welcomed for their manpower and firearms.

Ousemequin (Yellow feather), the Wampanoag chief whom the Pilgrims called Massasoit, made a pact of peace which he faithfully kept. Chicataubut, the Massachusetts sachem, along with six other sachems, signed a pledge of loyalty to King James in 1621. Although it is doubtful that they really understood what they were signing, the Indians certainly were not feeling threatened at this point.

The political organization of the northeast Indians was under hereditary chiefs. The terms *sachem* and *sagamore* were used almost interchangeably by the English; the native Americans used the term *sachem* almost exclusively. Today, the stated difference is that *sagamore* means prince, while *sachem* means king. Whatever the term used, there were in the political organization minor sachems who owed loyalty to grand sachems. The Punkapog Indians were descendants of the Neponset tribe whose local sachem had been Chicataubut.

Chicataubut, whose name means "house afire,"[11] was also the Massachusetts' grand sachem when the English arrived. Although he was one of the nine sachems who pledged loyalty to King James in 1621, ten years later he was reported by Thomas Dudley of the Massachusetts Bay Colony as the sachem who "least favoreth the English of any Sagamore we are acquainted with, by reason of the old quarrel between him and those of Plymouth, wherein he lost seven of his best men."[12] Chicataubut died in 1633 of smallpox, leaving several small children.

Cutshamequin ("big feather") assumed leadership as regent for Chicataubut's son.[13] Cutshamequin (also spelled Cutshamache and Kitchmakin) was Chicataubut's brother. In 1636 he sold to Dorchester the territory south of the Neponset River to the Blue Hills.[14] He also signed papers of submission to the Massachusetts Bay Colony in 1644.[15]

Wampatuck ("wild goose").[16] Chicataubut's son also known as Josias Chicataubut and as Josias Wampatuck, finally became old enough to assume his place as sachem. He sold the district around Quincy in 1665.[17] The men of Dorchester were not completely satisfied with the deed formerly given for their land and asked Wampatuck for a confirmation of their earlier deed. He promised this but died before it could be given.

Prior to his death Wampatuck had appointed Job Ahauton as his attorney. On December 10, 1666, Job Ahauton granted to Dorchester all the land beyond the Blue Hills within the Dorchester grant, reserving for the Indians Punkapog Plantation.

Wampatuck's son, Charles Josias, confirmed that sale of the Dorchester New Grant.[18] This son, also known as Wampatuck, received payment for the site of Boston and neighboring islands in 1685.[19]

Squamaug, acting as regent for Wampatuck's son Jeremy, confirmed in 1670 the deed given by Job Ahauton to the town of Dorchester.[20] He is also the one who met that same year with Philip to settle the boundary controversy between the Massachusetts and Wampanoags. Squamaug seems to have been a brother of the first Wampatuck. It is not clear whether Jeremy is the same person as Charles Josias, the second Wampatuck.

The signing of deeds by the last few sachems was merely a formality. After 1657 the Neponset tribe of the Massachusetts Indians had ceased to live on this land; they had been removed to Punkapog Plantation.

4

As the settlers took more and more of the land, it became a problem to know what to do with the Indians. Solutions ranged the whole gamut from absorbing them into English society to providing a separate place for them. Cotton Mather held the former opinion when he wrote in his diary in 1718:

> A Projection to putt out as many of the Indian children, as tis possible unto English and godly families, is what I would now prosecute, as most likely to answer all good intentions for the next generation among them.[21]

The Massachusetts Bay Colony had appointed overseers for the Indians, among them William Stoughton whose property bordered Punkapog Plantation. A friend of Stoughton, Judge Samuel Sewall, a frequent visitor to Sharon's Billings Tavern and more widely known for his participation in the Salem witch trials, was involved in some of the legal work for the Indians. In 1700 he had been appointed one of the commissioners of Indian Affairs in the New World. He wrote to Sir William Ashhurst, suggesting a separate place for the Indians, with natural boundaries such as rivers and mountains:

> Except this be done, I fear their own Jealousies, and the French Friers, will persuade them, that the English, as they encrease, and think they want more room, will never leave till they have crowded them quite out of all their lands. And it will be a vain attempt for us to offer Heaven to them, if they take up Prejudices against us, as if we did grudge them a Living upon their own Earth.[22]

Sewall's proposal for English policy toward the natives in the New World may have been influenced by the ideas of John Eliot fifty years earlier. Eliot had a genuine concern for the Indians as a people. He felt they would be better off if separated from their English neighbors.

Eliot, minister of the church in Roxbury, had sought earnestly to convert the Indians. He made a diligent effort to learn their language and then proceeded to translate a Bible for them. The Indians who became his followers were called "praying Indians," and the places he established for them were called "praying towns."

Natick, established in 1650, was the first "praying town." Eliot had begun his work there by preaching every other Thursday. His success among the natives led to the establishment of Natick. Indian influence declined there during the next one hundred years, but it was 1781 before it ceased to be Indian.[23] This did not take place until after Crispus Attucks, a Natick Indian, had become a victim of the Boston Massacre. Although Attucks' mother was black, his Indian father's name meant "deer" in the diminutive form.[24]

The second "praying town" was Punkapog. It was established because Natick house lots were all assigned and because the Neponset Indians did not wish to be there. John Eliot petitioned the Dorchester selectmen to set aside a place for them.

> Though our poore Indians are much molested in most places in their meetings in way of civilities, yet the Lord hath put it into

your hearts to suffer us to meet quietly at Ponkipog, for w^h I thank God, and am grateful to yourselfe and all the good people of Dorchester. And now that our meetings may be the more comfortable and favorable, my request is, y^t you would please to further these two motions: first y^t you would please to make an order in your towne, and record it in your Towne record, that you approve and allow ye Indians of Ponkipog there to sit downe and make a towne and to injoy such accommodations as may be competent to maintain God's ordinances among them another day. My second request is, y^t you would appoint fitting men, who may in a fitt season bound and lay out the same, and record y^t alsoe.[25]

Eliot had been preaching to these Indians on alternate Thursdays. It is interesting that his request included provision for a public record of the setting aside of the land. The town acted favorably on his request in 1657. Punkapog was set off, 6000 acres in what is now the north part of Canton.

Daniel Gookin left this description of Punkapog:

The next town is Pakemitt, or Punkapaog. The signification of the name is taken from a spring, that ariseth out of red earth. This town is situated south from Boston, about fourteen miles. There is a great mountain, called the Blue Hill, lieth north east from it about two miles: and the town of Dedham, about three miles north west from it. This is a small town, and hath not above twelve families in it; and so about sixty souls. This is the second praying town. The Indians that settled here, removed from Neponsitt mill. The quantity of land belonging to this village, is about six thousand acres; and some of it is fertile, but not generally so good as in other towns. Here they worship God, and keep the Sabbath, in the same manner as is done at Natick, before declared. They have a ruler, a constable, and a schoolmaster. Their ruler's name is Ahawton; an old and faithful friend to the English. Their teacher is William Ahawton, his son; an ingenious person and pious man, and of good parts. Here was a very able teacher who died about three years since. His name was William Awinian. He was a very knowing person, and of great ability, and of genteel deportment, and spoke very good English. His death was a very great rebuke to this place. This town hath within this ten years, lost by death several honest and able men; and some have turned apostates, and removed from them: which dispensations of God have greatly damped the flourishing condition of this place. Here it was that Mr. John Eliot, junior, before mentioned, preached a lecture once a fortnight, for sundry years, until his decease. In this village, besides their planting and keeping cattle and swine, and fishing in good ponds, and upon Neponsitt river which lieth near them; they are also advantaged by a large cedar swamp; wherein such as are laborious and diligent, do get many a pound, by cutting and preparing cedar shingles and clapboards, which sell well at Boston and other English towns adjacent.[26]

William Ahauton was spoken of in 1670 by John Eliot as a "promising young man, of simple and upright heart, and good judgment. He prayeth and preacheth well. He is studious and industrious and well accounted of among the English."[27] The name of William Ahauton and his father appear on the parchment deed of Boston, 1685.

The Punkapog town was not as large as the one in Natick. In 1674 there were 150 Indians at Natick, while Punkapog had only 60.[28] Over one hundred years later, 1784, the Stoughton tax list shows fifty-two Punkapog Indians (21 male, 31 female).[29] Seventy-five years after that in 1849 there was only one full-blooded Punkapog Indian.[30] By 1861 there were 117 descendants listed.[31]

The Punkapog Plantation was gradually absorbed by the whites surrounding it, especially as the population dwindled. In 1921, Indian Lane in Canton, near York Pond, was the center of the Indian residences. Descendants of these Indians continue to live in Canton and surrounding communities, but their distinctiveness as Indians is gone.

The Plantation which once extended from the present Route 128 southward to where Massapoag Brook crosses Washington Street in the center of Canton's business district is now represented by the small village of Ponkapoag in the shadow of the Blue Hill. The language of these people is also gone. An interview with Mary Chapelle, a Punkapog descendant in 1921, revealed that Mrs. Chapell's mother died in 1919 at the age of ninety and she could not speak the language. Mrs. Chapelle did not think her mother had ever heard it spoken.[32]

The native Americans who met the English settlers made uniform good impressions on the white men. Because a number of the early explorers and settlers wrote down their feelings, we have a fairly good picture of the life of the Indians. It would be extremely interesting if we had accounts of the Indians' impressions of the newcomers, but unfortunately the lack of a written Indian language in that day makes it impossible.

Almost without exception the early contacts were pleasant, and persons such as Roger Williams, Thomas Morton and Daniel Gookin speak highly of Indian hospitality. Roger Williams recorded, "There is a favor of civility and courtesie even amongst these wild American, both amongst themselves and toward strangers."[33]

Gookin stated, "They are much given to hospitality in their way. If any strangers come to their houses, they will give him the best lodging and diet they have; and the strangers must be first served."[34] Some of the Pilgrim Fathers took a trip into Ousemequin's territory, were treated with every courtesy, including a huge common bed, but left almost faint with hunger, not because the Indians refused to feed them, but because there simply was no food to eat.

As dangerous as it is to try to assign a national character to a race of people, the general impressions of the early writers cannot be ignored. And even though they judged the natives by the European standards they themselves carried, the writers' comments were most often good.

Seemingly everyone who saw these native Americans was impressed with their physique. John Smith spoke of their fine appearance. William Wood gave a graphic description to this fellow Englishmen in 1634:

> Of their Stature, most of them being betweene five or six foote
> high, straight bodied, strongly composed, smooth skinned, merry

countenanced, of complexion something more swarthy than Spaniards, black hair'd, high foreheaded, blacke ey'd, out-nosed, broad shouldred, brawny arm'd long and slender handed, out-brested, small wasted, lanke bellied, well thighed, glat kneed, handsome growne leggs, and small feete.[35]

This description sounds like something being advertised for sale, and perhaps Wood was trying to sell Englishmen on the idea of the new colony. The fact remains that the Indians' stature had to impress the rather short Europeans. In fact, over one hundred years later John Adams commented in a letter to Thomas Jefferson in 1812 about some Indians he had known:

Aaron Pomham the priest and Moses Pomham the King of the Punkapaug and Neponset tribes were frequent visitors at my fathers house —at least 70 years ago. I have a distinct remembrance of their forms and figures. They were very aged and the tallest and stoutest Indians I have ever seen.[36]

What evidence then is there of Indians within the town of Sharon? For one thing, arrowheads have been found in widely scattered sections of town — Mountain Street, East Street and Gunhouse Street.

When the Brothers of the Sacred Heart decided to dig a skating pond on the property now known as Deborah Sampson Park, their excavation netted a number of arrowheads which were mounted into a display.

A collection of arrowheads has been recovered near the Fish and Game Club Pond at the end of Billings Street and has been donated to the library.

The Drake family descendants have record of the Mattakesett Indians living about one-fourth mile off Morse Street near the old Morse homestead. These Indians moved from Sharon to Duxbury. There is a tradition of Indians having lived on what is now Highland Street.

Some years ago several unmarked graves in Rock Ridge Cemetery were investigated. It was discovered that three of the graves were Indians buried in the pauper section during colonial days.

A very interesting piece of evidence remains in the Tolman family. The Tolmans were among the earliest owners of property in Sharon. When the deed for their property on Mansfield Street was signed, the old Indian chief gave to the Tolmans a stone pestle which he told them to use to grind herbs if they were ever sick. The deed signed by the Indians was carefully preserved in a specially built cane with a hollow place in it. The deed has gone to one branch of the family. The stone pestle is in the possession of those members of the family still residing in Sharon. The pestle is about fifteen inches long, 3 inches in diameter, very smooth and rounded on one end, the other end shaped to fit the grip of the hand.

Indian names provide another evidence — Massapoag, Wolomolopoag, and Maskwonicut. The word Massapoag means "large swamp." Mashapoag Cedar Swamp and Mashapaog Pond are both shown on the map first surveyed in 1696 and completed in 1726, called "A Map Plat or Draught of the Twelve Divisions of Land, as they were Laid out, Bounded & Measured to ye Pfoprietors in Dorchester New Grant, beyond ye Blew-Hills."

Maskwonicut, which means "great white trail," may have referred to birch trees. On the 1696 map there is a portion of land east of Moosehill and north of Massapoag Pond which was sold to Matthew Hobbs. The brook running through it has been called Hobbs Brook and now is called Beaver Brook. A note on the old map states, "Within these lines is a meadow called Maskwonicut Meadow not belonging to ye lot sold."

The word Wolomolopoag is very interesting. "Deep pleasant water" has been given as its translation, but a problem arises because the Algonquin language has no "l" in it. The word, however is very similar to Wollomonopoag, the Indian name for the town of Wrentham. The translation of that name is given as "place of shells" — perhaps a reference to freshwater mollusks in Lake Pearl or Lake Archer. The Wolomolopoag Pond in Sharon appears without name in the correct place on the 1696 map.

One other place with an Indian name is Mohawk Hill, shown on a map originally laid out in 1713 and completed in 1730. This map is called "A Map or Plot of the Twenty-five Divisions of Land (so called because a Single Division or each Proprietor's Proportional part which was determined before the Quantity of Land to be laid out was known, Doubled Twentyfive times to take up all the Land that was to be laid out) late in ye Township of Dorchester and now in the Township of Stoughton, it being part of that Land commonly called Dorchester New Grant beyond the Blew-Hills."

Perhaps the most famous Indian place in Sharon is an interesting rock formation off Mansfield Street. This spot is considered to be the place where sachems of various tribes met to plan strategy in the uprising known as King Philip's War, 1675-76. At the present time preparations are underway to have the area preserved as an historic site.

Although Indian place-names remain in the town, nowhere in our town meeting records is there any reference to Indians, either as a group or as individuals identified as such. There probably is nothing strange in this because the records date from 1765, over one hundred years after Punkapog Plantation was provided for the Neponset Indians. It is also true that the Indians took English names and therefore would lose identification.

It is interesting to note, however, that in the census ordered by Congress in 1776 there is a column listing the "No. of Negroes & Molatoes in Each family." This document, the original of which is at the town hall, shows a total of 1271 "souls in Stoughtonham." Eleven were listed as black persons. There is no mention of Indians.

It is possible to find persons of Indian descent in Sharon, but the culture they represent has been absorbed and obliterated in the nearly 350 years since the Dorchester Proprietors bought the land from the Massachusetts Indians. A few names and a few momentos are all that remain of these first Americans.

Footnotes

1. Louis A. Cook, ed., *History of Norfolk County, Massachusetts, 1622 - 1918* (New York: S. J. Clarke, 1918), 13.
2. Hutchinson, *History of Massachusetts*, Vol. I, p. 402 quoted in William Dana Orcutt, *Good Old Dorchester, A Narrative History of the Town*, 1630 - 1893 (Cambridge: The University Press, 1908), 66.
3. *Massachusetts State Papers*, Vol. XXX, *Indians*, pp. 131 - 133 as found in Canton Historical Society, File C2.6, D2.

4. Cook, 21.

5. Dorchester Antiquarian and Historical Society, *History of the Town of Dorchester, Massachusetts* (Boston: Ebenezer Clapp, Jr., 1859), 220.

6. Clifford W. Lane, *That Was Forborough!* (Foxborough, Massachusetts: Rea-Craft Press, 1966), 10.

7. William Dana Orcutt, *Good Old Dorchester, A Narrative History of the Town*, 1630 - 1893 (Cambridge: The University Press, 1908), 65.

8. Alden T. Vaughan, *New England Frontier, Puritans and Indians*, 1620 - 1675 (Boston: Little Brown and Company, 1965), 28.

9. *Ibid.*, 54.

10. Daniel Gookin, *Historical Collections of the Indians in New England* ("Collections of the Massachusetts Historical Society for the Year 1792"; Boston: The Society), 148.

11. Frank G. Speck, *Territorial Subdivisions And Boundaries of the Wampanoag, Massachusetts And Nauset Indians* ("Indian Notes and Monographs" Edited by F. W. Hodges. No. 44. A series of publications relating to the American Aborigines; New York: Museum of the American Indian. Heye Foundation, 1928), 95.

12. Typed source reported from *The New England Historical and Genealogical Register, III* (1849), 332.

13. Dorchester Antiquarian and Historical Society, 11.

14. Speck, 103.

15. Vaughan, 342.

16. Speck, 97.

17. *Ibid.*

18. *Massachusetts State Papers*, Vol. XXXI, *Indians*, 2, p. 24 as found in Canton Historical Society, File c2.6, D2.

19. Speck, 97.

20. Dorchester Antiquarian and Historical Society, 218.

21. Cotton Mather, *Diary of Cotton Mather*, 1709 - 1724 ("Massachusetts Historical Society Collections, 7 ser." VIII; Boston: The Society, 1912), November 21, 1718.

22. Samuel Sewall, *Letter Book of Samuel Sewall* ("Collections of the Massachusetts Historical Society, 6 ser." I, pp. 231 - 232; Boston: The Society, 1886), May 3, 1700.

23. Vaughan, 321.

24. Speck, 137.

25. Orcutt, 65.

26. Gookin, 184.

27. Typed source in Canton Historical Society, File C2.6, D82.

28. Speck, 12.

29. Typed source in Canton Historical Society, File C2.6, D81.

30. *Report of the Commissioners Relating to the Condition of the Indians*, 1849 quoted in Dorchester Antiquarian and Historical Society, 13.

31. Speck, 8.

32. Speck, 141.

33. Roger Williams, *The Complete Writings of Roger Williams, I*, quoted in Vaughan, 43.

34. Gookin, 153.

35. Wood, quoted in Vaughan, 41.

36. John Adams, *John Adams Works*, Vol. X, p. 19 as copied in Canton Historical Society, File C2.6, D60.

Ancient Farm Site of the Billings' Family, Friend of the Indian   *Courtesy of: D. E. Clapp*

The Old Post Road

Photo by: J. K. Harris

TRAILS, TALES AND TAVERNS

By Mary D. Wade

CHAPTER 2

A narrow path climbs out of the cranberry bogs at the Sharon-Foxborough line. Not far up the rise is an ancient cellarhole. These remnants mark a post road whose origin is lost in antiquity. Across town a picturesque tavern and stone mile-markers are reminders of another post route known in early colonial days as the Way by Dry Pond. Running diagonally between these two is Sharon's Main Street — a road which is nearly ready to celebrate its Tricentennial.

OLD POST ROAD

The post road from Boston to New York undoubtedly started as an Indian trail. In time it also bore the name of the "Roebuck Trail," a tavern by that name having stood on the corner of Old Post Road and Coney Streets in Walpole.[1]

This early route forms part of Sharon's present western border. It then enters the town at the intersection of Route One and Walpole Street. In colonial times it branched at this point — the eastern section running over Walpole Street under Bluff Head to South Main Street. The western branch went along the edge of Moose Hill, dipped into the eastern edge of the cranberry bog at South Main and Interstate 95, and then turned to follow Mechanic Street into Foxborough.

On an undated map showing the land along the Neponset River in Dedham and Dorchester, this route is called "The Contray Road."[2] The map shows the "Ponset Bridge." This bridge was first built in 1652 by Henry Woodward and Roger Billings, the father of Ebenezer Billings, who ran Billings tavern on the route fifty years later.

Post roads were established to carry mail between the colonies. As early as 1673 post service by way of Springfield had run between Boston and New York, but the route lasted only a few months due to the Dutch take-over of New York and the unrest caused by King Philip's War.[3]

In the 1690's the colonists, prompted by the French and Indian War, again felt a need for closer contact. On May 1, 1693, a weekly post between Portsmouth, New Hampshire, and Williamsburg, Virginia, was estabished. The route chosen was the Country Road. Old Post Road was the First National Highway in America.[4]

Beginning in Portsmouth, the route went through Newbury, Ipswich, Salem, Marblehead, Lynn, Boston, Dedham, Rehoboth, and down to Bristol Ferry. From Bristol a ferry carried post and passengers to Newport. From here they rode to Mantunuck, New London, New Haven, New York, Brooklyn, Staten Island, Amboy, Burlington, Philadelphia, New Castle (Maryland) and James City (Virginia).[5]

Between Boston and New York there was a shuttle. The post rider went from Boston to Providence, New London and Saybrook, Connecticut. There he met the "mail man" from New York, exchanged mail with him and returned to Boston.[6]

Along the route the post rider not only delivered the mail and spread local news, he often had other duties assigned. Frequently he conducted travelers on their journeys. This, however, should not conjure up pictures of a driver with a coach-and-four. Announcement of the post departure at three a.m. meant just that. If a person wished to ride with the post, he must hire his own horse and would then accompany the post rider along the way. This service was free of charge — in line with the post rider's sworn duty to act always in the public good.

Guiding travelers was not time consuming, but brokerage and express activities could be. The post rider sometimes bought and sold bank notes and lottery tickets and even did shopping in the city for villagers.[7] The post rider also might conduct a special delivery service. One incident is recorded of a post rider conveying cattle for a customer.[8]

The Wainman's Ordinary

The 1794 map of Sharon shows the Old Post Road. A map based on the 1794 map has an interesting superinscription drawn in 1904 by Robert Tappan. At the point where the stream coming out of Wolomolopoag Pond turned to run through the cranberry bog, an "X" marks the site of the Wainman's Ordinary.

The term "ordinary" is an obsolete one meaning "inn" or "restaurant." The Wainman's Ordinary, whatever it was, was an identifying landmark in the southern part of early Dorchester. According to Solomon Talbot, Sharon historian at the turn of the century, the building was the shelter constructed by the immigrants from Dorchester who set out for the Connecticut Valley in October of 1635.[9] Stopping on a height of land between Massachusetts and Narragansett Bays, they built a shelter while the men were clearing a better path through the woods for them and their cattle.

Talbot's research showed Mrs. Rhoda Gore and Lieut. John Remington (whom she later married) came to the Wainman's Ordinary while getting lumber to finish the Roxbury meeting house.[10] That same year, 1658, the Dorchester selectmen appointed two men

> to require Mris Goer that she doe Desist from making any vse of any land at ore neare Wainmans ordinarie or any wher else in Dorchester for buildinge making of hay ore any other use.[11]

The first colonial owner of the land in the area was Roger Billings, the elder. This Roger Billings is mentioned quite often in the Dorchester Records as a person who built roads and bridges.

As previously mentioned, in 1652, he along with Henry Woodward was commissioned to build a bridge across the Neponset River, in present-day Norwood.

> The 8 day of the 6 mo:
> It is agreed by and betweene the Select Men for the towne of Dorchester for the tyme being and Roger Billinges and Henry Woodward of the same towne that the said Roger and Henry shall make a bridge over the river of Norponsit in the way leading from Dedham vnto Rehoboth sufficient and stronge the said bridge to be in bredth fower foote standing vpon three sufficient trussells being three foote high betwen the ioyntes or their abouts, and duble brased, the peeces that tye over to be very well pinned and fastned also a rayle on either side about twoe foot and a halfe high from the bridge. In Consideration whereof thay ar to have five poundes to be paid out of the next towne rate for the rayles of each side the bridge they are to be paid for over and above — to whic agrement we have subscribed our handes:
> > Rob[t] Howard with the consent and in the
> > name of the rest of the select men.
> > Roger Billing
> > Henry X Woodward
> > his marke[12]

The following year they were paid six pounds each for the bridge.[13]

In the succeeding years Roger Billings was called upon to build roads and cartways and to protect public property. He built a cartway between Milton and Squantum Neck and received five pounds for it.[14] He and Henry Leadbetter were empowered by the selectmen to keep residents from carting away stones from Squantum Neck[15] and to keep trespassers off Cedar Swamp around Braintree.[16] In 1670 he was chosen as one of five men "to Run the line from the top of the blew hill betwen Brantry and vs; and soe home to Plimoth line."[17]

It is not certain at what point Roger Billings first saw the area he later received as a farm, but it was certainly before 1672. A reference to his farm is given when the Dorchester selectmen leased on June 28, 1672,

> vnto Samuell parker of Deadham for this year all that Meaddow vp in the Contry neer to woodcocks well, which formerly he did vs to Mow Saveing what was laid out latly to Roger Billeng.[18]

In 1673 the Dorchester selectmen again leased meadowland, this time

> vnto John Farrington of Deadham all that Meadow vp in the Contray neer vnto the three hundred acres which Captain William Hudson had by Contract of Dorchester Select men; that Farme being excepted, and roger Billeng his farme lately laid out, the rest of the Meadow we do lett vnto the fore said John Farrington.[19]

By 1674 intruders had begun to encroach on this area so far removed from the settlement of Dorchester.

9 (9) 74 The same day it was Concluded by the Select men for the time being that shalbe, Shall Commence an action against some of thos that have entered vpon o^r lands beyond Wainmans ordinary and about wadeing river and bring it to a tryall and p'secut it to effect.[20]

The next year saw the beginning of King Philip's War. The people in outlying areas such as Wrentham returned to their former homes (Dedham, in the case of Wrentham), but the Billings seem to have stayed in this area. A folk tradition states that Indians on their way to burn Medfield in May, 1676, did not attack the Billings farm. The story relates that this was because of the friendship between Metacom (Philip) and Captain Ebenezer Billings.

The story has some basis in the fact that there was no recorded problem at the Billings farm during this troubled period. However, Ebenezer was only twenty-one years of age at the time — quite young to have established such a friendship. Nevertheless, he undoubtedly did live on the property, was married and had a son one year old.[21]

It seems more likely that Roger Billings, the elder, was head of the household. Two years after Metacom's death, Roger Billings asked the town of Dorchester for a deed to his farm.

At a publique Towne meeting the 15-11-78 being legally warned and Come together. It was Voted in the affirmatiue that (at the motion of Roger Belleng) the Select men should Sige a deede vnto him of the farme he had of the towne lying about Wainmans Ordinary and to secuer it to him from the towne and their Successors.

. . . .

The same day the Select men Signed to Roger Billeng Senr a deede of the farme about Wainmans Ordinary.[22]

It was not until 1682, however, just a year prior to his death, that Roger Billings received from Elisha Menunion, William Ahauton and James Maumition, Indians, a deed to seven hundred acres of land.[23] This followed the Massachusetts Bay Colony practice of securing deeds from both the Indians and the English.

In the meantime, Roger Billings had been appointed one of the "Commissioners of the Contry Rate" in 1675 and again in 1680.[24] In 1680 he was also appointed one of the twelve tithingmen for the town,[25] a job he held for the next four years, until his death. Interestingly enough after skipping 1684, the name of Roger Billings again appears as tithingman in 1685, undoubtedly carried on by his son.

Billings Tavern

Roger Billings, the elder, had two sons — Ebenezer, born in 1655, and Roger, born 1657. (His oldest son, Joseph, died in 1679 and his youngest son, Jonathan, had died two years before that.)[26]

Both Roger and Ebenezer were active in Dorchester town affairs. Roger was chosen in 1686 to "run the boundaries between Dedham and Dorchester."[27] From the period 1684 to 1686 Ebenezer Billings was on a committee appointed to work out the apportionment of the common land beyond the Blue Hills.[28] The assignment for Ebenezer kept him in the part of town where he lived — in the Dorchester New Grant.

At the death of Roger Billings, senior, in 1683, both sons were executors of his will. After specific grants were made to other relatives, Roger and Ebenezer were to share his estate equally, with a slight added amount given to Ebenezer.

> The Last will and Testament of Roger Billing Sen[r] within the bounds of Dorchester. I Roger Billing afores[d] in the County of Suffolke in New England liveing at m[r] Glovers Farme being senceible of bodily weakness and decay of body but of good and sound understanding and memory being desirous to Set my house in order do constitute and appoint this my last will & Testament.
>
> . . . .
>
> My whole Estate remaining after the former perticulars are taken out, I give to my Son Ebenezar and Roger to bee equally divided whether houseing household Stuffe or Land whither in Boston, Dorchester or houseing and land at Wainmans Ordinary or any other Estate either in this Jurisdiction that either doth or may to me appertain an[d] belong now or hereafter, with all my cattle horses Sheep Leases or revertions wth my Cartes wheeles chains and debts due to me, and all my Carpentry tooles and other movables and whatever did belong to me, my Sloope and little Boate and every thing thereto belonging and every thing that is mine whither mentioned or unmentioned I give all to my two Son's Ebenezar and Roger who have been very helpfull to me and tender in my old age: I do hereby constitute and appoint my two Son's Ebenezar and Roger Billing joint Executo[rs] of this my last will and Testament . . . when I say I appoint my two Sons Ebenezar Billing and Roger Billing Executo[rs] my meaning is that the two shall Administer and take my whole Estate into their hands with my Booke of Accounts and all my Deeds and writings which they are best acquainted with and all my Servants whither maid or men I commit to my two Son's Ebenezar and Roger Billing and all my Corne whither on the ground or in the house or any else that is mine wherever it bee, it is my will that my Son Ebenezar Billing have ten pounds out of my movables more than my Son Roger, and that the whole of my Estate bee then equally divided between Ebenezar and Roger Billing . . . Upon consideration of what I have done for my Son Roger more then for Ebenezar I can do no less than make that ten pounds formerly expressed, twenty pounds to my son Ebenezar more then Roger out of my Estate: . . .
>
> Roger Billing & a Seale[29]

In dividing the estate, Ebenezer then became owner of the property around the Wainman's Ordinary, together with the buildings. The house of Captain Ebenezer Billings is drawn on the Map of the Twenty-five Divisions of the Dorchester New Grant, as is the house of his son, Captain Billing, Junior. The senior Billings house must have been impressive — it is twice as large as any other house drawn on the map.

The site of Billings Tavern was in the northwest corner of the parking lot for the shopping center at the intersection of Interstate 95 and South Main Street. The building and its additions were obliterated by the parking lot and the relocation of South Main Street.

In its day the tavern was a regular stop for travelers on the post road. Judge Samuel Sewall, the diarist, mentions it many times, the first one about Billings farm being in a tragic report of a storm.

> July 15, 1685. One Humphry Tiffiny and Frances Low, Daughter of Anthony Low, are slain with the Lightning and Thunder about a mile or half a mile beyond Billinges Farm, The horse also slain, that they rode on, and another Horse in the Company slain, and his Rider who held the Garment on the Maid to steady it at the time of the Stroke, a coat or a cloak, stounded, but not killed. Were coming to Boston.[30]

The judge himself began regular visits to the tavern five years later.

> April 21, 1690. Mr. Stoughton and I set forward for New York . . . refreshed at Roxbury, Billinges and from thence rid to Rehoboth.[31]

Their return on May 8 notes a stop at Billinges also.[32]

The tavern so far removed from the meeting house in Dorchester was not overlooked by the church when they voted in 1696 to notify the General Court that they wanted only persons of "improved integrity" to be licensed, and they felt one tavern, besides Mr. Billing's and Mr. White's, would be sufficient for the town.[33]

About the time of the Dorchester church action, Judge Sewall began almost yearly visits on his way to hold court in Bristol, Rhode Island.

> Sept'r 9, [1695]. Set out for Bristow. . . . Baited at Neponset, din'd at Billeges, where were also Mr. Newton and Mr. Cary; went to Woodcock's, refreshed there so to Rehoboth.
> . . . .
> Sept 13, [1697]. We rid to Dedham and refreshed there: Dined at Billenges. Lodged at Child's at Rehoboth.
> . . . .
> Sept'r 27, [1699] [on the return]. Govenour Winthrop sets out for Boston, Pole of the Calash broken by the Horses frighted with a pistol. The making of a new one takes up an hour or two.
> Sept'r 28. Set out at 7 *mane*. Dine at Billenges. Set out at 2. Get to Dedham by 5.[34]

The calash of which he speaks is a two-wheeled [ehicle with a top. The stage still had not come into existence for public use. These small conveyances were very popular.

Sewall missed by two weeks being at Billings Tavern when Madam Sarah Kemble Knight came through on her famous journey. Her diary, recording her trip to New York in 1704, is a caustic record of the situations she encountered.

She relates in great detail her trouble in getting to Billings and how the accommodations did not particularly suit her.

> Monday, Octob^r ye second, 1704. — About three o'clock afternoon, I begun my journey from Boston to New Haven; being about two Hundred mile. My Kinsman, Capt. Robert Luist, waited on me as farr as Dedham, where I was to meet ye Western post.
>
> I vissitted ye reverd, Mr. Belcher, ye Minister of ye town, and tarried there till evening, in hopes ye post would come along. But he not coming, I resolved to go to Billingses where he used to lodg, being twelve miles further: ....
>
> In about an how^r, or something more, after we left the Swamp, we come to Billingses, where I was to lodg. My Guide dismounted and very Complasantly helpt me down and shewd the door, signing to me wth his hand to go in, wch I Gladly did but had not gone many steps into the room, ere I was interogated by a young Lady I understood afterwards was the eldest daughter of the family, with these, or words to the purpose. (Viz) Law for mee — what in the world brings You here at this time a night? I never see a woman on the Rode so Dreadfull late, in all the days of my versall life. Who are you? Where are you going? I'me scar^d out of my witts with much now of the same kind. I stood aghast, Preparing to reply, when in comes my Guide — to him Madam turn^d, Roreing out: Lawful heart John, is it You? — how de do! Where in the world are you going with this woman? Who is she? John made no Ans^r. but sat down in one corner, fumbled out his black Junk, and saluted that instead of Debb; she then turned agen to mee and fell anew her silly questions, without asking me to sitt down.
>
> I told her she treated me very Rudely, and I did not think it my duty to answer her unmannerly Questions. But to get ridd of them, I told her I had come there to have the post's company with me tomorrow on my Journey, &c. Miss star'd awhile, drew a chair, bid me sitt, And then run upstairs and putts on two or three Rings, (or else I had not seen them before,) and returning sett herself just before me, showing the way to Redding, that I might see her Ornaments, perhaps to gain the more respect, But her Ganam's new Rung sow, had it appeared, would affected me as much. I paid honest John wth money and dram according to contract, and Dismist him, and pray'd Miss to shew me where I must Lodg. Shee conducted me to a parlour in a little back Lento, wch was almost filled with the bedsted wch was so high that I was forced to climb on a chair to gitt up to ye wretched bed that lay on it: on wch having Stretcht my tired Limbs, and lay'd my head on a Sad-colored pillow, I began to think on the transactions of ye past day.
>
> Tuesday, October ye third, about 8 in the morning, I with the Post proceeded forward without observing anything remarkable.[35]

Zipporah, the eldest Billings daughter, was twenty-five years old at the time Madam Knight came as a late-night guest at the Tavern. Ten days later Zipporah was married to Samuel Man at Wrentham.[36]

Further Sewall diary entries show that in September of 1706, he again dined at Billings Tavern.[37] And the following year the tavern entertained newly-weds. Judge Sewall attended a party for two couples, one of which had come through a rainstorm and had lodged at Billings on their journey from Rehoboth. The bride had excused herself for the evening.[38]

Other entries show an annual visit and a growing friendship with Ebenezer Billings.

> Sept[r] 16, [1708]. [returning from Bristol] Dined at Rehoboth. Bait at Devotion's; get to Billinges a pretty while after Sun-set, where we lodge; viz. Walley, Corwin, Sewall, Dudley.
>
> . . . .
>
> Sept[r] 30, [1709]. [returning from Bristol]. Lodge at Billinge's; Many stars were to be seen before we got thither. Cornil, a Quaker, in company. From Billings's writt to Mr. Man, enclosing an oration.[39]

The presence of the Quaker must have been an experience for the Puritan judge. One wonders if he lectured this one as his diary records his having done with another.

The Mr. Man to whom he wrote was the minister in Wrentham and an ancestor of the family who built Mann's Mill in Sharon.

In September of 1710 the judge went to Bristol "by way of Punkapog . . . Got to Billinges before Sun-set."[40] The route he took went over what is now Main Street in Sharon.

The following September he returned to Billings Tavern, and then after a two-year absence had an interesting visit.

> Sept[r] 11, [1714]. I set out for Bristol with Jn° Cornish; Twas so hot and late that Lodg'd at Billing's.
> Sept[r] 12, [1714]. Rid with Capt. Billings to Mr. Man's. See his Sermons.[41]

It was the judge's custom to carry a small diary on journeys in order to make sermon notes and other notations he wished to remember. On the occasion of this visit, he recorded his expenses. It cost him five shillings, six pence for the night's lodging at Billings Tavern.[42] This was in line with the four to eight shillings he paid in other places.

September 12 was a Sunday. The Judge and the Captain took the "road to Wrentham," which branched off the post road about a mile south of the Billings farm, and went to hear Mr. Man preach. A notation in the small diary records a "contribution" of five shillings that day. He must have placed this in the offering plate at church.

The last two dates for lodging at Billings Tavern were in September of 1715 and 1716.[43] Two years later Samuel Sewall became Chief Justice of the Massachusetts Supreme Court and the Sewall visits to Billings Tavern ceased.

That same year the Judge noted in his diary the death of his friend.

> Jan. 28, [1718]. Tuesday, Capt. Ebenezer Billings esqr is buried this day on a Hill between his house, and his Sons in Punkapog Road, between 1 and 2 P.M. Jn° Arcus saw the Process.[44]

In the *Collections of the Massachusetts Historical Society*, where the Judge's diary is printed, is also found the *Boston News Letter's* obituary for the tavern keeper.

> Dorchester, Feb. 4 — On the 25th of January, died here, Capt. Ebenezer Billings, Esq: in the 63 Year of his Age, very much Lamented by his Neighbours both of this and the Neighboring Towns; He was a great Lover of the Religion and Liberties of his Country, a great Friend to Justice, very diligent to find out, and exact in punishing Vice, especially Drunkenness and Sabbath-breaking; He left behind him thirteen Children, one whereof viz. Mr. Richard Billings, he bred up at College, and is now a Minister of the Gospel at Little-Compton; he was Decently Interred on Tuesday the 28th of January past.[45]

The publication also notes that Roger Billings survived his brother by only two days.

The End of an Era

The *American Almanack* of 1713 gives "A Description of the High-ways and Roads. From New York to Boston, 278 miles thus accounted." Toward the latter part of the journey from New York, these entires are given: "To Providence 20. To Woodcocks 15. To Billends 10. To Whites 7. To Dedham 6 and from thence to Boston 10 mile."[46]

Although "Billends" is not the correct spelling, the mileage is accurate for Capt. Billings' place of business.

Woodcocks refers to a very popular tavern in North Attleborough. On July 5, 1670, John Woodcock had been licensed to keep an ordinary at the "three mile river (so called) which is in the way from Rehoboth to the Bay."[47] Judge Sewall stopped at Woodcocks as often as he did at Billings.

Whites is a reference to the tavern owned by Henry White at the bridge crossing the Neponset River. The map of the Twelve Divisions of the Dorchester New Grant shows on it the Dorchester School Farm (300 acres) leased to Henry White.

By 1751 Sharon's portion of the post road ceased to be on the regular route. A listing of stage stops as provided in the "Young Secretary's Guide" of that year shows the route from Boston "to Dedham 10, to King's Bridge 7, to Woodcock's 5, to Providence 15."[48] This new route led through Walpole and Wrentham — a savings of twelve miles just in the portion of the road from Boston to Providence. Billings Tavern had lost its main supply of guests.

The 1794 map of Sharon does not show the tavern on it, but the building had not ceased to exist. The structure was rebuilt on several occasions, and the Turner family, who in recent times cultivated the cranberry bogs, used portions of the tavern as the cranberry store house. With the construction of the shopping center, however, the building and its site have disappeared.

One interesting relic of the tavern is assumed still to exist. A wooden punch bowl used in the tavern was said to have been brought home from Jerusalem by a Billings ancestor who had gone on one of the Crusades. The following item is recorded in the Wednesday, June 7, 1865, meeting of The New England Historic Genealogical Society.

William R. Deane exhibited a punch bowl of the "olden time" —
turned out of lig num vitae, which was in use near 200 years since
at the noted Billings Tavern — on the road from Boston to New
York, in what was then Dorchester, — now Sharon. Rivers of
punch have flowed from this old fountain and moistened the
throats of thousands.[49]

As for the post road, Sharon's own town records show that on March 22,
1768, the town allowed a road "through Samuel Follit's land and part of
Thomas Clark's to Old Post Road at a stake and heep of stones."[50] Over two
hundred years ago the Old Post Road had already received its present name.

Once one of the busiest roads in the Massachusetts Bay Colony, the portion in Sharon is now distinguished by short, broken stretches of residences,
alternating with three tracks disappearing into the woods.

By 1830, the time of Sharon's second official town map, Old Post Road
stopped at South Walpole Street. Today a small park is being laid out at this
spot — a pleasant reminder of a bygone era.

BAY ROAD

Across town from the Old Post Road is another route coming from
Boston. A century after two-wheeled calashes stopped at Billings Tavern,
stages on this route, reaching the "parting stone" in Roxbury, turned more
directly south to come through present-day Milton, Canton, Sharon and
Easton on the way to Taunton in this southernmost direction of the Lower Post
Road.[51] Sometimes called Taunton Road in Sharon, this early way also took the
name Bay Path as the road between Massachusetts and Narragansett Bays.

Following a route shown on the Map of the Twenty-five Divisions as the
"Way by Dry Pond," Bay Road marks most of the eastern boundary of
Sharon. The road does indeed go by Dry Pond, but today the interesting
feature of that landmark, which was a reference point in early records, is that it
is *not* dry.

When Sharon separated from Stoughton, the road between them had to be
apportioned to each town for upkeep.

We ye Subscribers Being Chosen Committes by ye Town of
Stoughton and District of Stoughtonham; to Proportion and
Devide ye Road Called Dry pond Road Between ye Sd Town &
District; have accordingly met on ye 14th Day November AD:
1765: and Vewed the same and report as followeth (Viz) We have
Devided and assigned to Stoughtonham for their part of Sd Way:
begining at Easton Line near where mr Jeremiah Willes formerly
Lived Down the Road to a heap of Stones Erected the Westerly
Side of ye Road Between Two Gravely Ridges on Rattle Snake
Plain in Clifford Belchers Land; & also from a large Stone or heep
of Stones Erected on ye Easterly Side of the Road opposite or
against mr Elijah Bakers Lain that goes from ye Road to Said
Bakers house: So Down by Clifford Belchers to ye Lane that Leads
by mr Richard Hixsons; or So far as the Way goes between the
first Precinct of Sd Town and the District . . .[52]

The portion for Stoughton mentions the same places and adds the names of Deverix and Noyes as identification points. The common road ran from Cobb's Corner to Easton just as it does today.

It should be noted that Bay Road was not the complete boundary between the towns. Even on the 1830 map of Sharon there is a triangular section of Stoughton land which lay west of the road in the Dry Pond vicinity. This is now a part of Sharon, having been added in 1864.[53]

Noyes Tavern

Bay Road is noted for the taverns along it. Doty Tavern in Canton was the place where the Suffolk Resolves, forerunner of the Declaration of Independence, were formulated. May Tavern, also in Canton close to the First Parish Meeting House, was well known in early days. The stage register for the Boston-Taunton road in 1776 carried this list.[54]

Road to Taunton and Swanzey

Kent	Dorchester	4
Vose	Milton	3
Doty	Stoughton	2
May	Stoughton	3
Noyes	Stoughtonham	4
Howard	Easton	8
Godfrey	Norton	2
Crocker	Taunton	8
Whitmarsh	Dighton	6
Freebairn	Swanzey	4

Noyes Tavern was located on Bay Road at Chemung Street. It was also called "Widow Noyes's." John Rowe, the Boston merchant whose motion placed the sacred Cod in the state capital building[55] was a visitor there. Rowe was an avid fisherman and never missed the opportunity to try his luck in the numerous freshwater lakes of eastern Massachusetts. His diary records that he fished in Lake "Mossepong" on July 30, 1767, and stayed that night at Widow Noyes' in Sharon.[56]

Little else is known about Noyes Tavern, and the transcriber of John Rowe's diary does not elaborate on a comment about "Widow Noyes's in Sharon (then Stoughtonham, where one of the Edmund Quincys seemed to be an habitue.)"[57]

Edmund Quincy, Jr., noted for his partnership with Colonel Gridley in the foundry which cast cannon for the American Revolution, moved to Stoughtonham prior to the war and married as his third wife, Hannah Gannett, on April 30, 1767.[58] Her father, Benjamin Gannett — better known as Deborah Sampson's father-in-law — had a home on East Street about a mile from Noyes' Tavern.

Cobb's Tavern

Sharon's most famous tavern came into prominence several decades after that of Widow Noyes. In 1797, the year before his marriage to Sibel Holmes, Jonathan Cobb bought property on Bay Road from Elijah Fisher. According to the research of a former owner, the oldest part of the house was constructed in 1740 and may have been moved from across the road.[59] Fisher may even have run a tavern there; however, it remained for the Cobbs to give the tavern its name and present proportions.

Jonathan Cobb enlarged the structure considerably — perhaps to accommodate an increase in customers, but most assuredly to house his ten children, born between the years 1799 and 1821.[60]

Included among the children were twin girls, and all but one child lived to adulthood. A portrait of the oldest son, Jonathan Holmes Cobb, painted in 1830, hangs in the Dedham Historical Society. This son was one of a panel of speakers at his graduation from Harvard in 1817.[61] Soon after his graduation at age eighteen, he moved to Dedham and lived there the rest of his life.

Although the double doors of the tap room of Cobb's Tavern have not opened to admit patrons since the tavern closed three quarters of a century ago, the building has been preserved and restored. To step inside it is to be transported into another era.

The tap room remains intact. The dark, unpainted bar, fifteen feet long, its soft pine worn with use, boasts a money slot for customer payment. A long low seat in front of the bar and a straight-backed bench on the side provide seating near the hearth.

On one wall of the room is the remains of a circus poster advertising a performance at Cobb's Tavern, East Sharon, Massachusetts, on Tuesday, September 8, 1846. The name of the group is not identified but a tavern register, now lost, listed Van Amburgh's Menagerie, Howe's Trans-Atlantic Circus, and G. P. Bailey's as ones which performed there in succeeding years.[62] The troupe whose performance bill is preserved was composed of 125 persons. The tavern had many outbuildings at one time and these undoubtedly were called into service for so large a group.

A slot in the left front door of the tap room recalls another responsibility of the tavern keeper. On July 1, 1819, Jonathan Cobb was appointed postmaster.[63] Since the tavern was on the stage line, it was a logical place to leave the mail. Bay Road residents thus received daily mail, but other townspeople had to wait for the mail to come to the center of town once a week.[64] The center finally received a post office in 1828. A *Boston Globe* article in 1905 stated that school children were given letters to distribute on their way to school.[65]

In 1841, the year Warren Cobb took the job from his father, the name of East Sharon was officially given to this post office.[66] In the tavern hang two signs — the original "Post Office" sign and the one proclaiming "East Sharon." When Warren Cobb, Jonathan's youngest son, died in 1895, the Post Office closed, and the tavern became a private home for Warren's two daughters. The property left the Cobb family in 1935.

Besides the tap room, the tavern had other facilities. For overnight guests there were rooms for lodging. For the ladies who traveled, there was a parlor on the second floor to provide a retreat while the males enjoyed the sociability of the tavern.

That upstairs parlor was the scene of the romance between Keziah Cobb and John Duff of Lexington, Kentucky, a construction engineer staying at the tavern during the building of the Canton viaduct on the Boston-Providence Railroad in 1835. Through the thin partition, the family heard Mr. Duff pleading with Keziah to marry him.

Three years later she did marry him, but apparently her father was not happy about it.

24

This appears to have been a source of great grief for Jonathan, who on his deathbed, is said to have exhorted all who loved Keziah to take care of her, for "That Duff will never come to anything, I am sure." Engineering was a doubtful profession in those days, and railroading even more so. But Duff did better than Jonathan feared, for he became vice president of Union Pacific Railroad, and was one of those honored men who drove the golden spike that connected the East with the West when the two great railroads were joined. He also became wealthy, and packages from "Aunty Duff" arrived frequently at Cobb's Tavern.[67]

The Cobbs also encouraged use of their facilities by various organizations. The Old Stoughton Musical Society held meetings here. With members from several surrounding towns, the society varied its meeting places, often going to homes or places of establishment of members. For Jonathan cobb, however, it was strictly a business venture since none of his immediate family ever joined.

From the first meeting at Cobb's Tavern on November 12, 1804, to the last one on June 6, 1808, the Old Stoughton Musical Society held seven meetings there.

> A record of a meeting at Cobb's Hall, Feb. 13, 1807, closes with these words: After partaking an Elegant Supper with good Harmony, a motion was called for by the president for adjournment.
> Voted unanimously to meet at the same place at the Artillery Election, June next, at 10 o'clock A.M.
> Cobb's bill — Supper, 2/3 each; 1/3 for Drink
> Benj. Capen, Secretary[68]

Jonathan Cobb encouraged the Masons to use the tavern by constructing a large hall on the second floor. From 1814 to 1817 the Rising Star Lodge of Stoughton met under its arched blue ceiling.[69] In succeeding years the Cobb family used the hall as a bedroom, but later owners have converted it into two bedrooms.

Apparently veterans' groups also used the hall. Col. John Gay, whose diary is in the Canton Historical Society, notes on May 27, 1818, "Met at Jona Cobb's Inn. I was elected Col. Capt. James Blackman Lt. Col. Asa plymptin Maj."[70]

Not to be outdone by his father, Warren Cobb played host to the Boston Bicycle Club. In the latter part of the nineteenth century this sport was very popular, and the club held an annual "Wheel around the Hub." According to one participant

> In 1886, at the age of 24, I was a member of the Dorchester Bicycle Club, riding a 55-inch wheel. Dinner at the Tavern was a frequent occurrence. I shall never forget the exhilerating ride through the Blue Hills of Milton, but the Tavern itself was the chief attraction of the outing . . . including the long-disused bar room.[71]

Activities and merchandise for sale during the period 1822 to 1835 can be documented through the account book now in the historical collection of the town after being returned by the efforts of a former resident.[72]

The entries though difficult to decipher make very interesting reading. The first entry dated April 15, 1822, comes as no surprise.

Nathan Warren dr to a gill NE rum (amount obscure)[73] Many later entries deal with postage and carriage arrangements; however, the variety of other entries almost indicate a general store. Interspersed with the glasses of New England rum and the quarts of "ginn" are entries such as these.

```
Wednesday April 17 Thomas Shepard dr to a horse
                    collar 2/6                          42
June 22 [1822] Thomas P. Richards to 25 cts worth
               gingerbread and bisquits
July 11 [1822] Lieut. T Rich Dr to a cheese $1 =
               8 d Bushel corn                        2   8
Thurs 18 [1822] Mrs gardner Dr to 2 skeins white
                thread                                    4
                20 1/h lb pearl ash 2 oz
                salts                                    10
Oct. 30, 1822 Enos Gardner to 1 lb of soap by
              Mary Horton
              No amount is given, entry under
              it is for nails and the whole
              account is marked "Settled."
May 12, 1823 Sam¹ H Horton dr to horse & waggon
             to Boston                                2
             to horse & waggon to Wrentham            2
             Cr by horse to plow & Wᵐ work
             2/3 of day
Jan. 17, 1824 Peter Capin Dr to half a pint of
              wes rum                                   6
              Postage 6 cents
Sunday May 28, 1826 John Foster left a handkerchief
                    for 1/ if he returns
                    the money he his to have
                    the same
Oct. 7, 1830 Johathan Belcher to ½ lb ten-
             penny nails                               50
```

After 1830 most of the entries are for meals, lodging, drinks, postage and rental of horses and wagons or chaises. He did sell on commission knives for the Ames.[74]

```
March 5, 1834 List of Knives recd of Mr. Amez
   Recd 3 Doz Carving Knives ........at $3.00      9 00
   2 Doz Shiving ................Do. at $1.25      2 50
   5 Do Bread ...................Do. at $1.50      7 50
   16 Doz Shoe Knives at          $1.00          16 00
   1 Doz No 3 Shoe Knives at       4.25           1 25
                                                 ------
                                                 36 25
   Discount for Sales 10 per ct (per agreement)   3 62
                                                 ------
                                                 32 63
```

He then records the charges for Mr. John Amez, which left an unpaid balance of $8.41. A large note across the page indicates that the account was finally settled in 1839.[75]

The entries in the Cobb journal are not the neat, double-page entries such as those of Benjamin Hewins' account books. Those ledgers of the Hewins store, operated in the 1760's and 1770's, list the debits on one page and the credits on the facing page. Each entry in the Cobb ledger is entered and then marked paid or simply has an "X" marking them out. The handwriting is sometimes almost illegible and indicates several different hands. One wonders if the entries were made by different members of the Cobb family or by the patrons themselves. The same names appear again and again, indicating a regular clientele.

The furnishings of the old tavern were sold at auction, and little of the original movable items remain. The swing sign for the tavern, now in the Dedham Historical Society, featured a cobb horse — a natural for the name. It is doubly interesting in that it shows distinctly two signs having been painted on the same board. The cobb horse is quite weathered. A closer look reveals a layer of paint giving the distinct outline of a coach drawn by two horses. Jonathan Cobb's name is visible on both signs.

Bay Road Inhabitants

A mention of the persons living along Bay Road must include the Drakes, who owned property along much of the route. This family is supposed to have provided the largest number of soldiers for the Revolution of any family in town, but it was the elderly grandmother whose story is preserved.

> On the site where now stands the barn belonging to the estate of the late Benjamin Drake stood the modest farmhouse of a Mrs. Drake, the grandmother of the late Ashael Smith Drake of Sharon. She was an honest hardworking woman, caring for her family as best she could in those troublous times. On a certain day when she was standing at the door of her barn two British officers rode up and asked her for hay and grain for their horses. She replied that she had none to spare, she needed all that she had for her own use. One of the officers said, "Well Madam, since you refuse to give it, we shall take it," and advanced toward the door to put in execution his threat. Mrs. Drake stepped back, and seized an instrument with a long handle and many iron prongs called a coal crane, used to take charcoal from the kiln. She advanced again to the door waving the instrument aloft, and with these words to the Redcoats, "Cross this threshhold if you dare! I will brain the first one that makes the attempt." After a few whispered words the better part of valor was to flee from a plucky Yankee woman armed with so formidable a weapon.
>
> At some distance from the house was the well from which she carried water for daily needs. The well is still in use, situated on the farm belonging to Edgar F. Drake.[76]

Mrs. Edna (Drake) Field of Bay Road, whose grandfather was Ashael Drake, identifies the farm as the Tisdale Drake farm on the 1830 map of

Sharon. She states Mrs. Drake was perhaps 100 years old when the incident happened.

Another resident of Bay Road is better known for having lived on East Street. Deborah Sampson came back from the army without a home to return to. As a result she came to live with her mother's sister, Alice, who had married Zebulon Waters. The Waters property was then in Stoughton in that triangular section of land west of Bay Road near Dry Pond Cemetery. It was here Deborah was living when she married Benjamin Gannett, Jr.

Bay Road Today

Passengers riding in the carriages down Bay Road in the eighteenth and nineteenth centuries could mark off the miles with the stone markers beside the route. Several of these are preserved, but the ones along Sharon's part of the road have been destroyed, perhaps by the widening of the road or by being used for another purpose. The closest one to the north is the Nathaniel Leonard milestone, one-half mile from Cobb's Tavern. Erected in 1773, it marks the 17th mile from Boston. The Richard Gridley milestone is just south of town, where Mountain Street intersects Bay Road.[77] Col. Gridley helped survey Bay Road; he also owned the company which cast cannons in Sharon during the Revolution. The Gridley stone marks the twenty-third mile from Boston, and notes it was 13 miles to Taunton.

Passengers driving down Bay Road today in Sharon will find it straightened and widened, no longer looking like an early route. Cobb's Tavern, once eagerly sought by patrons of the tap room and customers at the post office, is now a beautifully preserved, private home, maintaining its integrity amid expanding shopping centers and multiple-family residences. Bay Road continues to be a major route for the town of Sharon.

MAIN STREET

Running diagonally between Bay Road and the Old Post Road, from Cobb's Corner to the Foxborough line, is Sharon's Main Street, laid out in 1700. A committee was chosen by the town of Dorchester to "lay out the highway between Milton line and Mr. Billings his house."[78] They started in Milton, came past the Blue Hills and marked oak trees along the way. The road was two rods wide, and near the middle of their surveying, they left a great white oak standing in the middle, giving the road one rod width on each side of it.

The street as originally planned did not come to Cobb's Corner, but followed a different route into Sharon. After proceeding down Washington Street in Canton until it came to High Street, the road then turned west and came into our town on Canton Street, joining present North Main Street at the box factory.

At this point the road begins a steep ascent to the center of town. The Savel family, who lived at the bottom of the hill in the 1800's, kept a pair of oxen yoked so that they could help teams pull wagons to the top.

From the box factory to the Foxborough line, Main Street runs very much the route laid out in 1700.

Taverns and Social Halls on Main Street

The center of town had several halls and taverns at various times. The records of the Old Stoughton Musical Society show they met in several of these.

For five rehearsals during the period 1802 to 1804, the musicians met at John Savels' Hall.[79] This meeting place was the upper floor of the old Pettee store, formerly in Post Office Square, now a residence on Station Street.

Samuel Johnson's was a meeting place for the musical society for seven times during the period from December 25, 1820 to December 25, 1830.[80] Johnson's Tavern stood on the corner across from the Unitarian Church, where the brick stores are. It was moved to High Street and now faces the telephone company building.

About a mile and a half closer to Foxborough, on the corner of East Foxboro Street and South Main, stood the Randall Tavern, which was in operation during the Revolution.

This tavern also had its diarist. Ezekiel Price, the Clerk of Courts of Common Pleas and Sessions for the County of Suffolk,[81] apparently was one of the persons who left Boston during the British military occupation. It is assumed that he went to live in Canton at the Doty Tavern.

> Wednesday, May 24 [1775]. — Went down to Roxbury in expectation that some of my effects had been got out; but was disappointed.
>
> . . . .
>
> Thursday, June 15. — Miss Becky and Miss Polly Gridley . . . called here in their way to Dr. Sprague's and went up with Mrs. Price and Mrs. Armstrong to the top of the Blue Hills. Mrs. Becky, in her way down, killed two small snakes.
>
> . . . .
>
> Saturday, June 17. — A pleasant morning. Report of the day, — that six hundred of the Continental Army last night opened an entrenchment on Dorchester Neck; that three thousand marched from Cambridge to Charlestown, and opened an entrenchment there; that no opposition was made to those at Dorchester, but the Regular Army fired from their battery on Copp's Hill; the ships also fired towards Charlestown; . . . The firing of cannon continually heard, and very loud. We set out, towards sundown, with our baggage, and reached Randall's, at Stoughtonham, about nine miles. In the evening, saw a great light towards Boston, the country people marching down; the firing of cannon distinctly heard till after eleven o'clock.
>
> Sunday, June 18. — At Randall's. The morning and forenoon, and towards sundown, heard the report of cannon. In the evening, some of the people who went down returned from Cambridge, &c. Reported that the town of Charlestown was burnt by the regulars that had landed there, and forced the Continental Army out of their entrenchment on Bunker's Hill; that the engagement was hot and furious on both sides: but, the ammunition of the Continental Army being spent, they were unable to oppose any longer; and the Regular Army then jumped into the entrenchment, and made considerable slaughter among the Continental Army. The loss is un-

certain either side. It is supposed that great numbers are killed on both sides. Dr. Warren is said to be among the slain, Colonel Gridley wounded in the leg, Colonel Gardner wounded badly, and a great number of others.[82]

The war did not seem to interfere with Mr. Price too much. His other diary entries speak of visits, fishing and watching the mowers in the fields. About six weeks after the Battle of Bunker Hill, he and his wife took a trip to Providence. On the way down and returning he "dined at Randall's in Stoughtonham."[83]

No established stage line served Main Street, but the following advertisement appeared in a Dedham paper in 1803.[84]

SHARON STAGE

The subscriber would inform the Inhabitants of this, and other adjacent towns, that he, from repeated solicitation, is induced to establish a STAGE to run from *Sharon* to *Boston*. It will start at 5 o'clock in the morning, every SATURDAY, from the MEETING HOUSEs and from Maj KING'S *Inn* home, at 3 o'clock, P.M. the same day. — This line he proposes to continue till the first of *September*, when he will go twice a week, *Tuesdays* and *Saturdays*; time of day the same. — Those who may favor him with their custom may depend on his punctual attention, and of having good accommodations.

JOSEPH CUMMINS

Sharon, July 11, 1803

The success of this business venture is not known; no record of it remains.

OTHER STREETS

An examination of the old maps of the town reveals that all but one of our major streets were in existence in 1794. The center of town shows the intersection of four streets — North and South Main, Depot and Pond.

Norwood Street, leading west and then turning north, displays some of its present peculiarities. The 90° angle turn where Depot Street/Upland Road become Norwood Street is clearly visible. The S-curve by the nursing home probably was not quite the problem it is today with high speed travel.

The "Road to Mashapoag" (Pond Street) continued along the east side of the lake with only slight deviation until it joined Mansfield Street. The 1858 map shows Massapoag Street running straight south rather than following Mansfield Street, but at the entrance to the community center it still followed Capen Hill Road and Morse Street on the 1876 map.

On the east side of town the 1794 map shows Mountain Street and East Street, much as they are today, but it is to be assumed that Mountain Street was traveled its whole length. On the west side of town Walpole, Furnace, and Wolomolopoag Streets are seen. The latter is called the Norton Road, having been called the "Path to Norton" on the Map of The Twenty-five Divisions nearly a century earlier.

East Foxboro Street and Mohawk Street joined the Norton Road in the early days. By 1830, though, East Foxboro had taken its present configuration.

Mohawk Street was cut off by the railroad. Recent housing developments and the construction of the railroad overpass have brought renewed traffic to East Foxboro and Wolomolopoag Streets.

Billings Street, totally absent in 1794, had by 1830 progressed as far as the curve near the present Cottage Street intersection. It remained this length until the Manns began to develop their mill. A survey made for the mill site in 1837 shows Billings Street as complete to East Street.

Ames Street, however, shown on the 1794 map as running between East Street and Pond Street, was not yet through to South Main Street even on the 1876 map.

Gunhouse Lane, which received its name from the arsenal where ammunition was stored during the Revolution, does not appear on the map until 1830. The arsenal stood at the corner of South Main and East Foxboro Streets.

Later maps show the development of some streets and the demise of others. Everett Street is just a path for most of its length. At one time it led to the town Poor Farm. The 1876 map also shows a road going from Massapoag Road by the present Community Center over to Lakeview Street although no such road exists today.

Evidence of an abandoned road which never got on any map can be seen near Chestnut Tree Cemetery.

> It is not known when this road was made (old abandoned road running from Viaduct Street [now called Edge Hill Road] a little west of Dedham Street and coming out on Richards Street a little south of Chestnut Tree cemetery, crossing midway in its course Puffer's brook at the "stone bridge") but it was the only road which the people who lived in Pigeon swamp used for fifty years for travelling from this corner of Sharon to any other place. (Pigeon swamp is the most northerly part of Sharon reaching from north of Viaduct street to Neponset river. . . .)[85]

Early Town Meeting Action on Roads

There is frequent mention of roads in early town records, and several persons were appointed each year as Surveyors of Ways.

When an old road was to be improved or a new one to be constructed, an article such as this one for the acceptance of Furnace Street appeared in the town records:[86]

> March 17, 1766 . Voted to accept of a Way Lay'd out by the Select Men by ye furness Provided there be no Demands for any pay for the Land on the District. A Return of a Way Lay'd out by us the Subscribers in Stoughtonham Begining on a Ridg Hill South Easterly from Royall Kollicks House and down by Said house to the furness as it is now Improved to the Sinder heep & from thence to the westerly end of the Dam Northeast of the BlackSmith's Shop; and then as the Way is improved to a bunch of White Oaks on the southwesterly Side of Said Way: then to a pine on the North Easterly Side, and thus to a White oak on the North Side; then to a gray oak on the South Side; from thence to a Scrubed top pine to be in the middle of the Way; and then to one

other Scrubed top pine on the South Side of the Way: and So to the Town Way Leading from Seth Boyden to Capt Billings; the above Said Way is Lay'd out two Rods Wide by us the Subscribers FebrY ye 15th: 1766   Job Swift   Select Men
                                      Thomas Randall

Three years later the town "Voted to Joyn with the Committee chose by the Furnace-owners in equal halves (as to the cost) in opning the Old Taunton road, thr° the Land of Mr Nathan Clark & Seth Boyden."[87] This probably was the old "Path to Norton" now the south portion of Wolomolopoag Street. The next article in the warrant that year voted Edmund Quincy, who had a vested interest in the furnace since he jointly owned Massapoag Lake and its iron ore, to join the furnace committee in opening that road.

The entry for the acceptance of Furnace Street bears record that the town fathers were careful about having to pay for the land on which a road was built. The standard phrase included in any acceptance was that there be no cost to the town.

Each year the rate for road repair tax was assessed to individual land owners. The person was then expected to work out the amount of the tax by his own labor since there was no Department of Public Works. If he brought his team of oxen and his cart, he could pay off his tax twice as fast. The following action, taken at town meeting on March 9, 1767, indicates a practice prevalent for many years following.

> Voted that the Ways in the District be mended the Ensuing year by Working out the Sum of Eighty Six pounds five Shillinges & Eleven pence; as follows, (Viz.) that Each one be Set in the Surveyors List the one-half that is Set to their names in the Last Ministeral County & District Rate: And that Said Sums be paid in Labor at two Shilling pr Day for a Man & four Shillings pr Day for Man & teem & Cart; And that Said Work be done on the Ways between the first Day of May and the first of october Next And that the Surveyors make Return of the names of those that have not Worked out their Sums to ye Select men in october next; in order for their being assess'd.[88]

Even at that repairs were not speedily done. Just a year after the formation of the District of Stoughtonham, the eleventh article on the warrant (October 13, 1766) called for the repair of Hobb's Bridge or its rebuilding.[89] The article was dismissed. Hobbs Brook was the former name of Beaver Brook. This bridge was in the area of the railroad station, on the major road leading to Dedham (Norwood). The same article appeared on the warrant in 1772 and 1786. It was dismissed each time.

In the era of furious turnpike building at the beginning of the 1800's, Sharon seemed to have had only one proposal for such a route. The Norton Turnpike Corporation submitted a proposal in 1806 to build a turnpike from Warren, Rhode Island, through Norton and Sharon to Bay Road in Canton.[90] There it was to connect with the Brush Hill Turnpike. The plans, however, were never developed and no construction was ever done. Sharon was one of the few towns in the state which had no turnpike.

Streets Today

It is not quite certain at what point streets began to have names, but an interesting exercise with the 1830 map is to look at the names of residents and compare these with the present names of streets.

The street numbering system was instituted by Gilmore Richards when he was assessor in the 1920's. According to local residents, Mr. Richards had the entire town surveyed and then instituted the first block system.

The evolution of Sharon as a residential community has continued steadily since its founding. Helped along by W. B. Wickes' promotion of Sharon as the "Healthiest Town in New England," there has been a steady increase in population since the boundaries of the town were fixed at the beginning of the nineteenth century.

Real estate development has caused numerous streets to be added to the ancient ones in town. During the 1940's the Heights area developed streets on the plain which was one of the finest vegetable farms in the state. Recently there has been much land development in the east and south portions of town. Sharon, as with any expanding residential community in this part of the country, has streets as old as Indian trails and as new as fresh-cut trees.

Footnotes

1. Willard De Lue, *The Story of Walpole, 1724 - 1924* (Norwood: The Ambrose Press, Inc., 1975) p. 202.
2. *The Dedham Historical Register* (Dedham, Mass.: By the Society, 1898) IX, 44 facing.
3. De Lue, p. 199.
4. *Ibid.*
5. *Dedham Historical Register*, VI, 130.
6. De Lue, p. 200
7. Stewart H. Holbrook, *The Old Post Road* (New York: McGraw-Hill Book Company, Inc., 1962), p. 23.
8. *Ibid.*, p. 24.
9. Solomon Talbot, "Historic Traces of the Wainman's Ordinary and its Location in Sharon, Massachusetts" (Sharon Public Library), p. 2. (Typed.)
10. *Ibid.*, p. 5.
11. *Dorchester Town Records, Fourth Report of the Record Commissioner of the City of Boston, 1880* (2d ed; Boston: Rockwell and Churchill, City Publishers, 1883), p. 94.
12. *Ibid.*, pp. 309-310.
13. *Ibid.*, p. 316.
14. *Ibid.*, pp. 125, 128.
15. *Ibid.*, p. 131.
16. *Ibid.*, p. 163.
17. *Ibid.*, p. 166.
18. *Ibid.*, p. 185.
19. *Ibid.*, p. 193.
20. *Ibid.*, p. 202.
21. Harold Ward Dana, "Roger Billings of Milton, Mass., and Some of his Descendants," *The New England Historical and Genealogical Register* (By the Society, 1938), XCII, 265.
22. *Dorchester Town Records*, p. 229
23. *The Sharon Advocate*, July 1, 1965, p. 8.
24. *Dorchester Town Records*, pp. 210, 250.
25. *Ibid.*, p. 239.
26. Dana, p. 264.
27. *Dorchester Town Records*, p. 279.
28. *Ibid.*, pp. 270, 280.
29. Dana, pp. 261-263.

30. Samuel Sewall, *Diary of Samuel Sewall, 1674-1729*, Vol. V, Fifth Series of the *Collections of the Massachusetts Historical Society* (Boston: The Society, 1878), I, 88.
31. *Ibid.*, pp. 317-318.
32. *Ibid.*, p. 319.
33. Dorchester Antiquarian and Historical Society, *History of the Town of Dorchester, Massachusetts* (Boston: Ebenezer Clapp, Jr., 1851), p. 267.
34. Sewall, pp. 412, 259, 502.
35. Sarah Knight, *Journal of Madam Knight*, ed. Malcolm Freiberg, (Boston: David R. Godine, 1972), reprint of 1920 edition.
36. Dana, p. 265.
37. Sewall, II, p. 169.
38. *Ibid.*, p. 203
39. *Ibid.*, pp. 237, 265.
40. *Ibid.*, p. 287.
41. *Ibid.*, p. 323.
42. *Ibid.*, p. 426.
43. Sewall, III, pp. 57, 103.
44. *Ibid.*, p. 162-163.
45. *Ibid.*, note.
46. *Dedham Historical Register*, IX, 46.
47. Frederic J. Wood, *The Turnpikes of New England* (Boston: Marshall Jones Company, 1919), p. 88.
48. *Dedham Historical Register*, IX, 46.
49. *The New England Historic Genealogical Society*, "Proceedings. Boston, Wednesday, June 7, 1865," (Boston: The Society, 1865), XIX, 373.
50. *Sharon Town Records*, I. 23.
51. Holbrook, p. 14
52. *Sharon Town Records*, I. 7.
53. Carroll D. Wright, *Report of the Custody and Condition of the Public Records of Parishes, Towns and Counties.* (Boston: Wright & Potter, 1889), p. 250.
54. Samuel Stearns, *The North-American's Almanack and Gentleman's and Lady's Diary for the Year of our LORD CHRIST 1776*, (Worcester: I. Thomas, 1776)
55. "Seals of Massachusetts" *Proceedings of the Massachusetts Historical Society, 1867-1869* (Boston: The Society, 1869), X, 104.
56. John Rowe, "The Diary of John Rowe," ed. Edward L. Pierce, *Proceedings of the Massachusetts Historical Society*, Second series, X, 48-49.
57. *Ibid.*, p. 47.
58. *Vital Records of Sharon, Massachusetts, to the year 1850* (Boston: Stanhope Press, 1909), p. 126.
59. F. S. Tobey, "The Tavern at Cobb's Corner," (Privately owned, 1955), p. 3. (Mimeographed.)
60. *Vital Records of Sharon*, p. 19.
61. *Proceedings of the Massachusetts Historical Society, 1889-1890*, Second series, V, 182, note.
62. Tobey, p. 13.
63. D. Hamilton Hurd, *History of Norfolk County, Massachusetts With Biographical Sketches of Many of its Pioneer and Prominent Men* (Philadelphia: J. W. Lewis & Co., 1884), p. 467.
64. Jeremiah Gould, *Annals of Sharon, Massachusetts, 1830.* (Sharon: The Sharon Historical Society, 1904), p. 5.
65. Tobey, p. 9.
66. Hurd, p. 467.
67. Tobey, p. 13.
68. *The Old Stoughton Musical Society*, (By the Society, 1928), p. 43.
69. Hurd, p. 404.
70. Diary of Colonel John Gay, Jan 27, 1818 - May 4, 1822. (in the files of the Canton Historical Society), manuscript.
71. Willard H. Fobes as quoted in Tobey, p. 10.
72. *The Sharon Advocate*, August 26, 1971.
73. Jonathan Cobb, Ledger, April 15, 1822 - September 5, 1835. (in the Sharon Public Library), manuscript.

74. *Ibid.*
75. *Ibid.*
76. H. Rebecca Johnson, "An Incident Which Occured on the Bay Road in Sharon During the Revolutionary War," *Sharon Historical Society Scrap Book, Vol. II, 1905,* (in the Sharon Public Library), pp. 43-44.
77. Easton Historical Society, "Old Bay Road Tour and Historical District Dedication, October 23, 1972," (Privately owned), (Mimeographed.)
78. *Dorchester Town Records,* quoted in Daniel T. V. Huntoon, *The History of the Town of Canton, Norfolk County, Massachusetts.* (Cambridge: John Wilson & Son, 1893), pp. 600-601.
79. *The Old Stoughton Musical Society,* pp. 40, 163.
80. *Ibid.,* p. 164.
81. Ezekiel Price, "The Diary of Ezekiel Price," *Proceedings of the Massachusetts Historical Society,* Second Series, (Boston: John Wilson, 1864), VII, 185 note.
82. Price, pp. 189-191.
83. Price, pp. 202-203.
84. *Columbian Minerva,* Vol. VII, No. 354, July 19, 1803.
85. Solomon Talbot, "Early Settlers on Viaduct Street," *Sharon Historical Society Scrap Book, Vol. 5, 1908.* (in the Sharon Public Library), pp. 54-55.
86. *Sharon Town Records,* I. 10.
87. *Ibid.,* p. 31.
88. *Ibid.,* p. 14.
89. *Ibid.,* p. 12.
90. Wood, p. 157.

The Boston Bicycle Club at Cobb's Tavern

The Grave of Captain Ebenezer Billings - Pioneer

Photo by: J. K. Harris

THIS HALLOWED GROUND: SHARON CEMETERIES

By Katharine M. Cartwright

CHAPTER 3

"Thousands of journeys I have gone,
  Both night and day to heal the sick
  I have traveled weary on the way
  But now I have gone a journey never to return."

This epitaph marks the grave of Dr. Samuel Hewins in the old Chestnut Tree Cemetery. Thus walking through these old burying grounds one gains an insight into the lives of the people and the hardships of those early times — the history of a town.

Many of the early gravestones in the old yards were made of flint-hard slate stone perhaps brought over from North Wales with the decorations and epitaphs carved there. This fine stone cutting, beautifully fashioned, has survived the years as if inscribed yesterday. Later white marble tombstones from the quarries of Vermont were erected, then came monuments and stones of native granite.

Not only can one judge the age of these graves by the stone used, but by their decorations, wordings and epitaphs. In the old Sharon cemeteries we find that the earliest stones, usually slabs of slate, simply bore names and dates upon them. A little later came the crudely carved death heads, carved as if done by a child, showing the morbid thoughts of death then held. More artistic are the graceful weeping willows, scrolls, and urns of a later period.

Epitaphs appeared during the era of the 1800's; a few, earlier. Some of these interesting verses seem unbelievable in that they grace the gravestones of loved ones in their crude humor. Some of the history and love inscribed bring tears to the eyes as they tell of the mortality of the times, especially of the little ones.

There are in Sharon nine cemeteries, with three more shared by Canton and Sharon. None of these were known as church yards. Instead there were family burying grounds and tombs. Originally there were several tombs close to the homes, the best known one being the "old village tomb located about six rods to the east of the Episcopal Church on High St. It was constructed of split stones built into the excavated side of a natural knoll and rounded over with a thin layer of earth and sods. The vertical side faced the south and in it were three low wooden doors which entered three separate vaults of the proprietors.

The westerly one belonged to the Curtis family and the middle and easterly ones to the two branches of the Billings family.

"The tomb stood upon Billings land but was erected and jointly owned by Philip Curtis and Jesse and Lewis Billings. Philip Curtis, the first minister of the town, who died in 1797 after a pastoral service of fifty-five years, was buried here. (Perhaps the first burial here was that of his wife Elizabeth who died in 1752.) There were no interments after 1860 and soon after that the bodies of the Curtis family were removed to the Chestnut Hill Cemetery and the bodies of the Billings families to Rock Ridge Cemetery."[1]

One interment was at the request of an early resident of Sharon who lived on land now occupied by the present Camp Wadsworth. Mr. Tolman was buried in the old pasture on the west side of Lake Massapoag, all alone. It was his wish to be buried there "so he could see the wild geese as they flew over the lake in the spring and the fall." About forty years ago some of his family had his remains taken up and put in Rock Ridge Cemetery.

The earliest marked grave in Sharon is that of our famous innkeeper, Ebenezer Billings, who was buried in the West or Dudley Hill Cemetery. Of course many of the early graves were unmarked or their stones destroyed by time or vandals.

In 1900 William R. Mann recorded in manuscript form all of the epitaphs in all of the cemeteries in Sharon with the help of Mrs. Mann, Mrs. George Kempton, and Eugene Tappan.[2] Through their labor we have preserved for us the history written on those tombstones. Many of the early graves were unmarked; many have disappeared through the years. Sadly, some cemeteries have been desecrated. An example of the value of this record of epitaphs is in the following cemetery.

THE OLIVER LOTHROP YARD

The Oliver Lothrop Yard is situated at the junction of Moose Hill and Walpole Streets. The last time I visited it, in 1975, one stone was left intact; the others were lying in pieces or had entirely disappeared. Lothrop and Billings families are buried here, and in 1900 eight graves and their epitaphs were listed. One of the epitaphs on a vandalized stone in this yard is of Hannah, the ten-year-old daughter of Oliver Lothrop who died in 1823.

"Too sweet alas for mortals here
Her Savior called her home.
Come sympathize and shed a tear
And mourn her early doom."

That is the earliest grave. The latest burial was in 1855.

THE FRIEND DRAKE CEMETERY

The Friend Drake Cemetery, a small family burying ground, is in the woods near the Job Swift house on Mountain Street. This is the smallest of the yards with only four marked graves, those of Friend Drake and his family. Little Emma Eldora, his five-year-old daughter, is remembered with the longest epitaph recorded in Sharon.

"Yes, thou art fled, and saints a welcome sing.
Thy youthful spirit soars on angels' wings.
Oer dar'ls affection might have helped thy stay.
The voice of God had called his child away.

In infancy she sought the Lord
And loved to pray and read his word.
She learned submission to his will
And wished his precepts to fulfil.
Gone where he gives, supremely good
Nor less when he denies
Even from his sovereign hand
Are blessings in disguise.

It surely is not in his nature
To be cruel as the grave
Believe not our divine Creator
Will destroy what he can save."

THE GEORGE DRAKE BURIAL GROUND

On the old farm of George Drake, this burial ground is hard to find, lying perhaps one-quarter of a mile in the woods on the left-hand side of Mansfield Street, opposite the road to East Foxboro. This cemetery, which has been badly vandalized recently, contains twenty marked graves. The earliest date is 1810. Here lies buried Melzar Drake who, according to his epitaph, "entered the service of his country at the age of 16 years and served in the war of her independence." He died January 10, 1812. Abial Drake, also a Revolutionary soldier who answered the alarm for Lexington and Concord, died November 13, 1824 in his 91st year.

THE ESTY CEMETERY

The Esty Cemetery, near what was the Esty home on East Foxboro Street, is well enclosed by a stone wall with nineteen marked graves and many unmarked ones. Estys, Clarks, Holmes, and Fishers, among others, are buried here, all of whom lived in the vicinity. The earliest marked grave is that of Thomas Clark who died in 1804. "The righteous perish and no man layeth it to heart" is the epitaph over the grave of Mary, wife of Jacob Fisher.

Three Revolutionary War veterans are buried here:
Thomas Clark, d. Feb. 19th A.D. 1804
John Esty, d. Nov. 27th, 1811 in the 78th year of his age
William Hewins, d. March 4, 1812 aet. 67 years

THE TISDALE CEMETERY

A larger cemetery, the Tisdale, is located in the southeast corner of Sharon on Mountain Street near the Easton line. It is on land formerly owned by that family, the old homestead built by Colonel Israel Tisdale in 1811 now being a part of Borderland State Park.

Many members of the Tisdale family are buried here with seventy-eight marked graves. The earliest marked grave is that of Zilpha, daughter of Ebenezer Tisdale, and Joanna his wife, who died Dec. 1, 1724. Colonel Israel Tisdale died March 24, 1852 at the age of seventy-two. However, Ann Tisdale, daughter of Captain Ebenezer, is called on her stone "the first tenant of this ground" although the stone was not erected until 1851.

Several infants are buried here, showing as do other cemeteries the high rate of infant mortality in those times.

The graves of four Revolutionary soldiers are here.
Captain Ebenezer Tisdale, d. Jan. 24, 1791 aged 68 years.
Lieut. Ebenezer Tisdale, Jr., d. May 28, 1785 in ye 38th year of his age.
Captain Edward Tisdale, d. Nov. 13, 1826 aged 71 years, 9 months.
Zebulon Holmes, d. Dec. 31, 1825 ae. 66 years.

THE CHESTNUT TREE CEMETERY

Land for the Chestnut Tree Cemetery, so known by the early settlers here but now incorporated as the Chestnut Hill Cemetery, was given by the Hixson family and laid out about 1730. This picturesque old cemetery is situated on a side hill, banked by an old stone wall with an early burial vault dug into the hill. It is well worth a visit, for so many of the names appearing in early Sharon history are found here. It lies at the junction of Canton Street and Richards Avenue. Up until the year 1900 about 540 people were buried here. In this burying ground appear the names of Hixsons, Cobbs, Johnsons, Richardses, Curtises, Monks, Goulds, Hewinses, Estys, Dunbars, Raynolds, Cumminses, Haweses, Everetts, Savels, Hobbses, Coneys, and Whittemores, all early inhabitants of the town. Rev. Philip Curtis, first minister of the town and his family were moved here from the family vault on High Street.

The earliest marked grave is that of Mehitable, wife of Elder Joseph Hewins "who died Sept. 14, 1733 in the 63rd year of her age." Both the Elder and his wife would have been born in the 1600's. Here, buried side by side, are John and Mehitable Hixson, John dying in 1751, his wife in 1743. John was the builder of the first church in Sharon and he and his brother Richard were undoubtedly the donors of the land for Chestnut Tree Cemetery.

Here is the grave of Dr. Samuel Hewins whose epitaph introduces this chapter. He died on April 14, 1794. The ardent patriot Dr. Elijah Hewins also rests here. He was influential in the town before and during the Revolutionary War. Acting in behalf of the town, he was one of two delegates attending the meeting of the adoption of the Suffolk Resolves which were the precursors of the Declaration of Independence. Throughout the war he served as a surgeon in the army, later a doctor in Sharon. His home was on North Main Street. He died May 21, 1827 in his 80th year. Jonathan Cobb, of Cobb's Tavern and an early postmaster, with many of his family are in this cemetery. Daniel Richards, an early Selectman, is also buried here.

A stone was erected in memory of Boston Randall, an aged Negro and perhaps the last slave in Sharon who died in 1835, eighty-five years of age. He was a servant of Benjamin Randall but refused to accept his freedom because he was being so kindly treated. He was buried in his master's lot.

One wonders what plague visited Sharon in 1775 when we read the epitaph of Clifford Belcher who died in the 30th year of his age.

"Three children in their youth cut down
  Their bodies buried in the ground.
  Their father and their mother too
  See what the hand of God can do
  They five in fourteen days did dye
  Their bodies here in graves do lye."

A commentary of the life of the times is the fairly common epitaph of Mrs. Abigail Harlow who died in 1752: "She was buried with her infant Susannah in her arms." A strange and gruesome decoration is on the double headstone of the twin babies of Philip and Rebecca Withington. Instead of finding cherubs pictured there, two small skulls with crossbones mark the graves.

Ebenezer Hewins who died July 22, 1751 aged 45 years fought in the French and Indian Wars.

Twenty one marked graves of Revolutionary soldiers are here.
Jonathan Belcher, d. May 26, 1812 aged 72 years
Benjamin Bullard, d. April 4, 1838 aged 79 years
Samuel Cummins, d. Dec. 11, 1804 in his 97th year
Deacon Philip Curtis, d. Nov. 12, 1844 aged 89 years
Lt. Jacob Estey, d. March 29, 1798 in ye 59th year of his age
Deacon Oliver Everett, d. July 28, 1827 aged 77 years
Mathew H. Harlow, d. Oct. 22, 1809 in the 60th year of his age
Benjamin Hewins, d. Nov. 18, 1826 in his 80th year
Lt. Ebenezer Hewins, d. May 8, 1806 aged 75 years
Lt. Enoch Hewins, d. August 10, 1821 aged 80 years
Capt. Increase Hewins, d. Sept. 26, 1822 aged 55 years
Lieut. Richard Hixson, d. Sept. 6, 1778 in his 49th year
Lieut. William Holmes, d. Aug. 8, 1801 in his 48th year
Isaac Johnson, d. Oct. 24, 1795 aged 66 years
Daniel Richards, d. Nov. 8, 1819 in his 78th year
Jeremiah Richards, d. Feb. 4, 1828 aged 74 years
Thomas Richards, d. April 27, 1813 aged 77 years
William Richards, d. Jan. 28, 1801 aged 67 years
Capt. Edward Bridge Savels, d. Dec. 2, 1792 in his 59th year
John Tolman, d. June 21, 1805 in his 81st year
Philip Withington, d. Oct. 7, 1796 aged 59 years
Edward French, Sr. is probably buried here as his son is found here. Edward French, Sr. was born in 1761, d. 1845

War of 1812
Amos Barden, d. April 7, 1854 aged 63 years
Capt. Richard Hixson, d. April 14, 1860

Civil War Veterans
Alonzo H. Clarke, d. June 15, 1863

Edward Cobb, d. Jan. 8, 1900 aged 43 years
William H. Cobb, d. July 3, 1867
John Murray Drake, d. 1863
Corp. John W. Godfrey
Robert Hamilton, d. Dec. 10, 1905
James T. Harradon, d. July 1, 1864
Benjamin Hewins, d. Nov. 14, 1869
Addison H. Johnson, b. Feb. 10, 1824 d. Oct. 31, 1863
George F. Lothrop, d. March 19, 1863 aged 26 years
Henry Parks
John Parks, d. July 1, 1887
John B. Parks, d. Aug. 14, 1864
Henry Peach, b. May 10, 1825 d. Oct. 1, 1890
Albert Pettee, d. 1908
Henry W. Pettee, d. Aug. 16, 1864
George W. Richards, d. Sept. 9, 1888
Albert E. Smith, d. Aug. 16, 1876 aged 35 years

MOOSE HILL CEMETERY

Seventy-eight marked graves are in the Moose Hill Cemetery lying at the foot of the hill on the corner of Moose Hill and Bertram Streets near Route 1. The earliest is that of Ruth, consort of Lemuel Fuller, who died on April 22, 1775. Here lie buried the families of the Goulds, Fishers, Fullers, Leonards, Smiths, Houses, Hewinses and Gays. Another grave is that of Mrs. Nancy Gould, widow of Deacon Samuel, who was the benefactor of the First Congregational Church, having left the church her farm of thirty-eight acres, more or less. This land was on North Main Street opposite the church.

Two Revolutionary soldiers are buried here:
Lieut. David Fisher, d. August 16, 1812 in the 80th year of his age.
Israel Smith, d. Dec. 27, 1839 ae 78 years.
Presumably Capt. Israel Smith his father is here also, in an unmarked grave, for other members of the family are found here.

THE WEST CEMETERY

Another ancient cemetery, the West Cemetery, also known as the Billings or Dudley Hill Cemetery, is on South Main Street in the southwestern part of Sharon near the Foxboro line. One hundred and thirty-three marked graves represent families who lived in this part of the town. Some of the families buried here are Billingses, Clapps, Fairbankses, Clarks, Rhoadses, Talbots, Curtises, Morses, Kingsburys, Holmeses, and Kollocks. The oldest marked grave is that of Ebenezer Billings, whose home was nearby, across the road. His stone is decorated with an hourglass and a head and reads "Here lyeth interred ye body of Capt. Ebenezer Billings, Esq. who departed this life Jan. ye 25, 1717/8 in ye 63rd Year of His Age." The year was written that way because of double dating. Before 1752 the new year began on March 25th, and these dates on his tombstone signified that the old innkeeper died in 1717 by the Old Style, in 1718 by the New Style. His son, Capt. Ebenezer Billing who "Died Oct. ye

27th, 1758 in ye 82nd Year of his Age" is nearby. The grave of Royal Kollock, whose name appears many times in the old town records, is here, the date being Nov. 20, 1806. Dr. Edwin R. Clarke who made and bottled the famous Clarke's Bitters in the southwestern part of the town is buried here. He died Aug. 20, 1868, aged 45 years.

Manson Sturtevant's epitaph reads "drowned June 12, 1867 ae 21 years. A freedman from Virginia."

An unusual epitaph is over the grave of a young man, Lemuel F. Hewins, who must have been a lover of music, as there is on his tombstone a complete staff and four measures of music with the words underneath "So fades this lovely blooming flower." He died in the year 1844 aged 23½ years.

So fades the lovely blooming flower

Revolutionary War soldiers
Capt. Elijah Billings, d. Mar. 31, 1810 ae 60 years
Timothy Clapp, d. Aug. 18, 1811 aged 78 years
Lieut. Amasa Hewins, d. Jan. 10, 1812 in his 46th year
Royal Kollock, d. Nov. 20, 1806 in his 81st year
Col. Ezra Morse, d. May 9, 1807 in his 67th year
Lieut. Nathaniel Morse, Jr., d. Jan. 1, 1816 in his 46th year

Civil War soldiers
Horace W. Clapp, d. April 3, 1905
Leander Clapp, d. May 6, 1864
Benjamin A. Fairbanks, d. Oct. 23, 1864
Henry Hewins, d. Dec. 10, 1862

ROCK RIDGE CEMETERY

Rock Ridge Cemetery has been for many years the main and best-known cemetery in Sharon. It is located at the junction of East and Mountain Streets. As its name implies, it is situated on a rocky ridge which geologists believe to have been man-made, perhaps 2,000 years ago.

The earliest grave was dated 1760, that of Elizabeth Capen. Up to 1900 there were 420 marked graves, with probably many others with no identification. There have been many more burials up to the present time.

The cemetery was not incorporated for many years; then it was changed from a private type community cemetery. The Rock Ridge Association some time between the years 1860 and 1870 acquired a charter from the Commonwealth of Massachusetts. It is non-sectarian, administered by a Board of Trustees, a President, Treasurer and Secretary, all serving without pay.

Of the many families represented there are Morses, Tolmans, Gannetts, Gays, Johnsons, Leonards, Raynolds, Dunakins, Harlows, Swifts, Gilberts, Glovers, and Manns. Through the years many people have pilgrimaged here to view the grave of Deborah Sampson whose grave is marked "Deborah, wife of Benjamin Gannett, April 29, 1827 aged 68y." On the side of the stone facing the DAR plaque is "Robert Shurtleff, Female Soldier service 1781-1783," although the correct dates are 1782-1783.

Job Swift, patriot and a leading citizen often mentioned in the early records of the town of Stoughtonham, is buried here.

JOB SWIFT Born in Wareham, October 2, 1711
          Died at Sharon, February 14, 1801
          Member First Board of Selectmen of Sharon 1765
          One of Committee of Safety 1774
          Delegate to Provincial Congress 1774 to 1775

In a jog of land at the rear of the cemetery lie the poor and unknown. Said "Sharon Potter's Field Uncovered" in the *Norwood Messenger* June 14, 1951:

A recent survey in connection with a mapping of the lots in Rock Ridge Cemetery has revealed that a row of flat field stones numbering more than twenty and for the past hundred years believed by visitors to the ancient burying ground to be a crudely tiled path to the southerly boundary is in fact the last resting place of the destitute people of the town who died in Colonial days. Many of the cemetery records were destroyed years ago by fire, and considerable research was necessary to establish the fact that the small area had originally been set aside as "Potter's Field" in the old cemetery. Investigation by the cemetery authorities indicate that the area includes the bodies of three Indians, original natives of the town, but no records of the identity of the remaining seventeen other bodies are recorded in any town or cemetery documents.

This epitaph for a beloved spouse is that of Peter Phelan who died Aug. 25, 1849 aged 69 years:

"Farewell, Farewell, my bosom friend
Thy loss has rent my heart.
But hope we'll meet in relms of bliss
And never more to part.
O may thy soul my beloved spouse
Fly up to God's bright throne above
To join the holy hosts of heaven
In praising of our Savior's love."

Fifteen Revolutionary soldiers are buried here.
Capt. William Billings, d. Febry 18, 1816 aged 73
Ebenezer Capen, b. Apr. 15, 1716, d. Jan. 4, 1787
Capt. Lemuel Capen, d. Nov. 26, 1805 ae 59
Benjamin Gannett, d. Jan. 9, 1837 in his 80th year
Deborah Sampson Gannett, d. 29 April, 1827 aged 66
Thomas Glover, d. July 10, 1845 ae 87

"Rejoice in glorious hope
Jesus the judge shall come
And take his servants up
To their eternal home."

Asa Harlow, d. Nov. 23, 1794 ae 41 y
Benjamin Harlow, d. Apr. 13, 1825 in his 66th year
Dea. Jacob Hewins, d. July 20, 1806 in the 75th year of his age

"Sleep here thy Dust while concealed in Earth
Til the glad Spring of Nature's second Birth
Then quit the transcient Winter of the Tomb
To rise and flourish in Immortal Bloom."

Joseph Hewins, son of Dea. Jacob Hewins and Mrs. Damaris his wife, who
died April 15, 1783 in ye 21st year of his age
Gilead Morse, d. Jan. 11th, 1809 in his 72nd year
Joseph Morse, d. Feb. 1, 1802 aet 71 y 6 d
Lt. Isaac Johnson, d. Oct. 24, 1833 in the 74th year of his age
Job Swift, d. Feb. 14, 1801 in his 90th year
Major Elijah Capen, d. in 1821

The most commanding monument in the cemetery, located on a rising spot of land easily visible from East Street, is the Soldiers' Monument. Its inscription reads:

Erected by the Town of Sharon A.D. 1908
Commemorative of her sons who fell in the Great Civil War 1861 - 1865
from the Bequests of George Washington Gay
and his wife Eunice Lyon Gay

The following excerpt is from *Massachusetts' Deborah Sampson* by Pauline Moody.

A Grandson's Gift

A huge crowd gathered in Rock Ridge Cemetery an afternoon in May 1908 for the dedication of an imposing monument, a memorial to Sharon's Civil War dead and to Deborah Sampson. Passengers alighted from surries with fringe on top, buggies, and bicycles.

The onlookers were reverent and perhaps curious. Some twenty years earlier, Deborah's grandson, cobbler George Washington Gay, son of Patience Gannett and Seth Gay, had left a life estate in his property to his widow with power to use the whole or any part of the principal. The will also provided that any residue remaining at her death was to go to the town of Sharon, one half for the common schools, and the other half for a monument to Sharon soldiers in the Civil War. Another provision was "I further request to have the name of Deborah Sampson Gannett with proper reference to her service in the war of the revolution inscribed on the same memorial stone." Inasmuch as the Sharon Friends School Fund had received well over $7,000, townspeople were eager to see the monument purchased with the other half of the Gay estate.

The Gay's son, George Herbert and another Sharon boy, Alonzo Artemas Capen, were killed in the spring of 1864. That

45

summer both were eulogized at the first anniversary and reunion of the Stoughtonham Institute where they had been students.

There were addresses before and after the unveiling of the monument. The donor's nephew, Edwin T. Cowell, delivered one of them. "The Spirit of 1776" was among the musical selections and the Norwood band rendered it with the same fervor that modern actors are performing the play *1776*.

The monument was the work of the celebrated sculptress Mrs. Theo Alice Ruggles Kitson. Miss Edythe Monk, Deborah's great-great-granddaughter, assisted in the unveiling.

The spectators beheld on a sightly rise in the cemetery the figure of a youthful soldier in front of a spreading semi-circle of light gray granite. They were too far away to read the eighteen names of Sharon's Civil War dead on a bronze plaque in an ornamental pillar at one end of the semi-circle, and a brief description of Deborah Sampson's military service below a bas-relief of her in the pillar at the other end.

These are the eighteen names on the plaque:
Louis Britton, Co. I. 5th Reg't Massachusetts Cavalry
Daniel W. Bright, Co. A. 4th Reg't Massachusetts Infantry
Alonzo A. Capen, Co. K. 33rd Reg't Massachusetts Infantry
Leander Clapp, Co. F. 29th Reg't Massachusetts Infantry
Alonzo H. Clarke, Co. A. 4th Reg't Massachusetts Infantry
John M. Davis, Co. K. 33rd Reg't Massachusetts Infantry
John M. Drake, Co. K. 33rd Reg't Massachusetts Infantry
John Daley, Co. C. 2nd Reg't Massachusetts Infantry
Amos L. Fuller, Co. E. 58th Reg't Massachusetts Infantry
John B. Franklin, Co. F. 51st Reg't Massachusetts Infantry
George H. Gay, Co. B. 33rd Reg't Massachusetts Infantry
George M. Gerrish, Co. B. 33rd Reg't Massachusetts Infantry
James T. Harridon, Co. B. 33rd Reg't Massachusetts Infantry
Henry Hewins, Co. D. 2nd Reg't Massachusetts Infantry
Norman Hardy, Co. A. 4th Reg't Cavalry
Addison H. Johnson, Co. K. 33rd Reg't Massachusetts Infantry
George F. Lothrop, Engineer Corps
John B. Parks, Co. K. 33rd Reg't Massachusetts Infantry

Other Civil War veterans buried at Rock Ridge are:
James Blackwood, d. Nov. 2, 1925
William Harrison Blanchard, d. Dec. 14, 1926
Henry Bohersack, d. July 23, 1870
Seth Boyden, d. Feb. 23, 1875
Charles F. Bryant, d. June 6, 1912
James N. Burrell, d. 1890
Herbert S. Capen, d. 1918
John D. Capen, d. May 21, 1909
Richard H. Chute, d. Sept. 25, 1933
Obed Cobbett, d. 1909
Charles Alonzo Dunakin

Stillman Dunakin, d. April 3, 1911
Alfred H. Evans, d. 1908
Nathan Russell Fuller, d. Sept. 25, 1901
Sgt. Charles E. Hall, d. July 24, 1914
Elbridge G. Harwood, d. June 14, 1886
Frederick Levi Holbrook, d. 1904
Alfred V. Johnson, d. Jan. 25, 1880
Jessie Johnson, d. 1883
Reuben F. Johnson, d. 1915
Warren Johnson, d. 1906
Samuel Mackay, d. Mar. 28, 1864
W. R. Middleton, d. Oct. 26, 1870
Capt. Esrom Morse, d. 1897
Jacob A. Morse, d. Dec. 23, 1875
Stillman H. Morse, d. Jan. 28, 1895
Henry L. Narramore, d. 1898
Josiah Wardwell Perry, d. Jan. 23, 1904
Charles F. Richards, d. 1905
Jessie S. Robinson, d. 1931
Otis S. Tolman, d. June 14, 1918
Leonard W. White, d. 1902

Five men were veterans of the War of 1812:
Col. Ramsel Jones, d. Nov. 21, 1827
Capt. Nathaniel Leonard, d. Nov. 17, 1843
George H. Mann, d. Oct. 25, 1847
Capt. John Morse, d. April 11, 1850
Jedidiah Snow

Dunakin died in 1911. He fought in the Spanish American War.

Rock Ridge Cemetery gave to the Charles R. Wilber Post 106 of the American Legion the land for the Legion Lot. The cemetery also gave the land for World War I and World War II memorials. These monuments erected in 1948 were the gift of Edmund H. Talbot who left a trust fund to maintain them. The World War II monument was in memory of Talbot's nephew Edmund A. Chapin.

The World War I monument is in memory of Charles R. Wilber, the only Sharon soldier to be killed during that war. The Charles R. Wilber Post 106 bears his name as does the Intermediate School on South Main St. Names of the 108 Veterans of this war are listed on the Memorial Stone in front of the Sharon Town Hall.

The World War II Memorial bears this inscription on its central portion.

They Live With Us In Grateful Memory Of Their Sacrifice
World War II
Dec. 8, 1941 to Aug. 15, 1945
Edmund A. Chapin Memorial
2nd Lieut. Q.M. Corps U.S. Army
Aug. 13, 1889 - Mar. 22, 1938

The names of those lost in action are inscribed on the side panels of the Memorial.

1918 Sgt. Francis M. Cunningham July 8, 1943 Sicily
1922 F 2/c Edward N. Hare Nov. 6, 1943 South China Sea
1922 Sergt. Warren H. Hickey April 21, 1944 England
1918 Sgt. James A. Keating Nov. 8, 1944 France
1917 Corp. Harold D. O'Neil Feb. 23, 1943 Dutch East Indies
1920 Lt. John H. Penning May 24, 1944 Austria
1922 P.F.C. Nicholas Savino July 17, 1944 France
1924 Lt. Horace K. Walter May 21, 1944 Germany
1917 Lt. Arthur E. White Feb. 22, 1944 North Sea
1913 Edward Stevenson Mar 17, 1944 U.S.M.M. at Sea

KNOLLWOOD CEMETERY

In 1898 a group of business men from Boston formed a promotional corporation to be known as "Knollwood Cemetery" and received a charter from the Commonwealth of Massachusetts. They planned and built a new cemetery after the plan of what is known as a rural cemetery, the land lying both in Canton and in Sharon. This was to be the last resting place primarily of families living in Boston.

Early burying grounds were located close to the communities which they served and were soon filled and surrounded by these cities and towns, such as King's Chapel and Old Granary grounds in Boston. In the 1800's the idea was conceived to have cemeteries outside of the cities, and in rural areas not apt to become thickly settled. The grounds were to be landscaped and made spots of beauty where families could come by train or horse-drawn vehicles to visit their family lots and to enjoy the beauty of their surroundings. The first of these rural cemeteries, Mt. Auburn, is brought to mind by the poet, James Russell Lowell who wrote "I think of a mound in sweet Auburn, where a little headstone stood."

Such was the plan and intention of what is known locally as "Old Knollwood," to differentiate it from Knollwood Memorial Park across the way. Located on Canton Avenue its land ran down to the railroad tracks. It covered an area of about four hundred acres, being twice the size of Forest Hills Cemetery and three times the size of Mt. Auburn. This same acreage now includes Knollwood Memorial Park and Sharon Memorial Park.

Great thought was taken to preserve the natural beauty of its surroundings. The paths and roads were given either Indian or historical names. As a portion of this land was owned by the patriot, Paul Revere, in 1801, a plot which contains a lovely natural lake called Ninigret was given the name of our Revolutionary War hero. An eminence of some thirty acres from which can be seen views of the Blue Hills, Dedham, Norwood, and other surrounding towns was named Mt. Gridley, for our famous Revolutionary War engineer.

To make the cemetery accessible to Boston a railroad station was built on the grounds, trains ran every two hours from Boston and Back Bay. The brochure tells us that "a magnificent special car 'Knollwood' was to be built to accommodate the mourners who would then be met at the station by a horse-drawn hearse and carriages." Roads were lined with cork so that the silence would not be broken.

A mausoleum or receiving tomb said to be the "largest, finest and most expensive mausoleum in the country" was for the use of lot owners. Pictures of the mausoleum and the railroad station appeared in the first annual report of the cemetery. A large lithograph in color showed the entire grounds with the buildings. Both the mausoleum and station were built of granite. Today a large plot of bare ground probably marks the site of the receiving tomb, since as many Sharonites remember ... both the mausoleum and the stations were destroyed — one by fire, the other by vandals. The old caretaker's house, whose original owner in 1822 is unknown, was moved a few years ago to Edge Hill Road where it was restored. Many prominent Bostonians as well as Sharon and Canton residents lie buried in Knollwood. Apparently only a small percentage of the acreage was cleared and landscaped, certainly none of the land on the otherside of Canton Street was used.

The promise in the thirties of a beautiful garden cemetery did not materialize due to the coming of age of the automobile. It was easier for families to travel to Mt. Auburn or Forest Hills by car than to journey to the station for a train.

Four veterans of the Civil War from Sharon are listed as being buried here: Harrison E. Harwood, Andrew Goodwin, Samuel Weir, and — Burnam.

KNOLLWOOD MEMORIAL PARK

The three cemeteries, Knollwood, Knollwood Memorial Park, and Sharon Memorial Park, are under the same management and cover the same acreage as the original Knollwood. In the 1940's a new Board of Directors was formed and today Knollwood Memorial Park is truly a place of beauty, it and Sharon Memorial Park being among the most beautiful cemeteries in New England, perhaps indeed the most beautiful. Its plans and care may be compared to the celebrated Forest Lawn in California.

Part of the non-sectarian Knollwood Memorial Park is in Sharon and part in Canton. The lawns show an unbroken green, for uniform bronze plaques marking the graves are set level with the lawn, enabling one to see its beauty. The landscaping has been planned by the noted landscape architect Mr. Harry Frazier. The natural contours of the land have been preserved, the trees and shrubs set at the best possible locations, the statuary and their approaches placed at eye-catching points.

Knollwood not only is a beautiful garden with its trees, flowering shrubs and lawns, but it has also been planned as a Biblical garden. On a rise in each section of the cemetery are statues of sculptured marble which in themselves warrant a visit in any season of the year.

In the Garden of the Word one sees on the hilltop a large open Bible in a frame of six Corinthian columns reminiscent of the words of Isaiah, "The grass withereth, the flower fadeth; but the word of our God shall stand forever."

On another distinctive knoll, the life-sized representation of the Saviour with extended hands overlooks the Garden of the Saviour. Purple junipers form a carpet leading to the feet of Christ. Eastern rosebuds signify the betrayal of Judas. From the road surrounding this knoll visitors obtain a view of the valley of the Neponset far below.

The Garden of the Last Supper is dominated by a 6½' x 14' marble bas-relief representation of Leonardo da Vinci's masterpiece "The Last Supper."

Made of Carrara marble, it is perhaps the largest piece of this marble in New England. On each side of the approach are twelve Japanese crab trees representing the twelve disciples.

The Garden of Gethsemane contains a life-sized statue, again in marble, which shows our Saviour kneeling in prayer by a great rock. Here are eight olive trees, the same number still remaining today in the Holy Land's Garden of Gethsemane.

The Garden of the Cross is shaped in that form, the focal point being a fourteen-foot iron cross silhouetted against the sky. Events in the life of Jesus are symbolized: the crown surmounts the cross; the three leaves of three fleur-de-lis represent the trinity; twelve rays radiating from the crown represent the twelve apostles, as do twelve dogwood trees planted here.

The newest memorial is in remembrance of veterans. Appropriately it is a white marble representation, again on a hilltop, of the soldiers raising the flag at Iwo Jima. It overlooks the graves of veterans buried here.

SHARON MEMORIAL PARK

The Greater Boston Jewish Community in the 1940's found a need for a new cemetery as the ones in the Boston area were being filled. So in 1949 Sharon Memorial Park, a part of Knollwood, seemed an ideal location and was established there. Now in 1976 it serves thirty-six sponsoring organizations, including Orthodox, Conservative and Reformed Congregations as well as many fraternal societies. These include members from Greater Boston and communities as far away as Worcester to the west and Providence to the south. Already over 10,000 lie buried here. Lots are owned by outstanding and famous Jewish people in every field of endeavor.

Memorial services are held annually at the High Holidays in the Jacob Grossman Chapel in the Woods, which will seat over 1,000 persons.

Obeying the Hebraic Law from Exodus 20:4 "Thou shalt not make unto thyself any graven image," no statuary is here. The graves are marked by polished bronze plaques which lie horizontal to the ground. In some plots there are stone benches marked with the family name. Enclosing many lots are well-cared-for yew hedges.

This is truly a garden cemetery filled with living memorials in the form of trees planted twenty-five years ago, which in the years to come will have achieved their ultimate stature. Crab and cherry trees, azaleas, rhododendrons, and andromeda are glorious to behold in the spring. The park is especially noted for its yews. All of these trees and shrubs are indigenous and thrive in the New England climate.

On a wall in the gracious reception center, which contains the staff offices and the reception rooms for the public, is a large bas-relief map of Israel. It shows many of the cities, the River Jordan, and Mounts Gilboa and Sinai.

Here then, in this beautiful cemetery, is comfort for those visiting the graves of their loved ones and beauty for the eye of the beholder.

Footnotes

1. John G. Phillips, "The Village Tomb." *Sharon Historical Society Phillips Scrapbooks*, Vol. I (Sharon Public Library)
2. William R. Mann and others, comp., "Sharon Epitaphs," compiled by William R. Mann, Mrs. Mann, Mrs. George Kempton, and Eugene Tappan for the New England Historic Genealogical Society (Boston: Mass., 1900)
3. Massachusetts. Secretary of the Commonwealth, *Massachusetts Soldiers and Sailors of the Revolutionary War* (Boston: Wright & Potter Printing Co., 1905)

The Knollwood Mausoleum

The Chestnut Tree Cemetery   *Photo by: J. K. Harris*

An Early View of Lake Massapoag

Lake Massapoag, 1976

Photo by: J. K. Harris

An 1898 View of the South Shore of Lake Massapoag Showing the Steam Launch Pier

Courtesy of: B. D. Ornell

52

LAKE MASSAPOAG
A GREAT POND

By Katharine M. Cartwright

CHAPTER 4

"Lake Massapoag lies in the heart of the town,
    With its beautiful face to the sky,
And its lover, the Sun, all the day time looks down
    And smiles from its station on high.
Surrounded by groves in its rural retreat,
    The wild flocks here assemble for flight,
And the moon and the stars are impatient to meet
    Where their beauty is mirrored at night.

In the far away time the red Indian came
    And his wigwam was built on the shore,
He fished on its waters and gave it the name
    Of Massapoag for evermore.
Then the Puritan settled on the banks of the lake,
    Tolman crossed in his boat to his cot,
And Gridley and Quincy in war learned to take
    Iron ore for their cannon and shot.

Where to slaken their thirst came the moose and the deer,
    The fond heart will oft turn with delight,
As bedecked with all charms that the senses can cheer,
    Lake Massapoag gleams to the sight.
From the bowl of pure water in nature's own hand
    We will drink to its health and our own,
For as long as the beautiful lives, it will stand
    The loveliest lake we have known."

Eugene Tappan[1]

Lying in the plain between Moose and Rattlesnake Hills is a body of water called Lake Massapoag. Long before the white man came, it was known to the Ponkapoags who gave it this Indian name and undoubtedly fished in its quiet waters.

In 1912 J. Eveleth Griffith, of the Sharon Improvement Society, hoping to attract newcomers to the town, wrote in his *Sharon the Beautiful* the following description of the Lake.

"This lake is exceptionally pure and limpid, and so close do the surrounding woodlands encroach upon it, making it sparkle like a gem in a dark setting, that in places they seem to have gathered at its edge for the express purpose of studying their reflection on its surface. At its southern end a sandy beach strikes in, surrounded by a noble grove of hemlocks."[2]

One of the very early white men to have knowledge of the lake was William Tolman whose home was nearby where Camp Wadsworth is located. His family tell that he hollowed out a great log in the Indian fashion and so fished or rowed across the lake.

This notice of the Lake appears in an old Gazetteer of Massachusetts, dated 1878: "A little south of the centre is a fair and a broad sheet of water, covering an area of about 460 acres, and known as 'Massapoag Pond.' It was a favorite resort of the aborigines. It rests upon a bed of iron ore, and is much frequented by the angler and the sportsman."[3]

In early maps and records we find various spellings: in the 1696 "Twelve Division Lots" it appears as "Mashipaog"; in the 1794 map of the town we find "Mashapoge pond put on by gess" — it was a poor one at that!

Because of its glacial origin it was formed during the time when the glaciers of the ice age were receding to the north, scraping out great holes. At its deepest point in the center where the glacial ice remained longest there is a trough 45 feet deep. One school of thought about the origin of the lake is that when the colonists were digging for bog iron they tapped springs in the center of the depression which filled and thus formed the lake. This theory was disproved by the evidence of the lake banks and by the fact that the bog iron was grappled for and not dug.[4]

Lake Massapoag is legally known as a great pond, meaning that it is over ten acres in size and thus is under the jurisdiction of the Commonwealth of Massachusetts. It covers an area of about 400 acres and is 300 feet above sea level. The old maps do not agree on the size of the lake probably because of the various methods used in the earlier days in arriving at the acreage. Because of its high elevation it is relatively free of fog. It lies in the depression of the Neponset Valley, is mostly spring fed, with ground water from the cedar swamps contributing to its size. From a newspaper clipping on an underwater survey of the lake we note "In the immediate vicinity of Lake Massapoag, there are three recognizable recharge areas which have a direct influence on Lake Massapoag and its water level. The first is the extensive swampy land traversed by glacial eskers (sandy ridges) lying to the east of Massapoag Avenue in the rear of the Salvation Army Camp. The second is the swampy area, also extensive, lying to the west of Lakeview Street near the southern end of the lake. The third is Great Cedar Swamp approaching the lake from East Foxboro Street."[5] Several small brooks enter it, Sucker Brook, in the vicinity of the Salvation Army Camp, being the largest. The outlet of the lake is Massapoag Brook, whose waters finally enter into the Neponset River.

Older residents claim that the water came up Pond Street as far as Ames Street so that boats could go up that far. The swamp level must have been much higher at that time. However, geologists believe that today it is approximately the same size as when the glaciers receded and the pond was filled in.

Frederic Endicott of Canton was employed in 1870 by the Revere Copper Company to make a survey of Massapoag Pond showing the line of water as it then stood, and the ancient line of the pond bank. He wrote an interesting article entitled "The Bank Around Massapoag Pond" which appeared in the Sharon Historical Society Publications. Much of it is quite technical, but of great interest to a geologist. A map accompanied the article showing the pond banks and the names of families living around the lake at that time.

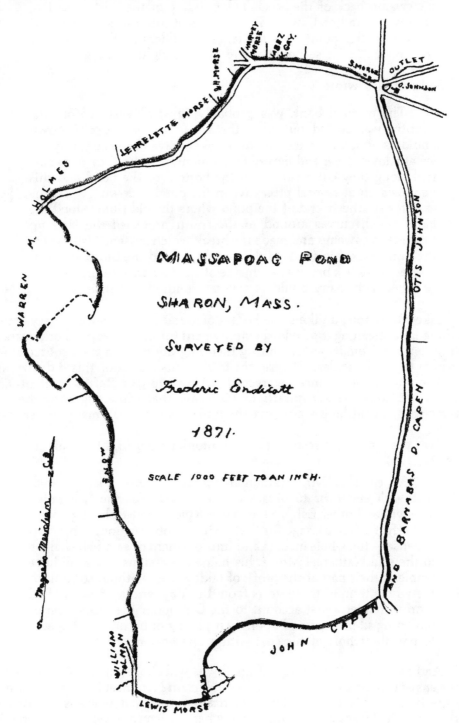

The improvements around the hotel have smoothed out the distinctive characters of the bank at that place and filled in a gap which existed in the original bank where in 1870 there was a dam and flume holding back the waters of the stream which flows from the swamp back of the hotel. The building of the Burkhardt Ice-houses and railroad swept away the most interesting part of the bank as at this point were the largest boulders on the borders of the pond. . . . These boulders were six to eight feet high.

Endicott also wrote:

The original bank was probably finished years before the country was settled but since the water has been drawn down boulders which were too low to be taken have been caught by the ice at a lower level and moved along many feet. As they were carried along they cut a furrow in the bottom of the pond and this may be seen at several places when the pond is down. . . . At the extreme southerly end of the pond where the old flume stood the bank which curves around to the south protected the land up towards the swamp and made the break which is seen. Also, where the pond makes in towards the swamp behind the Burkhardt Ice-houses there is a break at each side of the bay and we find a piece of bank with many boulders several hundred feet inland.[6]

Lake Massapoag unlike some bodies of water of its size was a very active working lake, meaning it provided employment for many people. For instance, taking alewives from its waters during their migration was a great source of income for the early settlers. References to the importance of this industry are found in the old town meeting records. Amy Morgan Rafter Pratt in *The History of Sharon, Massachusetts to 1865* says that while migrating the fish became so plentiful horses crossing the outlet would crush many under their hooves.

Two years after the records of Stoughtonham began, I find this record — Sept. 21, 1767:

Voted that Mr. Nathaniel Morse of this District shall forthwith endeavor to obtain a free passage for the fish called alewives and other fish up Neponset River into Mashapoge pond and effect a free passage for them without obstruction, at his own expense — the whole income and Improvement of said fish shall be to the said Nathaniel Morse, his heirs and assigns and shall have whole of their part of the profit of taking them without control for the whole term of three years from this day, and at the end of sd term to render a just account to the District of the prime cost of obtaining sd passage and upon their paying or becoming obligated to pay the whole of his cost within one year next after. . . .

And as late as 1809, "To see if the towns will choose an agent or agents to make answer to the petition of the mill holders on Neponset River for Shutting up the fish ways." The problem which arose was that whereas the fish in earlier times had free access to the pond, when settlements were made along the

Neponset, mills sprang up and mill dams prevented the fish going up stream to spawn. This controversy continued for many years, it being brought by the towns to the General Court so that laws were passed controlling the situation. Finally the mills increased so in size and number the people gave up the struggle.

Cedar swamps once adjoined the pond at its northwesterly and southeasterly portions and these were heavily wooded with large trees suitable for splitting into posts and rails which then were in demand. The second growth trees were not nearly as good as the primeval cedars as even fifty years growth gives soft wood without wearing qualities.

The next industry connected with the lake was taking bog iron from the lake bed. First the iron was used to make household and farming implements, and later, during the Revolutionary War, cannon and cannon balls. See Sharon's Cannon.

In 1724 Ebenezer Jones and other "owners of ye iron works" purchased 370 tons of iron ore from the lake. In 1727 Nathaniel Leonard was granted the right "of improving Massapoag to git iron ore." In 1770 the whole property (this was illegal) was sold to Edmund Quincy, a mining operator, for 30 pounds, six shillings. In this same year Richard Gridley purchased of Edmund Quincy one-half of Massapoag Pond for the procuring of iron ore from its bed.

Over the years mills were established to utilize the water power from Massapoag Brook, the lake's outlet. Later the lowering of the lake level by the Revere Copper Company led to a bitter dispute and a law suit which continued for five years.

On July 7, 1885 a committee of five men representing the inhabitants of Sharon filed a suit against the Revere Copper Company demanding that they be restrained from drawing water, without right or authority from said Massapoag Pond. They claimed that it, by greatly lowering the natural height of the water, impaired the rights of the public for boating, fishing, etc., and was also detrimental to health.

The plaintiffs based their suit on the Colony Ordinance, passed in 1647, providing that "no town shall appropriate to any particular person or persons any great pond," thus making the grant to Edmund Quincy in 1770 invalid.

The defendant claimed that it had, for over one hundred years, owned and held title to the pond, and was the absolute owner of the pond. They based their claim on the grant, given in 1637, which predated the 1647 Ordinance, from the Colony to the Dorchester Proprietors, who in turn had granted the rights to various persons.

However, the Court in reviewing the case said that due to the fact that the Defendant had had an unbroken chain of title to this privilege since 1637, and as the lowering of the lake was not detrimental to health, and a business of $1,800,000 was involved, settled in favor of the Revere Copper Company.

Toward the end of the 1800's a flourishing business sprang up to continue for many years, that of cutting ice, which provided work for many people. The first company, located at the southern end of the lake where the homes on Livingston Road now stand, was the Burkhardt Ice Company. Recently divers working at the lake found three large stone boats or sleds, perhaps 25' - 50' in size, resting on the bottom piled high with rocks. It was conjectured that these were to build a wall for the Burkhardt Ice Company. After a number of years the Boston Ice Company bought out this business. See The Boston Ice Company.

Brymer's Ice House was where the town beach is now. This was a local business selling ice in Sharon. Brymer's ice cart can be remembered by many people now living in the town.

The ice houses were the last of the history of Lake Massapoag as a working lake. From that era the purpose of the lake has been to give beauty to the observer and recreation for the people.

In 1931 the town purchased the land, buildings, and water rights to Massapoag Pond which were assessed to the Plymouth Rubber Company. Since that time the lake has remained full. Sometime in the 1900's the old wooden flume house was replaced with a stone one, built as a replica of an early powder house.

During the late 1800's the lake became a popular summer resort when people came in numbers to enjoy the scenery and the clear waters of the lake. A carriage ride around the lake was one of the pleasures of a sunny afternoon. Beautiful homes were built overlooking the lake.

Solomon Talbot described Burkhardt's Grove in the 1880's, situated at the corner of East Foxboro and Beach Sts. A branch railroad, connected with the icehouse, enabled people from Boston to come out and enjoy picnics and dances. Mrs. Mary McGrath remembers when she and her friends here in Sharon later enjoyed the weekly dances held here at "The Grove."

The most famous of the hotels overlooking the lake was the old Massapoag Hotel, since burned. Again Solomon Talbot tells of this famous hostelry: "Upon the southeast side of the lake stands the Massapoag House, located in a grove about thirty feet above the water, a summer watering place, large and roomy — a pleasant resort during the summer for people of business or leisure. A more pleasing situation cannot be imagined." Mrs. McGrath's father, Captain MacDonald, was the skipper of the steam launch, owned by the hotel, which plied the waters of the lake for five cents a ride. It was reported to me that this launch caught fire at its wharf and was towed out into the lake and there burned and sank. Another story, whether fact or fiction, tells that the pet of the hotel, a seven foot alligator, escaped about sixty years ago and was last seen swimming out into the lake. The town purchased the hotel, which replaced this earlier one, in 1967 and it is now known as the Community Center where townspeople of all ages gather for recreation.

There are several camps around the southern end of the lake where underprivileged children are brought from the cities for several weeks at a time. The largest of these is the Salvation Army Fresh Air Camp, "Wonderland," which had its first season around the year 1924. Here several hundred children come during the summer as well as mothers with babies, and senior citizens. Camp Gannett and the Kiddie Camp, now known as "Horizons for Youth," are two others which are doing fine work to bring happiness to these children.

Fishing through the years has been an important recreation at the lake, both on shore and in boats, making it a mecca for fishermen.

In 1912 Mr. Griffith wrote in *Sharon the Beautiful*, "Landlocked salmon, white perch and black bass have made it their home." Each spring the Massachusetts Division of Fisheries and Game stock the lake. Large and small-mouthed bass, rainbow and brown trout, yellow perch, sunfish, and hornpouts are caught. Four-, five-, and six-pound bass and a seventeen-inch rainbow trout were caught by lucky fishermen in 1975. For the past few years a Fishing Derby for children through the age of fourteen years has been an exciting event, sponsored by the Sharon and Massapoag Fish and Game Clubs and the Recreation Department, prizes being donated by the manufacturers of fishing equipment.

Iceboating, skating, and fishing take place in the winter. On a fair Saturday or Sunday the lake is beautiful with the fleet of sailboats belonging to the Massapoag Yacht Club.

The town has two beaches, one near the north end of the lake, the other near the Community Center. The Recreation Department has trained life guards at these beaches. Swimming and boating classes are held for the children in the summer.

Footnotes

1. Eugene Tappan's poem was sung to the tune of "Believe Me If All Those Endearing Young Charms."
2. J. Eveleth Griffith, *Sharon the Beautiful.* Issued under the Direction of the Publicity Committee of the Sharon Improvement Association (Boston: Griffith-Stillings Press, 1912).
3. Elias Nason, *Gazetteer of the State of Massachusetts* (Boston: B. B. Russell, 1878).
4. G. Duffy Bailey, "Environmental History of Lake Massapoag" (Sharon, Mass.: Lake Management Committee, 1972).
5. Editorial, *The Sharon Advocate*, February 11, 1971.
6. *Sharon Historical Society Scrapbook*, Vol. II, June 1905.

An 1898 View of the North Shore of Lake Massapoag   *Courtesy of: B. D. Ornell*

Burkhardt's Grove Picnickers at Sharon Heights Station

BURKHARDT'S GROVE

By Clifford L. Jerauld

CHAPTER 5

The Grove was originally established by the Burkhardt Brewery as a recreation area for its employees sometime in the late 1880's. Eventually it was sold to the Norfolk and Bristol Street Railway. It was rather common for street railways to own recreation areas on their lines to encourage people to travel to and from them at quiet times of day and night, and especially on weekends.

The name Burkhardt was dropped, and locally the area became known as the Grove. It was enclosed with a solid board fence twelve feet high and ran from the corner of Harding and East Foxboro Streets to the corner of Beach and East Foxboro, down Beach to the corner of Harding, along Harding to the corner of East Foxboro. This area is now occupied by Lake and Grove Avenues. There were three large gates: two of them located about where Lake Avenue is now; the other on East Foxboro Street about halfway between Harding and Beach.

There were buildings inside the fence. The larger was in the form of a T. The upper part of it was about 100 x 35 feet. The lower floor had picnic tables and benches, and the base of the T was a kitchen. The upper floor had a beautiful dance floor with an outside balcony which ran the full length of the building. The dance hall had a set of tuned bells. When the building was no longer used, the bells were stolen and broken up. Dances were held every Saturday night during the summer. The building swayed when a large crowd was dancing and some people felt it might be unsafe. It was discovered, however, when the building was torn down that the sills were of solid rubber one-yard square. This accounted for the bounce or sway of the building.

There was also a dance pavilion about 35 x 35 feet, a large refreshment stand, and a ticket booth. A pump supplied water which was drunk from a communal tin cup. A baseball field was tucked in one corner, and a scattering of eight swings with 25-foot ropes hung between pine trees. The whole grove was spectacular, consisting of pine trees with butts of 15 to 20 inches. They were destroyed when a development was put there.

Several times during the summer there would be picnics with people arriving from Boston by RR trains or large streetcars. Three to four trains or a dozen or more streetcars were necessary to transport the hundreds of picnickers. The one big local picnic was put on by the Catholic Church. It lasted from 10 A.M. until midnight, and people from surrounding towns came by streetcar. This was about the largest gathering the town would have throughout the year. There were band concerts in the afternoon and evening and a dance orchestra during the later hours. The priest behind all this was Father Costello. Other churches had their Sunday School picnics at the Grove, and for several summers settees were placed in the pavilion so evangelistic services could be held there.

Burton Bernstein's novel, *The Grove*, is about summer residents who came year after year to that section of Sharon.

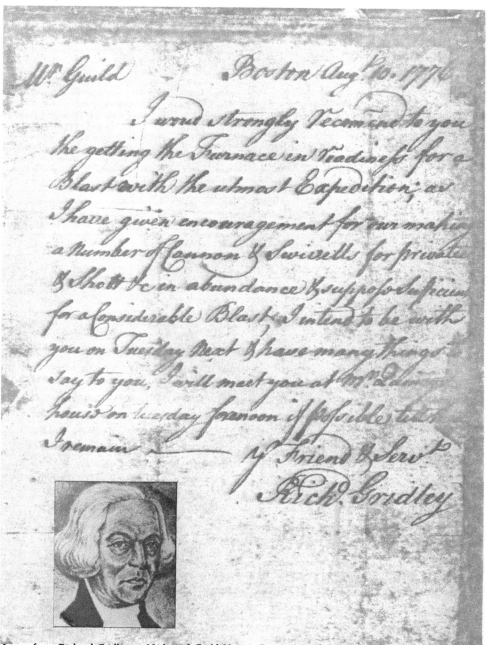

Letter from Richard Gridley to Nathaniel Guild Urging Furnace Readiness

Courtesy of: Stoughton Historical Society

SHARON'S CANNON

By Sydney S. Morgan

CHAPTER 6

Nestled in a valley of old Stoughtonham (now Sharon) between two ridges stood the Stoughtonham Furnace which according to tradition produced the first cannon cast in this country to be used in the Revolutionary War. The waters which flow southerly from Wolomolopoag Pond (an Indian name meaning "Deep Pleasant Water") passed by the furnace site and provided the power and cooling necessary for the furnace operation. Secluded in its forest setting, the necessarily clandestine operations conducted here were safe from prying Tory eyes.

Two men, Edmund Quincy and Richard Gridley, formed one of those unlikely partnerships that providently exist in our country's history just when they are most needed. Quincy was the business man, the promoter, the entrepreneur. Gridley possessed the technical skill, the practical experience, and the ability to get things done. Both were patriots who had cast their lot with the struggling American colonies. Together they founded a company that produced the heavy armament required in the forthcoming conflict with England.

Edmund Quincy V was descended from a wealthy and notable English family that had been distinguished in literature and public service. He was born in Boston on April 15, 1725. His father was a retired Braintree merchant. He came to Stoughtonham in 1767 to re-examine the area for minerals, since his grandfather had founded the first furnace in Canton in 1717 and had obtained ore from the vicinity. Quincy stayed at the home of Benjamin Gannett on the easterly side of Lake Massapoag. At forty-two, he was a self-styled "gentleman" and was described as having the style and manners of English nobility. He soon wooed and won the hand of the Gannett's sixteen-year-old daughter Hannah. They were married April 30, 1767. He bought a farm of 150 acres adjacent to that of his father-in-law, where he resided the rest of his life.

In 1770, being aware of the amount of bog iron ore laying on the shore and in the waters of Lake Massapoag, he approached the Dorchester Proprietors offering to purchase the ore, provided they would drain off the water from the pond. The committee appointed to investigate the expense reported that it would cost 500 pounds. The Proprietors considered this expense so great that they chose a committee to sell the pond. The records state:

To all people to whom these presents shall come. Joseph Hewins
of the district of Stoughtonham, Esq. Lemuel Robinson and
Richard Hall both of Dorchester, and all in the County of Suffolk
and province of Massachusetts Bay in New England and a committee chosen and fully empowered by the proprietors of
Dorchester and Stoughton at a meeting of said proprietors on the
fifth day of June, 1770, to sell a certain pond in the said District of
Stoughtonham known by the name of Mashapoag Pond provided
they can get for it what they shall judge to be the value thereof and
to pass and execute a good deed or deeds in the law for the con-
veyance of the same in the name and behalf of the said proprietors
as by their records will more fully appear . . .[3]

The proprietors conveyed the pond to Edmund Quincy on June 11, 1770,
for 30 pounds 6 shillings. The pond, which contained about 400 acres, had
been a part of the grant made by the Colony of Massachusetts Bay on
November 20, 1637, to the proprietors of Dorchester.

Whether they had the legal right to sell is questionable, since a Colony Ordinance in 1647 had defined "Great Ponds" as those containing more than ten
acres, making them public property "to lie in common for public use."

As a matter of interest, it took a case in Suffolk Court in 1890 to give the
lake in fact back to the people after a succession of private owners. The court
found:

Under the Colony Ordinance of 1647 providing that "no town
shall appropriate to any particular person or persons any great
pond containing more than ten acres of land," a deed made in 1770
by the proprietors of a town to an individual, and purporting to
convey a great pond within its limits, is invalid.

The Boston Massacre, which occurred on March 5, 1770, had made it clear
that armed conflict with the mother country was inevitable, and most colonists
expected hostilities to commence much sooner than they actually did.

Quincy knew of the Ebenezer Mann Furnace in Stoughtonham, having
supplied it with ore from his prospect in Wrentham. With an apparently inex-
haustable source of raw material under his control only two miles from the furnace, and with a sense of urgency brought about by current events, he approached Richard Gridley, the Artillerist, who was then in Boston.

Persuaded by Quincy, Richard Gridley came to Stoughtonham to look
over the furnace property and iron ore reserves. He was fifty-nine years old,
having been born in Boston on January 3, 1710/11. He had been apprenticed to
a Boston wholesale merchant, but having a bent for mathematics, he became a
surveyor and civil engineer. He studied military engineering under John Henry
Bastide, a British officer engaged in planning fortifications for Boston and
vicinity. On February 25, 1730, he married Hannah Deming, by whom he had
nine children.

In 1745 he was commissioned lieutenant colonel, and captain of the artillery train preparing to seige Louisburg, the French fortress on Cape Breton
Island. After many actions and commendations during the French and Indian
War, he went to England to adjust his accounts with the War Office. For his
services he was granted the Magdelen Islands with a valuable seal and cod

fishery, half pay as a British officer, and 3,000 acres of land in New Hampshire. He lived for several years on the islands and built up a profitable business in walrus oil.

He had returned to Massachusetts Bay sometime before the Boston Massacre, and this incident made it apparent to him also that armed conflict was inevitable. Gridley realized that a supply of heavy ordnance was vital for success.

Seeing the opportunity presented by the fortuitous combination of available iron ore and usable furnace, he agreed with Quincy to enter the business of cannon manufacture.

On September 25, 1770, Edmund Quincy conveyed by deed to Richard Gridley one half of his title to Mashapoag Pond for 15 pounds, 3 shillings.

The purchase of the furnace property was somewhat more complicated.

On October 26, 1770, Quincy, together with Richard Gridley and Joseph Jackson, a truckman of Boston who provided the money, purchased the Ebenezer Mann Furnace at the southerly end of what is now known as Gavin's Pond for 360 pounds. No iron had been produced in the colonies since 1750 when the English Parliament decreed, at the behest of English merchants who were feeling the competition of Colonial hardware manufacturers, that iron manufacture in the Colonies should cease.

It was natural that the early colonists, in order to provide for their needs, would start the industries that would furnish what was required. As colonial production increased, the English manufacturers viewed their dwindling export profits with alarm, and prevailed on the government to pass restrictive legislation.

In 1699 Parliament enacted a law prohibiting any woolen yarn from being shipped or transported any place whatever. In 1731 a law was passed that no hats should be shipped or laden upon a horse cart or other carriage whatever to be transported to any other colony places.

The 1750 law relating to the manufacture of iron prohibited the erection or maintenance of any mill or other engine for slitting or rolling iron, or any plating forge to work with a tilt hammer, or any furnace for making steel in the Colonies under a penalty of five hundred pounds. Every such mill or plating forge was declared a common nuisance, and the Governor was directed to cause the same to be removed within thirty days or forfeit the sum of five hundred pounds. As a result most furnaces in the colonies stopped production.

Nevertheless, on March 27, 1762, Royall Kollock conveyed three acres of land to Jonathan Ripley, Daniel Dunbar, Perez Ripley, High Knox, and Swift Payson. Owners of adjacent lands were Seth Boyden, Nathan Clark, and Benjamin Fairbanks. Members of the company lived in Halifax, Walpole, Wrentham, and Foxboro.

On June 1, 1762, they recorded an agreement to build a furnace for casting hollowware in Stoughtonham, on land bought from Royall Kollock, to be done November 1st, next. All were to have one-eighth shares except Ebenezer Mann and Nathaniel Guild, who were to own one-sixteenth share each. Several changes of share ownership were recorded during the life span of the Mann Furnace, but the Gridley Company had purchased a controlling interest of nine-sixteenths of the furnace, land, buildings, utensils, dam waters, etc., from Nathaniel Guild of Walpole, Joseph Pratt, John Comee, Swift Payson of Foxboro, Nathaniel Morse and Benjamin Billings of Stoughtonham, and Ebenezer Britton of Raynham.

SHARON, MASSACHUSETTS: A HISTORY

Further transactions are recorded on the same date, October 26, 1770; by another deed Swift Payson conveys one thirty-second part to the same three men for twenty pounds; Ebenezer Mann of Shackstand Hill conveys one thirty-second part with price of twenty pounds, by another deed, another one-sixteenth share with price of forty pounds; James Russell of Holliston conveys a one-eighth share for eighty pounds. On November 13, 1770, Ebenezer Mann conveys another one-sixteenth share for forty pounds. On November 22, 1770, Josiah Morse and Nathan Tarbell Prentice sold one-sixteenth share each for forty pounds each. On January 28, 1771, Richard Sanger of Sherburne also conveyed a one-sixteenth share of the Stoughtonham Furnace.

The early settlers believed that there were valuable minerals to be found under the surface of the ground, and these were mentioned in the early deeds. On April 7, 1772, Edmund Quincy conveyed all his interest in all mines, mine ores, minerals, and other hidden treasures of the earth in the farm of Barnabas Thurston of Wrentham, stated to be a two-sixteenth part, to his partners Richard Gridley and Joseph Jackson. The price was two hundred pounds or about $1,000 making the mineral rights worth $8,000.

To obtain the ore from the lake bed, the water level had to be lowered. At the time, the main outlet from the spring-fed lake was through the cedar swamp at the southwesterly edge. The tradition is that the townspeople assisted in digging the present outlet at the northern end, partaking of a roasted ox while they dug, being sustained through their labors with a keg of New England rum. Additional channels were dug "herringbone" pattern, joining the main channel, to further lower the level.

Gridley's Diary informs us: "Aug. 24, 1773, Began to get ore out of the pond." The ore was "mined" by fishing it up from the bed of the lake by means of long-handled tongs, similar to those used by oyster fishermen.

The tongs were manipulated by a man standing in a rowboat or raft, reaching down to the shallow bottom to bring up sand, weeds, and nodules of iron ore. A second man would separate the ore from the stones, wash the sand out, and load it into another boat. A day's work would fill the boat and make a tenth of a cannon. It would then be carted to the furnace site.

The bog iron nodules had been formed through the action of bacteria, which abounded in stagnant swamps and absorbed their sustenance from the water. The iron in solution could not be digested, and precipitated in microscopic quantities against their outer membrane. It took billions of these tiny particles to make a nodule. The result was pure hematite (Fe_2O_3) which was about seventy percent iron.

Gridley had personally surveyed and supervised the lowering of the lake, being assisted by his son Scarborough, who lived at the Quincy farm in Sharon while the work was going on.

On September 23, 1773, he records in his diary: "Moved from Quincy's house to the forge house in Canton." This was on a farm owned by Jacob Leonard and purchased by Gridley, who put up the furnace as security for the purchase. It is from the records of this transaction that we have a description of the furnace property.

The furnace works, as they were set off by the court to Jacob Leonard on the 17th of September 1773, consisted of the following property:

Three acres of land bounded northerly by the land of Seth Boyden, westerly by the land of said Boyden and Benjamin Fairbanks, viz A small Dwelling House and Warehouse One Furnace, mall, with all the utensils Two Coal houses with all the Ore and Stock now lying there One small Dwelling house. Also a Blacksmith Shop with all the Tools and Scales, which stands upon the land of Benjamin Fairbanks, and is held by a lease during the time said furnace shall stand.

Solomon Talbot comments: "This property was placed in the name of Jacob Leonard as security for the farm sold Col. Gridley in Canton, and also to prevent interruption in the business by litigious claimants."

On January 24, 1774, the Committee of Safety and Supplies voted that all the cannon mortars, cannon balls, and shells be deposited at the towns of Worcester and Concord.

They also voted that 450 of four-pound cannon balls be brought from Stoughtonham to Sudbury. Also, that one ton of grapeshot be carried from Stoughtonham to Sudbury. Also that one ton of three-pound cannon balls now at Stoughtonham be carried to Sudbury. Voted that one-half a ton of two-pound cannon balls now at Stoughtonham, exclusive of what is for the use of the matrosses, be carried to Sudbury.

Production from the furnace was up, but delays in payments kept the company in financial difficulty, as evidenced by entries in Gridley's diary. "May 20, 1774 Quincy's place was attached by a Sheriff who took possession. Quincy and family came here" (to Gridley's in Canton). On August 24, 1774, the sheriff attached Gridley's place at Canton and it was set off by order of court to James Russell. This suit was brought for a share of the furnace which had not been paid for at the time it was purchased.

On January 26, 1775, Jacob Leonard surrendered the furnace property to Richard Gridley & Co., as he had bought a farm near Foxboro center and wanted the money to pay for it. The property was now mortgaged, to raise the money, to a man in Boston. In spite of the problems, the work continued.

The furnace was situated on the side of the hill and consisted of two parts. The top part was circular in section, constructed of naked fire brick bound with iron hoops to retain the weight of the charge. The lower part, the crucible, was cone shaped and operated at white heat during the blast. The front of the crucible opened into a rectangular box or "sump" at ground level. This box had an open top with a "tymp" or inverted dam on the wall nearest the crucible which extended down into the molten iron and slag. The front of the box had a hole at the bottom through which the iron was drawn off when ready into metal ladles, which had a pouring lip for transferring the molten metal into the molds. When no metal was running, this hole was plugged with clay which soon baked into rock like hardness.

Heat for the furnace came from charcoal, which was prepared on the site by firing wood piled in mounds or pits which were covered with turf or soil in such a way as to exclude the air. When the wood was thoroughly charred, the air was completely cut off and combustion ceased. The charring process took from ten to twenty days, but they obtained thirty-three bushels of charcoal for every cord of wood. Charcoal was a good fuel for the blast furnace because it had great porosity and very little ash or sulfur content.

The furnace fire was started with cord wood lit from the hearth, and allowed to burn or preheat for twenty-nine hours before the blast was put on. A forced draft or "wind" was maintained by means of a "blowing engine" or bellows, which consisted of a single compressing cylinder operated by a water wheel. This produced one hundred cubic feet of air per minute, which allowed the making of one ton of iron for each twenty-four hours.

The furnace was charged from the top of the hill in alternating layers of the charcoal fuel, and the bog iron mixed with limestone to serve as a "flux" to render the earthy matters fluid so they would melt away from the metal.

Two wheeled "barrows" of the reddish stony lumps of ore were pushed over a ramp to the furnace top and dumped onto a metal plate called a "bell." When sufficient amounts were in place on the bell, a lever rotated the plate and the charge was dumped into the furnace. The charging was regulated so that the furnace was always full, the level being determined by poking an iron rod down through a hole in the top until it struck the charge. Thus the furnace had a constantly descending column of solids being acted on by gases and heat from below.

As the molten iron and slag flowed down into the sump they separated, since the slag was lighter and floated on top of the iron. The slag was continuously skimmed or "raked" off, allowed to cool on the ground, and taken away to the slag pile as a waste product. Since the crucible temperature was so intense, it was necessary to continually spray water on the outside walls to cool them down. Once started, the smelting of the iron (or blast) was a continuous process night and day, with new raw material being put in the top as the molten iron was drawn off below.

When the furnace was "tapped" by poking out the clay barrier at the bottom of the sump, the molten metal flowed into the ladles, which were carried by two men by means of a double long-handled yoke to the casting area. Here the metal was carefully poured into the compacted sand molds. The building where the casting was done was some distance from the furnace, probably on the top of the hill on the east side of the stream, because the road to the furnace site which the selectmen authorized Quincy to construct passed by this location.

Some historians state that the patterns for the molds, because of their value, were hidden in caves to protect them from sabotage by local Tories. This is doubtful because the humidity of a cave would affect the wood from which they were made. It is more likely that they were stored in another of the buildings on the site, well guarded by the company of matrosses assigned to the furnace by order of the Committee of Safety.

In April 1775, the Massachusetts Provincial Congress commissioned Gridley chief engineer and colonel of artillery with the rank of major general.

On May 18, 1775, he records in his diary: "Let Nathaniel Guild have forty pounds for carrying on the Furnace. It was between this date and the following March that the First Guns were cast and finished." It is not surprising that this is a retroactive notation.

In June Gridley laid out the fortifications for Breed's Hill in Charlestown, and was wounded in the ensuing battle. The end of June he was at army headquarters in Cambridge pleading for supplies for his men. On July 3, 1775, he threatened to withdraw from the army in a strong letter addressed to the Provincial Congress because of lack of support.

In September 1775, Gridley received from the Continental Congress reaffirmation of the rank of major general bestowed upon him by the Massachusetts Provincial Congress.

In February 1776, Gridley was back at Stoughtonham testing mortars. This is attested to by the following story from the Memoir of Nathaniel Curtis, Esq.

The Rev. Philip Curtis, the first minister of Sharon, had a daughter who married a relative of her father's. The couple had a son born the 17th of March, 1774. During the occupation of Boston by the British, they came to Stoughtonham for safekeeping and lived in her father's house. The husband, a sea captain, had a vessel lying at Salem and while the family stayed with Rev. Curtis, he took the ship to Gloucester, loaded her with fish, and running out under the cover of night, evaded the British cruisers and proceeded to the Island of Barbadoes, as it was supposed to be under the French. Arriving in the evening, he was boarded from a British frigate, and his vessel brought to anchor under cover of her guns. But his crew was not taken out, nor were an officer and men put on board. Fortunately for him, a heavy gale blowing out of the harbor accompanied by squalls of rain sprang up that night, causing vessels to drag their anchors. The frigate's crew being occupied with her, Capt. Curtis cut his cable and drove to sea without being discovered. The Island was then in the possession of the British. Running down to St. Eustatia, a neutral Dutch Island, he sold his cargo very favorably for Spanish dollars. Not deeming it prudent to return to Massachusetts Bay, he made for Stonington, Conn., arriving there safely, and returned through Providence to Stoughton.

At this time, Col. Richard Gridley, the chief engineer of the army, was engaged at Mashapoag Pond with a number of men, proving some mortars which had been cast to be placed on Dorchester Heights, to bombard the town or ships in the harbor. Capt. Curtis, having some knowledge of gunnery acquired in the French War, volunteered to assist Col. Gridley.

Meanwhile an imposter rode through the country, stating that the British had marched out of Boston; had then reached Milton bridge, and were devastating all before them.

Captain Curtis returned home to find the family fled to the woods, except a faithful Negro, who had put out the fires and armed himself with a heavy club, with which he said he was determined to defend the house. He said that the bags of money were in the well, and pointed out the hiding place of the family.

On March 4, 1776, it was decided to fortify Dorchester Heights and Gridley, according to all accounts, performed miracles in erecting the breastworks. Needing cannon, he sent a rider to Stoughtonham for all available at the furnace.

The story is told that Uriah Atherton, one of the workers at the furnace, started for Dorchester Heights with a wagon so laden with cannon that his team could not pull it. Atherton's father-in-law, Seth Boyden who lived adjacent to the furnace site, brought to his assistance a yoke of bulls and a stallion that had to be worked in fetters. Boyden assured Atherton that with this combination the transportation of the cannon would be safe; for if he should meet the redcoats, all he would need to do to rout them would be to unhitch his warlike cattle.

Seth Boyden returned to Stoughtonham with his unlikely team but Uriah Atherton, on the way home, decided to join the army. He answered the muster roll with Captain Josiah Pratt's company, marching from Roxbury in Col. Gill's Regiment on March 5, 1776.

The story is also told of Sally Leonard who lived with the Talbots in Sharon in her declining years. When she was thirteen years old she carried a message from Col. Gridley in Canton to the furnace in Stoughtonham, the purport of which was to hurry up the manufacture of the cannon as they were needed for use at Dorchester Heights.

After the evacuation of Boston, General Washington offered to Gridley his choice of a place of residence in that city where he remained many months, and was entrusted by the commander-in-chief with the duty of demolishing the British entrenchments in the Neck.

On August 10, 1776, he wrote to Nathaniel Guild, the foreman at the furnace, as follows:

"Boston Aug. 10, 1776

Mr. Guild

I would strongly recommend to you the getting of the Furnace in readiness for a Blast with the utmost Expedition; as I have given encouragement for our making a number of Cannon & Swivells for privateers. If Shott be in abundance and supposed sufficient for a Considerable Blast, I intend to be with you on Tuesday Next & have many things to say to you. I will meet you at Mr. Quincy's house on Tuesday forenoon if possible . . .

I remain
Yr Friend & Serv.
Rich Gridley"

Nathaniel Guild was a Walpole man who had been one of the original Ebenezer Mann Furnace owners, and a delegate from Walpole to the convention in Milton which produced the "Suffolk Resolves." As a result of Gridley's letter, Mr. Guild petitioned the Massachusetts Provincial Congress as follows:

On the petition of Nathaniel Guild presented Sept. 18th, 1776:

Resolved that the prayer of the petitioner be so far granted, that the Committee of Correspondence of Walpole be directed to sell to Mr. Nathaniel Guild as much wood of the estate belonging to Isaac Royall, Esq., Sir William Pepperrill, and George Erving, lying within two miles of Stoughtonham Furnace as they think necessary, not exceeding one hundred cords, Provided that said Committee of Correspondence see that it be cut where it will be the least damage to said lots, the said Guild paying the full value for the wood to the said committee being accountable to this court for the sum or sums received.

And it be further
Resolved that sixteen such men as Mr. Guild most wants to carry
on his furnace business, it being of so great importance for the
defence of this, and the United States of America, be excused from
service in the present alarm if drafted agreeable to the resolve of
this Court to assist said Guild in his furnace works.

The men named were British sympathizers or Tories whose estates had
been confiscated when they fled at the outbreak of hostilities.
On November 2, 1776, the Provincial Congress voted:

Resolved that the Committee for Casting and boring large cannon
for the use of the State be empowered and directed to import from
Philadelphia 200 tons of Pig Iron.
Resolved that said committee are hereby empowered to employ
Monsieur de Maresquells, a French engineer now in Boston in the
business for which they were appointed and to make such agree-
ments with him as they shall think proper for overseeing and
directing therein under them.

Under the power conferred upon them, the committee submitted the following propositions which were accepted as follows:

Proposed contract, Marie Louis Amand Anstart de Maresquells,
an old captain of infantry, having been brought up in the forges of
France (his father there, Marquis of Monte Surbert having fur-
nished for many years all the iron cannon in the service of the
French king) proposes to the Honorable Council and House of
Representatives to establish furnaces in the State of Massachusetts
Bay on account of the Government for the furnishing the State
with such iron cannon as they may need.

He has some particular methods of softening the iron by mixture of ores and minerals, and also of casting cannon solid, and
boring the same, by which means they are less massive and
stronger than others with a cylinder. Formerly all cannons were
cast with a cylinder, which always occasioned many little holes or
cavities in the pieces which frequently occasioned their bursting.

His father having observed how prejudicial those cavities were
to the service of the artillery, he in the year 1750 cast many solid
cannon and found them superior to those cast with a cylinder, and
at present no other but solid cannon are cast in the forges of
France. His father is the inventor of the machine for boring solid
cannon and with it a twenty-four pounder may be bored, polished,
and the sprue cut off in twenty-four hours.

If the state will furnish the land, buildings, machines, and
necessary apparatus and iron ore, he will construct the furnaces,
and superintend the building of the machines, and everything
relating to iron foundry, which being ready and the guns prepared
for boring.

He will then furnish one cannon for service every twenty-four hours; out of the common ore within the state; it being understood that he shall cast a few beforehand to give them time to cool. The calibre or bore of the cannon will depend on the largeness of the furnace.

He will prove his cannon before commissioners of the state. He will disclose at any time his knowledge in the premises to any such persons as the state may order, and no others. And if he does not fulfill the whole promised upon his part in these proposals (unavoidable casualties excepted) he agrees not only to forfeit all claim to everything by virtue of these presents, but also to forfeit the sum of one thousand pounds to satisfy the damage the state may sustain through his failure in fulfilling his proposal aforesaid.

He expects from the state to recover three hundred dollars in hand to compensate the expense he had to be at, in removing from Europe to this country, and also one thousand dollars yearly from and after date hereof until the end of the present war with Great Britain and the United States of America; and after that time the sum of six hundred and sixty-six and two-thirds dollars yearly during his life, he doing and performing his part in all respects as aforesaid. He also expects the honor of a colonel's commission to give him rank, but without any command or pay in virtue of said commission.

Witnessed his hand at Boston, December 6th, 1776.
(Signed) Demarquells

Signed by the above Demarquells after being fully interpreted to him in the presence of James Rice.

We the subscribers, Committee of Honorable House of Representatives.

N. Cushing
F. Palmer.

Read and approved.

Gridley had been casting cannon with a core, that is, the iron was poured into a mold which not only had the shape of the outside of the cannon, but also had a mold which was an inner cylinder, so that the molten iron filled up the space between the two molds. The idea seemed logical, but the cannons were poor, many breaking on testing. Air bubbles and cracks had resulted from the unequal cooling of the cannon as the iron hit the cool sand core. Colonel De Maresquelles showed them how to cast the cannon in one piece and cool it slowly, avoiding the strains which caused flaws and cracks.

Because of the power required to bore the large castings they were probably bored in the vertical position by a drill directly coupled to a water wheel at the flume adjacent to the furnace.

Since the casting was done some distance from the furnace, the story is told that De Maresquelles, fearing that the metal would cool before being poured into the molds, would tell the men carrying the ladles to "Hooray! Hooray!" In his imperfect English this meant to hurry before the metal cooled down.

It is not certain where De Maresquelles lived while working at the furnace, but we do know that he was married to Polly Wimble of Boston on December 23, 1779, by Philip Curtis, the Pastor of the First Congregational Church in the center of Stoughtonham.

On February 14, 1777, Congress empowered Robert Treat Paine to contract with Gridley for forty-eight inch howitzers to be sent to Ticonderoga.

Gridley and Quincy sold the Stoughtonham Furnace on September 4, 1777, for 350 pounds to Uriah Atherton, who continued to contract for the casting of cannon for the balance of the war. He also was one of the founders of the Foxboro Foundry in South Foxboro in December, 1782.[30]

De Maresquelles continued his efforts on behalf of the colonists, assisting at several furnaces in the area as "Inspector General of Foundries." He moved to Dracut, Massachusetts, in 1784, became an American citizen and changed his name to Louis Ansart. He became active in that town's affairs, and died there at age sixty-two.

Edmund Quincy died in 1781, before the war was over, but his burial place is not known.

Gridley, because of his advancing years, had resigned his Continental commission and served out the war as Major General in the Provincial forces. Charged with improving the fortifications of Boston harbor, he spent considerable time at Castle Island which was under the command of Lt. Col. Paul Revere.

His declining years were spent in Canton in the company of his wife, who died in 1790, and his two daughters, Becky and Polly. He was almost constantly in financial trouble since his modest pension would not cover rising expenses. The aftermath of his partnership with Quincy and Jackson also caused financial drains. Among his creditors was John Hancock, who was Quincy's brother-in-law. He died on June 21, 1796, strangely enough from blood poisoning caused by cutting some poisonous bushes.

He is buried in Canton where a suitable monument, erected by the citizens of Canton, marks the spot.

"It is said that America commenced her Revolution with but ten pieces of cannon, and to the mechanical science and ingenuity of Gridley was she indebted for the first cannon and mortars ever cast in this country."

Today the waters from Wolomolopoag Pond still flow between the twin ridges on their way to the ocean, but of the Stoughtonham Furnace there is no sign. A succession of mills, including Deacon Clapp's Shingle Mill, were built on the site, their machinery powered from the dammed up waters of what is now known as Gavin's Pond; but of them there is no trace either, except for the stones forming the flume and spillway.

In another, less secluded, spot this site of America's first defense industry would probably be much more frequently visited by societies and individuals interested in our nation's heritage.

Perhaps, as a symbol of changing times and needs, it is better this way. It was there when it was needed to help make America. It served its purpose.

Deacon Clapp's Shingle Mill on the Gavin's Pond Site of Gridley's Foundry

Pitcher Decorated with Foundry Scene and Legend   *Photo by: C. W. Jones*

Seth Boyden's Wagon Loaded With Cannon Enroute From Stoughtonham to Dorchester Heights, March 4, 1776.
Drawing by Vera Cross

Cannon Cast at Stoughtonham Furnace Mounted on Fixed Carriage.
Drawing by Vera Cross

Only Drawing of Deborah Sampson Made From Life

DEBORAH SAMPSON

By Pauline Moody

CHAPTER 7

Late in October 1783, a youthful figure in an army uniform sailed down the Hudson River in a sloop of war, took a packet to Providence, and then started to walk to Stoughton.

That figure was Deborah Sampson. At West Point she had just been honorably discharged from the 4th Massachusetts Regiment by General Henry Knox, and commended by her officers for her bravery and good conduct while serving some seventeen months as a foot soldier in the American Revolution under the name of Robert Shurtlieff.

Homeless, the sturdy Deborah headed for the Cape Cod cottage of her aunt Alice Waters and husband Zebulon in the Dry Pond section of Stoughton which was later annexed to Sharon. As the young woman strode along — she was almost twenty-three — she must have wondered how she would be received wherever she went. She had joined the army, leaving no clue for her mother and sisters and brothers in Plympton or for the Thomas family in Middleborough with whom she had lived eight years as an indentured servant.

Certainly it never entered the thoughts of the tall Deborah — she was five feet seven and one-half inches when the average height of men was five feet four and of women four feet nine — that in two hundred years she would be u-nique in United States history and a forerunner of something called Women's Lib.

The story has come down that the Stoughton relatives accepted Deborah's statement she was her brother Ephraim (also a soldier in the Revolution) and soon she was working on their farm. The young woman knew all about farm work.

Born in Plympton, Massachusetts December 17, 1760 — the year George III became King of England — Deborah was one of seven small children Jonathan Sampson, Jr. had deserted before going to sea. Although well-to-do Jonathan Sampson, Sr. had several daughters, there was only one son and his inheritance would have been sizeable had he not felt a brother-in-law was mismanaging his father's estate, begun to drink heavily, and then left Plympton. While old histories report Junior was lost at sea, there's evidence and some proof he lived in Maine long enough to have one and possibly two common-law wives.

Though Jonathan lacked courage and will power, he was, nevertheless, the great-grandson of Miles Standish and of John Alden. His wife, Deborah Bradford, was the great-granddaughter of Gov. William Bradford.

Butter was only six cents a pound, meat twelve, and a whole cod four, yet without a helpmate Mrs. Sampson could not feed Deborah, Sylvia, Ephraim, Hannah, Jonathan, Elisha, and Nehemiah. She was forced to "scatter" some of them.

Deborah, rather plain in spite of her sparkling hazel eyes, fair skin, and blonde hair, lived with a cousin, Mistress Fuller, until that loving relative's sudden death. Then shelter was provided by highly intelligent but elderly, ailing Madam Thacher, a minister's widow residing in Middleborough. By the time Deborah was ten, the patient required more care than the child could give her. Once again the little girl was homeless.

THE BOUND GIRL

Since child labor was accepted as a way of life in colonial times, there was nothing opprobrious in Mrs. Sampson's obtaining a permanent home for Deborah by binding her out until she became of age. The new home was in the Thomaston section of Middleborough with Farmer Thomas and his considerate wife. In their large household — there were ten sons — the bound girl was well fed and comfortably clothed.

The indentured girl helped Mrs. Thomas do household chores, make candles and soap, fill feather beds, and spin and weave. She thoroughly enjoyed outdoor life, however, and undoubtedly preferred working on the farm with the ten boys. She handled farm implements skillfully and could fashion baskets and other articles as needed. As Sharon poet (Mary) Josephine Folsom Lamprey wrote in *America's Woman Soldier, Deborah Sampson*:

In the field, oftimes, with the men she toiled,
And, though tanned her visage, her garments soiled.
It was thus she gained the endurance great
Which her served so well in her future state.

Perhaps the girl couldn't be spared to go to school regularly; or Farmer Thomas may have agreed with the prevailing idea that women shouldn't be educated. But the plucky Deborah early formed a lifelong habit of solving seemingly unsolvable problems. She was determined to master the three R's of the time — reading, 'riting, and religion — and she did. Fortunately, her mother had taught her to read; Mistress Fuller and Madam Thacher had encouraged her to continue; and Rev. Sylvanus Conant, pastor of the local Congregational Church, had awarded her a few precious books for learning the Catechism of the Assembly of the Divines so well. Farmer Thomas gave her sheep and fowl with the understanding all profits were to be channeled into worthy causes, and she could have mastered "cyphering" by accounting for the profits. Although paper was in short supply, she managed to learn to write a good hand. Like Benjamin Franklin before her, each night she checked a list of the good and bad qualities she had expressed throughout the day.

After Deborah's indenture was completed, she was asked to teach in a schoolhouse two miles from the Thomas home. In spite of holding a pen peculiarly — possibly because of a felon on her forefinger — she drilled the pupils, particularly the boys, in penmanship. She taught the girls to sew and knit. For teaching two summers she was paid $12.00. Expert at spinning and weaving, she worked winters in Middleborough homes, and also in Sproat Tavern.

FOOT SOLDIER

No one will ever know exactly what prompted Deborah Sampson to become a soldier. As a small child she must have heard again and again how war had affected her mother's people, the Bradfords. For instance, Governor Bradford's son William, commander of the Plymouth forces in King Philip's War, had received a musket ball in his flesh which he carried the remainder of his life (surely Deborah never dreamt she'd have a similar experience). Zebulon Waters of Stoughton, who married Deborah's aunt Alice Bradford, had helped remove the Acadians from Nova Scotia.

Simeon Sampson, cousin of Deborah's father, was already America's first naval captain; all ten Thomas sons had enlisted; and news could have reached Middleborough that Margaret Corbin and "Molly Pitcher" Hays had rendered emergency service in the Revolution by taking over their husbands' guns and fighting valiantly after the men were killed or disabled.

Not only was the soldier-to-be tall; she was also very masculine. When Mrs. Gardner Derry came to Sharon as a bride, her husband's grandmother told her she had known Deborah and could understand how she got away with being in the army. She had associated with the Thomas boys so long she was decidedly masculine in both mannerisms and appearance.

Deborah enlisted first in Middleborough as Timothy Thayer of Carver. The whole performance was more or less of a lark. She appropriated a suit of men's clothing — after which the owner vowed he'd never wear it again — signed up, received her bounty money, went to an ordinary (perhaps Sproat Tavern) and spent some of it for liquor. It was not until "Timothy" failed to join the departing recruits that an elderly lady, carding wool in the room where the enlistment had taken place, admitted she had noticed how strangely "he" held "his" pen. Only Deborah Sampson held a pen like that.

The culprit was excommunicated from her church because of her "unchristian" behavior in the tavern. The Thomases forgave her. The members of the Third Baptist Church were less tolerant. On coming to Middleborough, Deborah attended the Congregational Church. There she listened spellbound while the Declaration of Independence was read — it was read in every church and copied in the records of every town in the Commonwealth. After the death of the beloved pastor, Rev. Sylvanus Conant, a series of revivals attracted the girl to the Third Baptist Church, and she joined it in November 1780. Rev. Asa Hunt was the regular minister, but Rev. Noah Alden, great-grandson of John and Priscilla and a native of Middleborough, often came from Bellingham to exchange pulpits with him.

The young woman in men's clothing took herself out of Middleborough before she enlisted again. First she signed up on a privateer at anchor in New Bedford, but vanished as soon as she heard that the captain mistreated his men. Then she tramped for days, often over wretched roads and through sparsely populated areas, finally arriving weary and penniless in the Crimpville section of Bellingham.

"I have a hunch," writes historian John Lundvall of Mendon, "that she came to be in Bellingham because she knew Rev. Noah Alden, and also to be with Baptist friends. This would give her a chance to prove her ability to conceal her sex and also to survey the area for a higher bounty in exchange for her services. Surely Rev. Alden knew who would pay the highest bounty around there — he had been around the countryside preaching. It seems he helped her in that manner and when she signed up in Bellingham, that he took her to Uxbridge where Noah Taft completed the deal."

John Adams Vinton explained in one of his excellent footnotes in the edition of *The Female Review* he edited and which was published in 1866:

> The male population of every town, capable of bearing arms, was at that time divided into classes, and each class was obliged to furnish a soldier for the army. The class sometimes paid a very considerable bounty. Deborah enlisted, and was accepted, for a class in Uxbridge. Bellingham is separated from Uxbridge by the town of Mendon. The man who enlisted Deborah is called a speculator, because he withheld from her a part of the bounty-money to which she was entitled.

Signed up as Robert Shurtlieff to serve three years in the Continental army, Deborah received a bounty of sixty pounds and gave Noah Taft a receipt dated "Worcester, May 23, 1782." Soon Robert was one of some fifty recruits marching the long, dusty route from Worcester to West Point. There he was assigned to Captain George Webb's Company, in Colonel William Shepard's 4th Massachusetts Regiment, and General John Paterson's Brigade. Early in 1783 Colonel Shepard was promoted to Brigadier-General and Colonel Henry Jackson was given command of his unit.

The uniform issued the female soldier is described as consisting of "a blue coat lined with white, with white wings on the shoulders and cords on the arms and pockets; a white waistcoat, breeches or overhauls and stockings, with black straps about the knees; half boots, a black velvet stock, and a cap, with variegated cockade, on one side, a plume tipped with red on the other, and a white sash about the crown." She needed certainly her "endurance great" to carry, along with other things, a good firearm, bayonet, hatchet, cartridge box and cartridges, buck shot and leaden balls, flint and powder, jack-knife, canteen, haversack, and blanket.

The Female Review: or, Memoirs of an American Young Lady by Herman Mann, a book about Deborah published in Dedham in 1797, contains glowing accounts of her action at Yorktown when Cornwallis surrendered in October 1781. And it's incredible that so many years of research — and numerous hassles and misunderstandings — passed before Jan Lewis Nelson recently thought of a way to determine whether or not Deborah was at Yorktown. In the Massachusetts State Archives Mrs. Nelson consulted the "Muster Roll of Captain George Webb's Company of Light Infantry in the 4th Mass. Regiment in the Service of the United States Commanded by William Shepard Esq. Col. From the first of February to the last of November 1781. Inclusion being 10 Months." Robert Shurtlieff's name is not on it. His name is on Captain Webb's muster roll made up in Worcester November 17, 1782.

Seemingly this is what happened. With the British occupying what is now New York City before and after Yorktown, the Infantry scouted in Westchester County to spy on the movements of the enemy. Inevitably there were skirmishes with Tories. When Deborah and her comrades came head on with Tory Colonel James De Lancy and his forces near Tappan Bay, between Sing Sing and Tarrytown, the patriots would have been routed had not Colonel Ebenezer Sproat and his 2nd Massachusetts Regiment come to their rescue. (Of course the Colonel did not recognize Deborah among the rescued although he had often seen her spinning in his father's tavern in Middleborough.)

Years afterward Deborah Sampson Gannett swore she was wounded at Tarrytown. She received a sabre slash in the head and a bullet — perhaps more than one — in her thigh. It has been reported that in a hospital she managed to keep the surgeon's attention on the sabre slash. After his departure she found a silver probe and extracted a bullet herself. There's also a legend she remained alone in the woods, removed a ball from her left leg with a penknife, and rested until able to rejoin her company. Prolonged suffering much later would indicate at least one shot never was removed.

The jig was up when the soldier's sex was discovered. Unpaid soldiers mutinied in Philadelphia and threatened Congress so drastically General Washington dispatched troops to protect them. Among those dispatched, Deborah had not been in Philadelphia long before she was in a hospital with a raging fever. She was unconscious when Dr. Barnabas Binney placed his hand over her heart and did not see him recoil with utter astonishment as he felt the binders about her breasts. The Doctor, a native of Boston, was so concerned about this girl from Massachusetts he is said to have had her removed to his home for her convalescence.

On her way back to West Point, Deborah was more terrified of what might be ahead of her because of her deception than she had been of gunfire. Her fears were groundless; she was not punished but given an honorable discharge.

BRIDE

During the Bicentennial it was discovered that a rather elegant two and a half story house on Bay Road was once the Cape Cod cottage to which Deborah came following her discharge from West Point. She had lived there a year when intentions of marriage were announced between Deborough Sampson of Stoughton and Benjamin Gannett, Jr., a farmer in Sharon. They were married in April 1785. Presumably they moved in with the groom's parents who lived in a small farmhouse Benjamin, Sr. had built after coming from East Bridgewater about 1750. It stood opposite the present junction of East and Billings Streets — at that time there was no Billings Street, only Billings Lane.

Earl Bradford, Mary, and Patience were born to the young Gannetts, and with them they reared orphaned Susanna Baker Shepard. With a growing family and post-war prices exorbitant, in 1792 the ever-resourceful Deborah petitioned the Commonwealth of Massachusetts for back pay. Her petition stated, "Hitherton I have not received one farthing." She was awarded thirty-four pounds and commended for her heroism.

LECTURER

A decade later, ignoring the disapproval of her family and friends, the individual who never lacked ideas again trod what was then only a man's path. She appeared on public platforms in Massachusetts, Rhode Island, and New York. In doing her own thing she was perhaps the first American female to earn money as a public lecturer. At a time when many women couldn't read and counted on their fingers, she was her own business manager and press agent.

Astonished readers of *The Columbian Centinel* learned that Mrs. Gannett, the American heroine of the Revolution, would perform in the Federal-Street Theatre in Boston March 20, 24, 27, and 29, 1802.

The ghost-written narrative was little more than an apology for renouncing household duties to fight for her country and neglected to mention the exhausting marches, the loss of her toenails after her feet were frozen, and the lonely hours on night duty, but Deborah delivered it clearly and flawlessly. Then, equipped in complete infantry uniform, the middle-aged woman went through the manual exercise so expertly "she could almost make the gun talk every time it came to the ground from her hand." The programs in Boston usually concluded with the singing of "God Save the Sixteen States."

The lecturer, having been successful in both Boston and Providence, left Sharon in July to exhibit in Worcester, Holden, Brookfield, Springfield, and Northampton, Massachusetts before performing in Albany, Schenectady, and Ballston Springs, New York. She kept a diary throughout her tour. In it she described traveling by chaise, in private carriages, "with the Mail," and once six days by wagon. Understandably, as the months passed and the mother continued her exhibitions, more and more entries in the diary were about fatigue and illness. At one point she wrote, "Only God knows how happy I shall be to see my Dear Children."

Deborah Sampson Gannett also listed all but one of her lodgings. "At Sudbury one night. I forgot the Land Lord's name." If the traveler was a guest at Wayside (then the Red Horse Inn) the old Barroom is still much as she saw it. And she must have responded with a warm smile if she were told Dorothy Quincy spent a night at the Inn en route to Fairfield, Connecticut, to marry John Hancock. Hancock's bold signature graced the document awarding the ex-soldier the thirty-four pounds. Another matter of personal interest was that Dorothy was a sister of Edmund Quincy, Jr. whose third wife was Hannah Gannett, Deborah's sister-in-law.

At last the weary woman arrived in Lisle, New York. Along the way she had been a guest in Captain Webb's home in Holden; now in Lisle another of her former officers, Major General Paterson, his family, and the "negbourhood" entertained her for the entire month of November.

PENSIONER

Apparently the visit in Lisle was beneficial in more ways than one. For the next two years Judge Paterson was in the U.S. House of Representatives. It is thought that he, with the assistance of Massachusetts Congressman William Eustis, to whom Paul Revere wrote on Mrs. Gannett's behalf, was largely responsible for having the female soldier placed on the federal roll of invalid pensioners.

The first pension of four dollars a month, retroactive to January 1803, was increased to six dollars and forty cents. Years later, the invalid pension was relinquished for the eight dollars Congress voted for soldiers who had served continuously nine months or longer, and were in need of financial assistance.

Paul Revere purchased the site of the old powder mill in Canton and "established a plant for the manufacture of copper, bell metal, ship fastenings, etc." A receipted bill for charcoal he and his son bought Sept. 23, 1803, from Joseph Gannett, brother of Benjamin, Jr., is still in Sharon. It was left when Joseph, his wife, and their numerous progeny departed for Pompey, New York, in a covered wagon drawn by oxen.

In his saddlebags Revere may have brought Mrs. Gannett her money from the Boston office of the agent for paying pensions. Gossip, relayed from generation to generation, has it that the two met occasionally for a cup of cheer at Cobb's Tavern.

Deborah died April 29, 1827 in her son's home and was buried in Rock Ridge Cemetery.

The veterans' agent in Sharon has no record of a military funeral. Miss Marion K. Conant, former librarian of the Dedham Historical Society, did considerable research before reporting, "I have found no information about Deborah Sampson Gannett's funeral. *The Village Register* of May 3, 1827 did print an exceptionally long obituary but I can find no account of her funeral in that issue or later ones."

Benjamin, described as "lacking initiative" and also as "very upright and hard-laboring," was saddled with staggering medical expenses for his wife. His own health was "broken by constant labor and watching with the one he so dearly loved, for he seems to have been entirely devoted to her." At the urging of concerned friends, the elderly farmer petitioned for his wife's pension. Congress, baffled by such an unprecedented request, hemmed and hawed so long that the announcement it had been granted reached Sharon after Benjamin was beside Deborah in Rock Ridge Cemetery. He died January 9, 1837. Years later Ripley, of *Believe It or Not* fame, drew a picture of a solemn Benjamin and gave it the caption "His Wife Went to War — He received a Widow's Pension."

By special act of Congress the amount due the widower was divided among Earl Bradford Gannett and his sisters Mary Gilbert (Mrs. Judson) and Patience Gay (Mrs. Seth).

A FINE NEW HOME

Earl Bradford Gannett married Mary Clark. Mary's home was near Wolomolopoag (or Billings) Pond, and deeds to her family's property were signed by an Indian chief. The Clark's ancestor Thomas arrived in Plymouth on the *Anne* in 1623, along with Barbara Thorne who succeeded her deceased sister as Mrs. Miles Standish, and widow Alice Southworth who became Governor Bradford's second wife.

Earl and his wife joined his parents and grandparents in the old farmhouse. There their first child, Mary, was born. According to notes left by another daughter, all the Gannetts in 1813 moved into Earl's newly constructed mansion at what is now 300 East Street. Built on land Benjamin, Jr. had purchased in 1786 and cleared — recently the deed was given to the Sharon Public Library by the Cowell family descended from Patience Gannett Gay — it was several rods north of the old home and on the other side of the street. Well-preserved and considerably modernized, today the house is diagonally across from the man-made pond created for the Sharon Fish and Game Club. Beside another pond, not visible from the highway, is a sign "Deborah Sampson's Spring."

Benjamin, Sr.'s farmhouse was sold to butchers Smith and French of Canton and moved there for a slaughterhouse. The doorstone was embedded in the wall skirting the front lawn of Earl's new home.

The mansion was none too large. Patience; Deborah; Rhoda; Warren; Earl, Jr.; Benjamin; Thomas; and Joseph Warren were born there. When their sister Mary was fourteen she began teaching in the East School, not far from Bay Road. She couldn't shield her brothers and sisters from their schoolmates' taunts about the soldier grandmother; she could give them deserved rewards of merit.

After the death of Earl's son Benjamin in 1901, a newspaper noted changes in the stately old house: the substitution of modern chimneys for those containing the great fireplaces, the present hip roof in place of the original gable, and the addition of a verandah. It did not mention that the brick ends had been replaced with clapboards.

Passing out of the Gannett family more than a century after it was built, the spacious dwelling had a series of owners in rapid succession. During prohibition, police were forced to shoot into it before they captured the bootlegger holed up there. And sometime in the course of those uneasy years, a fire destroyed the ell connecting the house and barn. The pantry was untouched and at ninety-five, the late Mrs. Edith Leonard Johnson, Deborah's great-great-granddaughter, relished memories of the molasses cookies kept in a jar behind the pantry door.

Young Daniel H. Arguimbau, the present owner, takes as much pride in the mansion as if he had been one of the children who bounced their toys on its low window sills. He is descended from Thomas Southworth, son of the widow who was the second wife of Governor Bradford.

RECOGNITION

The Town of Sharon voted in 1860 to "accept the report of the selectmen in laying out a road over the land of H. A. Lothrop & G. R. & W. R. Mann" — land donated by those gentlemen. Thus a lane became a street, and it was local historian Solomon Talbot who suggested it be named after Deborah Sampson. Occasionally the question is asked if land along that street was given to the soldier in addition to her pension. The National Archives reports that Deborah Sampson Gannett received no land from the government.

Historian Talbot had a memorable background of his own. On his mother's side he was descended from one of the three Hessian soldiers settled in Sharon. The founder of his father's family was a knight who fought in the Battle of Hastings. Also in that Battle was Albertus Greslet from whom Col. Richard Gridley was descended. Since the Sampson ancestry dates back to Ralph de St. Sampson, chaplain to William the Conqueror, the Talbot, Gridley, and Sampson forbears may have been acquainted. "I love my God, my country and my fellowman as myself" is on Gridley's tomb in the Canton Corner Cemetery. "Disgrace is worse than death" is the translation of the motto on the Sampson coat of arms.

DAR Chapter 323

Records stashed away in Sharon since 1896 say the "antiquarian" was impelled at that time to win more recognition for Deborah Sampson. Whoever he was, he mounted an American flag on her grave. And the following year eligible women in Brockton organized Chapter 323 of the Daughters of the American Revolution and named it after soldier Deborah Sampson.

A number of the Brockton ladies called at the mansion one summer afternoon to talk with grandson Benjamin about Deborah. The elderly host told them she was a strict disciplinarian and kept a whip hanging on the wall in case the numerous little Gannetts became too frisky. "Generally," he added, "the vision of the tall, dignified grandmarm, sternly pointing to the whip was sufficient to subdue the most exuberant."

The guests saw Deborah's pewter teapot and Bible, and were given bouquets of flowers and branches from the huge willow on the lawn. (Teapot, Bible, and tree have disappeared.) After the callers tactfully reminded their host of his offer of a door to use in framing their DAR charter, he produced one from his grandmother's cupboard. A piece of an elm from Boston Common became the head of the Chapter's gavel; wood from Brattle Street Church, the handle.

The Brockton Chapter placed a small boulder, bearing a descriptive plaque, in back of the woman soldier's tombstone in Rock Ridge Cemetery. Later, with the Town of Plympton, it gave a "fine granite boulder with a bronze tablet to commemorate the valor and patriotism of Deborah Sampson." The memorial is on Plympton Green, once a training ground where Minutemen, including Bradfords and Sampsons, drilled. Several years ago, a Sharon newspaper announced: "On Saturday five members of the Deborah Sampson Rebekah Lodge went to Plympton to help celebrate Deborah Sampson Day there where on the Village Green an old time Church Fair was being held. Visitors saw the old plaque commemorating her feats."

While the First Parish Church in Brockton was celebrating its 175th anniversary in 1913, the local DAR dedicated a plaque in recognition of "the patriotism of Deborah Sampson." The plaque was set in a huge boulder on the church green. Brought from the Simeon Cary farm, it also memorialized Col. Cary who had drilled Revolutionary soldiers on that same green. It was necessary to remove the stone after the building burned to the ground in 1965 so at a stirring rededication ceremony the plaque was placed on an outside wall of the new church.

For several years, on Memorial Day Chapter members gathered at the mansion and then proceeded to visit Deborah's grave. For the occasion in 1913 Josephine Lamprey composed *America's Woman Soldier, Deborah Sampson* and dedicated it to the heroine's great-granddaughter Susan Gannett Moody, who with her husband and four children lived in the homestead. By that time George Washington Gay's gift of a monument in memory of his grandmother and Sharon's Civil War dead had been erected in Rock Ridge Cemetery (see *This Hallowed Ground*). The women preferred, however, to meet at Deborah's grave. There they placed flowers, mindful of the last stanza of Mrs. Lamprey's long poem.

Dear my Friends, as, tenderly, now, you lay
Fairest flowers on graves, this Memorial Day,

Oh, forget not her, by the southern gate,
Who lies, mute and still, by her earthly mate,
With the Stars and Stripes soaring 'bove her breast,
In her long, unending, and well-earned rest.

A Posh Banquet

In April 1902, a century after Deborah Sampson Gannett became a lecturer, state and local officials, reporters from Boston newspapers, descendants, and many others gathered in Sharon for the specific purpose of bringing "more fully to notice the fact that Mrs. Gannett was an early woman lecturer and her efforts as such."

Some came by trolley. On attractive folders, along with the catered menu, was printed: "Electric cars run two miles to Cobb's Tavern, there connecting with electrics for Canton and Norwood, or for Stoughton. At Stoughton, connection is made with Brockton electrics."

The first of several distinguished speakers was Mrs. Mary L. Livermore of Melrose. In her address she said:

> I am sorry that Deborah felt obliged to apologize for having fought in the army, because if war is right, then a woman has just as much right to fight as a man has. She had real grit, for she did whatever came to her hand, whether in the line of housekeeping or lecturing.

The speaker's quip, "She held her tongue at all times, and if there is anything I admire it is a woman that can hold her tongue," produced "great laughter."

To supplement a copy of the diary Deborah kept while lecturing, the secretary of the Sharon Historical Society, Eugene Tappan, recorded the names and addresses of those attending the banquet and copied all of the speeches in a bound volume. There is also other pertinent matter in the book and this introduction:

> It is interesting to know why there is an absence of tradition about the lecturing tour. The explanation is offered that Mrs. Gannett was in advance of her time, and leaving home and family to ride about the country and deliver an oration upon the public platform was not according to the taste of her neighbors and friends. She, therefore, would not care to say much about the matter.
>
> George Washington Gay, a grandson of Mrs. Gannett, was ten years old when his grandmother died, and remembered her well, having often visited her. He was accustomed to treasure up what appeared from time to time in print concerning Mrs. Gannett, was fond of her, and provided in his will for a permanent memorial to her. Yet his widow was surprised to learn a few months ago that Mrs. Gannett had ever delivered a public lecture, and was quite sure that her late husband had never mentioned the fact, and did not know it.
>
> A former resident of Sharon intimate with the Gannett family, writes, "I was well acquainted with Mrs. Anna Holmes, a

granddaughter of Mrs. Gannett. She told me among other facts that her grandmother, during all the years that she knew her, was very sensitive to any allusions even to her life as a soldier, and was very unwilling to speak of it. If then in 1802 she regarded that part of her life with approval, it is certain, as Mrs. Holmes told me, that in later years she did not regard her disguising herself as a womanly or a truthful act."

A letter copied in this unique volume was one written by Mrs. Zilpah Tolman of Fitchburg, Massachusetts. Mrs. Tolman was a granddaughter of Revolutionary veteran Jeremiah Thomas whose third wife, Sylvia Sampson, Deborah's niece, related to her "incidents of the army life of her aunt and my grandfather as she heard them from her lips."

This letter clarified some of the puzzling aspects in the life of the woman soldier. Other valuable information was supplied by Mr. Charles H. Bricknell as he went painstakingly through the old handwritten records of Plympton before he recently published them in twelve volumes.

Liberty Ship S.S. Deborah Gannett

The soldier was recognized, too, in the interval between the banquet and the nation's Bicentennial. With pomp and ceremony the U.S. Government launched Library ship *Deborah Gannett* at the Bethlehem-Fairfield Shipyard in Baltimore, April 10, 1944. Among the notables present was the founder of the Gannett group of newspapers and radio and television stations, Frank E. Gannett of Rochester, New York. Gannett was descended from the Joseph who left Sharon in a covered wagon.

Also in the forties, "A lovely creamy throated gladiolus of blush pink, with rich florets thick on strong stalks and the name of Deborah Sampson" won Wendall Wyman of Sharon a coveted prize in a large flower show.

More enduring than the Liberty ship and the gladiolus is a stone in the Altar of the Nation at Cathedral of the Pines in Rindge, New Hampshire. Stone number 46 in the eastern end of the Altar Rail is from the grounds of Deborah's home in Sharon.

Deborah Sampson Week

Early in 1975 the Cranberry Players in Middleboro presented *Portrait of Deborah*, a drama playwright Charles Emery and researcher Clemice Blackington Pease wrote and published in 1959. In August the Plympton Bicentennial Commission and the Plympton Historical Society hosted a celebration in which a ten-woman detachment of the Women's Army Corps from Fort Devens participated. At the end of the year during Deborah Sampson Week in Sharon, William Appel directed *She Was There*, a play he wrote especially for the occasion. The cast was large, ranging from "townsfolk to bloodied soldiers, from an aging Paul Revere to Joan of Arc in a dream sequence, from the militia presenting arms while their small drummer boys beat a tattoo, to the notables John Adams, Patrick Henry, and Benjamin Franklin."

Deborah Sampson Week was, as the Selectmen's proclamation indicates, action-filled and impressive.

DEBORAH SAMPSON WEEK PROCLAMATION

WHEREAS, The Town of Sharon will celebrate Deborah Sampson Week from December 14 through December 20, 1975; and

WHEREAS, The Town's American Revolution Bicentennial Committee will sponsor a Deborah Sampson Art Festival on December 14, 1975, a Deborah Sampson Play on December 17, 1975, and a Deborah Sampson Entertainment Marathon on December 20, 1975; and

WHEREAS, Ceremonies will be conducted on December 14, 1975 at the final resting place of Deborah Sampson at Rock Ridge Cemetery; and

WHEREAS, The former Sacred Heart land will be officially re-named "Deborah Sampson Park" on December 14, 1975;

NOW THEREFORE, The Board of Selectmen of the Town of Sharon proclaims the week of December 14 through December 20, 1975 as:

"DEBORAH SAMPSON WEEK"

and urges residents of our community to join in active recognition of the only woman veteran of the Revolutionary War — Deborah Sampson.

GEORGE E. DONOVAN, Chairman
ROBERT F. CURRIE
NORMAN KATZ
BOARD OF SELECTMEN
SHARON, MASSACHUSETTS

Medals and Portraits

Before the Bicentennial actually arrived, Deborah had appeared on the reverse side of the Carter Braxton medal which was issued in platinum, silver, and bronze, the forty-sixth in a series honoring the Signers of the Declaration of Independence. Connie (Mrs. Sherwood W.) Steere of Sharon had won a local competition by designing a pewter medal of the patriot. And a third medal, also in pewter, was yet to be produced for members of the national DAR in a series "Great Women of the American Revolution."

The only portrait of Deborah ever made from life was drawn rather crudely by Joseph Stone of Framingham in 1797 to illustrate *The Female Review*. Using the original as a guide, a few years ago Sharon artist Virginia Chase Earle painted a charming portrait descendants believe resembles the real Deborah. Albert J. Forbes's recent portrayal in *The Christian Science Monitor* is similar to but an improvement on Stone's, now in the John Brown House in Providence. Reproductions of the Stone drawing are also on Bicentennial souvenirs such as posters and T-shirts!

Herbert Knotel's water color reconstruction of Deborah Sampson as a Continental soldier hangs in the West Point Museum Collections. And beside a unit of the exquisite handpainted miniatures in the Military Museum at Heritage Plantation of Sandwich a sign reads: "4th Mass. Regiment Continental Line 1776-1783. The Light Company of 1782, stationed at West Point, in which served the adventurous girl, Deborah Sampson of Plympton, Mass."

THE QUERIES CONTINUE

Ever since the *Ladies Home Journal* in May 1900 ran "The Girl Who Fought in the Revolution," historians, teachers, DAR members, dramatists, television personalities, and others have sought information about this resourceful woman from her descendants, town officials, and the public library in Sharon.

A decade ago, a lady wrote from California, "It seems strange that so many conflicting reports are written about Deborah Sampson Gannett for certainly she lived but one life and was but one person although she took the part of two. It will be interesting to see what more research brings forth."

Henceforth will Deborah's buffs, influenced by the current revolution, be more concerned with her as a herald of Women's Lib rather than the bound girl who became a unique figure in U.S. military history?

This chapter is a condensation of *Massachusetts' Deborah Sampson* privately published in 1975.

Deborah Sampson Homestead   *Boyden Collection*

Soldiers' Monument at Rock Ridge Cemetery

SHARON AT WAR

By William F. Connors

CHAPTER 8

In attempting to write the military history of our town, I decided against preparing a lengthy listing of Sharon wars and warriors. There are a number of sources available, however, for those of you who desire such information. I chose instead to do the following research on the subject:

Visit a war-related site within the town; chat with a Sharonite who lived through an American war; and relate some recorded experiences of Sharon boys in the Revolutionary and Civil wars.

I heartily recommend this approach to those of you who desire to make history "come alive." I found it the next best thing to actually being there.

A Visit to Rock Ridge Cemetery

With the exception perhaps of some skirmishes with the Indians in the early 1700's, there have been no actual wars fought on Sharon soil. The closest battle to our boundaries was the engagement of the British and American forces in the battle for Boston in the early years of the Revolution. As a result, our war-related sites are limited to:

Monuments: The most prominent ones are the two in front of the Town Hall dedicated to those who served in World Wars I and II.

Veterans Organizations: At present, our only organization is the Veterans of Foreign Wars post on South Main Street. The American Legion post, named in honor of Charles R. Wilber, the only Sharonite to die in World War I, was destroyed by fire in 1975.

Cemeteries: The many cemeteries in town contain a number of monuments as well as being the final resting place for Sharon veterans for nearly all of America's wars. Of all the cemeteries in town, Rock Ridge is probably the best known. Within its borders are the graves of soldiers from the Revolutionary War up to and including the Vietnam era. The grave of Revolutionary-War Captain William Billings (died 1816) lies less than 100 yards from that of Lance Corporal Daniel Dabreu, killed in Vietnam in 1968. Although the war veterans are buried throughout Rock Ridge, there are three sections which have a distinctly military flavor. The veterans' section, nearest the golf course, faces East Street. There are two large monuments here, one for each of the World Wars. See This Hallowed Ground: Sharon Cemeteries.

The land area to the rear of this section, between the golf course and the woods, is believed to be the site of the Edmund Quincy homestead. During the Revolution, Quincy and Richard Gridley helped to provide cannon and ball for the colonial forces. Quincy also served as moderator and surveyor of Stoughtonham (the town name prior to 1783), in addition to being a private in Captain Edward Savel's company of militia. There is a possibility that Quincy and one of his daughters are buried somewhere in Rock Ridge.

Also facing East Street and not far from the monuments commemorating veterans of World Wars I and II, is the famous Civil War memorial. Deborah Sampson's grandson gave it to the Town in memory of Sharon men who fell in the Civil War (his son was one of them) and likewise of his grandmother, a foot soldier in the American Revolution. However, the female soldier is buried in the oldest part of Rock Ridge Cemetery. And so is patriot Job Swift who lies within musket range of his house on Mountain Street.

On April 18, 1775, Swift, like Paul Revere and William Dawes, rode out of Boston with the news that the British planned to march to Lexington and Concord on the 19th. Arriving in Sharon before daybreak, he aroused his sons and all of them spent the remainder of the evening spreading the alarm through the town. The morning found Job and his three sons in the ranks of Captain Tisdale's company, on the march to meet the forces of King George.

One Who Took Part

The rock monument in front of the Town Hall, faces East Chestnut Street and contains the names of nearly 500 Sharon men who took part in the Second World War. These men went to all parts of the world to fight and ultimately defeat the combined forces of Germany, Italy and Japan. Unfortunately, no monument exists to honor those patriots who remained at home yet still supported our country's war effort every bit as avidly as any front-line soldier. Let Babbie Erkelens tell you what life was like in Sharon during the war years (1940-1945).

"We were aware of the possibility of attack or invasion, but we were too busy to worry about it. Many of the women worked in local factories and small assembly plants making war materials for the troops. Those who stayed at home were active in home nursing or as members of Red Cross instruction teams. Everything, and I mean everything, which could be of any conceivable value was contributed to the salvage collection bins set up in the center of town. Old cans, tin, scrap iron, clothing, and especially silk stockings used for making powder bags, were among the most valuable items. I remember that the Gillespie house on Pleasant Street served as a collection center for old clothing. The clothing was sent to the people of Russia who at that time were one of our most staunch allies.

"Bomb shelters were provided long before the atomic bomb scares of recent years. For those who didn't have one in their own house, there were well-stocked ones in the local churches. In addition to being a place of worship, the church served as a bastion of safety and common meeting ground for people to share the hardships of the times. Food coupons and fuel rationing were, of course, strictly enforced. We would bring our coupons to the local store in return for our allotted share of groceries, meats, and fats. Most everyone used margarine because even when butter was available nobody could afford it. Victory gardens similar to the one at Deborah Sampson Park sprouted all over town.

"The thought never left our minds that the Germans might some day land on the east coast of the U.S. Reports of Nazi U-boats off the beaches of Martha's Vineyard and Nantucket were not uncommon. I served with honor and excitement as a ground observer, watching for enemy planes from the heights of the old Sacred Heart tower near the center of town. As Sharon is a relatively high spot in Eastern Massachusetts, we could cover many miles of air space as we watched and identified all flying objects in our area. Fortunately we never spotted any unfriendly aircraft. Air raid warnings, practice alerts, and black-out curtains also combined to bring the realities of war closer to home. There was an air-raid warden in each 'bloc.'

"The children of the town were also very involved in the events of the times. In addition to their schooling and chores at home, they would scurry around town collecting materials for delivery to the salvage bins. I can't remember any youngster who was not a Junior Commando, and proud of it. Their energy and industry was an inspiration to us all.

"Everyone was involved. You either had a son, daughter, or relative in the service, or you knew someone who did. True, the war was a dreadful affair, but it drew the townspeople much closer together, probably closer than we have ever been since."[1]

Sharon in the Revolutionary War

In order to maintain the power and influence of the Empire, England was forced to place an increasing tax burden on its colonies around the world. As we all know, their revenue raising efforts were anything but popular in the American colonies. Stoughtonham's sympathy with the anti-British movement was shown in 1768 when they chose Job Swift to represent the district at a general convention to be held at Faneuil Hall in Boston. Clearly the citizens did not plan to sit back and be intimidated by the acts of Parliament or the soldiers of King George III. In 1775, the District voted to raise a group of minutemen in case of possible conflict with the British. In less than a month, 28 men and 2 officers had been enlisted and were drilling two half-days a week. Their training would soon be put to good use, for some 20 miles away on the other side of "Big Blue" forces of the mightiest army in the world were preparing to subdue the patriots once and for all.

When war erupted on April 19, 1775, Stoughtonham responded by sending nearly 200 men; this out of a population in the district of less than 1,000 people. Of those who took part in the Revolution, 20 were veterans of the French and Indian Wars. Few if any of these men were present for the fighting at Lexington and Concord, but marched instead to the vicinity of Dorchester and Roxbury. The records of those who served at Bunker Hill in June likewise contain no names of Sharon men. They probably watched the battle from the fortifications at Dorchester Heights, unaware that the Heights had originally been the primary target of British attempts to break out of Boston. Could it be that the British changed their attack plans when they realized that Dorchester Heights was well fortified with cannon made in Sharon?

Our soldiers participated in many of the major engagements of the war. The exploits of Gridley, Swift, and Robert Shurtlieff (better known as Deborah Sampson) are known to most readers. Here is an account of the experiences of one Benjamin Tupper of Stoughtonham who became a general during the war. Born March 11, 1738, Tupper joined the army at Roxbury and shortly after the Lexington alarm was promoted to major. He was soon ordered with his men to prevent the rebuilding of the lighthouse by the British in Boston Harbor. Major Tupper marched his men to Dorchester and there informed them that he was about to proceed down the harbor to drive the British troops off the island.

"Now," said the Major addressing his company, which consisted of about 300 men, "if there is any one of you who is afraid and who does not want to go with us, let him step two paces to the front"; and turning to the sergeant he quietly said, "If any man steps two paces to the front, shoot him on the spot." It's needless to add that every man kept his position.

The major then proceeded with his men from Dorchester down the Neponset River, taking their field pieces in whale boats. They arrived at the lighthouse about two o'clock in the morning, attacked the guard, and killed the officers and four privates. The remainder of the English troops were captured. Having demolished the lighthouse then in the process of construction, the party was ready to embark when the major himself was attacked by several of the enemy's boats. But with his field piece he succeeded in sinking one of the boats and, happily, escaped with the loss of only one man killed and one wounded. He killed or captured fifty-three of the enemy, among whom were 10 Tories who were sent to jail at Springfield. General George Washington personally thanked Major Tupper and the officers and men under his command for their gallantry and soldier-like behavior.

In 1776 he was appointed colonel of a Massachusetts regiment and was at Valley Forge during the memorable winter of 1778. It was at Valley Forge that he wrote the following letter to the General Court of Massachusetts to protest the deplorable conditions which his troops were forced to endure.

> In obedience to the order of the Legislature of Massachusetts State, I have collected as exact returns as I was able which are enclosed, and hope it will be found intelligible — it is observable that some of the officers under the head of remarks have given a sketch of clothing wanted, others have not. I wish it were in my power to picture to both houses the extreme sufferings of the poor unhappy soldiers for want of clothing, etc. I am sure it would move a heart of steel. I can't but think if the friends and relatives of the sufferers knew their distress some method could be found to relieve them. I am sure that neither distance nor any obstacle I can conceive (while alive) should prevent me from relieving a friend of mine. I am worn out in giving encouragement to the soldiers, that they will soon be relieved, and should scarcely be believed, if I was to declare that clothing had actually arrived, and thus our hands are weakened, with respect to government, so absolutely necessary in an army, would most humbly entreat that some method may be come into, to relieve us, or I could wish to leave the service, and not be a spectator of such complicated distress.
>
> I am your Honor's most obedient humble servant,
>
> Benj. Tupper, Col.

(In response to the pathetic and urgent letter, the people of Sharon responded immediately by the hand of Capt. Israel Smith, one of the committee of the town who procured for the suffering soldiers 42 shirts, 42 pairs of shoes, and 42 pairs of stockings for the army at Valley Forge under Washington.)

Jack Coggins, in his book *The Fighting Man*, tells us that the ideal soldier is one with "an intangible spirit which welds a unit together into a close knit society assured, in its sense of superiority, of invincibility." Such a description seems appropriate for Sharon's Benjamin Tupper.

Sharon in the Civil War

As a schoolboy, I memorized this poem to help me put the events and dates of this terrible conflict into perspective.

In 1861, the war begun;
In 1862, Lincoln told them what to do;
In 1863, the slaves were free;
In 1864, the war was over.

Sharon in 1860 was a town that had not known war for nearly fifty years; their last encounter having been the War of 1812. This decision to disrupt their peaceful existence in order to take arms against other Americans must have been most difficult for them. On April 26, 1861, however, a town committee of five prepared the following resolutions:

1. These resolves are necessary because of the war.
2. Good citizens must favor law, authority, and good government.
3. The loyalty of the citizens who are sustaining these laws is appreciated.
4. Sympathy is expressed for those who have or will have to leave home for this purpose and a promise is made to help them.
5. The town is to borrow a sum not over $5,000 to pay additional wages to enlisted men.
6. Each man enlisted is to receive $12.00 per month for each month of service.
7. A committee is to be chosen to look out for the needy families of those enlisting.

Records indicate that Sharon provided 146 men for the war, this figure being 8 over the quota for the town. The recruitment effort was ably handled by a young Sharon man named William Rufus Mann. At the age of sixteen, Mann was injured while driving a yoke of oxen and from that time on he was forced to go about using a cane. Because of this he was not in the active service, but was appointed an enrolling officer and evidently was quite successful in this task. During the day he visited many military hospitals in Maryland and Northern Virginia and assisted in processing furloughs for the sick and the wounded. No injury was going to prevent William Mann from making his contribution to the Union cause and to the boys of Sharon.

Sharon men fought at such places as Antietam, Second Bull Run, Vicksburg, Fredericksburg, the Wilderness, Spotsylvania, Cold Harbor, Petersburg, Richmond, Five Forks, and Appomattox.

At least 13 men served in the well-known 33rd Massachusetts Infantry Regiment. The regiment was organized at Camp Edward M. Stanton in Lynnfield during June and July 1862. On August 14, 1862, it left the state by train bound for Washington, D.C. I wonder what were the thoughts of those men as the train slowly rolled through Sharon, probably on the same roadbed as the present Penn Central line. For eight of those on board, this would be their final glimpse of Sharon; they would soon give their lives in battle with the Confederate forces. Here is a brief account of the unit's engagements:

October 1862 - The regiment arrived at Fairfax Station, Virginia.

November 1862 - They moved to Thoroughfare Gap and took part in a reconnaissance to White Plains, Virginia.

May 1863 - Took part in the Battle of Chancellorsville which proved to be Confederate General Robert E. Lee's greatest victory of the war, though costing the life of Stonewall Jackson.

June 1863 - Fought a rear-guard action in the retreat from Chancellorsville.

September 1863 - The regiment moved farther south and became part of the Army of the Cumberland in Tennessee. Here they faced their severest test in the Battle of Lookout Mountain when assigned to assault the heights. The men succeeded in their mission, but with heavy losses including John Davis, John Drake, and Addison Johnson of Sharon.

Early 1864 - The regiment was assigned to the 20th Corps coming under the command of General William T. Sherman. Under his command, it moved to battle at Resaca, Georgia, where more Sharon men were to die.

Mid-1864 - With the end of the war in sight, the 33rd participated in the seige of Atlanta and shared in Sherman's infamous march to the sea.

The company now turned north and finally reached Massachusetts on June 3, 1865. On the night before the 4th of June, the men were discharged from their encampment at Readville. Needless to say, the 90th anniversary of American independence was a joyous one that night on the road from Readville to Sharon.

It should be noted that the Sharon contingent in the 33rd Regiment possessed certain other abilities over and above their fighting skills. Most of them had been members of the Sharon Massapoags, the Massachusetts baseball champions for 1857, and they were quite fond of telling their soldier friends of the exciting occasion in which they defeated their rivals, the Olympics, in three straight games. They had borrowed red flannel shirts from the Stoughton Fire Department and contended for the championship on Boston Common. The last train for Sharon left around four o'clock, but by special arrangement with the Providence Railroad, they had been allowed to ride home in an empty freight car attached to a regular train.

Merely telling their fellow soldiers, however, was not enough to satisfy their pride and ambition. They formed a nine of their own and soon defeated every team in the regiment.

In further contests, they defeated some New York boys of the 136th regiment and at Atlanta they were victorious against the best of the Cumberland Army. Neither Confederate cannon balls nor Yankee fastballs were able to put our boys down. Quite a bunch they must have been, these Sharon men of the 33rd Regiment.

Veterans' Monument at the Town Hall, World War I   Photo by: Kennan

Veteran's Monument at the Town Hall, World War II   Photo by: Kennan

97

The Militia Fires a Volley at the Soldiers' Monument - 1975

THE SHARON MILITIA 1775-1976

By William F. Connors

CHAPTER 9

The first Sharon Militia was created by the town fathers of Stoughtonham on February 3, 1775 when they voted to raise 28 men and two officers in answer to their country's call for volunteers. During the Revolutionary War, upwards of 200 residents served in the Continental forces, many of them being members of the Sharon Militia. It's believed that the Militia disbanded after the war and that a related organization, the Sharon Artillery Company, was active well into the 1800's.

The modern day Militia was re-activated on June 13, 1974 by proclamation of the Board of Selectmen of the Town of Sharon. While the 1775 version was formed for fighting against the British, the present group has as its objective, the reliving of the revolutionary heritage by re-enacting those events which led to the formation of our country and a free and great nation.

PROCLAMATION

WHEREAS   the Town of Sharon recognizes the important contribution to the American Revolutionary War by the citizens of the town, then known as the District of Stoughtonham, who, as members of the militia company, were called to defend the cause of freedom for which they stood; and

WHEREAS   fitting preparation should be made for the commemoration of the bicentennial of this most important event;

NOW THEREFORE, the Board of Selectmen of the Town of Sharon does hereby reactivate the Sharon Militia Company for the purpose of participating in the Bicentennial celebrations.

> NORMAN KATZ, Chairman
> GEORGE E. DONOVAN
> ROBERT F. CURRIE
>   BOARD OF SELECTMEN,
>   SHARON, MASSACHUSETTS

June 13, 1974

What does the Sharon Militia do? Along with other Militia units from Massachusetts, we join together from early spring through late fall to take part in colonial parades, musters, fairs, fife and drum concerts, historic ceremonies, colonial balls, and battle re-enactments. Our dress and weaponry is as close as possible to that which was used by our colonial ancestors. The fife and drum music which is played during our events is identical with that played by the colonial minutemen as they marched to battle.

All the riflemen in the Sharon Militia are well versed in the handling and care of the "Brown Bess" musket which they carry. Prior to accepting invitations to events in which black powder would be used, members of the company traveled to the Milford National Guard Armory in February 1975 for instructions in the firing and safety procedure for the colonial musket. As a result, the present day Militia is confident that it could quickly step into the firing ranks of its 1776 predecessors without any problem.

After an initial parade on April 12, 1975, the company has grown and become quite active in a number of events in New England and even New York. Within the Town of Sharon the company has been active in the following events:

a) Fourth of July parades in 1975 and 1976
b) Memorial Day parades in 1975 and 1976
c) Annual town meetings in 1975 and 1976
d) Sharon country fairs in 1975 and 1976
e) Participation in the senior citizens' play (April 1975) and the Deborah Sampson play *She Was There* (December 1975)
f) The opening of Deborah Sampson Park and the wreath-laying ceremony at her grave site in Rock Ridge Cemetery
g) The Sharon Chapter Road Racers' Club race (for women) in October 1975
h) A number of lectures and demonstrations on colonial life and events before the schoolchildren of Sharon

What's the future of the Sharon Militia? The company is now a strong, well established unit and will be marching in Sharon long after the Bicentennial furor is over. The company has a long list of future commitments within the State and is hopeful of attending Bicentennial events in New Jersey, Pennsylvania, and New York as those states re-enact the battles which took place there in 1777 and 1778. The increase in membership among our younger Sharon residents coupled with the recent formation of the Sharon Militia Women's Auxiliary insures that the Militia will continue to function.

The ranks of the company through 1975 and 1976 include

Captain Edward Roach	Sergeant Gilbert Charlette
First Lieutenant Albert Blackler	Sergeant William Haviland
Second Lieutenant Gordon Hawes	Sergeant Gordon Hughes
Adjutant William Connors	

Militia:

Doris Annis (Deborah Sampson)	Cindy Hughes
Timothy Buyer	Frederick Jones
William Buyer	John Kilkus
Thomas Cavanaugh	James McAllister

Cheryl Connors
Timothy Donovan
Robert Ford
Arnold Holmes
Donald Holmes
Merilyn Holmes
Merrill Holmes

Patrick McCarthy
Gary Morris
Carol Newcombe
Raphael Nelson
Paul Patten
Walter Roach, Jr.
Lee Sacco

Militia Activities, 1975

Cobb's Tavern on Bay Road

TAVERNS, HOTELS and INNS

By Phyllis Brookfield

CHAPTER 10

Of those inns, taverns, hotels, and boarding houses which have been active through the years of Sharon's growth, first as a township and New Grant, then as Pole Plain, then as Stoughtonham and finally as the Town of Sharon, the first one and probably the most famous one was Billings Tavern. Otherwise known as Wainman's Ordinary, it was owned by Ebenezer Billings and built around 1670 or earlier. On the Old Post Road between Boston and Providence, it was used by many travelers after a day's trip from Boston. It was also used as a meeting house on Sundays until the local Community House was built. When King Philip and his band of Indians devastated Medfield and the surrounding countryside in 1676, they left Wainman's Ordinary unmolested, probably because of the kindness of Ebenezer Billings toward all the Indians.

There may have been other inns at this time too, but the next one of importance was Cobb's Tavern which was started as an inn around 1790. It was located on what was then the turnpike from Boston to Taunton and, "as one of the last hospitable road houses of olden time, Cobb's Tavern was a general favorite, particularly in its later years with bicyclists." Jonathan Cobb, the owner of the tavern, was also the Postmaster of Sharon. His son succeeded him in the business which flourished for over a century and the inn was finally closed when he died.

Sharon gained a reputation as being "the healthiest town east of the Rockies." The ozone count in Sharon's air was the highest anywhere and the water was considered the purest around. This encouraged people to come here for summer vacations and in the 1800's a great many inns, taverns, and boarding houses were started. These were in active use until some time in the early 1900's when with the increase in automobile travel, many summer homes became permanent year-round homes and the hotel business became so slack as to necessitate the closing of the last of the old hotels sometime in the 1940's.

In some cases, a building which has part of an inn still in it, is being used today. One such is Johnson's Tavern which was built around 1800 and became a private home in the late 1800's. It is now the home of the Harold Buckbees on North Main Street. The Stoneholm on the corner of Ames Street and East Street, opposite the County Club, was built about 1848 and was "open the year round for summer and winter boarders giving fine service." This building was built with stones from a local quarry.

The Quaker Inn was built as a private house around 1831 and became a hotel and tavern during the latter part of the 1800's until around 1900, and then was used as a private home until the Sharon Co-operative Bank bought it and used it as a bank until they built the present structure. The Savage Tavern on Bay Road was active at this time, although there does not seem to be much information available about it. The Crescent Ridge Farm had a boarding house which would accommodate 20 people. Other boarding houses in the 1800's included the Calledonian located on Billings Street and Mrs. Wicks's Boarding House on Pond Street, both of which catered to the workmen in the business establishments on Pond and Tolman Streets.

The Massapoag Lake House was one of the finest and largest hotels in Sharon. It had a hundred rooms, good boarding, livery stables, tennis courts, croquet, billiards, pool, boating, bathing, bowling, hunting and fishing. This hotel was built probably around 1880 and boasted of "Electric Bells, telephones, gas, steam heat, a good laundry and new iron fireplaces." Sometime in the 1920's it became Sunset Lodge when owned by the Dubinsky family. It was originally owned by A. Park Boyce & Co. and was a popular summer resort, being reached by taking the train or the trolley to the Sharon Heights station and then being met by a carriage. This took one to the edge of Lake Massapoag where a steamer would take passengers across the lake to the hotel. It was considered an excellent hotel and dances, parties and many different gatherings were held there. In 1955 the Catholic Church bought the lodge and it became the St. Francis Retreat which was used as such for twelve years.

In 1967 the Town of Sharon bought the St. Francis Retreat and converted it into the present community center. Dave Clifton became the Director of the Center in 1968 and has been largely responsible for the many activities that take place there. The townspeople feel this has been one of the best investments the town has made, for the Center is in constant use throughout the year. In 1973, the town also voted to purchase the Sacred Heart school area which has been renamed Deborah Sampson Park and it too will be widely used for town activities.

At this time, too, there was a hotel on the corner of what is now called Cedar Street and Beach Street. This hotel was called "Lake View Hotel" and was also very popular and well known. On the corner of East Foxboro Street and South Main Street there was a hotel called Elm Lawn. This hotel, also known as Randall's Tavern, had cottages for its guests.

The Tudor Motor House was a fine place for eating and their specialty was chicken dinners. This house was beside Wolomolopoag Pond and was a favorite with the Bicycle Club of Boston and those interested in the newfangled automobiles. This was built around 1890 and burned around 1915. It is now owned by Mrs. Finn who lives in a part of the original building. The Winship House which was considered a good inn, was built around 1840 on Pond Street and is now the site of the Executive Apartments. The Ingleside, which was on the highest point of land in Sharon, accommodated twelve people. The going price for lodging was from six to twelve dollars per week.

The Sharon Inn on the corner of Station Street and South Main Street was one of the most prominent and beautiful hotels in Sharon. It was taken down in the 1920's and the Charles R. Wilber School was built on its site. This was later enlarged to be the Sharon High School for many years, and is now the Intermediate School.

Other inns of this era were the Seven Gables Inn which was run by the grandmother of Mrs. Marion Hawkins, who lives in a part of the original inn and says it was an inn until about 1900 when it became a private home again.

One of the several inns that were active in the early 1900's and which will be remembered nostagically by many Sharonites, was the Glendale Inn which was on the corner of Glendale Road and North Main Street. This had originally been the home of Deacon Philip Curtis until it became an inn. Sometime in the 1930's, a fire destroyed most of the inn and eventually the site was bought by the Eliot Washburns who have their home there now. The Lawn Crest Inn on North Pleasant Street was one of the last of Sharon's old inns to go. Sometime in the 1940's it was torn down and a more modern single family house was put up. This had been a large hotel, well situated near the center of town and near the railroad station.

With the establishment of the Sanatorium for tubercular people around 1880, the reputation of Sharon's clear, clean air and pure water was more enhanced than ever and this probably was responsible for a number of these hotels, including summer hotels, being built.

Among these were Singers' Inn located on Capen Hill Road, which has been the Booth Memorial Home of the Salvation Army Camp until recently. Also Carvin's Hotel which was a popular summer resort and is now The Green Manor on Massapoag Avenue. The Mansion House, which was a private home for years was bought and used by the congregation of Temple Israel on Pond Street until they were able to build their present temple.

Sharon Inn on the Site of the Present Middle School

Lawn Crest Inn Formerly on North Pleasant Street

Stoneholm on Corner of East and Ames Streets

The Glendale Formerly on the Corner of North Main Street and Glendale Avenue

Main Lobby, Sunset Lodge, Now the Recreation Center

Massapoag Brook at Ames and Cottage Streets. Source of Water Power for Early Industries

Photo by: J. K. Harris

INDUSTRIES IN SHARON

By Mary D. Wade

CHAPTER 11

The resources of a community determine its industries. The first surveys of the Dorchester New Grant, besides identifying the persons to whom lots were assigned, carefully noted streams and roads.

Two streams rising in Sharon empty into Boston Bay. Another rising less than two miles away flows out of Sharon into Narragansett Bay. This phenomenon is caused by the elevation creating a watershed. In the current nuclear age this curiosity has no bearing on the industry, but in the early days of our country's development it set a pattern for the type of community Sharon is today.

Equally prominent on early maps were designations of meadows, iron mines, and cedar swamps. The meadows provided easy cultivation of hay while the cedar swamps were prized for the tall trees which were cut for ship masts, shingles, and clapboards. Iron ore had an even greater commercial value.

Bog iron formed in a sedimentary process from animal, vegetable, and mineral sources proved profitable enough to mine. This type of ore, although not of high quality, was used extensively during the Revolution because it was an available source for cannon and shot.

According to one town historian, iron ore was taken from the ridge east of Lake Massapoag as early as 1724.[1] Hixson's iron mine is located in this area on the Map of the Twenty-five Divisions, completed in 1730.

An interesting project sponsored by the Sharon Historical Society around the turn of the century was a handwritten notebook kept on geographic features, streets, cemeteries, etc. On the subject entitled "red dirt" there is this interesting note.

> A strip of Massapoag Street where the soil impregnated with iron
> is of a red color. It used to be used for trial of speed of horses.[2]

The bed of Lake Massapoag yielded bog iron in great quantity. As early as 1762 the Dorchester Proprietors had voted "to let Mr. Nathaniel Linnard have the improvment of Massapoag pond for one year to git Iron oar."[3] Leonard, for being allowed to take 100 tons had to post two pounds security for each twenty tons of ore and was to pay two shillings for each ton mined. Officials were appointed to check the operation and report to the Proprietors about it. Leonard's lease was renewed for seven years, but in 1770 the Dorchester Proprietors voted to sell the lake rather than go to the expense of lowering the level to obtain more ore.[4]

On June 6, 1770, Edmund Quincy, who had recently moved to Sharon, bought the lake. In partnership with Colonel Richard Gridley he mined the lake to supply ore for their furnace on what is now Gavin's Pond. Two men would go out in a boat. Taking large iron tongs with wooden handles eight to ten feet long, one man brought to the surface a mixture of ore, sand, and gravel and dumped this onto a screen. The other man picked out the stones, washed away the sand and placed the ore in the boat.[5]

Obviously the lower the level of the lake, the easier the mining operation. The new owners undertook the task of lowering the outlet channel and tradition says that a great ox roast was held to celebrate the occasion of its completion.[6] According to Gridley's diary, they began to take iron ore from the lake on August 24, 1773.[7] Not bothered about conflict of interest, the town of Sharon appointed Quincy to a committee to build a road to the furnace.[8]

Another resource for the early settlers were the fish which came up the streams to spawn. As mill dams were erected, passage of the fish was so interrupted that citizens sought ways to protect them. One of the first acts after Sharon received status as an independent town was to elect Richard Hixson, Jr. to "treat with the owners of the dams across the Neponset River about makeing a way for the fish called alewives & other fish passing up & down sd river."[9]

The fish at one time had been quite numerous. Jeremiah Gould, writing in 1830, described how during the running season, a horse crossing Massapoag Brook would kill the fish by stepping on them. However, he notes that by the time he was recording all this the alewives had been gone for many years.[10] Industry took precedence.

The streams were essential to industry at this period. Along each stream were established "privileges" which gave the owner the right to use the water power of the stream at that point. Dams were usually constructed at these sites and a manufacturing process begun. Sharon streams, although not numerous nor of large volume, provided enough power to run several mills. A number of ponds in town bear evidence of mill sites.

The right of ownership of the water could present interesting problems. The Revere Copper Company of Canton came into possession of Lake Massapoag and thus could control the flow of water all the way down Massapoag Brook. A serious conflict arose when Sharon citizens became irate over the extremely low level of the lake. In an injunction against the company in 1885, they claimed this served to impair

> greatly the right of the public in the use and enjoyment of the water thereof for the purposes of fishing, boating and other lawful uses, and to create and expose upon the shores of said pond a large quantity of slime, mud and other offensive matter very detrimental to the public health.[11]

The company responded that it was doing no such thing.

The map accompanying this litigation contains a legend giving the names of privilege owners. Since the legend is not dated, it presents a problem as to the ownerships in 1885 because the two Leonards listed had been dead thirty or more years. However, it does mark sites and is an interesting study for that reason.

MASSAPOAG BROOK

Massapoag Brook, the largest stream in town, also known in places as Devil's Brook and on maps of the late 1800's as Sapoo Brook, provided enough force to power six privileges along its route before entering Canton and emptying into the Neponset River. The ponds giving evidence to these sites of industrial activity take their names from some former activity at that site. Starting at the lake and following Massapoag Brook down, there is Hammershop Pond on Ames Street, another small pond sometimes called Knife Works Pond out of view behind houses on Ames Street, Mann's Pond on Billings Street and Trowel or Car Works Pond on North Main Street.

Hammershop Pond

The first water power on Massapoag Brook was on or near Hammershop Pond. Nathaniel Leonard (1764-1843) is shown as the person who had a privilege at the inlet to the pond according to the Revere Company litigation map. This Leonard seems to have been the son of the man who mined ore at the lake in the 1760's. He was a blacksmith who made superior edge-tools such as hoes, plow shares and other farming implements.[12]

On or close to the Leonard site, Deacon Samuel Bird, whose house appears on the 1730 map at the outlet of the lake, had a saw mill and grist mill.

> He continued to run these for many years, even after he had become old and feeble. His wife had bundled him up nice and warm to grind a grist for his neighbor but the upper gate of the raceway was hard to start and putting forth all his power it started suddenly throwing the Dea. into the water and he was drowned.[13]

Because no evidence of these first uses of the first privilege along the brook remain today, it is difficult to determine whether they are the same as that of the so-called second privilege at the outlet of Hammershop Pond on Ames Street. The town map of 1794 shows a saw mill on this site.

It is known that P. Eldorfe & Company manufactured fire arms of some nature here in 1776.[14] Mr. Eldorfe was a Frenchman, and he used French newspapers under the wallpaper on his house. A portion of this curiosity appeared when the wallpaper was being removed around the turn of the century. The combination of French printing and the wallpaper pattern may be seen today in the historical section of the public library.

About 1787 Nathaniel Morse and his son-in-law Leonard Billings erected a saw mill and grist mill which they continued for a number of years.[15] The section of present day Ames Street extending from Pond Street to Quincy Street was called Sawmill Road at one time, and later called Reupke Road. John Christian Reupke, stated to have owned a grist mill, is shown as owner of the house across Ames Street from the sawmill in 1794. Afterward Isaac Johnson put in another saw mill. About 1812 Samuel D. Hixson operated a grist mill

111

and also put in a carding machine to make cotton batting, later adding a couple of tack machines.[16] The local joke was that you were likely to get all of these in any bread made from the corn ground at the mill.

It was the last activity at the pond which gave it its name. The knife industry was started by John Ames, brother of Oliver Ames of Easton, and Ames Street was named for him.[17] In a catalog prepared in 1909 prior to the sale of the Revere Copper Company and the Kingsley Iron & Machine Company in Canton, the following information was given to prospective buyers.

> This privilege one-fourth mile from Massapoag Lake (Pond) and on the waterway to the large plants described herein, is at the junction of Quincy, Ames and Cottage Streets, Sharon, about a mile from the railroad station and three-fourths of a mile from the Post Office at Sharon village. There are over nine acres of land, one-third of which is in a storage pond. The privilege has been active as a manufacturing site since previous to 1800. About 1825 there was a textile mill here and in 1835 J. Ames of Easton established the present industry which was taken over in 1857 by H. A. Lothrop & Co., and under their management it has never been idle unto this day. Their lease does not expire until April 1st, 1911, an occupancy of 50 years, with never a question arising between lessor and lessee. They make the "J. Ames" and the "J. Sanger" market, butcher, and shoe and other knives, which are largely exported, but a great many are sold throughout this country. The employees number from 12 to 20 and at times there have been even more upon the pay roll. The immediate settlement about the privilege numbers about 100 people. There never has been any difficulty in securing good labor. The newer buildings belong to H. A. Lothrop & Co., the older buildings are part of the privilege and include a cottage house facing Quincy Street and now used as an office, and for the storage of stock and supplies. Below the property, on Ames Street, is a house lot containing 52 sq. rds. of land. The location of this privilege is certainly well adapted for a nice little manufacturing plant, is the first privilege below Massapoag Lake and therefore has the first use of all the water from this lake that goes to the Kingsley Iron & Machine Co. and the Revere Copper Co. The only power used is the water and there is an old Russell 30 inch horizontal water wheel in iron case, which was originally rated as 20 h.p. It operates the entire plant.[18]

At the Hammershop the water power was used to pound the blades into shape. Older residents recall the tremendous noise made by the hammer.[19] It apparently was the custom of at least one worker to cool the unsharpened blades by thrusting them through the wooden walls of the building. It became the delight of mischievous boys to stand outside and grab hold of the blade so that it could not be drawn back.[20]

Statistics show that 40 persons were employed here in 1855[21] and ten years later 70 persons turned out 30,000 dozen shoe and butcher knives.[22] The factory burned a few years after the sale described above, and the water power is now idle. The pond remains intact, with the dam and spillway in good repair. It makes a good addition to the Griffin Playground. The house at 5 Quincy Street is a private residence.

Third Water Power

The third water power on Massapoag Brook is now obliterated, but it clearly shows on the 1830 and 1858 maps of the town. The small pond directly across Ames Street from Hammershop Pond was cited by one historian as the earliest use of Massapoag Brook for water power.[23] Deacon Jacob Hewins, the son-in-law of Deacon Samuel Bird, ran a sawmill here. The account books of Benjamin Hewins' store show that between 1764 and 1776, the sawmill operator either paid cash or provided lumber to pay his bill at the store.[24]

It also was the site where Nathaniel Leonard, Jr. (1796-1849) had an axe factory.[25] Solomon Talbot recorded a high estimate of the company as a business establishment and told how a number of Sharon boys learned the iron business from the Leonards. He singles out one pupil, however, as an unwilling apprentice.

> The last mentioned [David Manley] was always trying to invent some machine to get rid of hard work and it was soon found out that he was too ingenious to make a successful iron worker.[26]

The third water power disappeared when the bed of the brook was deepened to furnish additional power for the knife works above it.[27]

Knife Works Pond

The fourth water power is still evident in a small pond in the valley behind the buildings along the north side of Ames Street between Quincy Street and Deborah Sampson Street. Several of the houses along here were built for Knife Factory workers.[28]

As with other sites, the privilege has been the scene of several different activities. The 1794 map shows a grist mill on the site. A man named Spencer Everton ran a grist mill here at one time. He caused some consternation by claiming through his Indian heritage the right to all the natural water in the region.[29]

Pictures still exist of the grinding shop for the Lothrop Knife Works, but a concrete dam and a broken sluice gate are all that remain as evidence of this arm of the parent factory upstream.

The natural stream flows out of this pond at the north side while the sluice gate is on the east. Both outlets are clearly marked on the 1830 map. On the channel from the sluice gate Seth Boyden and later Lemuel Capen manufactured patent leather. Seth Boyden was also reported to have had a foundry for making steel and maleable iron castings, but whether this is the site is uncertain.[30]

The 1830 map shows a satinet factory on the site, but this industry, operated by a man named Jenks, burned on October 23, 1834.[31] After the factory was rebuilt in 1837, James Carpenter moved his mill from the pond on North Main Street to this place and manufactured cotton shirting and sheeting until the time of the Civil War.[32]

Mann's Pond

The fifth water power of Massapoag Brook was located at Mann's Pond on Billings Street. A walk over the area below the dam reveals the foundation of several buildings. John G. Phillips, a member of the Sharon Historical Society at the beginning of this century wrote this article which was published in *The Sharon Advocate* on February 4, 1911.

The brook flowing from Massapoag pond in Sharon northeasterly to Canton and thence out into the Fowl meadows, where it joins another stream from west of Moose Hill to form the Neponset river, has supplied power for manufacturing purposes more than 200 years. Paul Revere, then living at Canton, purchased this water power from the Commonwealth, and thereafter claimed the control of all the water that came from the pond.

There have been six mill privileges utilized on this stream in Sharon. The fifth power from the outlet at the pond is now known as Mann's Mill, and I have the following account of its history from Mr. William R. Mann:

This privilege was first purchased by Jedediah Morse, who built a dam and commenced putting in the foundations for a water wheel, but he struck quick-sand and had to give it up. Not having the capital to overcome this trouble, the property reverted to Revere.

In 1831 George H. Mann bought the water privilege from Joseph Warren Revere, who was the son of Paul, erected a factory building, and put in machinery to manufacture "tickings." The building was located where now the wheel pit covered by an old roofing can be seen on Deborah Sampson street. This business was carried on until 1840, when the factory was destroyed by fire. The old stone mill, still standing, was built in 1833 for coloring the blue stripe in the ticking.

The year after the fire a new building was erected on the canal where the old foundations now mark the spot. The water wheel, the only thing saved from the fire was moved, and a "run of stones" put in to grind corn and rye. Oliver Ames & Son, having heard of the new grist mill, sent over from North Easton a load of seventy-five bushels of corn, and wanted to know how soon they could have it ground. The man was told that if he went home and when he got there turned about and came back, by the time he got back the meal would be ready for him. He concluded to wait.

Mr. Mann and his sons went to work building some looms and twisters to manufacture "cotton sail duck," and having an order for the same on hand, sold this lot and built more machinery. In 1844, having renewed their machinery, they commenced the regular manufacture of "cotton duck," and continued it until 1846, when the father retired and the two sons, George R. and William R., took charge. They enlarged the business, put in looms of double the width of sail duck to 44 inches, and contracted with

114

a Boston company for the delivery of 150,000 pounds.

In 1856 the sons found that the expense of keeping the works in repair was too great, on account of the settling of the building. They consequently decided to rebuild in a new location, and the present brick factory was the result, built on a solid foundation of decomposed granite. Here they found a fall of water of 23 feet and the present dam was built on the old one. They put in a water wheel 26 feet in diameter with 9 ft. buckets, and had everything in readiness to start by June, 1857.

They commenced delivering the finished goods weekly, averaging 3000 pounds per week. This was continued with success until 1900, when the competition of the Southern cotton mills made manufacturing unprofitable and the Manns retired from business.[33]

None of the buildings Phillips describes are standing today. The first building created by the Manns was under the bank of Deborah Sampson Street about half way to the dam, this being prior to the construction of Deborah Sampson Street in 1860. The three rooms of the factory are plainly visible, with the stone rear wall almost complete on the north room.

A large colored map in the Dedham Historical Society shows this factory as having a power source on a channel at the very eastern end of the dam. The other two streams from the dam are visible, but the power source is not recognizable today. The north chamber has a stone covered outlet through which the water rejoined the natural stream, the only indication that water once flowed through the mill.

Phillips does not mention the blacksmith shop which stood at the bridge on Billings Street. This probably served as the "Maintenance Department" for the mill. Nearby was the dye house, whose stone foundations are somewhat disarrayed. A picture of the building remains, however.

The site of the second Mann's mill is somewhat of a mystery. Phillips mentions a foundation close to the stream, and something answering this description is found on the land between the two streams a little way upstream from where they join. The land is wet there much of the time which may account for the settling which they encountered.

The "new" mill is the one which has left the most impressive mark on the landscape. Although there is no trace of the building which stood on the western end of the dam, the stone chamber for that tremendous breast wheel still retains its integrity, with a graceful stone arch as silent sentinel. The metal conduit pipe which brought water from the pond to turn the wheel is now stopped, but the stone channel which served as outlet for the water now carries a little stream brought into it by a drainage pipe from the road.

A comparison between the activity of the two mills can be found in statistics for the years 1855 and 1865. In 1855 the old mill had 608 spindles, consumed 103,552 pounds of cotton, manufacturing 48,247 yards of cloth (belt ducking, for machine belting, 37½ inches wide). The cloth was valued at $23,411.70. There was a capital investment of $10,000 with nine males employed and eleven females.[34]

In 1865 the mill used 121,523 pounds of flax yarn with a value of $70,439. There were 69,470 yards of cloth manufactured by three male employees and forty-four female employees.[35] Mr. Mann personally went to Maine to hire girls to work in his factory. They would work until they married and then he would go recruiting again.[36]

A survey[37] taken for insurance purposes on May 29, 1886, reveals the following information:

960 spindles
Main building: 40 x 85 ft., 2 stories, basement and loft
   Slate roof, stairs in the tower, elevator.
   Basement room = wheel, small upright boiler and repair shop
   First floor = spooling and weaving
   Second floor = carding and spinning
   Loft = not used
Building 2 - picker house, one story and basement
   Basement = store cotton
   First story = picker and lopper
   Powered by shaft from main building
   Covered passageway between main and this building
Heating = steam
Lighting = Kerosene in Westland Safety Lamps suspended by chains
Sperm and Paraffine oil used as lubricants
Work hours = 10 per day
Had no fire pump, hydrants, nor sprinkler but buckets of water
   were kept filled on each floor of the tower and in picker room
Lightning rods on mill
"Mill was built in 1856 and is of good substantial construction
   and kept in good order. Rooms neat. Business evidently well
   managed. Limited fire appliances."

The decline of the mill came and it was sold. Cotton thread and cotton waste were made for a few more years, but the mill was destroyed by fire in 1919.

In the display cases at the Sharon Public Library there are interesting relics of this industrial effort. Shuttles, spools of thread and small machine parts can be found. There are several examples of fabric woven at the mill, including the machine belting and some of the blue and white ticking.

William R. Mann's home was at 228 East Street, and the old house retains much of its dignity. The houses on Mann's Hill Road were built for the workers. An interesting feature of the road is that it turned sharply and plunged down to Billings Street between the second and third houses. The map in the Dedham Historical Society shows this clearly. There was also a cistern shown, and the ten-foot deep stone walls are still in tact on Deborah Sampson Street.

Trowel or Car Barn Pond

The sixth water power on Massapoag Brook was located on North Main Street. The pond was created when Joseph Hewins and others petitioned the town for the right to build the dam.[38]

The following article written by John G. Phillips appeared in the April 1, 1911 issue of *The Sharon Advocate*. It was entitled "The Trowel Works."[39]

This is the name commonly given to the sixth water power of Massapoag brook.

In 1800, before the dam was built, Oliver Lothrop operated a tannery here. NOTE: This probably was Oliver Curtis, not Lothrop.

In 1809 Joseph Hewins and others petitioned the town for leave to build a dam. The petition was granted on condition that the road across the dam be kept in repair. Jona Belcher built the dam.

The same year a factory was built for the manufacture of cotton goods, by the Sharon Cotton Manufacturing Company. Darius and Gilbert Lothrop, mason and carpenter, built the mill.

In 1821, James Carpenter of Attleboro, hired the mill and continued the business of making fine cotton cloth, shirtings, etc., until 1837. In the meantime the Reveres of Canton had purchased the property, leased the "Ministerial Meadow" for additional flowage, and increased the water power.

Carpenter moved his plant up stream, and the firm of Manning & Glover of Boston, occupied the factory for the manufacture of bedding and upholstered goods, for several years.

About 1852, Frank Bisbee of Canton, took possession, changed the works into an iron foundry and made trowels.

At the time of the war, H. A. Lothrop & Co., the proprietors of the knife works at the second water power above, bought the factory and made trowels and knives. This business prospered for many years.

In 1880, the old building burned down and a new one was built. Jonathan Packard and others, continued the manufacture of tools for some ten years, after which the business was conducted by the Packards, in connection with the knife works.

About 1900, the property was sold to the Norwood, Canton & Sharon Street Ry. Co. For the last ten years the water power has remained idle.

Pictures of the car barn which stood on the north side of North Main Street can be found, but there is little physical evidence to show where it was. The road, of course, is now maintained by the town and has been for many years. The sluice gates for the factory are in good physical condition but are fully open. The site today is a favorite fishing spot, and Phillips has preserved in his scrapbook a local news item recorded by "Benjamin" at Sharon on August 4, 1873, showing that fishing on that site is nothing new.

> The pond at the Trowel works has been drawn down, to facilitate repairs of machinery — making splendid fishing — and berries being very plenty.[40]

Wintertime brings hockey players to the scene, but industrial activity has long ceased.

BEAVER BROOK

Beaver Brook, rising a mile or so southwest of the center of town, flows northeastward until it joins Massapoag Brook. Its earliest name was Hobb's

Brook, a name undoubtedly taken from Matthew Hobbs, whose ownership of a large area surrounding the brook is shown on the Map of the Twelve Divisions of the Dorchester New Grant, dated 1726.

Although not so large as Massapoag Brook, the stream was sufficient to power several industries along its banks. One of these is still in operation.

Activity near Railroad Overpass on Depot Street

The first dam on Beaver Brook was some distance below the railroad overpass on Depot Street. John G. Phillips, writing in *The Sharon Advocate* in 1911, gave this information.

> About 1725, Matthew Hobbs sold 50 acres or thereabouts of land covering the locations inquired about, the purchasers being Benj. Hewins, John Hixson, (a mason), and Ephraim Payson, (a carpenter). These men formed a company and built a dam and a bloomery, or furnace, to make wrought iron. Fragments of slag may now be picked out of the ancient dump just below the dam. The ore treated was the kind called "bog ore," and probably was hauled down to the furnace from the iron mine on the right of Upland Road, just after passing the end of Crossmore Road. Several such iron mines were worked in Sharon in the early days. This company operated the bloomery until about 1740, when it was sold to Benj. Johnson (a blacksmith) who followed the business for a few years. Until the restrictions of Great Britain became so severe regarding the manufacture of iron goods, that it soon proved an unprofitable industry. Afterward the mill was operated as a fulling mill by one Everton, and still later by Ebenezer Mann. When the road was built in the thirties the old mill disappeared.[41]

At the forge on this site were fashioned the iron hinges for the first meeting house in town. In 1905 Solomon Talbot gave the following history of the land bought from Matthew Hobbs, whose house in 1725 was the only one within a mile.

> He [Hobbs] had two daughters; the oldest married Benjamin Harlow of Plymouth, who was a bloomer in the iron works, and one of the first workmen employed; the other daughter married Isaac Johnson, whose father Benjamin bought the forge property in 1744 and carried on the iron works. It was he who made the great hinges for the doors of the church. At his death in 1760 the forge lot was left to his son Isaac.[42]

Both the 1830 and 1858 maps show a paint mill at this site, while the 1794 map had indicated a fulling mill, as Phillips had mentioned. By 1830 the paint mill was owned by Elijah Hewins, a local Justice of the Peace and also the man who surveyed the town for the 1830 map.[43]

Maskwonicut Street

The next privilege down Beaver Brook was at Maskwonicut Street. The Sharon Historical Society took a "ramble" to this site on June 24, 1905, and published this report.[44]

> Mr. Talbot was our leader. The first stopping place of historical interest was the railroad bridge on Maskwonicut street. Here Mr. Talbot gave us some interesting points. In 1737 a sawmill held the place of the present bridge, and was in existence until all the logs in that vicinity had been cleared away, which was about 1760, when it changed hands and became a grist mill until about 1835, when the railroad company had to get a special act of the legislature before it could destroy the mill privilege.
>
> The bridge was made double, one section for the railroad and the other for the brook. It has been raised twice to avoid accidents and as we crossed we were informed by our leader that in former times there had been a residence between the brook and Mr. Luff's house. In this house lived Edward French who ran the mill until after 1800. He was a musician and it was he who composed the tune known as "New Bethlehem" for the ordination of Rev. Mr. Whitaker who was the second minister in Sharon.

The 1830 map shows Johnson's Mill on this site, with houses for E. French and J. Johnson next to the mill. Josiah Johnson owned the mill[45] and Edward French the fine singer and composer was the miller. Not only was his tune "New Bethlehem" sung at Rev. Whitaker's ordination in 1799, it was sung again by the Old Stoughton Musical Society at the celebration of Old Home Week in Sharon in 1906.[46] It was also Edward French who, when the mill was destroyed, saved the broken mill stone, giving half to the Johnson family and keeping half. Each family used the pieces as their doorsteps.[47]

Canton Street

The third power on Beaver Brook occurs at the Sharon Box Company, the oldest business established and currently in operation in town. For 120 years there has been a sawmill at this site.

In 1856 Asa and Ira Billings built a dam across the brook and erected a "one story water powered, grist and sawmill. . . . What had originally been a meadow and apple orchard was converted into an attractive, scenic pond, furnishing power for the mill."[48]

The farmers brought their logs to be sawed with an old-fashioned upright saw and a long carriage which pushed the logs forward into the up and down motion of the blade. Grain was ground in the grist mill on the lower level.[49]

> Twice, during the first few years after it was built, the dam broke down and the stones and gravel were spread over the fertile meadows below. A just judgement upon the owners for working the mill on Sundays was the common sentiment. At any rate the business proved unsuccessful and in 1865 the plant passed into

the hand of Mr. Emmons Leonard. Mr. Leonard made many improvements and conducted a prosperous business for 32 years when he sold it.[50]

Statistics for the year 1865, when Leonard bought the mill, show that two sawmills in town prepared 265,000 feet of lumber and 45,000 shingles. Combined, they employed four hired hands.[51] One mill was obviously this one on Beaver Brook, and the other would have been the Holmes Mill on Billings Brook.

During Leonard's ownership, the sawmill on Beaver Brook was converted into a box factory. One of the principal customers was the Morse Brothers of Canton, who manufactured the "Rising Sun" Stove Polish.[52]

Elijah A. Morse, whose extensive factory was on Sherman Street in Canton, started this successful business in Sharon. John G. Phillips, writing in *The Sharon Advocate* in 1911 states

> Hon. Elijah Adams Morse was not born in Sharon, but came here with his father and two brothers when a boy. The father was an itinerant preacher and gatherer of genealogical information. Probably the latter profession did not pay much better than the former, at all events, the sons were forced to provide for themselves at an early age.
>
> I remember Elijah well when he was perhaps 16 and I was 8 years old. At that time he worked in Calvin Turner's store, now called the Quaker Inn. He was the sexton of the Congregational church and also took care of my father's horse. As his boarding place was with a neighbor, he frequently took me fishing down to the Ministerial Meadow . . . I liked him very much.
>
> Within a few years after this period, Elijah began to make stove polish from a recipe which he came into possession of in some way. The small building used for this purpose then stood a little back from Pond street, but is now the woodshed behind the Middleton house on Depot street. Some of the boys would turn the crank for him and after making a small batch of polish, he would take a basket on his arm and peddle it out from door to door. One day he surprised the boys by appearing on the square with a freshly painted old "tin cart,'" a white horse and a yellow dog. The boys helped him load up the wagon with Rising Sun Stove Polish and set him going. He soon outgrew the town.[53]

Several persons have recorded memories of Elijah Morse in the scrapbooks kept by the Sharon Historical Society. George F. Leonard, writing in 1904, tells about taking a May Day walk with his chums and seeing Mr. Morse painting the sign for his stove polish in the year 1860.[54]

Perley B. Davis, writing in the same publication, states

> My first acquaintance with Sharon dates from a beautiful Saturday afternoon, June 8, 1861. I had come from Andover to occupy the pulpit of the Congregational church on the following

day. I then met for the first time a young man who afterward became the Hon. Elijah A. Morse. He had returned that afternoon from his first trip with horse and wagon selling stove polish. Being informed that I was a theological student, and assuming therefore that I could unravel every theological difficulty, he plied me with questions Biblical, historical and metaphysical far beyond my ability to answer.

. . . I then formed a high appreciation of the intelligence of Sharon people.[55]

At Elijah Morse's death, 1898, came this obituary.[56]

The death of Elijah A. Morse of Canton removes one of the best known and most influential citizens of Norfolk County, and a splendid example of the self made man. Years ago in Sharon he laid the foundation of a fortune. In the little shop, now standing in the rear of John Middleton's on Depot St., he made his first stove polish and peddled it from house to house about the country. Soon he was able to buy a horse and cart, and so he climbed by push and shrewd advertising methods, to a world wide business and success. Sharon should have had that business but her citizens did not then foresee its growth and so refused him the land he sought.

He reached the goal of his ambition on his election to the Congress of the United States. There his vote and influence were always on the side of strict party loyalty and good citizenship. To his death he took a vital interest in the welfare of his town and in public affairs.

The funeral ceremonies, at his request, were, like his life plain and unostentatious. His life and example will not soon be forgotten by the people of this vicinity.

In the same year that Elijah Morse died, Ralph Brown bought the box factory, built a new story on it, only to watch it burn in 1903.[57] He sold it to Charles F. Smith but continued to operate the mill for several years.[58] Smith expanded the business, but economic hard times and another partial destruction by fire led to the sale of the building and equipment. George Durell, manager at the time, bought some of the equipment, kept five employees and ran the business until 1937, when Arthur Rhodes purchased it.[59]

Mr. Rhodes expanded, bought equipment and trucks, and cleared land just east of the factory in order to air-dry stacks of lumber, mostly eastern white pine.[60] Today, Mrs. Rhodes continues to act as president of this corporation which produces crates, skids, pallets and wooden shipping boxes, using 4½ to 5 million board feet of lumber per year.

A big change has occurred on Beaver Brook from the 1830 map, which shows ponds at Depot Street and Maskwonicut but nothing at Canton Street, to the 1876 map which shows only the Sawmill Pond at the Box Factory. On this site now the dam still holds the pond intact, but the broken spillway allows a flow of water whose power is no longer needed.

BILLINGS BROOK

Billings Brook, rising from the natural pond shown on the 1794 map as Billings Pond and now called Wolomolopoag Pond, provided water for agricultural and industrial uses.

Cranberries

The first use of the brook is that of a cranberry bog. This industry, still very active today, is on the site of a natural bog at the intersection of South Main Street and Route 95. Billings Tavern stood at the ancient junction of Old Post Road and the Road to Punkapoag.

The cranberry business was started here about 1860. The statistics for 1865 show 550 bushels valued at $1,650 were grown on twenty acres of land in Sharon.[61] A little over half this acreage was at the "Paradise Meadow" on Billings Brook.

An undated newspaper account in the *Foxboro Reporter* provides this information about the harvest.[62]

> There were about 100 men, women and children, all on their knees, crawling along in their alloted space, which is marked by white cord drawn from stake to stake. Peck measures are used in which to pick, and after the picker has filled one, they are taken to the cashier, this position being filled by Miss Mabel F. Turner, who pays them a one-peck check. After receiving four of the peck checks, a silver half dollar is given in exchange. . . .
>
> A team is constantly employed during the day transporting the filled bushel crates to the storehouse. On Monday last the berries were being gathered at the rate of 40 bushels per hour. . . . It is estimated that the entire crop this season will amount to about 1500 bushels.
>
> At the close of picking, the berries remain in the crates in the storehouse, just as they were taken from the meadow, until November, when they will be sorted, graded and placed in barrels ready for shipment to the firm of E. L. Minzer of Philadelphia, who takes the entire crop each season.
>
> A barrel of cranberries which bears the trademark, "Paradise Meadow," always finds a ready market. The peculiarity of this berry is its rich color, fine flavor, and large size. It is peculiar to this meadow, which by the way is a natural "bog," having been greatly enlarged and improved. Comprised in the meadow is 12 acres of land. There are three artificial ponds, one above the other, backed by a never failing supply of water which is so essential in cranberry culture.

Clapp's Turning Mill

Farther downstream from the cranberry bog is a tributary feeding into Billings Brook. On this small stream a pond provided power for Reuben Clapp to have a turning mill for making bedsteads in 1830.[63]

Gavin's Pond

Directly on Billings Brook is the pond which gave Sharon its fame. Known now as Gavin's Pond, the dam on its southern end is thought to be the site of the furnace which cast the first cannon for the Revolution.

A short while before Edmund Quincy bought Lake Massapoag in 1770 in partnership with Colonel Richard Gridley and Joseph Jackson of Boston, he bought "three acres of land and a dwelling house together with furnace, bellows, walls and all other utensils, two coal houses with all the ore and stock therein."[64]

At this factory a great quantity of shot was manufactured. A company of matrosses was assigned to guard the activities here.

> On January 24, 1774, the Committee of Safety and Supplies voted that all the cannon mortars, cannonballs and shells be deposited at the towns of Worcester and Concord. Voted that four hundred and fifty of four pound cannon balls be brought from Stoughtonham to Sudbury. Voted that one ton of grape shot be carried from Stoughtonham to Sudbury. Voted that one ton of three pound cannon balls now at Stoughtonham be carried to Sudbury. Voted that one half a ton of two pound cannon balls now at Stoughtonham, exclusive of what is for the use of the matrosses be carried to Sudbury.[65]

Colonel Gridley, who helped fortify Bunker and Breed's Hills, ran the furnace with the assistance of Louis de Maresquells, whose father had developed a method of boring cannons in France. This method was adopted by the Americans because the cannon were more reliable than the cylinder-cast ones which often had flaws causing them to explode. Gridley's cannon were bored by placing them perpendicular over a drill driven by a small water wheel. After cooling the cannon were taken to Lake Massapoag to be proved by Colonel Gridley and Captain Nathaniel Curtis, son-in-law of Philip Curtis, the town's first minister.[66]

Edmund Talbot added one interesting sidelight to the story of Sharon's cannon going to Dorchester Heights to help drive away the British from Boston. In a paper read before the Historical Society in August, 1905, he stated

> There lived with my father sixty years ago an old lady by the name of Sallie Leonard. Aunt Sallie as she was called was born in 1762, and during this very period was about thirteen years of age. She related to my father that she carried a message from Col. Gridley in Canton to the furnace in Sharon, the purport of which was to hurry up the manufacture of the cannon as they were needed for use at Dorchester Heights.[67]

The exact site of the furnace has been elusive. A slag heap at the south end of Gavin's Pond was reported in 1905,[68] but recent use of metal detectors has not brought a full answer. The pond, however, continues to exist.

The 1830 and 1858 maps show that J. Holmes had a mill on this site, and in 1876 the estate is still in his name. He operated a saw mill here. Pictures of this mill and the lake appeared on several souvenirs for Old Home Week at the beginning of this century. Cups bearing the picture are displayed at the library, as are cannon balls manufactured at the furnace.

OTHER WATER-RELATED INDUSTRIES

1830 Water-powered Industries

Two other small factories can be found on the 1830 map, both south of Lake Massapoag. One was a carding mill on the upper branch of the Canoe River. A dam had been built and a channel coming out of the west side of the dam powered the activity here. An interesting thing about this pond and mill site is that they are now in Foxboro. Sometime between 1830 and 1858 the boundaries between the towns changed. Today the pond can be found on the extension of East Foxboro Street into Foxboro. The road has been straightened to go behind the old house at the site, but the pond and channel carrying water are still visible.

The other factory on the 1830 map was on a small stream in the southeast part of town, coming out of what is now Briggs Pond. The brook rises in Stoughton, crosses Bay Road and Mountain Street before emptying into Leach Pond. The factory was on the southwest side of Mountain Street with a small reservoir on the opposite side formed by Mountain Street.[69] In 1906 the Historical Society took a ride to the spot and found the remains still visible.[70] No indication of the type of activity at this mill site is available. The site is now under water.

Spring Water

Promoters of the town of Sharon nearly a century ago spoke of the purity of its water. William B. Wickes, real estate agent, wrote in 1883

> The springs in Sharon at and near the source of Beaver Brook have long had a local celebrity for their medicinal qualities. The waters of a spring on the railroad company's land, near the station, have the reputation of having cured diseases quite recently, and for some years a few families in Boston have had a regular supply of this spring water sent them.[71]

Charles Walcott, a resident 1888-1890, shipped six to eight casks a week to his store in Roxbury.[72]

Later Mr. Wickes modified his claims a little.

> Tradition tells us that the Indians and early settlers believed its use would cure dyspepsia and jaundice and dissolve gall and bladder stones, and even in our own day intelligent people ascribe wonderful cures of different diseases to its use. Chemical analysis, however, shows no special medicinal qualities, but a remarkable absence of all deleterious qualities, and as far as I am able to discover it is simply very pure water which remains ever the same summer and winter.[73]

The source of the pure water which he acclaimed was a spring just north of the railroad station under the railroad bed.[74] The size of the spring was variously estimated to be eight feet in diameter up to thirty feet.[75] The output was never measured, but it was enough to disturb the surface of the spring.

When the spring was dug out and filled at the building of the railroad, it burst out on the west side of the railroad bed in a spring hole four feet in diameter.[76] The Sharon Water Company located the town's first pumping station there, and it remains today.

This also was the site of the Sharon Hydraulic Company about 1840. William B. Wickes, writing in 1880, stated

It is now 40 years since the Hydraulic Company first brought water into this village. The subject was agitated for a long while before it was accomplished. A half century ago the village contained but a few scattered houses, and though the need of good water was severely felt yet it was a great and seemingly impossible undertaking to pump water to the height of 100 feet as it was necessary to do. When the project was first taken up certain persons agreed to join if a company of ten could be secured. At first this seemed possible, but there was so much talk against the success of the undertaking, and so many pronounced it impossible to raise water to that height with a pump, that the majority of those engaged in it backed out. Four men decided they would go on and build the works at their own expense. These men deserve special mention and their names should be kept in remembrance: they were Captain Chas. Ide, who kept store where Mr. Turner now lives; Dea. Joel Hewins, the village blacksmith, who lived where his son, J. P. Hewins, now lives; Dea. Philip Curtis, who occupied the farm H. A., Lothrop owns and Mace Hixson, who lived where Albert G. Hixson now lives. To fully realize what these men did we must remember that this was 15 years before Boston had a supply of water, and that there were very few places supplied with water by pumping. Nearly everyone even while the works were being constructed, prophesied that the thing would not work and that all the money put in would be sunk. We can well believe, as these four men met from time to time in Captain Ide's store to talk it all over and carry out their plans, they must have felt some anxiety, but they never wavered but as they met with unexpected obstacles and more money was called for they cheerfully contributed it. The first pipe was of lead, hand made, by one Littlefield of East Walpole. A gentleman who was present when the water was let in tells us the excitement was intense. Few present believed that the pumps could be made to throw water so high. As the pipes had not been connected with the houses the water was first let out on the common. When it was seen to spurt into the air, anxiety and suspense gave way to joy, and the few stockholders felt repaid for their trouble. . . .[77]

The houses served by the operation were where the Sharon Co-operative Bank, the Post Office, and the brick house by the Unitarian Church are. The

Christian Science Church stands at the corner of the farm also served.

Other springs were bottled in various forms. The Sharon Alta Spring water[78] was a carbonated beverage which came in ginger ale or sassafras and pine flavors, according to lables which still exist. F. W. Mansfield and Sons promoted their products by stating, "SHARON PINE is *NOT* a nerve tonic, an opiate or stimulant. Cures nothing but thirst."

Plans were made to build a resort hotel on the corner of Belcher Street and Bay Road, beside the spring which furnished the Alta water. A prospectus was drawn and a floorplan of the hotel circulated; however, the grand project never came to be.

Bitters, in the form of Clarke's Sherry Wine, were bottled in Sharon. The aqua bottle which was associated with the product here were valued at $50 each in 1973.[79]

Icehouses

Before the era of refrigeration, people had used various methods of keeping food cool. The simplest way was to place the food in containers and place them in spring water. Nearly every farm had this kind of facility.

Then the era of ice boxes came. Large chunks of ice were placed in a sealed cabinet and food was placed in the same area to keep cool. Before the days of refrigeration the ice was cut from lakes, made into cakes of standard size and stored in ice houses, covered with hay. According to one historian ice shipping was the idea of Bostonian Frederick Tudor, who in 1805 traveled in the Caribbean and got the idea of shipping ice to other countries. After experimenting with hay, cornstalks, wheat straw, tanbark, and finally sawdust, he built efficient ice houses. Then with Nathaniel Wyeth, who invented a saw operated by horse power, he cut blocks of ice from ponds, packed them in storage houses, and shipped them around the world.[80]

Lake Massapoag was a source of ice which was shipped into Boston. Burkhardt's Icehouse stood on the western bank of the lake. The 1876 map shows the railroad spur which served the business. Diving expeditions at the lake in November, 1975, yielded ice hooks, splitting bars, and the idling wheels for the chain which carried the ice from the lake to the ice house.[81]

OTHER EARLY INDUSTRIES

Charcoal

The earliest record of charcoal being produced in Sharon is during the Revolutionary War. Richard Hixson had a large farm on North Main Street, after his death Mrs. Hixson ran the farm.

> When the mother of Capt. Richard Hixson, born in 1774, on the Hixson homestead, North Main st., was left a widow with 5 daughters and one son, she successfully conducted the business in varied lines which her husband Richard Hixson, dropped at his death. The farm was made productive, small fruits were cultivated, and the charcoal pits at Rattlesnake Hill were kept burning, and the business of making and marketing charcoal was managed, the widow employing 5 men in the work.[82]

126

The names of the persons who continued this work are not known, but statistics show that in 1855 there were 20,480 bushels produced by 12 employees.[83] Ten years later production ran half that at 12,600 bushels produced by eight employees.[84]

Leather and Shoes

Tanning pits in Sharon seemed to cluster close to North Main Street with a few exceptions. Some of the sites have now been covered with mill ponds. A water source was important to tanning not as power but as a soaking agent. Hemlock bark and oak bark were used to cure hides of animals, usually ones slaughtered for food.

Captain Richard Hixson had tan pits which were still visible at the turn of the century. Oliver Curtis had pits close by where he cured white leather from the skins of trapped animals. He eventually went farther west to get better supplies of hides. A man named Gilbert and later Jeremiah Richard had tan pits at the sawmill. On Viaduct Street Lemuel Estey had a tanning operation, and a man named Eberley cured calf skins by a new process in a factory on Morse Street.[85]

Although the tanning pits seem unlikely to have supplied all the leather for the boot makers in Sharon, this industry flourished here in the first half of the nineteenth century. The area along Upland Road, Norwood Street, Maskwonicut Street, and Richards Avenue was known as Shoemaker Valley.[86] Boots made in Sharon sold in Boston, Philadelphia and New York.[87] During 1855, 29,604 pairs of boots and 1,000 pairs of shoes were manufactured by 84 male employees and sixteen female employees.[88] Ten years later the number of pairs of boots had risen to 33,847, but the employees had dropped to seventy-one males and eight females.[89] By 1892 the business had died out.[90]

Although Joshua Whittemore, a glazier living on Norwood Street, seems to have been the earliest shoemaker, dating to the late 1770's, later manufacturers seemed to concentrate near the center of Sharon, on Depot and Pond Streets.

On Depot Street, Warren Bullard had a shop near the railroad track, with Albert Middleton close by.[91] Joel Pettee, a tall dignified man, had a shop on the same street[92] as did George Gay and Joel Hewins for several years.[93]

Pond Street was also a popular place. The three Hixson Brothers, John R., Albert G. and Charles D., built a shop in the first block. Their former shop had been in an attached room on Savels Tavern, now moved to High Street.[94]

Charles Winship and Addison Johnson first set up shop on South Main Street but then moved to Pond Street.[95]

One of the first boot manufacturers on Pond Street was Amasa Dunbar, who built the stone cottage which still stands. He started business in 1837, adding his shop on the south side of the house.[96] As a later sideline he made coffins, and the story is told that he visited the gravely ill to estimate the measurements for future use. It is true that in 1865 there were 25 coffins manufactured in a business employing one male.[97] Amasa Dunbar died in 1874 at the age of eighty-two.

"Home" Industries

Before 1830 the tedious job of braiding straw for bonnets began to be done by females in Sharon.[98] During the winter months the women made straw bonnets from the long strands which they had braided.[99] The children were often set to the task of braiding. According to one Foxboro resident, the young girls who had lived in her house a century ago had been required to braid a length that would reach the ground from the second story window before they could go out to play.[100]

The bonnets were also manufactured by Benjamin S. Leonard in the village[101] but the operation never reached the proportions of the factory in Foxboro.

An interesting display of straw materials in various stages of being braided, including two different styles of braiding, can be found in the historical section at the library.

Another interesting occupation not confined to females was the separation of cotton seeds from the fibers prior to spinning. Deborah Sampson was one who did this in her later years. Elisha Horton, at the age of 64, wrote this account on January 1, 1858.[102]

> The first cotton factory in Massachusetts was built about fifty four years ago (if I remember right) by Mr. James Beaumont. The Factory was located where the rolling Dam of the Neponset Factory now is. This factory was the first in Mass and second in the United States of America.* In the year 1809 or 10 it past into the hands of Mr. Richard Wheatley and the writer of this was Overseer, under the direction of David Wild, of Wild and Waterman who run the Factory on shares or, so much pr lb for yarn, no cloth, was made at this time in the Factory. . . .
>
> Some may wish to know something about the Machinery of those days. Let me state a few things which I well recollect —
>
> The Cotton was receiv'd from Market in Bags from 2 to 300 lb Packed by hand by the growers South and consisted of Sea Island (Best) Georgia Upland (2d best) Purnhambuea (Very strong and course). The cotton was weighed out in lots of from ten to fifty and old and young ladies children and old Men of every Class and Station took the Packages to their several places of abode and with there hands and fingers separated the bad cotton,† Dirt, Seeds and etc. and Returned the Cotton and it was ready to Pass to the Breaker, from the Breaker to what was called Finisher, from thence to the drawing Frames, after passing through 5 heads of the drawing Frames and Doubling sixteen times, it went to the Roping Frames, from thence it was taken by Children and wound by hand on large Bobbins and sent to the Struker from the struker to hand Mule, or Throstle, or Water Frame and then made into yard No 5 [or 8] to 12 worth from 60 to 75 cents pr lb.
>
> *Mr. Samuel Slater Built the First Cotton in the U.S. at Pawtuckett, R.I.
>
> †Many controversies occured Respecting the difference in weight, in many Instances its loss was grate. in many Instances, I adopted the plan, to return all waste and have it weighed, still it fell short with some. I well remember two persons that I considered honest, one was old Mrs. Ganett (of Sharon called Old Souldier) and the other is now Elijah Endicuts Widow.

Silk Production

There was an attempt at one time to raise silkworms in Sharon for the production of silk cloth. As late as the beginning of the twentieth century there were old mulberry trees on the south corner of Bay Road at Cobb's Corner, remnants of the industry which Jonathan Cobb had tried to introduce here.[103] In the library is a collection of silk and silkworm cocoons belonging to Olive Richards in 1830.

Granite Quarries

Nature has been generous to Massachusetts in giving it large amounts of granite. In Sharon these deposits were not helpful to the farmers, but stone quarries off Morse Street have supplied stone for several houses in town — one on North Main Street and the other on the corner of Ames and East Street.

The largest operation to use the granite from the Moyle Quarry was the Canton Viaduct. Originally, it had been planned to use stone quarried in Canton to build this tremendous span. However, the stone proved to be difficult to dress properly and it became Sharon stone which is still serving after 140 years.

Hotels

Sharon's location on the Boston & Providence Railroad provided the impetus for an activity which, although not an industry, provided a source of income for Sharon residents. The "pure air and water" promoted by real estate agents such as William B. Wickes appealed to city dwellers. It became fashionable to spend summers in Sharon, much as people go to the Cape now. Several large hotels were built and large houses were turned into inns to house the paying guests. In addition, people needed places to stay while they visited persons confined to the Sharon Sanitarium for the treatment of tuberculosis.

All this combined with recreation around the lake brought people to Sharon. A large number of dwellings in town were originally summer cottages which now are year-round homes. The special trains which brought cars full of persons ready to enjoy Burkhardt's Grove no longer run, and most of the hotels have disappeared — the most prominent one remaining is now the community center for the town.

Carriages

In the days of more leisurely travel there was a carriage shop on the corner of Tolman and Cottage Streets. Harper's Carriage Shop made wheels noted for their excellence. "His buggy wheel was the despair of carriage makers of Europe and not one on that continent was ever able to equal it for its combined lightness and endurance."[104]

An older Sharon resident recalls that as a young boy he disliked the work of sanding the spokes for these carriages. The painting was done by experienced workers and much care was given to painting the stripes.[105]

Hothouse Gardening

The broad plain at the intersection of Moose Hill Street and South Main Street was the site of a large operation that involved gardening under hothouse conditions. Around 1900 Oscar L. Dorr, living beside Wolomolopoag Pond, raised vegetables here. He heated his houses by steam, using a smokestack as large as one necessary to operate a factory. Dorr also maintained a water tank which he filled from the pond.

From the several acres of crops in his greenhouses he sent loads of fresh vegetables to Boston daily. He also took pride in delivering lettuce to the Foxboro depot each day in time for it to be sold in New York the following morning.[106]

MODERN INDUSTRIAL PARK

In more recent times the Bay State Film Company was organized to produce film for motion pictures, but it is no longer operating. Other than craft-type industries which have become popular in the past few years, there is little industry in Sharon. With the exception of the Sharon Box & Lumber Company on North Main Street, large industry is now confined to the Industrial Park on Route 1 near Walpole Street.

On the 360 acre industrial site there are nine firms employing an average of 469 people, providing a payroll of approximately four million dollars.[107] The largest company manufactures metal products. Sharon's industry has come full circle with metal products. But industry does not now, and never did, provide the economic base for the town.

Footnotes

1. *Sharon Historical Society Scrapbook*, Volume 3, December 1, 1905, p. 23.
2. *List of Localities and Places in Sharon, Massachusetts*, p. 91 (manuscript).
3. *Records of the Dorchester Proprietors*, quoted in *Phillips Historical Scrapbook*, Vol. II, p. 17.
4. *Ibid.*
5. *Sharon Historical Scrapbook*, III, 16.
6. *Ibid.*
7. *Ibid.*
8. *Sharon Town Records*, I, 31.
9. *Ibid.* p. 10.
10. Jeremiah Gould, *Annals of Sharon, Massachusetts, 1830* (Sharon Historical Society Publication, Vol. I, 1904) p. 10.
11. Commonwealth of Massachusetts. Supreme Judicial Court. Suffolk County, Massachusetts. *Attorney General, at the Relation of William R. Mann and others v. Revere Copper Company*, July 7, 1885.
12. Solomon Talbot, "First Mill on Massapoag Brook," (Manuscript).
13. *Ibid.*
14. *Sharon Historical Society Scrapbook*, Volume II, June, 1905, p. 75.
15. Talbot, "First Mill on Massapoag Brook."
16. *Sharon Historical Society Scrapbook*, Volume I, September, 1904., p. 48.
17. *List of Localities*, p. 2.
18. J. E. Conant & Co., *Catalogue* (Lowell, Mass.: Butterfield Printing Company, 1909), pp. 21, 23.
19. Interview with Alice Packard, November, 1975.
20. Interview with Lawrence Peck, July, 1975.
21. Commonwealth of Massachusetts, *Statistical Information Relating to Certain Branches of Industry in Massachusetts, for the year ending June 1, 1855* (Boston: William White, 1856), p. 402.
22. Commonwealth of Massachusetts, *Statistical Information Relating to Certain Branches of Industry in Massachusetts, for the Year Ending May 1, 1865* (Boston: Wright & Potter, 1866), p. 464.
23. Talbot, "First Mill on Massapoag Brook."

24. Benjamin Hewins, *Account Books, Volumes I and II*, 1760-1778, I, p. 13, II, p. 141.
25. John G. Phillips, *Historical Scrapbook*, Vol. II, p. 17
26. Talbot, "First Mill on Massapoag Brook."
27. Phillips *Scrapbook* II, 17.
28. *List of Localities*, p. 57.
29. *Sharon Historical Scrapbook* I, pp. 47-48
30. Unidentified manuscript (in the Vertical File of the Sharon Public Library)
31. *Ibid.*
32. Phillips *Scrapbook* II, 17.
33. *Ibid.*, p. 14.
34. *Branches of Industry*, 1855, p. 402.
35. *Ibid.*, 1865, p. 463.
36. *Sharon Historical Scrapbook* II, p. 110.
37. *Barlows Insurance Surveys* No. 8771 "G. R. & W. R. Mann's Cotton Duck Mill, Sharon, Mass." (in the files of the Merrimack Valley Textile Museum, North Andover, Massachusetts)
38. Gould, p. 20.
39. Phillips *Scrapbook* II, 19.
40. John G. Phillips, *Historical Scrapbook*, Vol. I, p. 36.
41. Phillips *Scrapbook* II, 20.
42. *Sharon Historical Scrapbook* III, 33.
43. *List of Localities*, p. 50.
44. *Sharon Historical Scrapbook* III, 20.
45. *Sharon Historical Scrapbook* I, 47.
46. *Sharon Historical Society Scrapbook*, Volume IV, March 12, 1907, p. 96
47. Phillips *Scrapbook* II, 14-15.
48. *The Sharon Advocate*, May 17, 1965.
49. Phillips *Scrapbook* I, 19.
50. *Ibid.*
51. *Branches of Industry*, 1865, p. 464.
52. *The Sharon Advocate*, May, 17, 1965.
53. Phillips *Scrapbook* II, 20.
54. *Sharon Historical Scrapbook* I, 24-25.
55. *Ibid.*, p. 12.
56. Derry Scrapbook, undated (private)
57. The Sharon Advocate, May 17, 1965.
58. Sharon Historical Scrapbook II, 38.
59. *The Sharon Advocate*, May 17, 1965.
60. *Ibid.*, May 31, 1965.
61. *Branches of Industry*, 1865, p. 464.
62. *The Foxboro Reporter*, undated
63. *List of Localities*, p. 11
64. *Sharon Historical Scrapbook* III, 16.
65. *Ibid.*
66. *Ibid.*
67. *Ibid.*, p. 17.
68. *List of Localities*, p. 39.
69. *Ibid.*, p. 11.
70. *Sharon Historical Scrapbook* IV, 99.
71. *Ibid.*, II, 36.
72. *Ibid.*, p. 37.
73. *Ibid.*, p. 36.
74. *Ibid.*, p. 33.
75. *Ibid.*, pp. 34-35.
76. *Ibid.*, p. 36.
77. *Ibid.*, p. 108.
78. Sharon Alta Spring bottle labels (private)
79. Ralph Kovel and Terry Kovel, *The Official Bottle Price List* (New York: Crown Publishers, 1973), p. 34.
80. The Dodges, *New Puritan Paths from Candle to Countdown* (The Newburyport Press, 1964), p. 12.

81. *The Patriot Ledger*, November 3, 1975.
82. *Sharon Historical Scrapbook* I, 16.
83. *Branches of Industry*, 1855, p. 402.
84. *Ibid.*, 1865, p. 464.
85. *Sharon Historical Scrapbook* IV, pp. 46-48.
86. *Ibid.*, 46.
87. *Sharon Historical Scrapbook* II, 116.
88. *Branches of Industry*, 1855, p. 402.
89. *Ibid.*, 1865, p. 464.
90. *Sharon Historical Scrapbook* IV, 46.
91. *Ibid.*, II, 115.
92. *Ibid.*, I, pp. 24, 29.
93. *Ibid.*, II, 113.
94. *Ibid.*, 112.
95. *Ibid.*, 113.
96. *Ibid.*, 110-111.
97. *Branches of Industry*, 1865, p. 464.
98. *Gould*, p. 20.
99. *Sharon Historical Scrapbook* II, 116.
100. Interview with Dorothy Johnson, Foxborough, Massachusetts, June 17, 1970.
101. *List of Localities*
102. *Elisha Horton*, "Recollections of Past Events," (in the files of the Canton Historical Society) pp. 1-3. (manuscript).
103. Gould, pp. 20-21.
104. Reprint in *The Sharon Advocate*, July 1, 1965.
105. Interview with Walter Seaver, Sharon, Massachusetts, January 26, 1975.
106. Reprint from *The Sharon Advocate*, July 1, 1965.
107. Massachusetts Department of Commerce and Development, *City and Town Monograph. Town of Sharon* (Boston, Massachusetts) Revised, 1973.

Mann's Mill on Mann's Pond   *Boyden Collection*

The Hammer Shop, Formerly at Ames and Cottage Streets   *Boyden Collection*

The Knife Shop, Formerly on Massapoag Brook   *Boyden Collection*

133

Sharon Box and Lumber Co. Inc., 1976   *Photo by: J. K. Harris*

Sawmill at Corner of North Main and Canton Street about 1898   *Courtesy of: B. D. Ornell*

134

THE BOSTON ICE COMPANY

By Clifford L. Jerauld

CHAPTER 12

December 21 is the first day of winter. Shortly after that a contingent of the harvesting crew arrived, consisting of 24 horses and a pung (wagon mounted on runners) loaded with equipment for the horses. The animals were hitched in pairs in line. Bill Huntley rode one of the lead horses and guided the line from Boston. They were stabled on the corner of Mohawk Street and East Foxboro Street.

As the ice thickened on the lake, the next contingent arrived, consisting of about 20 men with Homer Lightbody in charge. These men were known as the bosses. They had rooms in the boarding house (across the street from the stables) which was operated by Ma Prue, whose husband, Pa Prue, was the permanent manager of the plant. The men were charged $3.50 per week. Their rooms were on the second floor.

At this time all unemployed males in Sharon checked in with Homer and were given a number, and most of them were put to work at once making repairs, etc. Most of these men were in the building trades and were well-known from year to year and had key jobs in the operation. Among them were steam engineers and a blacksmith. Norm Whitney operated the gasoline engines and miscellaneous motorized equipment. Norm was a local boy who, at the age of twelve, was a genius with gasoline engines at a time when mechanics were not as common as now.

The thicker the ice became, the more it insulated the water from the cold. The ice did not freeze as quickly, so sometimes other means had to be used to bring the water to the top of the ice. Every time there was a snow storm all the men would be lined across the ice and snow about 6 feet apart with punch bars, and do what was called sinking the pond. The men would punch a hole through the ice and then move forward 6 feet and punch another row of holes until a large area was covered. The weight of the snow and the men would cause the water to bubble up and saturate the snow and create more weight until it was possible to create from 4 to 6 inches of ice on top of the existing ice, which would freeze solid in a few days, the ideal thickness being 12 inches before harvesting. Should there be additional snow, large horse-drawn scoops would be brought into play, and the field would be cleared of snow.

With the building repaired and the discharge doors closed in, the intake doors were opened to receive the new ice. The engineers had filled the steam boilers with water, steam raised, and a long, endless chain that dragged the ice up from the lake had been loosened from the ice at the lower end, that was just below the level of the lake. The chain was started, bearings and the chain links were greased, and any cross bars that were cracked or broken were replaced. The blacksmith had repaired and sharpened the tools. Norm Whitney had all of the motorized pieces ready. The channel and the field had been surveyed and marked. All that was needed was 12-inch ice.

The third contingent now arrived, which consisted of a crew of men picked from skid row by an employment office and shipped out to make up the full crew needed when the harvest started. A more bedraggled group of men has not been seen in Sharon. They were relegated to the third floor of the boarding house, which consisted of rows of cot beds, and was known as the "ram pasture." The smoking room became off limits for the youngsters, and Joe Rose, the night watchman, began his patrols of the house to guard against fire, theft, or drinking.

Usually harvesting started the next day. The grooving crew started cutting the channel and the field at about 2:00 in the morning with their motorized saws, which cut grooves in the ice measuring 44 inches by 44 inches. The grooves left about 3 inches of ice to hold the cakes together. Large ice floes were then cut with hand saws and floated down the channel to the sluiceway. The individual cakes were split off and fed into the chain that carried them up to the runs and into the houses.

The plant consisted of a main building 300 feet long, 150 feet deep, and 50 feet high, with four runs along the front of the building and a sawdust room at the top, and separated into 8 rooms. All walls were double, with a 12-inch space between, that was packed with sawdust for insulation. Each room had an opening at each end. There was an enclosed incline that extended into the lake which was about 200 feet long and carried the chain that dragged the ice up from the lake. Halfway up the incline, the ice cakes passed through the planer that kept the ice to a consistent 10-inch thickness. As the ice arrived at the run being used, it would drop out of the chain and slide around a corner to be picked up by another single chain that carried it along the run. This chain was operated by a large single-cylinder gasoline engine through a belt that had to be extended from time to time as the upper runs were brought into play. This was Norman Whitney's responsibility. He stayed in the engine room 24 hours a day and slept on his workbench to start the engine every few hours to keep it from freezing, and to be available should the motor equipment used by the groovers at night give trouble. As the ice in the houses reached even with the first run, a section was placed in the incline that allowed the ice to be carried up to the next run. A trough under the planer collected the chips in a flow of water, and they were carried out onto the ice and became what was known as the chip pile (this extended several hundred feet out onto the lake).

Only four houses were worked at a time, and each opening had a man known as a switcher. He would hook a corner of the cake and switch it onto the run into the house. The first switcher took every fourth cake; the second man every third cake; the third man every other cake; and the last man, the only cake left. If a cake had cracked on the way up, it was allowed to go off the end of the run into the waste pile. This pile lasted until July before it melted. It took about 4 to 5 weeks to fill the houses, then everything shut down. The engines and boilers were drained of water; the doors of the houses were closed up and packed with sawdust; the tools were stored in the blacksmith shop; and payday had arrived.

Homer Lightbody and some men from the Boston office had brought the cash, and the pay envelopes were filled and numbered. They would sit behind a long table in the dining hall, and the workers would form a line giving their name and number, and would receive an envelope containing their earnings. Even the skid row group would leave the picture of health. Good food and no liquor for a month had made quite a difference. Bill Huntley would line up his horses and leave for Boston at daybreak and things would return to normal at the lake.

About April, a summer crew came to remove the stored ice into rail cars and have it shipped to Boston. The 44-inch cakes were sawed down the middle, making the shipping size 22 x 44. The cars were drawn into position by horses. Only one or two cars a day were shipped in the beginning. The number was increased as the temperature rose to a peak of 10-15 cars a day during the summer months and tapered off in the fall until the houses were emptied.

About 1923 it was found to be more economical to manufacture ice in Boston, and the operation was shut down. Building wreckers came in about 1926 and removed all of the iron, and one night the rest of it burned. This was the most spectacular fire that could be imagined. It was a mass of flames when the fire was discovered. The heat generated by the wooden building, plus the sawdust in the walls, was indescribable. It was impossible to get within 300 feet of the building because of the heat, especially when the fire would burn a hole in the wall, allowing the sawdust to pour out and create a fire fall that, by the time it reached the ground, would be ashes. The members of the Fire Department could not get near enough to fight the fire and limited themselves to containing it. The fire burned all night and part of the next day, and so the Boston Ice House went out in a blaze of glory.

Boston Ice Co. Formerly at South End of Lake Massapoag   *Courtesy: W. B. Roach*

Sharon Co-operative Bank

Photo by: J. K. Harris

Norfolk County Trust Co. Now Bay Bank Norfolk

Photo by: J. K. Harris

Sharon Credit Union

Photo by: Kennan

BANKING IN SHARON

By Dwight P. Colburn

CHAPTER 13

During the 1700's and 1800's Sharon was principally a farming community. Although essentially a farming town, enterprising men started factories for making carriages, cotton goods, cutlery, files, woolens, boots and shoes, trowels, machetes, banana and boot knives. There were sawmills and corn and grist mills.

Along about 1865, out of a population of about fourteen hundred, 276 people were engaged in farming and 253 in seven small industries or trades.

There was little need for banking then, and any monies taken in by the farms or small industries was kept in small cast iron safes. Daniel Webster Pettee maintained the central store in what is now known as Post Office Square and with an 1850 revolver in his pocket took the Saturday night cash home for the weekend.

In the late 1890's and the early 1900's many Boston business and commercial persons came to Sharon and made their homes here. It has been mainly a residential community since. Most of the farms have disappeared, and dwellings have been built on them.

There was, therefore, a need for home financing, and a group of Sharon residents organized the Sharon Co-operative Bank. On January 19, 1912 it was chartered and opened for business on February 19, 1912. J. Eveleth Griffith was the first president and William D. Wheeler, the first treasurer. The "office" was opened the third Monday evening every month at 8:00 P.M. at William D. Wheeler's drug store in Post Office Square. It had deposits of about $10,000.00 at the end of the first year, and the first annual statement is shown at the end of the chapter.

The first Board of Directors were J. E. Griffith, F. V. Brittain, A. C. Sampson, W. T. Maher, W. J. Roach, W. E. Clark, H. F. Nelson, and A. E. Wright.

One month after the bank opened, the first loan in the amount of $3,500.00 was auctioned off and bid in at 5½%. For the first thirty years the home mortgage loans were in the vicinity of $3,500.00 to $4,500.00.

The presidents since J. Eveleth Griffith have been John J. Rafter, William B. Brigham, Frederick V. Brittain, Dwight P. Colburn, and Robert F. Currie. The principal executive officers and treasurers since the original opening have been Nathaniel Wheeler, George Hall, Archie Kingsbury, John J. Rafter,

Dwight P. Colburn, V. Belle Winchester, and Robert F. Currie. The attorney for the bank and Chairman of the Board of Directors for many years and to this date is A. Clinton Kellogg. With one exception, all members of the Board of Directors have been Sharon home owners and residents. The bank has grown over the years and has undertaken many new banking services in addition to the original savings and home mortgage services. The total assets on the latest published statement show them to be $13,200,147.00.

From time to time commercial banks outside of Sharon studied the need for a commercial bank in Sharon, but inasmuch as it was a residential community, none had undertaken a commercial bank branch or new bank. The Stoughton Trust Company for several years during the 1920's and 1930's sent a representative once each week to pick up deposits from local merchants and other customers.

In 1952, however, Mr. Edwin R. Marshall who was president and who had established the Norfolk County Trust Co. in Brookline by combining several small banks with the Boulevard Trust Co. of that town, visited Sharon with the Executive Vice President, Mr. Elmer Cappers. They consulted with many about the need for a commercial bank. As a result, a branch of the Norfolk County Trust Company was opened at 15 Post Office Square on August 18, 1952. The original manager was Robert T. Sheldon. Mr. Dwight P. Colburn opened the first account at Norfolk County Trust. This branch has grown steadily and in January, 1976 had deposits of $8,000,000.00 and about 5,000 accounts. The branch still stands on this site. It is a substantial commercial bank furnishing all banking services for industry and industrial enterprises.

A group of Sharon residents saw the need for savings and personal borrowing soon after World War II. The Sharon Credit Union was incorporated by the Commonwealth of Massachusetts on April 26, 1956. It was founded by a group of eleven local men, with the first accounts opened on May 16, 1956. Depositors were permitted to borrow $100.00 for each $5.00 deposited in savings. Eli Krovitsky was the first President of the Board of Directors. He was followed by Lou Plonsky, and Lou Sweet, who presently holds that office.

The first location of the Sharon Credit Union was the home of its first treasurer, Max Lubin. After a short time, the Credit Union moved to a small office on East Chestnut Street. The next move was to P. O. Square in an office over the stores. Some time later the Credit Union rented a store at the Sharon Heights Shopping Center. Before moving to the present location, 10 Billings St., the Credit Union was also located at Washington Place.

The Credit Union was run by the first founders until February, 1966 when the first paid employee was hired to work one night a week for three hours. In June, 1966 the hours were increased to two hours one afternoon and three hours one evening each week.

Until October, 1967 the Sharon Credit Union paid a yearly dividend. Beginning in 1968 a quarterly dividend was instituted. In January, 1967, when the Credit Union moved into its present location on Billings Street, the hours were changed again, and it was open Tuesday and Thursday from 1:00 P.M. to 3:00 P.M. and Wednesday 7:00 P.M. to 9:00 P.M.

A second employee was hired in February, 1968, and in September of the same year, the hours were again extended to five afternoons and one evening each week.

The Credit Union's 1000th account was opened in April, 1970 by David Goldberg, fourteen years after its incorporation. It was not until May, 1970 that the Board of Directors voted to open for five full days and one evening weekly. Depositors now number over 8,000, and the Credit Union's assets are over $19,000,000.00.

Upon the opening of the Sharon Shopping Plaza at 700 South Main Street, the South Shore National Bank with headquarters in Quincy, Massachusetts opened a branch office. This bank was originally the Granite Trust Company, which in recent years converted to a national bank. The early presidents of the bank were Theophilus and Delcevare King of Quincy. This bank offers all commercial bank services and is a full service bank.

The most recent banking organization to open a branch in Sharon was the First Federal Savings and Loan Association of Boston. This institution with main headquarters at 50 Franklin St., Boston opened an office at the Sharon Shopping Plaza on South Main Street near the Foxboro border on January 27, 1975, and the present manager is Mrs. Karen V. Ross. The president of the association is Richard E. Hale.

This savings institution was originally the Suffolk Co-operative Bank of Boston, organized in 1885. It became the Suffolk Federal Savings and Loan Association in 1937 and finally adopted the name of First Federal Savings & Loan in 1955 when Ernest A. Hale was the president.

Sharon is now well supplied with banking services appropriate for a residential community.

Sharon Co-operative Bank

Incorporated Jan. 19, 1912   Began Business Feb. 12, 1912

SALE OF MONEY, ROOM 7. DENNETT'S BLOCK, SHARON, MASS.
THIRD MONDAY OF EACH MONTH AT 8 P. M.

ANNUAL REPORT

ASSETS		LIABILITIES	
Permanent expense	108.68	Dues Received	$9796.00
Real Estate Loans	6,700.00	Surplus	92.37
Share Loans	30.00	Guaranty Fund	3.73
Cash on hand Jan. 31, 1913,	3320.52	Profits	267.10
	10,159.20		10,159.20

Series	No. Shares	Dues Paid	Profits last quarter share	Total Profits share	Withdrawal Value share	value share	Loans authorized but Not paid
No. 1	694	$12.00	$0.15	$0.34	$12.34	$12.26	1 for $6,000
							1 for $1,300
No. 2	121	9.00	.11	.19	9.19	9.14	1 for $1,000
No. 3	153	6.00	.07	.09	6.09	6.07	Rate of interest paid: 1st quarter: 5%
No. 4	23	3.00	.03	.03	3.03	3.02	2d quarter: 5½% 3d quarter: 5½% 4th quarter: 5½%

ADVANTAGES OF THE CO-OPERATIVE BANK.

Offers unequalled security. Is most economically managed.
Invests its funds only in first mortgages.
Provides a legitimate plan for savings.
It pays good dividends.
Can afford to loan more money on real estate than a savings banks or individual.
Has helped many to buy homes.
Borrowers share in the bank's earnings receiving interest on their dues the same as non-borrowers.

Save now. Save regularly. Save in the Co-operative Bank.

President, J. Eveleth Griffith.   Vice-President, F. Edwin Walter
Secretary, A. Presby Colburn,   Treasurer, William D. Wheeler

The Railroad Station at Sharon - Past and Present

Boyden Collection (old)
Photo by: J. K. Harris (new)

SHARON AND ITS TRANSPORTATION

By Adolf W. Arnold

CHAPTER 14

Sharon, Massachusetts, is located 18 miles southeast of Boston and comprises an area of about 25 square miles. Sharon is a nice place to live and a nice place to visit. This means that whichever you want to do, you have to get to and from and also through Sharon.

Since its incorporation, Sharon has had two major attractions: Lake Massapoag and Moose Hill. There was plenty of fresh, clean air and crystal-clear water in the spring-fed Lake. Lakes made streams; streams meant power to drive equipment. That was one reason for people to settle and get started. Another good reason was that Sharon is in a scenic, beautiful area, with trees aplenty to give us fresh air.

Nowadays, Sharon is considered a suburban community. It is a bedroom town. There is very little industry of consequence as of the date of this writing (1976). This means that most Sharonites have to travel to and from work to make a living. Many work in the surrounding towns of Stoughton, Foxboro, Walpole, and Canton, but most commute daily either to Boston or Providence. This requires a network of transportation.

Circa 1800, Sharon had less than 24 roads and highways in all. As late as 1890, the old Town map shows that there were less than three dozen streets at that time. Most of them were dirt roads. A later street map shows the names of two hundred and twenty-seven (227 — yes, count them) streets and roads all within Sharon. From less than 15 miles of roadway to a total of about 95 miles, roads in Sharon developed rather suddenly after the 1930's.

Sharon's transportation network consisted of the streets and highways, the street-car system, and the railroads. Let us take a look at these one at a time in order to better understand their importance to us.

STREETS AND HIGHWAYS

The major artery in Sharon is called Main Street. It runs from the northeast corner of the town to connect us with Stoughton and Canton. From Cobb's Corner to Post Office Square, this section of the street is called North Main Street. It then continues in a southwesterly direction until we enter Foxboro. This section is called South Main Street. It is the major thoroughfare.

North Main Street is also known as Route 27 which turns in a westerly direction at Post Office Square and then changes to a northwesterly course to bring us to U.S. Highway Route 1, with Walpole as our neighbor. Route 1 is the longest highway in the United States of America, stretching from Northern Maine all the way down to the keyes in Florida. In less than twenty minutes by car, a traveller can be in Boston on Route 1, or in Providence within about 30 minutes. If we stop for a moment to remember the horse-and-buggy days, we find that this meant a strategic location to go either north or south.

Route 27 winds its way northwards through Walpole and other towns. It connects with Brockton on the easterly side and ends up near Plymouth.

During World War II, numerous industries began operation on the western outskirts of Boston. Electronic firms started up like mushrooms. Nearby MIT and other educational facilities set up laboratories. The new nuclear age brought about rapid changes, and the demand for new industrial products grew steadily. A new highway was created, Route 128. Many Sharonites make their living in one of the many companies that mushroomed along Route 128. Massachusetts was blessed with ever-increasing business, especially during the days of the "Outer Space Programs." Our astronauts flew in spaceships that were produced in large part from components made and developed right along Route 128.

As traffic increased, more highways were needed. U.S. Route 95 was developed to relieve the traffic congestion along U.S. Route 1. Both highways run in the same general direction. Route 95, however, is a limited-access Interstate highway. This means that there are no restaurants, gasoline stations, or other stores readily accessible from 95. Sharon borders Route 95 and has two access roads to it.

But Route 128 began to get too crowded. This was the reason for yet another major highway to be developed, U.S. Route 495. This outer-belt highway connects the southern part at Mansfield with Lowell, Lawrence, and Haverhill to the north, in a gentle sweep at about an equal distance from the semi-circular Route 128. In a few minutes driving time, Sharonites can be on Route 495 and on their way to Worcester, or to head westward on the Massachusetts Turnpike.

Sharon is also not very far from U.S. Route 24 that goes through adjacent Stoughton. Route 24 is a major north-south highway that connects with Brockton, Taunton, and Fall River, and also with U.S. Route 25 that brings you to Cape Cod.

Ever since the days of the stagecoach, it appears that Sharon has been and still is in a strategic and ideal location when it comes to highway traffic. Gone of course are the dirt roads. The well-built and maintained streets and highways in and around Sharon also provide work for numerous people in the Sharon Department of Public Works. The approximate 95 miles of streets and highways within Sharon consume approximately 1,000 tons of salt and 3,000 to 4,000 tons of sand that protect the motorist from the hazards of the icy roads during an average winter. In addition, there are 15 snowplows, 4 sand trucks, and other vehicles owned by the town in addition to the road-building equipment, and maintenance equipment, such as sweepers.

One of the amazing facts is that Sharon really does not have any traffic lights. Yes, there are a few blinking lights suspended over some intersections along Main Street, but that's about all until we come to Cobb's Corner. There the traffic lights serve three towns at the same time: Sharon, Canton, and Stoughton. All major roads through Sharon are well lit at night. In general, Sharon roads and streets are extremely well maintained and clean.

THE STAGECOACH IN SHARON

Long before the steam railroads came into Sharon, there were many stagecoach lines. One such line came from Boston to Washington Street in Canton, to Cobb's Corner, thence via Bay Road to Taunton, Fall River, and Newport. Also, before the Norfolk & Bristol Turnpike was established, a stagecoach line ran via the Old Post Road in Sharon, near Routes 1 and I-95, where the Pancake House is now, then through South Walpole Street and on to Attleboro and Providence areas.

Stagecoaches had the advantages of flexibility. No one bothered to watch a clock, when the coach was filled up, away it went. It was not until the mid-1840's when coaches carried passengers who had to connect with trains that they had to resort to somewhat of a time schedule.

THE RAILROAD IN SHARON

The railroads, as we know them now, came into being on June 22, 1831, when the Boston & Providence Railroad Corporation was officially incorporated in this Commonwealth of Massachusetts. That corporation had the authority to construct a railroad from Boston to a place near India Point on the east bank of the Seekonk River.

On July 11, 1831, another company called the Boston and Providence Railroad and Transportation Company was organized. That company was officially incorporated on May 10, 1834 in Rhode Island. It constructed a bridge across the Seekonk River and established its terminal station at India Point, Providence, to connect with the Boston & Providence Railroad.

On June 4, 1834, the Boston & Providence opened the line from Boston (Park Square Station) to Readville. During 1835, it opened the Dedham Branch from Readville to Dedham Center, a 2.1 mile stretch. In August of 1835, the Boston & Providence Railroad opened its line from Readville through Sharon to East Junction which is just south of Attleboro. That same month, the Railroad opened from East Junction to India Point, Providence (India Point Branch), a 7.5 mile-long line.

On March 16, 1844, the Stoughton Branch Railroad Company incorporated. It constructed a railroad from the Boston & Providence main line at Canton Junction to Stoughton (Central), where it later connected with the Easton Branch Railroad for a distance of about 4 miles. This line was operated by the Boston & Providence Railroad from the time of opening on April 17, 1845.

On May 16, 1855, the Easton Branch Railroad Company had opened a line from Stoughton Central to North Easton, a distance of 3.8 miles. It, too, was operated by the Boston & Providence Railroad until September 23, 1866.

As soon as it was recognized that the railroad system was here to stay, lines around Sharon were expanded. After all, Sharon is on the line of the major rail system between Boston, Providence, and New York. So it was no surprise that the Boston & Providence Rail Company established various lines and sections in this area to meet the growing demand for fast public transportation.

Before the incorporation of the Boston & Providence Railroad on June 22, 1831, several preliminary plans were conducted to establish the best possible route between the two cities, Boston and Providence. As a result, the company decided that the assault upon the Sharon Hill be made from the eastern edge of the Neponset Valley, passing close to Canton. While perhaps shorter, it had some drawbacks: A westerly approach to Sharon Hill would have taken the line through Dedham, with a more gentle ascent of the hill. The Sharon route required several cuts and many embankments. It also meant crossing the east branch of the Neponset River (then called the Canton River) which lay in a wide and relatively deep valley.

It should be noted here that the Canton route was unquestionably more difficult than a route through Dedham. But there were "other considerations." For example, one of the six members of the railroad's Board of Directors was Joseph Warren Revere, son of Paul Revere. In the latter part of his life, Paul Revere had moved to Canton and established a copper works and brass foundry on the site of the Revolutionary-War powder mill. The Revere Copper Works, operated by Joseph W. Revere, lay within one-quarter mile of the new railroad's route through Canton.

Mercifully, the original idea of using inclined planes to get across the Neponset Valley did not last long. After a fatal accident involving several well-known businessmen on the Granite Railway at Quincy, Mass. (which used inclined planes), all thoughts of inclines were discarded and it was decided to build a stone viaduct over the valley instead. The firm of Dodd & Baldwin was contracted to build the structure according to the specifications set forth by the Boston & Providence Railroad engineers.

Much has been written about the viaduct, which now stands as one of the earliest surviving multiple-arch stone railroad bridges in the United States. Furthermore, its design and history make it unique in its own right. It surpasses the notoriety of the B & O's much-acclaimed Thomas viaduct. The superstructure consists of two walls extending the entire length of the viaduct, connected at intervals of 27½ feet by buttresses 5½ feet thick extending transversely across the walls, and projecting 4 feet beyond their faces. The main wall is 4 feet thick and 4½ feet below the grade of the road.

Captain William Gibbs McNeill was hired and charged with the construction of the railroad. The foundation stone of the viaduct was laid April 20, 1834, commencing an eventful two years of building. Construction of the railroad itself was started at both the Boston and Providence ends, working toward Canton. The viaduct proved to be the railroad's largest and most difficult project, and it was the final link in connecting both cities.

Initially, it was thought that a local quarry in Canton could provide all the necessary stone for the structure. As it turned out, however, the quarry (located near Dunbar Street in Canton) contained stone which was not suitable for finish stone, just for foundation and backing. It was necessary to obtain face stone from a quarry in Sharon, on the westerly slope of Rattlesnake Hill. The stone was hauled over the road some three miles by oxen or horses to the railroad near what used to be Sharon Height station, then loaded on a flat car that rolled downhill by gravity another four miles to the viaduct side. An elderly white horse named Charlie hauled the empty car back to Sharon once its load of granite had been removed.

The "Stone Bridge" as the viaduct was also referred to, is 615 feet in length, 22 feet in width, and the rails are about 70 feet above the surface of the river. Originally, there was a single highway pass, a semi-circular arch 22½ feet wide. Six rounded arches of 8 feet 4 inches each allow the river to pass through the viaduct. As the structure neared completion a stone bearing the names of the Railroad Officials was set in the western part of the parapet. The inscription reads:

> This viaduct erected by the B & P R. R.
> T. B. WALES, President
> Directors: J. W. REVERE
> C. H. RUSSELL, J. P. LORING
> C. POTTER, J. G. KING

Tuesday, July 28, 1835 saw the first regular passage over the viaduct. The *Boston Advertiser* of July 30, 1835, reported the event as follows:

> We understand that the magnificent Viaduct at Canton is so far completed that the locomotives with their trains of cars pass from Boston to Providence without interruption. The train which left this city at four o'clock on Tuesday afternoon arrived in Providence in an hour and forty-seven minutes. It returned the same evening with about a hundred passengers in two hours and three minutes.

In 1860 it became necessary to lay a double track on the viaduct. This of course required major alterations. Thanks to the foresight of the designers, it was possible without major alterations to the superstructure. In 1910 the Railroad Company, at this time known as the New York, New Haven and Hartford Railroad, reinforced the arches on both sides of the structure with concrete.

During the last few days prior to completion, a great debate occurred (as you might expect) as to who should have the privilege of being the first to cross the viaduct by rail. The need to call the militia out again was averted when all agreed that the unsung hero of the viaduct's construction would have the privilege. So, with great ceremony and laughter, Charlie, the old white horse that had hauled the flat cars between the viaduct and Sharon, was placed upon the flatcar and hauled across the viaduct, thus becoming the first passenger to cross the structure.

On March 14, 1844, the Old Colony Railroad was chartered to build a railroad from Plymouth to Boston. The Boston & Providence, leased for 99 years, was one of the more than 60 railroads that eventually formed the empire of the Old Colony.

The Old Colony Railroad, in turn, was leased in 1893 to the New York, New Haven and Hartford. In 1896 the New Haven issued a timetable for the Old Colony System. As of October 4, Sharon was on it 23 times for stops to and from Boston and Providence. Mind you, the timetable stated "Trains run Week Days only unless otherwise noted." So, with less population then we had lots more trains to choose from.

In spite of government control of railroads during World War I, that decade, and the one following it, are often referred to as the "Golden Age of

Public Transportation." The only alternative the public could use at that time was the trolley.

Don't feel sorry if this seems or sounds confusing so far. It just goes to prove that this is the way it was from the infancy of a railroad system, however well-intentioned, to the current mess. The New Haven, as we would like to call it, of course had its day in court. Now called the "Penn Central," the future of the road is uncertain. But before we begin to explore the present-day problems, let us once more get into the nostalgia of yesteryear, the time we would like to remember most (provided we are in the middle-aged group).

Here then are some quips and stories at random about the trains that ran through Sharon at one time or another:

When the first steam engine came through the town of Sharon, two sisters reportedly walked down to the old gravel pit and boarded the slow-moving train so they could say they were the first residents riding through the town. The only question is, who were the sisters?

Before 1930, there was no overpass above the Sharon Railroad tracks. For years there had been talk that there should be an overpass but it took a tragedy to bring it about. One rainy day, Burton Peck, a senior in High School, was asked by his mother to drive over and pick up his younger brothers and sisters who were at school. After dropping off the children at home, he went up town where he picked up Henry Stone, a junior in High School. The boys headed down Depot Street and saw Martha Burlingame, a sophomore. Because it was raining, they decided to give her a ride. She lived on a street off Norwood Street. No one is sure if the gateman forgot to stop them or what happened, but the New York Express came through. Peck died within minutes, and the other two were killed instantly.

August 1897. Sharon was a prosperous summer resort with many Sunday visitors. On Sundays, the trains ran every hour and the 7 P.M. train was coming in to take some of the tourists back to Boston. No one had realized the train was coming in two parts, and all were loading the first section when the engineer of the second train went through the light and hit the first train. Nine people were killed and eighty injured.

Fortunately, not all incidents were tragic. For example, certain Sharon residents long remembered the train that left Boston on February 13, 1899, at 5:40 P.M. and reached Sharon the following day at 12:25 P.M., going 18 miles in 18 hours. This is slower than the oldest-fashioned way of travelling, unless tradition can tell how a former representative of this town was three-quarters of a day in taking news from the State House to his constituents.

The train was stalled for the night at Canton Junction. In car number 2,400, love songs were sung for Valentine's Day. The singers remembered the "Maine" and that its anniversary was near. Merry were the quips and cracks, with a touch of what was called "Sharon sarcas." A solo ended, and a Sharon man, who had been talking of something entirely different, exclaimed, "After this I can appreciate anything that is barely decent." "Thank you," tartly cried the singer. She was not of Sharon, and she soon asked, "What did you say is the name of that little town where most of you live?" For refreshments, there was a new style of sandwich, consisting of bologna sausage at midnight and bread to go with it the next forenoon.

Of course the train had been stalled due to one of the worst snowstorms that ever hit this part of New England. Rodney E. Monk remembered it well because his father, Loring Monk, was on that train. He said a man named Hawes lived just above the railroad on the west side. He repaired watches in his shop in Canton. He and his wife stayed up all night. Mrs. Hawes made doughnuts and her husband took them in a half bushelbasket and coffee in milk cans to the train. No charge, just to help people stuck.

"Whist Players" is an undated entry in a Derry scrapbook.

> A favorite pastime with business men on the cars between their homes and the Hub is that old and intellectual game of whist, and they tell occasionally of some close plays. On the 8:01 A.M. last Thursday, Capt. C. T. Derry and Alfred K. Hall, with Messrs. E. B. Wolston of Sharon and Wilson of Mansfield as opponents, captured all thirteen tricks in two consecutive deals. A very unusual combination of cards and skill, an occurrence the Captain said he did not remember happening in the thirty-five years of his experience at whist on the road. Among other notably good players are Messrs. E. H. Adams, G. A. Copeland, A. E. Crafts, and Fred Burnham.

On January 1, 1899, the large, magnificent, and very beautiful new South Station, in Dewey Square, Boston, was opened to the public. The New England Railroad and the Old Colony System had moved from their smaller stations on Kneeland Street and the foot of Summer Street to make use of the new station.

Sharon had its first station on the southbound side of the double track. It was a combination of passenger and freight station. Then, in 1936, a new station was built on the northbound side of the track. This building is still standing.

After a campaign started in May 1975 by Sharon's Transportation Authority, Penn Central/Con Rail, and the Town itself, Sharon residents who called themselves "Paintriots" began repainting this station the last weekend in May 1976 in order to finish by Bicentennial Day, July 4. The MBTA furnished the paint, and ConRail assigned a flagman for their safety. While Senior and Junior "Paintriots" covered the station with paint, TV and newspapers covered them with news stories.

Sharonites can see the new Turbo-train running through their station. To get aboard, one has to go to 128 station or into Boston. This is supposed to be the answer to a major traffic problem of hauling large numbers of people through one of the world's worst traffic corridors from Boston to New York and on to Washington. One passenger summed it up recently by saying, "Too little too late."

Sharon also had another station at Sharon Heights. This station was used very often, and in 1936 it was finally torn down since traffic no longer had any use for it.

On January 12, 1975, a group of Sharonites, Mal Farquhar, Gordon Hawes, Ross Morgan, and Syd Morgan went to the woods off Maskwonicut Street. On the west side of the railroad tracks (about 200 feet) and about ¼ mile south of Maskwonicut Street bridge, Gordon Hawes had discovered a marble plaque in the woods. Besides the plaque are numerous bridge stones that extend for about 200 feet. It looks as if they had been tipped off flat cars on a siding. Also found were shovel blades with burned handles in that same area. The granite stones are all cut and formed ready to form a bridge. The question as to where they came from and why they were stored in Sharon remains unanswered so far. Why was that bridge in Dedham never built, and where was it supposed to be?

On the plaque, a beautiful slab of marble, are the names of the officers of the Boston and Providence Railroad Company and others connected with the proposed construction. Below is

THE FOUNDATION FOR THIS BRIDGE WAS LAID
A. D. 1886
THE 250 ANNIVERSARY OF
THE INCORPORATION OF THE TOWN OF DEDHAM

About the only railroad system in Sharon that does not seem to be frustrated or in any type of jeopardy is the A & D Railway Museum. It is owned and operated by the author of this article, open to the public at no charge, but by appointment only. The museum has over 3,000 toy trains on exhibit from many nations, ranging in age from 1860 to 1976. These trains are made of cast iron, wood, cardboard, plastic, tin, steel, and even glass. Many other railroadiana items are also on display. Many people come from great distances by car to see the trains from yesteryear. Trains always seem to make fascinating conversation. They definitely make for countless friendships.

SHARON STREET RAILWAY TROLLEYS

Carl L. Smith of Norwood, Massachusetts is one of the most authoritative sources of information on the subject of Railways and Trolley. He compiled, among other items, the following:

The Norwood, Canton & Sharon Street Railway was incorporated on March 15, 1900, to build from Norwood to Canton and from Cobb's Corner (East Sharon) to Sharon, Sharon Heights, and Lake Massapoag. Four months later, the Blue Hills Street Railway was given permission to build from Canton to Norwood. The matter rested until 1901 when the two companies settled on a compromise, providing for a connection at the Neponset River Bridge, and the operation of through-service between the two communities.

Operation of the 4.7 mile Canton-Norwood line commenced on or about May 17, 1901 with Blue Hills conductors and motormen operating the line. As the line on the east side was owned by the Blue Hills, and the section into Norwood owned by the Norwood, Canton & Sharon, they each received half pay from each company. The crew was supposed to change their hat badges when operating on each of the two roads. A few months later, in September 1901, the Norwood, Canton & Sharon opened a 3-mile route from Cobb's Corner to Lake Massapoag, the line stopping at the near corner of Garden Street. There was a two-track carbarn on North Main Street near the pond beyond Sharon Box Company. Power was purchased from the Blue Hill Street Railway power house at Springdale near the pond on Bolivar Street. Norwood, Canton & Sharon was an independent small trolley line and Dr. William O. Faxon, a well-known doctor of Stoughton, was one of the directors. The road owned about 5 or 6 cars and could borrow cars from Blue Hill Street Railway whenever they needed extra equipment. They owned two 4-wheel RR roof closed cars and one 4-wheel 10-bench and one 8-wheel (No. 9) car. They also had one snowplow and one 4-wheel flat car.

During the heyday of the trolley years before World War I, trolley parties would come all the way from the city in Boston El surface cars over the Blue Hill line from Mattapan, through Cobb's Corner and end up near Lake Massapoag to enjoy a Saturday, Sunday, or holiday outing in the countryside away from the heat of the city. People hired electric trolleys then like chartered buses today.

Disaster struck the Blue Hill Street Railway shortly before seven o'clock in the evening Sunday, February 21, 1909, when the Canton Junction carhouse was destroyed by fire. Every car in the barn, numbering 16 open and 5 closed cars, was lost. The only equipment not burned were 6 double-truck closed cars of the 34-46 series out on the line at the time of the blaze, and some work cars which were stored out of doors. Two open cars, one 10-bench and one 12-bench, of the Norwood, Canton & Sharon were also burned. To replace destroyed cars, Blue Hill placed an order with the Wason Manufacturing Company of Springfield, Massachusetts. All were equipped with GE80 motors, K-11 controllers, and hand brakes. The passenger cars and the work car had standard trucks at first, but were later replaced by Taylor trucks.

Foreign cars were frequently seen on the Blue Hill line, particularly between Mattapan and Blue Hill station, conveying special parties to or from the Blue Hill Reservation. Boston Elevated and Bay State specials occasionally ran through to Sharon on the Norwood, Canton & Sharon line.

After the carhouse was destroyed in 1909, it was decided to build a new carhouse at Cobb's Corner where Canton, Sharon, and Stoughton meet. While the new building was under construction, Blue Hill cars were serviced at the Norwood, Canton & Sharon's small barn in Sharon.

LAST DAYS OF THE NORWOOD, CANTON & SHARON

Since the operations of the Norwood, Canton & Sharon were so intimately connected with those of the Blue Hill, some mention must be made of the former's last years.

The NC&S properties were sold to a Fall River junk dealer, one William J. O'Connor, in 1917 and he announced plans to scrap both the Norwood and Cobb's Corner-Sharon Heights lines. However, O'Connor ran into trouble when residents of Sharon demanded that he post a $50,000 bond to furnish a state highway between Canton and Sharon, to take the place of the street railway they were about to lose.

This was too much for the Fall River man and he forfeited his deposit on the purchase price, the NC&S reverting to its previous owners.

Then, in March, 1918, as previously stated, the Public Service Commission condemned the NC&S trackage between Norwood Center and the Norwood-Canton town line. This forced the suspension of service between Norwood and Canton; and operation of the Cobb's Corner-Sharon Heights route was discontinued at the same time.

Later in that same month the NC&S was again sold — this time to the Dominion Wrecking Company of Canada. This firm immediately tore up the Norwood to Canton rails, but when the wreckers moved into Sharon they ran into trouble. The local constabulary forced a halt to dismantling operations so as to give the town an opportunity to buy the line.

As it turned out, the town of Sharon didn't purchase the property, but one of its selectmen, Frederick A. Prince, did. He paid $10,000 for the 3.04 miles of track from East Sharon to Sharon Heights and Lake Massapoag and also obtained one passenger car and a snowplow in the deal.

Prince reorganized the NC&S under the name of the Sharon Street Railway and sold shares of stock to townspeople. The town itself voted a tax of $1 on each $1000 of valuation to raise money for the costs of rehabilitating the line. Many residents gave freely of their spare time to work on the railroad, and on August 1, 1919, the grand re-opening of the line took place.

The town was in gala array for the momentous occasion and the entire length of the line, from Cobb's Corner to Sharon Heights, was illuminated with red lights. The first car was in charge of William Anderson, motorman, and Charles Harding, conductor, both veteran employees of the Blue Hill Street Railway.

On the following day, regular service on an hourly schedule commenced between Cobb's Corner and Sharon Heights. Prince intended to extend service from Sharon Heights to Lake Massapoag and it was also his plan to run through cars from Sharon to Canton Junction — but these plans were never carried out.

Power was purchased from the Blue Hill Street Railway and George Spaulding, receiver of the Blue Hill, served as superintendent of the Sharon Street Railway. The line had two six cent fare zones, one from Cobb's Corner to Sharon Square and the second from Sharon Square to Sharon Heights.

During the five months from August 1 to December 31 the Sharon Street Railway wound up with a deficit of $1077.01. This was offset by non-operating income of $3.89 and the town of Sharon came through with $1373.12 as a contribution. The $300 surplus thus produced was used to pay liability insurance premiums in advance.

The same storm which tied up the Blue Hill also closed down the Sharon Street Railway. Service was never resumed and the tracks were torn up after formal abandonment of the line took place in September, 1920. Without power from Blue Hill it was impossible to operate.

Prince salvaged much of his investment from the sale of the rails and overhead as scrap. (Reprinted from *A History of the Blue Hill Street Railway* by O. R. Cummings and published by the Electric Railway Historical Society of Chicago, Ill., 1957. Bulletin No. 25.)

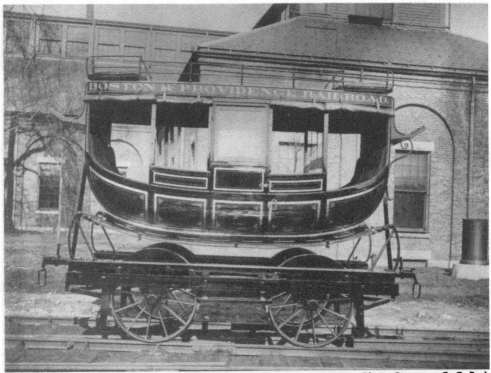

An Early Coach Used on the Boston and Providence Railroad   *Photo Courtesy: G. C. Peck*

Cornerstone of a Railroad Bridge Which Was Never Built   *Photo by: J. K. Harris*

A Passenger Train on the Grade at Sharon   *Courtesy of: A and D Railroad Museum*

These Worthies Pose at the Sharon Heights Station   *Courtesy of: C. L. Jerauld*

Sharon's Third Station Formerly Located at Knollwood Cemetery

A 1939 Passenger Train Stops at Sharon in a Snowstorm   *Courtesy of: A and D. Railway Museum*

155

Sharon Heights Station

Cliff Jerauld's First Delivery Truck

Courtesy of: C. L. Jerauld

RAILROADS, TROLLEYS AND OTHER TRANSPORTATION

By Clifford L. Jerauld

CHAPTER 15

It was midnight sometime in the 1600's when a man arrived home in what is now Sharon. He had left for Boston or Squantum the previous midnight and followed Indian trails and paths to his destination and return. Although some rode horses, he had walked. It was obvious that going to Boston and returning was a major project. As time progressed, the paths were widened so wagons, carriages, and stagecoaches could be used. While most of the growth of the country had been along the seashore or on waterways that had access to the ocean, Sharon was lucky and had two roads, Bay Road and Old Post Road.

The population of Sharon in 1800 was 1018 and in 1850 had only grown by 110 people to 1128. About 1830 a railroad was opened and the growth increased until by 1900 it had about doubled. This allowed Sharon to enter the commercial field, and also provided a means of shipping farm produce to Boston.

There were two stations here, one at Sharon and the other at the Heights. The freight yard and house were at Sharon Heights. Most passenger trains had express cars that carried a mixed load of smaller shipments that were dropped at the stations and were delivered to their destination by a local carrier. The mail and newspapers were shipped the same way. Most of the farm produce was shipped from Sharon and Sharon Heights by express to the Boston market. Originally, Sharon had Adams Express which was consolidated into American Express and in the end became Railway Express Agency and was owned by the railroads. This company went out of business recently although during its later years it used trailer and air freight to move the express better between cities, and trucks for local delivery.

By far the larger part of shipments into Sharon Heights came in at night by what was known as the way freight. This freight train was made up of way cars which were cars of mixed freight from Boston, plus carloads of other commodities. Coal was the principal item in carloads followed by lumber, grain, cement, and water pipe. There were other cars from time to time with special loads of other commodities needed in the town.

The way car was interesting because its load was a real mix of commodities used in the town everyday. Each town along the railroad would have from one to three of these cars delivered each night. The cars were loaded in Boston with merchandise ordered by merchants and people in the town. The merchandise was picked up by wagons all over the city and delivered to the railroad and distributed to the car designated for that town. The largest users of this service in Sharon were the stores which were operated by Pettee and Colburn, Stuart and Kincaid, and Long Brothers. Their wagons would arrive about six in the morning to remove their merchandise. The other pieces of freight would be picked up during the day by their owners. Any freight left over would be hand trucked into the freight house and picked up at a later date. This allowed the car to be removed that night and replaced by another loaded car. Harry Briggs was the agent and handled the express shipments, passenger tickets, and the freight. He was later transferred to Rhode Island and was replaced by Robert Stratton who stayed until the Heights station was closed and he in turn transferred to Clinton, Connecticut.

There were two way freights, one from Providence and one from Boston. The one from Providence picked up the cars of ice from the Boston Icehouse and the cars of sand and gravel from Nawn's Pit and took them to Boston. Working the way freight was a dangerous job and most of the conductors were killed in the line of duty. Some names that come to mind were Pop Nason, Jimmy Reeves, a man that I only know as Memo, and Bert Capen from Sharon. There may have been others. The one to escape was George McMillan who transferred to the passenger service. Most of these men performed their duties at night and were killed in South Boston railroad yards.

The railroads were set up in what was known as a block system; a series of blocks was a division. Each block had a signal tower; each division had a dispatcher. The tower man notified the dispatcher by telegraph when a train passed the tower. The tower also had a series of semaphores activated by levers with wires that extended from the tower to the semaphore; it also had control of all main line switches and was known as an interlocking system. Sam Davidson was the maintenance man for the system and lived in Mansfield. He was Betty Odiorne's father.

Young men in the Heights gathered at the signal tower and had a game of trying to steal the conductor's lantern. Sometimes they would win; most of the time they would lose. One night they hid in the attic of the tower, left the trap door partly open, and lowered a hook to get the lantern which was on the floor. About this time the conductor reached and closed the trap door and put a flagstaff through the latch and left them there. He let the men out later and they were covered with dust and perspiration. That was one they lost.

There was a crew of several men known as a section crew that maintained the right of way. The crew was made up of a section boss and a track "walker" although he rode a hand-operated velocipede. All lights on the railroad were powered by kerosene which was known as coal oil. A multitude of lamps was used by the RR, namely the stations, platforms, signal towers, and all the semaphores including the small so-called pot signals which were small semaphores located at the switches. An engineer could read ahead by the color showing on the semaphore concerning the conditions he was approaching: red light, stop; green light, clear.

About 3:00 P.M. the track walker would take his velocipede and a can of oil and service all the signals, cleaning, lighting, and refilling the reservoirs with oil. As he pumped his way along with his velocipede, he would watch for defects in the roadbed to be repaired. The electricity used to operate controls and the telegraph was supplied by dry cells; wet cells and storage batteries were used to activate remote switches; otherwise the switches were activated through rods and levers directly from the signal tower. Even the headlight on the engine was oil powered. The section crew transported themselves with a handcar that was activated by handles geared to the wheels.

The switches off side tracks were activated by the brakeman on the train involved, but he had no control over switches from the main line. Sharon Pit tower had no switch, only signals. Sharon Heights had fourteen switches plus several miles of side track. Charles Luff was the tower man on the 3 to 11 P.M. shift off Sharon Pit. Charlie was excitable and one night a train stayed at Sharon station for a long time. The dispatcher telegraphed to ask Charlie what he could see. Charlie answered that they were all out running around the lantern with engines in their hands! Powerful men, these railroaders! At Sharon Heights Bo Sheehan worked the 7 to 3 shift, Al Jerauld worked the 3 to 11 shift, and Henry Hickey worked the 11 to 7 shift.

Before I leave railroads, let me get this story to you: Most everybody knows who Whistler's mother was but few know that his father was an engineer on the Boston-Lowell RR.

The gravel used to fill in the South Boston rail yards was hauled from Sharon Pit which was in an area south of Maskwonicut Street. The gravel used to fill the Army Base during World War I came from an area south of South Main Street. Most of the sand and gravel used in construction on the south side of Boston came from Nawn's Pit in what is now Farnum Road. There is a great deal of Sharon in Boston!

There was another railroad station in Sharon at Knollwood Cemetery where the railroad would transport complete funerals from Boston.

Several times each summer trains loaded with people came for picnics at Burkhardt's Grove in Sharon Heights on the lake.

Although we always think of Ellis Island, New York, as the port of entry for immigrants, Boston was also used for the same purpose. The trains that transported these people passed through Sharon to areas where they would settle.

The boat train passed through Sharon at 6:00 P.M. so connections could be made with the Fall River line.

For the Century of Progress Exposition in Chicago in 1933-1934 the British shipped their crack train "The Flying Scot" to Boston for a tour of the United States which started from there. It was discovered then that the U.S. coal could not make steam fast enough. The train was just able to crawl up the grade to Sharon. British coal, which had more BTU's was obtained, and the tour was a success after it arrived. "The Flying Scot" was a beautiful train, but it was not seen in Sharon as it passed through at night.

Many of the prisoners of World War II were landed in Boston and shipped out through Sharon in army trains to prison camps around the United States.

Airplanes in the early days followed the New Haven tracks to New York and would fly over Sharon. The Hindenburg dirigible used this route to reach Lakehurst. It is possible that Sharon was the last to see the Hindenburg on the day it crashed, for from Sharon to New Jersey it was hidden by fog and clouds. One moonlight night Harry Hickey, who worked the third trick (11:00 P.M. to 7:00 A.M.) at the Heights signal tower, noticed what seemed to be the headlight of an engine approaching although there was no record of a train in the vicinity. Then he realized the light was passing over the South Main Street bridge rather than under it. It turned out to be the Hindenburg feeling its way along the railroad to its destination, probably our first UFO!

Herb King was in New Haven, Connecticut, to fly the first pictures of the Harvard and Yale football game to the *Boston Record* by chartered plane. The pilot was in the plane when Herb got to the field with the plane engine running and they took off at once. Two hours later, they saw a roof sign of Lowell and being low on gas they landed. The pilot had followed the branch line from Mansfield instead of the main line! Herb took a taxi back to Boston and arrived long after the rest of the people had returned from New Haven, but Harvard had lost so the pictures were not needed.

About 1900 a streetcar line was built from Cobb's Corner to the corner of Garden Street and East Foxboro Street by the Norfolk and Bristol Street Railway which purchased Burkhardt's Grove on the lake. The line connected at Cobb's Corner with cars for Stoughton which connected with lines covering most towns on the South Shore. Another line ran from Cobb's Corner to Boston with a branch line to Norwood which in turn connected with lines to most inland towns.

The track was on the right-hand side of Main Street until it reached Glendale Road, at which point it followed the center of the road through the Square and returned to the side of the road at a point where Dr. Schneiderman lives now. It then continued on to Peck's Corner where it turned down East Foxboro Street to the corner of Garden Street which was the end of the line. The rails and ties were embedded in the ground so that only the top of the rail was visible. The power came from a single overhead wire and was transmitted by a trolley to the electric motor which drove the car.

The cars were quite small, seating about 25 or 30 people. In those days there was a newspaper cartoon known as the Toonerville Trolley and our cars were exact duplicates of it. The car had one set of trucks which had four wheels very close together, and the electric motor was built into the trucks. The body of the car was mounted on the trucks, with doors and controls at each end of the car. Instead of turning the car around at the end of the line, the trolley pole was mounted on a pivot in the center of the roof and had a line attached near the trolley wheel and it would be swung around to the opposite end of the car. The motorman would take his handles to the other end and proceed in the other direction for the return run.

The first man in the morning left Cobb's Corner at 6:15 and left Sharon Heights at 6:45. This schedule was maintained every hour until the last car arrived at Cobb's Corner at 11:15 at night. Barney McGuire was the day conductor and Pat Donahue was the motorman. Tim O'Donnell was the night motorman and Ralph Crocker was the conductor. Barney and Ralph came from Sharon; Tim and Pat, from Canton. The conductor collected the fares and the motorman operated the controls.

The car barn was located across the street from the pond on North Main Street and contained spare cars and a maintenance car equipped with a snowplow. Long before Sharon plowed the streets, this plow cleared the tracks after a storm. During the day the power in the barn was shut off, and when the operating car came back from the last trip at night the conductor would reach in through a small door and put on the switch to supply power to put the car away. One night the switch was put on and the conductor turned to open the large doors to let the car in. One of the cars inside burst through the doors and took off with no lights for Sharon Heights. The conductor tried to pull off the switch before it reached the main line but all in vain. It reached the main power and kept going. The crew started after it with the other car but both had equal speed. The runaway never was caught. It ran off the end of the line and smashed into a large oak tree on the corner of Garden Street. Subsequently the tree died from the blow.

Joe Poirier was just arriving back from a round trip to Boston with his horses and wagon when he heard the first car coming and pulled over to the side of the road. It had room to pass but he didn't see it go by because it did not have any lights. Then he heard the second car coming and saw it pass. He continued on home much confused with the sudden traffic in street cars in Sharon.

During the summer months, open cars were used. They had no sides except a bar which the conductor raised and lowered to allow access to the seats. The conductor walked along a catwalk outside the car, gripping the handholds while collecting fares, ringing them up, ringing bells to stop and start while the car dashed along at 15 miles per hour and his coattails blew in the wind.

One summer day Helen Bowman dropped her teddy bear out of an open car and began to howl. Whereupon conductor McGuire rang for the car to stop, retrieved the toy, and returned it to its grateful owner.

Several times during the summer, 8 to 12 large open cars arrived from Boston for picnics at Burkhardt's Grove. They took up most of the tracks on East Foxboro Street. When it came time to return, the cars had to leave ten minutes apart; otherwise the power drain would be so great none of them could move.

Eventually traffic became so light it did not pay to continue running street cars although the Town subsidized the last year of operation. The wires and rails were removed and so ended another era. A couple of years later the car barn burned and no vestige was left of the trolley line except a few old ties left in the ground which created bumps. The ties were removed later.

Charlie Brymer operated the carriages that met the trains and did other local carrying of people. There was a great deal of this type of carriage work in those days because of the hotels on the lake and around the town. One hotel operated a steam launch that met the people at the north end of the lake and carried them to Boyce's hotel. The launch burned and later the hotel burned and was rebuilt as Sunset Lodge which is now the Community Center.

Alec Robb operated another type of stable known as a livery stable and was the original U-drive-it as he rented horses and carriages for people to drive themselves. Salesmen used this means to go to the surrounding towns to get orders. Some of these salesmen would stay in Sharon for several days at a time because Sharon seemed ideally located to get to adjoining towns. This probably accounted for the fact that we had several small hotels.

The heavy hauling was done by Archie and Howard Peck. Archie's work was mostly furniture moving and Howard's was miscellaneous heavy hauling.

After World War I trucks came into the picture, carrying goods to and from Boston and taking the place of wagons. Sharon had Bremner's Express and Hixson's Express which in turn took over Byam's Express from Canton. This operation was taken over by Ginger Morse. These trucks plus the closing of Nawn's Pit and the Boston Icehouse finally eliminated the way freight. The earlier express companies had what was known as a pony express license which gave them the right to transport alcoholic beverages into a dry town on order.

In time those having pony express licenses began to keep a stock of liquor on hand although it was illegal. They were never prosecuted so it was possible to purchase liquor directly from them.

Although there were wagons coming out of Boston with specialized merchandise during the days of the horse and wagon, they were not common. As trucks became common, more and more shippers began sending in their own trucks and the local express companies were doomed unless they specialized in one commodity and expanded their territory. Ginger Morse specialized in wool, but Bremner's Express went out of business. Sharon Parcel Delivery was always in a specialized business from department stores and kept on, but was finally crowded out by a larger carrier. Archie Peck's business was a specialized furniture moving business and is still being carried on by his grandson, Eddie Peck. Howard Peck's operation has gone out of business.

While Sharon was using horses, there were half a dozen blacksmith shops around town. As trucks and automobiles came into being, the blacksmith shops closed although some became garages. The principal one was Millard's on Cottage Street. Mr. Millard, while driving a Stanley Steamer, was, I believe, the first person killed in an automobile accident in Sharon. Arthur Nelson took the garage over and subsequently moved it to Pond Street and became the Ford dealer known as Sharon Motor Sales. After changing hands several times, it is now the Citco Station operated by Gardner. To my knowledge, the last blacksmith shop in Sharon was operated by Bert Forsyth on Ames Street. A garage was built on the corner of Station Street and South Main which was taken over by Jim Taylor. It distributed Studebaker cars and Stewart trucks. Later it became the Chevrolet distributor as it is today. It is still in the family. The Poirier Brothers built a garage on Pond Street opposite East Chestnut Street and distributed Durant cars. This garage passed through several hands and was converted into an office building as it is today.

The Foxboro Mansfield Bus Company operated buses from Foxboro to Canton Junction, but after several years business was so poor the company closed down.

The Sharon Heights section that for years was the center of freight and some passenger traffic is now a ghost town. The miles of side tracks and the 14 switches along with the station, freight house, platform, signal tower, and coal sheds with their scales have been removed, and the area is overgrown with weeds and brush. The signal tower at Sharon Pit is gone and all that is left is the main line. Remote control has taken over the signal system. The gates that guarded the Garden Street crossing have been replaced by an underpass.

Last night a man arrived back from commuting from Boston and sat down to a warmed-over supper with the remark that the traffic on the southeast expressway made commuting almost impossible. Two hundred years later, and the same problem still exists.

A Trolley Car Terminal at Garden Street

Car Barn and Tracks on North Main Street

Boyden Collection

Dr. Walter Alden Griffin, Physician, Humanitarian, Benefactor

THE SANATORIUM ERA

By Norma G. Ackerson

CHAPTER 16

Like a proud and gracious lady worthy of her good background and fine upbringing, Sharon long extended her leafy arms to greet the stranger. Passers by on the Boston-Providence trains could not help but feel impressed, many aware of a flickering sense of longing, as they read the hospitable words on a dignified sign at the railroad station proclaiming this a beautiful town, a good place to live.

Nature had been so generous in her endowments, the loveliness of the community was so great, householders felt an added inducement to keep their property attractive and it was rare indeed that the passing motorist, cyclist or stroller could behold a view that was lacking in eye appeal.

It was a good and beautiful place to live and Sharon people, be they old residents or newcomers, wanted to keep it that way. But there was another, less tangible asset that played a role in the growth of this Massachusetts town. In fact, its impact on the development of the community could not be underestimated.

Sharon, it was firmly believed, was a healthy place to live. In the *Boston Traveler* of Nov. 11, 1871, under the heading Healthfulness and Ozone with a subhead Hay Fever and Rose Cold Cured there appeared the words, "In a work on local causes of Consumption, by Dr. Bowditch, in 1862, he speaks of Sharon as likely to be free from lung diseases. The correctness of his judgment is now shown by the Town Records from which it appears one-fourth of all who have died in the town for the last five years were over 80 years of age, and more have died of old age than of consumption. In the four months of this year, ending April 30, one-half of the deaths were from old age, and were of persons over 87. It should be added, Sharon is a growing town with twenty per cent of its inhabitants between five and fifteen, and many of its inhabitants engaged in sedentary occupations."

In literature extolling the virtues of the town put out by a real estate developer of the 1880's there appeared the prideful claim that "The wonderful effects of Sharon air on those suffering from almost any form of disease has long been known, but it is not until quite lately that it has been learned that this is due to the large quantity of ozone which is constantly in the air here. Why there is much more ozone here than in other places is still a mystery."

165

The promoter quoted at length from an article in the *New York Medical Tribune*, explaining that ozone is a condensed form of oxygen, possessing greater activity with a peculiar, penetrating odor, somewhat resembling that of chlorine. It was described as "the most energetic oxidizing agent known," and afforded the land owner an opportunity to use hundreds of words to issue the call to health.

Indeed the developer claimed that "the curative qualities of Sharon air are so well known that medical men are sending their patients here from New York, Newport and New Haven, as well as from places nearer home."

With a flash of foresight the developer told of the magnificent air on Sharon's Moose Hill. "Persons with weak lungs enjoy it much," he wrote. "Invalids, by carrying a lunch and spending some hours on the hill, are often benefited. I regret there is no boarding place there. Perhaps some time there will be a sanitarium or hotel on the hill."

February 9, 1891, saw the formal opening of the Sharon Sanitarium for Pulmonary Diseases on Moose Hill. The first patient was admitted February 16.

The first annual report published in March, 1892, listed Alfred Bowditch as president of the board and Dr. Vincent Y. Bowditch and Dr. Robert W. Lovett as medical directors.

Its object was clearly specified: "To supply a suitable institution for the treatment of incipient pulmonary diseases only, arising in those who are unable for pecuniary and other reasons to seek distant health resorts. Only patients who are in reduced circumstances are received, and no advanced cases admitted. Price of board $5 per week, exclusive of washing. Medical attendance and medicines are given free of charge. Visiting days Tuesdays, Thursdays and Saturdays, from 2 to 5 P.M. Applications must be made to the matron, Mrs. M. E. Small, Sharon, Mass."

In the first year the sanitarium reached its capacity of *nine* patients. Many applications were refused for lack of room, according to the report.

"The success of the experiment of placing this sort of institution in a healthy country town near Boston has been fully shown . . . for the relief of a class most difficult to reach . . . women of very limited means and obliged to depend upon their own exertions for support."

From the beginning each patient had a separate bedroom affording every opportunity for privacy.

In 1896 the fifth annual report pointed out that America was far behind Europe in sanitaria for treatment of consumptives. "The Sharon Sanitarium is the only one for this special purpose in New England," the directors revealed.

A substantial gift in 1897 marked a turning point for the unusual hospital on Moose Hill. Thus far an assistant physician had made daily visits from Boston. The sanitarium now had "sufficient funds to pay an able resident an adequate salary."

The sanitarium had instituted a form of treatment that was rare in the United States and unheard of in its area: patients slept year round on porches out of doors. In the daytime they were bundled in furry robes and spent long hours reclining on the porches. Constantly they filled their weak and sickly lungs with fresh air and as the months went by they became better and better.

Interest in this form of therapy spread through the town. Many houses built in these years had sleeping porches and entire families used them even on the most bitterly cold night of winter. A Sharon resident in 1975 told of the many nights in which she saw a neighbor, swathed in about five layers of nightclothes, scurry from the warmth of her house to the bed on her porch for a healthy sleep.

Residents of the town did not forget their visitors on Moose Hill. An article in the *Boston Transcript* in 1900 about the work of the sanitarium mentioned that "Residents of Sharon as well as people from Boston are in the habit of furnishing weekly entertainments through the winter months. By no means is the sanitarium a dull or gloomy place with a sickly atmosphere. On the contrary, there is good cheer continually."

Directors in that year reported, "The projected enlargement of the sanitarium is now well under way and will give room for ten more patients." A $20,000 bequest had been received and a Ladies Auxiliary was constantly working to raise money.

In July, 1901 the sanitarium obtained the services of a resident director, Dr. Walter A. Griffin, who became a legend in his own lifetime and was still practicing medicine in Sharon at the age of 102 years when this book was written. More about Dr. Griffin will appear later in this chapter, but from the outset his imaginative, thorough treatment of patients under his care earned the respect and praise of the medical profession and the public.

The thirteenth annual report published in 1904 noted that the name had been changed from "sanitarium" to "the more modern and now almost universal Sanatorium," which meant, "to heal." Applications continued to far exceed the capacity of the institution. Dr. Vincent Y. Bowditch was medical director and Dr. Griffin was resident physician.

At the St. Louis Exposition in 1904 the sanatorium exhibit in the department of hygiene received a gold medal from the committee on awards.

Careful records were kept by the new resident physician and the 1905 report contained information about the weather. It was pointed out that the altitude was only 250 feet, not high in general terms but with the exception of the Great Blue Hill in Canton the highest spot between Boston and Providence. In records kept for three years the sun shone all day an average 168 days each year, there were 85 days with no sunshine and 112 days with sun one-fourth the time or longer. In a one-and-a-half-year test the average mean temperature at 8 A.M. was 46.5 degrees. The highest, in July 1903, was 94, and only three days registered more than 90 degrees. The lowest was 14 below zero. Relative humidity was high and reached above 90 per cent about six times each month, rarely going below 35 per cent. The average was 73 per cent. The physician's report pointed out that there was rarely less than two inches of rainfall a month. "The sanatorium is so well protected by woods that there is seldom any hardship to patients from winter winds," the report concluded.

In 1906 the directors happily proclaimed, "Recently the Edison Electric Company have extended their wires to the sanatorium and we have the advantage now of this method of lighting in the newer portions of buildings." The superintendent's report referred to the potato crop: "As yet I have not had to buy any potatoes and what I have on hand are excellent." In that year from its own gardens the sanatorium canned 600 quarts of butter and string beans and 475 quarts of tomatoes, and sold $21 worth of vegetables.

By 1907 applications were being received at such a rate that the institution could have been filled to five times its capacity. "The Sanatorium has never been in debt but the great increase in the cost of living has made the outlay necessary much greater than in former years in spite of earnest endeavors to economize." Later in the report appeared the statement, "After sixteen years of work it has been referred to by many medical men from different parts of the Union as a model of its kind . . . [which] should be sufficient to bring increased funds for its support and for enlarging its capacity."

Reference was made to patients being wheeled out of doors to sleep in the open air. "It is astonishing to see how the patients enjoy sleeping in the open air, even in the coldest weather," the report observed.

"The picture, 'A Sun Bath in Winter,' published in our annual reports has been copied far and wide throughout the United States, several state boards of health having requested that a copy should be placed in their own reports to induce the various legislatures to establish similar institutions for tubercular patients in other states."

At this time the resident physician sought funds to establish a scientific laboratory "which would greatly enhance the value of the work done at the Sanatorium in the crusade against tuberculosis." The healing center on Moose Hill practiced every possible economy. A new ice house made it possible to store about 120 tons of ice for summer use. All the fresh vegetables that could be used during the summer were provided by a thriving garden, and enough for the entire winter were canned with a little left over to be sold. Pictures of a sleeping balcony began appearing in the annual reports, as well as of an open air pavilion with hammocks.

In 1907 emphasis was placed on the need for a suitable X-ray apparatus and the following year fear was expressed that the $5 per week still charged as board to patients would have to be raised.

Some of the trials and successes of the early years were summarized in the 19th annual report in December, 1909. "One can hardly realize now how radical the suggestions seemed then to a great many people, who now take it as a matter of course that tuberculosis can be successfully treated in and around Boston. The Sharon Sanatorium was for several years unique. We demonstrated that tubercular patients need not necessarily be sent to distant parts of the country to be cured. The success of the Sharon Sanatorium was largely instrumental in the founding of the State Sanatorium at Rutland." But the Sharon Sanatorium was always full. Patients "often women of refinement in poor circumstances, obliged to earn their own living get accustomed to some of the niceties of life. For example, the mere fact of each patient having a bedroom to herself at the Sharon Sanatorium insures a certain sense of privacy."

Again emphasis was placed on inflation: food costs were soaring; it might be necessary to increase the price of board to $7 or $10 a week. The board of directors reported that "as the Sanatorium was the first of its kind in the community and a model, it has been visited by many scientists and other interested in the subject of relief and control of tuberculosis."

The next year the first institution of its kind in New England increased its board to $10 per week, but in many cases this amount was paid by philanthropic people.

In its first 20 years the Sanatorium proved a number of points and noted its progress.

1) Tubercular disease, if taken early in its course, can be arrested by comparatively simple means near at home in a much greater number of cases than

was ever thought possible before its foundation.

2) It has been shown that even in the cases which are too far advanced for permanent arrest of disease the patients have often become wage-earners again for a longer or shorter space of time and have, moreover, acted as missionaries among their families and friends.

3) Scientific investigation has been done in the use of whatever methods have been thought to give promise of aid in combating the disease.

4) Instruction has been given to medical students to enable them to treat their future tubercular patients with intelligence.

In 1911 there was a report on "an interesting experiment" during the year: manual labor in the open air, graduated according to the patient's condition, now being more and more resorted to.

Harvard Medical School students visited the Sharon institution in small classes and were taught by the staff the principles of sanatorium treatment. In a self-spoken comment of the health of former patients, it was mentioned that "forty braved stormy weather to attend the annual reunion day in October."

In 1912, Dr. Griffin's title was changed from resident physician to medical superintendent. He reported, "In our treatment we still rely chiefly upon the trinity of fresh air, good food and rest, combined with regulated exercise. Graduated manual labor is used as a therapeutic measure with marked success. During the past year we have resorted to the operation of producing 'Artificial Pneumothorax' which is now claiming the attention of the profession."

The following year the report listed among things "greatly desired at this time: a good strong horse for farm work; a new piano to replace the present one; a small automobile which would save much of a man's time in marketing and when going on various errands." It was pointed out that "the X-ray has been found of very considerable value in both diagnosis and treatment of lung conditions," and a request was made for a gift of X-ray apparatus and funds for operating it. A memorial donation of X-ray equipment was made the following year.

Gradually, more dreams were coming true. The 1916 annual report showed a drawing of the Children's Pavilion being erected through contributions.

In 1918 the report told of "a most gratifying professional tribute. Harvard Medical School having decided to add to the staff if its graduate school has asked our able and efficient Dr. Griffin to become a member of the staff in order to teach physicians the methods of treating tuberculosis in medium-sized, well-related sanatoria. This invitation came without solicitation."

Sharon Recollections, published by the Sharon Historical Society in 1904, had an article, "Sharon, Massachusetts, The Healthiest Town in New England" by W. B. Wickes, General Business Agent. Sharon was described as "a pleasant, healthy town, as rural as the back woods of Maine and yet but 35 minutes ride from Boston," adding that it "has good markets, good roads, good soil and low taxes."

Earlier, in 1901, a booklet has been put out by Colonial Park development. It pointed out that Moose Hill is 530 feet above sea level and Great Blue Hill in Canton 635 feet. It added, "Local doctors have claimed contagious diseases do not become epidemic here, and that all diseases under medical treatment respond more readily than in other localities. Hundreds of people visit here through the summer season. Hotels and boarding houses are taxed to their limit.

"This is the highest land between Boston and Providence. Having acres of pines, a dry gravel soil, a small water area, there is no rank growth of vegetable decay; no manufacturing, there is no filth, and for these reasons the oxygen in the air carries with it plenty of ozone, being that form of oxygen made by the Creator to destroy disease-producing germs which breed and multiply in decay and filth. The air is dry and invigorating, making the well strong, while the weaker ones feel this influence and grow in strength."

The elaborate claims of real estate promoters were coming true on Moose Hill.

From 1919 to 1921 there were constant appeals for money and reference was made to the open air school at the Children's Pavilion. This pavilion, referred to as a preventorium, was depicted in the 1922 annual report which declared that its "success is now very bright."

Their place was defined in the 1925 report. Children under 14 years of age, exposed to tuberculosis in their homes and showing signs of malnutrition and debility, could be placed in the Children's Pavilion and carefully watched under eminently favorable hygienic conditions.

In 1927 plans were announced to build a set of seven dressing rooms adjoining a large sleeping balcony, chiefly for patients well on the road to recovery. In the autumn classes were begun for the children in "Rhythmic exercises."

Time after time reports shed their formality for warm, human touches. In 1931 reference was made to a new hen house "to take care of our very useful hens who have furnished eggs . . . and roast chickens and fowl for the table."

Changes were to come at the sanatorium on Moose Hill, brought about by the Great Depression. The 1932 report told of a difficult year because of the general financial depression. Patients returned home to convalesce; children did not stay so long for treatment. A fire that November caused some damage to the kitchen, toilet rooms above it, and the roof.

In 1934 it was reported that the institution was not filled to capacity, although there were frequently not more than two beds vacant. The report noted, "The depression has certainly kept away some patients who might otherwise have found it possible to have sanatorium care, and a number of cases went home sooner than was desirable because they could not finance a longer residence." Reference was made to "three delightful entertainments of music by the E.R.A. (Economic Recovery Administration) bands and orchestras."

Money worries still kept people away from the needed health care in 1935. The following year attention was focused on the Children's Pavilion which housed 22 children, 11 boys and 11 girls. "Children with active pulmonary tuberculosis are not admitted," the report emphasized. The building was for "undernourished, run down, delicate children."

In June of 1936 a young woman, bride of only a few months, journeyed from Cambridge to Sharon to begin what was to be a three-year stay at the sanatorium in search of health. She had been fatigued and had a severe cough. Examination revealed that one lung was seriously involved, an advanced case; the other lung was moderately advanced.

When her health was restored to the point where she could be discharged she and her husband decided to make their home in Sharon, where they eventually built a lovely home in which they still lived at the time of this writing.

Her clear recollections give an excellent picture of life at the sanatorium.

The doctors tried vaccines in the early years to try to get the body to produce antibodies to fight it, she recalled. To her delight Dr. Griffin let her go to a little house with her books and radio. The house had rooms and porches for just two patients and was connected to the rest of the institution by the tunnels under the buildings.

Three years were spent in bed, three years she remembered as being "so tired." Every three months there was a trip to another building for X-rays and this was very exciting, for nothing else ever happened.

"The food was perfectly delicious," she recalled. Dr. Griffin had to be careful in the expenditure of money to keep the sanatorium going but he never scrimped on food and all patients had nourishing meals. She remembered tenderloin steaks, kidney lamb chops, garden fresh vegetables — the best of everything. "It was like an exclusive hotel so far as food was concerned," she laughed.

This was the only place in between the very expensive and the public institutions. Her treatment included pneumothorax. Adhesions had formed which held the lung partially open. The phrenic nerve could be cut and automatically collapse the lung temporarily. She recalled a visit to Dr. Edward Churchill, chest surgeon at Boston hospitals. "I don't need to ask where you've come from," he told her. "I know you come from Sharon. Dr. Griffin never sends us a patient who isn't ready." Unfortunately, state institutions frequently sent patients for surgery when they were not ready for it.

One of the reasons for establishing the sanatorium was to prove you didn't have to go to the Alps to get well, the Sharon woman pointed out. "Dr. Griffin never wanted me to go back to Plymouth (her original home) to live because of the East wind," she said with a tinge of regret.

She was proud of the hospital administrator. "Dr. Griffin got through medical school in two years instead of three," she beamed. Although others who did it had studied under him at Harvard Medical School, the way he did pneumothorax was not at all the way anybody else did, she recalled. He took a long needle and blunted the end, using just the one needle and not causing the pain experienced by patients elsewhere. "He said he taught it that way but people would rather do it in a more complicated way," she explained.

This former patient told an anecdote to illustrate the deep conviction of the Sharon doctor who lived to become a legend in his community and in the practice of medicine. "Dr. Griffin laid his job on the line at Harvard in 1936 or '37 to have a black student admitted to the graduate school. Dr. Griffin opened all his records to him and did everything he could to help him."

The patient learned of the incident one day when Dr. Griffin visited her and brought with him the black student. Dr. Griffin was called away to another building and his student waited in the patient's room for the director's return. He identified himself as the administrator of a sanatorium for blacks in the South who had come to add to his knowledge of care and treatment of tubercular patients. He told her the Sharon physician had made it clear that he would not remain on the faculty unless the graduate school accepted the black applicant.

At the sanatorium, the former patient said, the general impression was that Dr. Griffin did not accept a patient whom he considered hopeless. "It was always an experiment because of the nature of his mind," she explained. "He was always probing into the nature of the disease and ways to overcome it."

The open air school for children at the sanatorium attracted much attention, according to the former patient. Children and teachers were warmly dressed on cold days and, like outdoor sleeping, the open air classroom did not bow to the thermometer.

A different note was sounded in 1937. The sanatorium was 47 years old when the board president reported: "These are new times. Since the founding of the Sharon Sanatorium medical science has made great discoveries. In the early days tuberculosis was a dread disease. Today it is under control.

"Part of its facilities should now be used to meet the medical needs of today. After consultation with leading physicians, it was decided that the care of sufferers from arthritis was one of the most urgent problems. The situation and facilities of Sharon make it admirably adapted for the medical treatment of convalescent arthritic cases. Accordingly it has been decided to reserve some beds at the sanatorium for this type of patient."

The Children's Pavilion was not being so much used. It was suggested that it could well be used for juvenile arthritis or heart disease. There was a need for money to pay for this care.

In 1938 the directors reported: "A new pioneer effort beckons us. We are now admitting nonacute rheumatism cases for treatment and study." Women patients were still treated for tuberculosis, however. In the winter the sanatorium took twenty rheumatic children in the Children's Pavilion. They came from Children's Hospital. "Treatment consisted of living in the open air, having good food and plenty of rest. No parent or friend showing the slightest sign of a cold was allowed to visit the children, and the extraordinary thing was that during the past winter, when colds were so prevalent, these twenty children kept absolutely free of this infection," the board report proclaimed.

Reference was made to the fact that "the September hurricane wrought havoc in our lovely woods and did a lot of damage to our buildings."

Dr. Griffin's report stated that the hurricane caused partial wrecking of three verandas and four chimneys for which the cost of repairs was estimated at about $1,000. Pine trees in the forest were an almost total loss. "Pine groves were considered by many of therapeutic worth," he noted.

Regarding care of rheumatic children he described this as a "pioneer movement. . . . [which] will endeavor to show that the best convalescence and the best guarantee against the return of symptoms of rheumatic pains is the open air type of treatment such as can be given at Sharon. Aside from one institution in New York State and one in England this idea has not been tried on any large scale with accurate check-ups, and nowhere, unless possibly in England, has open-air treatment been pushed to the extent that it will be used in our Pavilion. The results so far have delighted" all physicians involved, his report concluded.

The 1939 report, paying tribute to Dr. Bowditch who had died a year earlier, stated, "Dr. Trudeau had started an institution in the Adirondacks in New York State to furnish a place for the open-air treatment of tuberculosis at a considerable altitude, several years before the Sharon experiment was started. Dr. Bowditch wanted to determine if an Institution at Sharon — nearer the ocean and at a lower altitude — where the sandy loam dried out quickly after rain would be suitable."

The report referred to writings in Dr. Bowditch's diary at the time the sanatorium was 25 years old.

"In his diary Dr. Bowditch spoke of his many hopes and discouragements and then how, with persistence, he had new hopes and then some discouragements, but always he finally decided to push forward again. He wrote that at times he felt that he would like to set fire to the buildings and end the experiment — just as Dr. Trudeau had felt at times that he would like to put dynamite under his experiment in the Adirondacks.

"But as 'sunshine still must follow rain,' Dr. Bowditch always decided finally to persist because he was trying a worth-while experiment that must succeed. So, with new hopes and new plans he pushed forward again and again — until at the end of twenty-five years he writes that he felt well repaid for the long and arduous years of work, discouragements, renewals of effort, with finally most encouraging results at the end of the quarter of a century."

In the medical report, Dr. Griffin noted that the sanatorium was in the second year of its experiment in treating children convalescent from rheumatic fever "and the results are certainly encouraging."

In 1941, directors quoted from a report published in the *New England Journal of Medicine:*

"In Massachusetts, there are only 200 (beds) for rheumatic fever. Of the 200 beds, 30 per cent are at the Sharon Sanatorium in Sharon, 19 miles from Boston, where a pioneer experiment in open-air treatment has been carried on for three years. As a result of the Sharon experiment rheumatic fever specialists now have reason to hope that with sufficient beds and adequate funds, the disease can be controlled."

The directors' report said the board had decided "to use all the facilities of the sanatorium for the study and cure of children suffering from this disease."

The sum of $40,000 needed to remodel the old building was received in the form of two bequests, one for $15,000 and one for $25,000. Work was completed on schedule and at a cost below estimates. Dr. John P. Hubbard of Children's Hospital, who had been in charge of the experiment at Sharon, was appointed medical director, and Dr. Walter A. Griffin agreed to remain as associate director.

"Rheumatic fever is accepted as one of the great scourges of modern life," the report stated. "It not only kills but it cripples permanently. The disease was considered incurable. Today the medical profession rejects that dictum and is making a bold attack on it. We at Sharon do not claim to have the final solution, but we do claim that over a period of three years our treatment has been far more successful than any other known method and we claim further that if this experiment continues to prove successful, the open-air treatment can be used in sanatoria throughout the country. The children get well at Sharon."

The last published report available was printed in 1943 and in the mid-1940s the sanatorium was closed, care of the children reverting the Children's Hospital.

July 2, 1947, the property was sold to Norwood Hospital and for a time it was hoped that institution could make use of it for the care of children. It was sold to Henry P. Kendall Dec. 21, 1950. The building that had been the Children's Pavilion, after alterations, became the home of the Kendall Whaling Museum.

It can only be speculated how many of the thousands of people who visited the museum over the years had been on the Moose Hill property as patients in the highly successful experiment in treating victims of tuberculosis in another time.

In 1940, when the Sharon Sanatorium was completing 50 years of service in the treatment of victims of tuberculosis, its story was told in abbreviated form in the directors' report. From it we quote:

"Ten years ago Ingersoll Bowditch, a cousin of Vincent Y. Bowditch M.D., founder of the Sharon Sanatorium, wrote as follows: 'During this long period of forty years, we have had most loyal and generous support. It has been our policy to afford the patients better equipment and facilities toward health, and to encourage a longer stay at the Sanatorium rather than to expand our work.'

"Recently the diaries kept by the founder, V. Y. Bowditch M.D., have been located and this annual report of the Sharon Sanatorium — now FIFTY YEARS OLD — contains a number of items of considerable interest put together by Walter A. Griffin M.D., who has been the resident physician now for forty years.

"The idea of treatment of tuberculosis of the lungs at a low altitude and near a large city was first brought to the attention of the medical profession and the public at large by Vincent Y. Bowditch M.D., and it was the little institution at Sharon that proved that cures could be effected in such adverse conditions of climate. There were only nine beds in the original sanatorium.

"The sanatorium has never been large, but it has blazed the way in the treatment of tuberculosis and has had a mighty influence in moulding sentiment for control of this disease."

Dr. Bowditch wrote, "The trustees of the Rutland Sanatorium in their annual report kindly said that to the success of the methods employed at Sharon is due partly the decision to build a large state sanatorium. How glad I am that my faith kept me strong in spite of heart-sickening discouragements at the outset."

In 1921, following the thirtieth anniversary of the institution, Dr. Philip Jacobs wrote, "I congratulate you personally on the success of Sharon and congratulate Sharon on the inspiration it has been to thousands of patients and to thousands of other workers in the tuberculosis field." Dr. Charles J. Hatfield wrote, "If you had accomplished no other wonderful thing than what is represented by this institution, you would have cause to be proud." *The Journal of the Outdoor Life* was quoted as saying, "The results achieved at the Sharon Sanatorium compare favorably with those achieved at the best climatic resorts in the United States or anywhere else in the world. . . . While the results of Sharon Sanatorium have in themselves been significant, the educational value of this early experiment . . . has been far greater."

An editorial in the *Boston Medical and Surgical Journal* in 1921 said, "The results accomplished by the Sharon Sanatorium show how much can be done in the treatment of tuberculosis regardless of climate. Until recently the means of meeting the tuberculosis problem in France have been entirely inadequate; but now that the experiment has been tried at Sharon, successful efforts have been made in climates formerly thought to be unfavorable to recovery. In this connection a letter received from one who has been working in Brittany is of interest: 'When I went to Finistere, those (tuberculosis patients) who could not go to an altitude or a warm climate, prepared to die at the hospital without any attempt to recover. Morlaix is called 'le puit de la tuberculose.' With its narrow valley always full of fog, morning and evening, and lack of drainage, it is not an encouraging outlook for recovery. But the nurses had heard of Sharon, and a Mrs. Ewing and others, and books had told of your effort to cure in any climate, and so, to prove it, I bought Porsmeur, situated on the hill but in the town of Morlaix. Needless to say, what had been proved at Sharon proved true in France as well . . . In France they say, 'L'idee, c'est la force eternelle,' and Sharon has it and holds it. We all owe an unbounded gratitude for the conception of such a place.' "

The Sharon Sanatorium proved to the world of medicine that the tuberculosis patient could be treated and cured not far from his or her own home. It made for Sharon a significant place on the map of healing. And it verified the old declaration that Sharon was, indeed, a healthy place in which to live.

It would be impossible to conclude the story of the Sharon Sanatorium without some mention of the story of a man it brought to Sharon, one of the most remarkable residents in the history of the town and a highly esteemed practitioner of medicine, Dr. Walter Alden Griffin.

Most of the information about him comes from *The Sharon Advocate* of Thursday, Aug. 22, 1974 which devoted almost its entire front page to a "Happy 100th Birthday Today, Dr. Griffin" article by Walter and Esther Reeve, and an article by Mrs. Rachel Baker of Sharon in *The Patriot Ledger* of Aug. 21, 1974 in anticipation of the physician's centennial.

As these words are written in December of 1976 Dr. Griffin, 102 years young, is still living at his farm on Norwood Street and still practicing medicine at his office on North Main Street in the center of town.

Born in Bradford, Massachusetts, he graduated from Haverhill High School and from Harvard College, magna cum laude, three years later. He then attended Harvard Medical School, from which he was graduated cum laude in 1900. He interned at Boston City Hospital. At the invitation of Dr. Vincent Y. Bowditch, founder of the Sharon Sanatorium, he came to be physician and later superintendent.

In addition to his work at the sanatorium he had a private practice in Sharon and maintained an office in Boston for many years. He was a member of the faculty of Harvard Medical School and the professional honors accorded him were many.

A tenor of solo quality who enjoyed choral singing, he was for many years a member of the Handel and Haydn Society of Boston and at the time of this writing still sings each Sunday in the choir of the First Congregational Church of Sharon, of which he is deacon emeritus.

Children found a special place in his heart, and although he had none of his own, all children he encountered were very special to him. In 1911 he became school physician for a salary of $25 per year and still held that position when he reached the century mark.

Healthy recreation facilities and cultural advantages for everybody were his dream. He formed the Sharon Civic Association to provide recreation for the community in 1931, long before towns took over that responsibility. He gave to this foundation land he purchased on Ames Street where summer sessions were operated for youngsters for many years.

Children had long gone to a shallow pond on the sanatorium grounds for safe skating in winter. To add to their pleasure he bought Pettee's Hill so they could enjoy their sleds and skis in safety.

A golf and tennis enthusiast, he played both until he was 95. He drove his own car with the familiar registration number 69 until about the same time and never hesitated to go out at any hour of night in response to a call to the bedside of someone who was ill. Over the years he purchased a number of older houses in the town and restored them for rental, largely because he did not like to see a fine old house slip into a state of decay.

Many of the seeds of American history were sown in Sharon and many fine citizens called the town home. When Dr. Walter A. Griffin was 100 years old more than 2,500 townspeople turned out to pay him homage and wish him well, not because he sought center stage, not because they were there when he accomplished his great achievements, but because he was a good man.

More could not be said of any man.

The Sharon Sanatorium

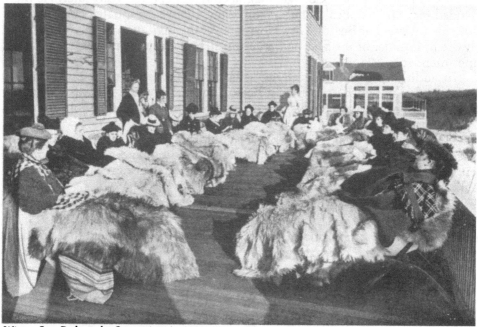

Winter Sun Bath at the Sanatorium in 1902

The Parlors

The Dining Room

Founder of the Sharon Historical Society

Eugene Tappan,

THE SHARON HISTORICAL SOCIETY

By Katharine M. Cartwright

CHAPTER 17

During the century following the Revolutionary War there was interest in researching and recording the history of the town. The Sharon Lyceum seems to have been the first organization to do this. *The Annals of Sharon*, written by historian Jeremiah Gould in 1830, was read before this Lyceum. By 1846, when the group disbanded, names such as Elijah and Joel Hewins, Richard Hixson, George Washington and Warren Gay, Joel Pettee, and Edwin Richards were in the records.

The next forerunner of the Historical Society was the Antiquarian Committee. Interest in local history was triggered in 1886 by the gift to the town of many articles of ancient origin owned by the family of William Richards who lived in that part of Sharon known as Pigeon Swamp. This town committee was formed to take charge of these relics and curios and any other gifts which might be added.

The committee members in 1888 were historians Solomon Talbot, Joel Hewins, and Jonathan Packard. Later, in 1895, the Public Library Trustees were added: Mrs. Emma Bowman, Mrs. George Kempton, Miss Alberta Felt, Mrs. Mary Ella Hixson, Sanford Waters Billings, W. O. Arnold, George R. Mann, and George H. Whittemore. They met quarterly in the Town House.

Many more gifts were presented to the town by the families of Hixson, Johnson, Packard, Tolman, Bullard, and others. These were placed in the Town House and later transferred to the Public Library and are on display there. One notable gift was a beautiful grandfather clock now in the Library, presented by Miss Elizabeth Morse.

In 1900 William R. Mann, Mrs. Mann, Mrs. George Kempton, and Eugene Tappan compiled the epitaphs of every grave in Sharon. The original manuscript is in the New England Historic Genealogical Society Library in Boston, and a copy is in the Sharon Public Library.

On April 1, 1903, the Antiquarian Committee appointed Eugene Tappan and Loring Monk to organize an Historical Society, for a need was felt at that time to have a history of Sharon written. Solomon Talbot, George Whittemore, and Mrs. Emily Capen were appointed to obtain data for this work, and to formulate plans for the incorporation of an Historical Society.

The newly formed Sharon Historical Society held its first meeting for the election of the following officers on August 27, 1903: President, John G. Phillips; vice-presidents, Solomon Talbot, William R. Mann, and D. Webster Pettee; recording secretary, George H. Whittemore; corresponding secretary, Eugene Tappan; treasurer, Arthur D. Colburn; custodian, Loring Monk; directors, Edmund H. Hewins, Mrs. Alice M. Drake, Timothy F. Quinn, and Miss Emma A. Baker. These officers included the names of those who through the years were interested contributors to the history of the town. On September 11, 1903, the Sharon Historical Society was incorporated under the laws of the Commonwealth of Massachusetts.

Meetings were held four times a year in January, April, July, and October, the July meeting being during Old Home Week. At its first quarterly meeting held in the Town House, Don Gleason Hill, the Dedham historian, spoke appropriately on the subject "Study and Use of Ancient Records." Within the year the society had 149 members. By 1907 the membership had swelled to 245. Programs were printed for each meeting. This was an extremely active group, its most productive years being from 1903 through 1910.

Following the death of William R. Mann in 1913, his widow, Mrs. Julia A. Mann, offered the gift of a building situated on the Mann estate to house the society's collections with the stipulation that the building be moved. The gift was gratefully accepted and a suitable location was found on Station Street.

Looking through the records one finds year after year the deaths of those who had been most active in the society. After the passing of Eugene Tappan in 1908 interest waned; the meetings were held semi-annually, and finally this fine society ceased to exist. The last meeting was held on June 15, 1923. Its building was sold, and the historical collections were passed to the Sharon Public Library to be held in trust, along with funds to be used for their preservation and maintenance.

During its active years the society published six books averaging about forty pages each. The principal article in Vol. I was *The Annals of Sharon*. A reprint of "An Address . . ." by Mrs. Deborah Gannett, with an introduction by Eugene Tappan, appeared in the next volume. Another contained Frederick Endicott's "Massapoag Pond Bank." Probably the most valuable was the printing of Rev. Philip Curtis's Church Records from 1742 to 1797 which are used today by many historians and genealogists. The sixth volume was a memorial to Eugene Tappan. In Tappan's memorial service he was called the father of the Sharon Historical Society. From its inception until his death he was its corresponding secretary.

In addition to the printed books were the society's scrapbooks, six in number, which are in the Public Library. These are bound manuscripts containing historical articles of Sharon's past contributed by society members. Some of the accounts preserved are "History of the Tolman Family" by Deacon Samuel Tolman; "Sharon Land Owners in 1798" by Eugene Tappan; "The Stoughtonham Furnace" and "The Old Cellar Holes of Sharon" by Solomon Talbot; "Sources of Sharon History" and "Shoemaker Valley" by John G. Phillips; "The Town Church Bells" by William R. Mann; "Some of the Early Tanneries" by Mary E. Hixson; and "The Sharon Spring" by William L. Haskel. This short list is but a sample of the many accounts of early Sharon.

In April 1905 a committee consisting of Solomon Talbot, Eugene Tappan, and John G. Phillips was asked to prepare a list of the men of Stoughtonham (Sharon) who fought in the Revolutionary War, together with their service records. This list of 211 soldiers took four years to complete.

The society was noted for its "Rambles." These took place in the pleasant weather, either on foot, in carriages, or by electric car. Among the many noted in the records were rambles to Moose Hill when fifty-six people were transported there in eleven carriages (afterward some of them visited the Robbers' Cave at Bluff Head); along Uncle Amasa's Path by Wolomolopoag Pond; over North Main, Bay, and Mountain Streets by coach, with lunch on Rattlesnake Hill; on South Main Street to the old John Randall farm and the Benjamin Randall Tavern; near the junction of East and Mountain Streets, the Benjamin Tupper birthplace; and, duplicating Madam Knight's ride, a carriage drive to the old Roebuck Tavern in East Walpole, then back to the site of Billings Tavern.

This account shows just a portion of the work accomplished by these dedicated historians in the early part of the twentieth century. Without their zeal and labor much of Sharon's history might have been lost.

The John Randall House Formerly on South Main Street

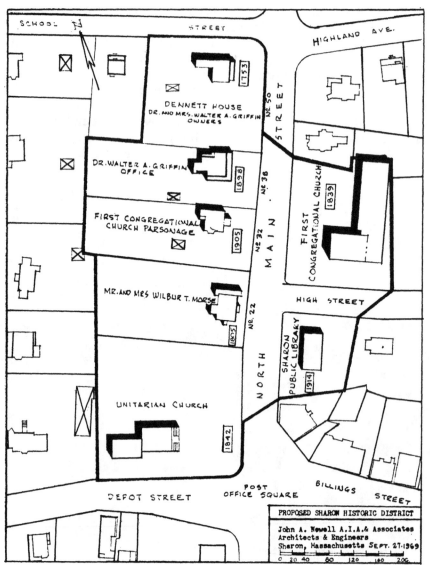

Map of the Sharon Historic District - Established 1970 Dennett House - Formerly Philip Curtis Parsonage
Mr. and Mrs. Wilbur T. Morse - formerly Aaron Fisher House

HISTORIC PRESERVATION

By Chandler W. Jones

CHAPTER 18

The need for preserving the early structures and areas in this nation which are indicative of our cultural, social and economic development, has long concerned scholars and historians. This concern has been shared by the Federal Government, which has set aside a variety of national monuments, historic sites, and parks for future generations. Related programs have been undertaken by state and local governments to a limited extent. Of importance, also, has been the effort of private associations to preserve early buildings and sites, although the scope of those activities has been restricted by financial limitations. Two such organizations are the National Trust for Historic Preservation and the Society for the Preservation of New England Antiquities. There are several large scale undertakings designed to preserve large areas and to develop typical villages such as Williamsburg, Va.; Shelburne Village, Vt.; Sturbridge Village, Deerfield and Plimouth Plantations, Mass.; and Strawbery Banke, N.H.

A recent approach toward the preservation of the exterior architectural features of buildings, structures and sites of historical value in Massachusetts while still in private ownership, has been the establishment of Historic Districts. Chapter 40C of the General Laws, entitled "Historic Districts" as established by Chapter 372 of the Acts of 1960 authorizing cities and towns to establish Historic Districts for the "preservation and protection of buildings, sites and districts of historic interest through the maintenance of such as landmarks in the history of architecture, of the commonwealth and of the nation, and through the development of appropriate settings for such buildings, places and districts."

In 1963 Massachusetts, recognizing the importance of recording the historic resources of the Commonwealth as a further step in preservation, enacted legislation which created the Massachusetts Historical Commission. One of the responsibilities with which the commission was charged was the compilation of an inventory of the historic assets of the Commonwealth. In 1966 the Federal government broadened its span of concern with man-made environment by passage of the National Historic Preservation Act. This act established the National Register of Historic Places, provided a program of matching grant-in-aid to the states for historic surveys and planning and for preservation projects, and established the Advisory Council on Historic Preservation.

Upon the recommendation of the Town Government Study Committee, the Board of Selectmen on May 23, 1967 voted to establish an Historic District Study Committee as provided by Section 4 of Chapter 40C of the General Laws. The committee was established for the purpose of making an investigation of the feasibility of establishing historic districts within Sharon. The committee held its first meeting on June 17, 1967. At this time the Massachusetts Historical Commission, in carrying out its responsibility for compiling an inventory of the historic assets of the Commonwealth, urged the Historic District Study Committee to make a complete inventory of buildings and structures which are of historical, architectural, or archeological significance to the town. This inventory was recorded on forms supplied by the commission, and the location of the buildings and structures recorded on the U.S.G.S. map of Sharon.

The inventory provides the information with which the Massachusetts Historical Commission can help to defend historic properties from adverse effect caused by publicly funded or licensed projects, such as highway construction, urban renewal and subsidized housing. The commission can comment on, and help to defend, only those historic properties which have been properly documented and recorded in the state inventory.

The inventory was very useful to the study committee in its search for groups of buildings that could be recommended for an historic district. The only group that met the qualifications for an historic district was located on North Main Street at Post Office Square.

The study committee prepared a preliminary report, submitted it to the required state and local agencies for comment, held the required public hearings, and on December 31, 1969 filed the final report, with recommendations, with the Board of Selectmen.

At the adjourned annual town meeting on March 10, 1970, it was voted unanimously to add Article 18 to its By-Laws which established the Historic District and Historic District Commission.

Article 18. Historic Districts.

1. There is hereby established an Historic District Commission under the provisions of the "Historic Districts Act," General Laws, Chapter 40-C, consisting of five members, and three alternate members, appointed by the Selectmen, including one member, where possible, from two nominees submitted by the Society for the Preservation of New England Antiquities, one member, where possible, from two nominees, one of whom shall be submitted by the Massachusetts State Chapter of the American Institute of Architects, and one of whom shall be submitted by the Boston Society of Landscape Architects, and one member, where possible, from two nominees of the board of realtors covering Sharon. One or more of the foregoing shall be, where possible, a resident of an Historic District established in Sharon pursuant to the Historic Districts Act. When the Commission is first established, one member shall be appointed for a term of one year, two shall be appointed for a term of two years, and two shall be appointed in like manner for three years, and

their successors shall be appointed in like manner for terms of three years. When the Commission is first established, one alternate member shall be appointed in like manner for a term of one year, one alternate member shall be appointed for a term of two years, one alternate member shall be appointed for a term of three years, and their successors shall be appointed in like manner for terms of three years.

2. There is hereby established an Historic District under the provisions of the Historic Districts Act, General Laws, Chapter 40-C, bounded and described as follows:

   The land shown on a plan entitled "Proposed Sharon Historic District" by John A. Newell A.I.A. & Associates, dated September 27, 1969, filed in the office of the Town Clerk, and comprising the parcels labeled on said plan "Unitarian Church," "Mr. and Mrs. Wilbur T. Morse," "First Congregational Church Parsonage," "Dr. Walter A. Griffin Office," "Dennett House," "First Congregational Church," and "Sharon Public Library" together with that part of North Main Street and that part of High Street enclosed by the heavy line drawn around the above premises on said plan.

3. The Historic District Commission shall have all the powers and duties of historic district commissions as provided by the Historic Districts Act, General Laws, Chapter 40-C, and of subsequent amendments thereto.

4. The Historic District Commission shall adopt rules and regulations for the conduct of its business not inconsistent with the provisions of the Historic Districts Act, General Laws, Chapter 40-C, and may, subject to appropriation, employ clerical and technical assistants or consultants and may accept money gifts and expend same for such purposes.

5. When taking action under the provisions of the second paragraph of Section 7 of the Historic Districts Act, General Laws, Chapter 40-C, the Historic District Commission shall make a determination within fifty days after the filing of the application for a certificate of appropriateness, or such further time as the applicant may in writing allow.

6. In case any section, paragraph or part of this By-Law be for any reason declared invalid or unconstitutional by any court of last resort, every other section, paragraph or part shall continue in full force and effect.

Members of the Historic District Commission are Chandler W. Jones, Chairman; John A. Newell, Vice Chairman; Katharine M. Cartwright, Secretary; Eleanor M. Herburger and William B. Crawford. Alternate members are Karl A. Gelpke, Edward Lyons, and Sydney S. Morgan.

Since the Sharon Historical Society had ceased to function in 1923 and had turned over all its historic records, artifacts, and memorabilia to the Sharon Public Library for safe keeping, there was no organized group to be concerned with local historic assets. The Massachusetts Historical Commission was urging cities and towns to organize local historical commissions to be concerned with the historical assets as conservation commissions are with the protection of the natural resources of the town.

The law provides that an historic district commission, which had been previously established, may be given the duties and responsibilities of an historical commission by vote of a town meeting.

At the adjourned annual town meeting on March 20, 1972 it was voted: "That the Historic District Commission be, and hereby is, given the powers and duties of an historical commission as provided in Section 8-D of Chapter 40, together with the title of Historical Commission, all as provided in Chapter 40C, Section 14 of the General Laws, as amended."

Among the duties of the Historical Commission are to

1. Compile and maintain an inventory of the historic assets of the town.
2. Coordinate the activities of unofficial bodies organized for similar purposes.
3. Keep records of its meetings and actions.
4. File an annual report to be printed in the annual town report.
5. Recommend to the Board of Selectmen buildings, structures, and historic areas that should be protected.
6. Make recommendations of Massachusetts Historic Landmarks.
7. Acquire in the name of the town property of significant historic value.

The Historic Preservation Act of 1966 said in part: "The Secretary of the Interior is authorized to expand and maintain a national register of districts, sites, buildings, structures, and objects significant in American history, architecture, archeology, and culture, hereinafter referred to as the National Register."

The National Register is the official schedule of the nation's cultural property that is worth saving. Being listed in the Register affords a high degree of protection against damage from projects involving federal funds.

The Massachusetts Historical Commission and the Sharon Historical Commission made application to the National Park Service of the United States Department of the Interior for listing of the SHARON HISTORIC DISTRICT and COBB'S TAVERN in the National Register of Historic Places.

The applicants were subsequently informed by the National Park Service that Cobb's Tavern was listed on August 29, 1974 and the Sharon Historic District was listed on September 22, 1975.

The Dennett house shown on the map of the Sharon Historic District at 50 North Main Street originally was the manse. An old account describes what Rev. Jonathan Whitaker, pastor from 1799-1816, could see from there: "When he arose in the morning and surveyed his glebe only two houses met his view, the home of Captain William Billings, on Billings Lane, and an Estey house which stood on North Main Street. There were but two other houses which stood down the hill near the forge; one where Isaac Johnson lived, and the other the old Hobbs house in which Obed Johnson lived — four houses within one-half mile of the Meeting House."

Plaques on Historic Houses

Early Owner	Date	Early Owner	Date
Cobb's Tavern	1740	Snow House	1810
Joel Hewins House	1785	H. A. Lothrop House	circa 1848
Bullard House	1808	D. W. Pettee's Store	1852
Samuel Cummins House	1733	Plimpton House	circa 1800
Deborah Sampson		Thayer House	1799
Gannett House	1813	Holmes House	circa 1800
Gay House	1798	Hannah Leonard House	1776
Aaron Fisher House	1805	Norton House	1822
Job Swift House	1735	Samuel Hixon House	circa 1800
Amasa Dunbar House	1828	Mace Hixson House	circa 1785
Philip Curtis Parsonage	1753	Archippus Drake House	1738
Dr. Daniel Stone House	circa 1805	Sylvanus Clark House	circa 1797
John Savels House	circa 1730	Augustus Hixson House	circa 1765
Darius Lothrop House	1835	Johnson House	circa 1755
Asahel Drake House	circa 1800	William Baker House	circa 1770
Col. Israel Tisdale House	1812	Benjamin Reynolds House	1741
Solomon Talbot House	1735	Elijah Estey House	1852
Mann's Mill House	1831	Col. Ezra Morse House	1780
Mann's Mill House	1831	Elijah Hewins House	1845
Mann's Mill House	1831	Amasa D. Bacon House	1851
Mann's Mill House	1831	Hixson Homestead	1748
Lewis Morse House	1817	West School Site	1766
Johnson House	1770	East School Site	1766

The Job Swift House   Boyden Collection

Dennett House -
Formerly Philip Curtis
Parsonage Built 1753

Photo by: C. W. Jones

Mr. & Mrs.
Wilbur T. Morse House
Formerly Aaron Fisher
House - Built 1805

Photo by: C. W. Jones

Dr. Walter A. Griffin
Office Built - 1898

Photo by: C. W. Jones

"SCHOOL DAYS"

Part I

By Walter L. Reeve

CHAPTER 19

In the good old "Golden Rule Days," when the three R's were taught "to the tune of a hickory stick," Sharon had its share of educational institutions in keeping with those rugged times and conditions.

As was then the custom, our town was divided into school districts, and we find still standing some of the stones which were set to mark the boundaries of these designated areas. One such, a squared, granite stone, similar to those used for marking town lines, may be seen on the northwest side of Quincy Street about midway between Ames Street and Massapoag Lake. This stone is set in the end of an ancient dam which crosses the swamp and Massapoag Brook at this point. It is marked "C" on the swamp (northwesterly) side, and "E" on the street side, thus signifying the line between "Central" and "East" School Districts. A similar stone set by the roadside about midway along the easterly shore of Massapoag, is marked "C" on its easterly side, and "S" on its southerly side indicating that the "South School District" extended to this point.

In 1765 two "School farms" were appropriated by the Dorchester Proprietors for the support of educational work in the town of Stoughton and its separated District of Stoughtonham (now Sharon). Ten years later, when Stoughtonham became a town, a division of these school bonds was made, leaving as Stoughtonham's share the sum of $460.41. This amount was to be kept as a reserve fund, and the interest only used for schools. In 1778 one of these farms, the "Hewes Farm," then in Wrentham, was sold, and twelve years later the other, known as "White's Farm" and annexed to Dedham, was also sold. Meanwhile, in 1783 the name "Sharon" had supplanted that of "Stoughtonham" as a name for our town.

In "Records of the Second Precinct of Stoughton" (referring to our district) we find that at a meeting held October 2nd, 1754, "It was put to vote to see if the Precinct Wold Grant any sum of money for the soport of ye School in the Precinct and it passed in the Negative." This seems to indicate that the Precinct contained at that time but a single school. It is also natural to suppose that our first Central District School might have been the one referred to. This, we understand, was originally located on the westerly side of "The Great Road" (now North Main Street) about midway between Post Office Square and Maskwonicut Street, and it is so designated on our first Sharon map of

189

1794. Some time later this schoolhouse was moved across the street onto the property of the Calvinistic Meeting House (now Congregational Church) and is shown thus on the official town map of 1830. After being discontinued it was again moved, this time on a longer journey, and at present it comprises part of a house on the southwesterly side of Quincy Street not far from the lake.

Five other schoolhouses are shown on the 1794 map, and also on the 1830 map. On the latter these are designated as "N. Schoolhouse," "E. Schoolhouse," S. Schoolhouse," "W. Schoolhouse," and "Old Schoolhouse." Of this Old Schoolhouse we know very little, excepting that it stood at the junction of the Old Post Road and Walpole Street for at least thirty-eight years. It may have been the first West Schoolhouse. Across the meadow and swamp to the west of the "Old Schoolhouse" location is a brook which flows northerly and easterly, emptying into the Neponset River at Walpole. This stream, for about three-fourths of a mile, marks the boundary line between Walpole and Sharon, and is noted on our maps as "School Meadow Brook," the meadow adjoining being marked "School Meadow."

The North District Schoolhouse was located on the easterly side of the county road (Norwood Street) just north of present Edge Hill Road. This building stood until March 25th, 1910, when it was burned down in a forest fire which ravaged this section. Advantage was later taken of the stone foundation for the erection of a bungalow upon this spot, now a part of Mr. Edmund Brown's property, 10 Edge Hill Road.

The old schoolhouse still standing on the southeast side of East Street near Bay Road, formerly the Stahnke residence, is not the original East District School. The first East School was built on the opposite side of the road (shown thus on 1794 map) and was later remodeled in the 30's, and was occupied by a Mr. Grant. The second schoolhouse representing this district was built, prior to 1830, on the site of the former Stahnke house. This was destroyed by a fire of unknown origin on March 3rd, 1877, immediately after which the third, and existing one was built. This schoolhouse has also been remodeled, and is now the home of Mr. and Mrs. Clarence E. Cormier at 347 East Street.

The South District Schoolhouse, which stood at the corner of Mansfield Street (now Massapoag Avenue) and Lake View Street, was destroyed by fire some 50 years ago, leaving a balance of one cellar hole to the credit of educational institutions in that vicinity. The burning of this schoolhouse — apparently unwitnessed and of incendiary origin — is enshrouded in considerable mystery. Added to this mysterious event is the fact that a schoolhouse in Foxboro, and another in Easton also succumbed to the torch in the same manner, and on the same night. Our schoolhouse here referred to was sometimes known as the "New South School," and was not the first in this District. As early as 1794, and probably much earlier, one was located at the corner of former Morse and Mansfield (Lake View Street) Streets near the old Tolman house, about a quarter of a mile northerly of the above. This was called the Mashepoag School.

In our West School District we had a "little red schoolhouse," built some time before 1800, which stood until 1869 on the westerly side of Moose Hill Road near South Main Street, and which in that year became supplanted by a new and better building. The incident of this change is referred to somewhat emotionally in our school report for that year. The later building still stands, in excellent condition and remodeled as a dwelling, at the Belden Farm. Mention has also been made of an "old schoolhouse" about a mile and a half northwest of this point, on the Old Post Road.

It is difficult to trace, through scattered records, maps, and documents covering a period of more than two hundred years, the definite locations and periods of existence of some of our valued relics, and in many instances we have been unable to locate the time of the starting of these District Schools. They have, however, played an important part in the educational development of our town, and we have still with us many who had attended them, either as teacher or scholar.

In the ancient, handwritten "Records of the Second Precinct of Stoughton" for the year 1744 we find under date of October 15th, a vote passed to divide this Precinct (which was to become the town of Sharon) into three school precincts: "the first to include all inhabitants to the northward of the meetinghouse, the second, all to the southward of Mr. Thomas Randals, and the rest of the inhabitants to make the other division, and each part to draw such a part of the money as is proportionable to what they pay to the province tax." The meetinghouse here referred to is our First Parish Church (Unitarian) in the square; while Randals probably referred to what was in 1794 called Randall's Tavern, near the junction of present South Main and East Foxboro Streets. Such a plan applied to our 1831 map, nearly a century later, would bring the "Central" and "North" schools within the area covered by that ancient "first precinct"; while the second precinct," to the south, apparently included all that area later served by the "West" and "South" district schools; thus leaving for the remaining, or central "precinct," that part later covered by the "East School" and the territory around the ancient schoolhouse which stood on the Old Post Road.

In 1826 a number of Boston residents, formerly of Sharon, donated the sum of $1860.00 to aid in the support of public schools here, thus establishing the Sharon Friends School Fund, which was placed under the care of a board of trustees to be chosen annually by the town, and the interest only used for schools. This fund has continued, with occasional additional legacies, and at the present time amounts to $12,210.00.

In 1835, at a precinct meeting on March 2nd, it was "voted to raise $650.00 to support the schools." Some interest had evidently been aroused in the eighty-one years since such support was refused in like meeting.

In 1863 we find a new institution of learning making its appearance in Sharon. This was known as the Stoughtonham Institute and was located on the southerly side of 63 Billings Street between Stone and Cottage Streets, the present home of Mr. Walter Seaver. This was a sort of High School before the active days of the Sharon High School. It was organized by Sanford Waters Billings, owner of much of the surrounding property at this location, and received students from several of our surrounding towns. The Sharon High School started late in 1877, holding forth in the lower rooms of this same building, and Billings became its first principal. The High School at this time comprised one teacher and thirty-four students. These were organized into three classes with graduating terms of two-, three-, and four-year courses respectively.

In 1869 an Act of the Legislature abolished the district system of schools in Massachusetts, although the people of our town sought to keep up the interest in the outlying sections, and some of these schoolhouses continued in use for many years thereafter. In our Town Report for this year we find the following appraisal of school property.

Central District School and land	$4500.00
North District School and land	835.00
West District School and land	2000.00
South District School and land	840.00
East District School and land	1250.00

These items from the same report are also of interest:

Expenses & teaching, repairs, etc.:	
Centre School (23 weeks' teaching, at $9.00)	$446.35
East School (23 weeks' teaching at $8.00)	259.63
North School (23 weeks' teaching, at $7.50)	205.50
West School (23 weeks' teaching, at $9.00)	257.50
South School (23 weeks' teaching, at $7.00)	161.00

About this time another school fund was started. This was known as the Dorchester and Surplus Revenue School Fund, and at the end of the fiscal year, 1934, amounted to $3,130.00. This fund is also under the care of trustees, and the interest is annually available for school work.

In writing of our schools, Jeremiah Gould in his *Annals of Sharon*, 1830, states: "The people have always been liberal in the support of schools, and are generally well informed. Societies and associations have been formed to diffuse knowledge and cherish social virtues, which in their little circles have been productive of much good."[1]

The Old East School, East Street

Bowden Collection

PUBLIC EDUCATION IN SHARON

Part II

By Shirley Husselbee

CHAPTER 20

The first School Committee was elected by the town in 1827 and was charged with allocating the available funds among the districts. However, each district continued to have its own Prudential Committee.

In 1838, teachers were furnished by the State with a "register," a booklet to aid the committee, and others in town in recognizing the correct school conditions, in tabulating punctuality of attendance, in recording classroom work and noting the correctness and incorrectness of students' recitations.

In those early rural times, poor attendance was the greatest problem. In the first printed report, the total absent days in the five schools amounted to 2,752 student days in a school year of 287 school days! There were 2,350 reports of tardiness.

The Committee was deeply concerned that only 60% of children were attending school for an average of seven months, although nine months of schooling were provided. But when the attendance increased to 85%, there was such a shortage of space that it was found necessary to move the upper classes to Mr. Billings' Stoughtonham Institute.

The first Superintendent of Schools was employed in 1860. In 1868, in order to qualify for state aid, the district system with all its inadequacies was abolished, and town funds thereafter were divided.

In 1873, Mr. Sanford Waters Billings, founder of the Stoughtonham Institute on Billings Street (also Superintendent of Schools and Representative in the Great and General Court) was largely instrumental in having state legislation passed which authorized local school committees to buy books "to be the property of the town and to be loaned to the children." Sharon has the distinction of being the first town in Massachusetts to take advantage of this act.

By 1876, there were 70 grammar scholars with an average attendance of 93%, so the Committee decided that some of the pupils be "ordered to descend to the Primary School."

A limited high school was established on November 6, 1877, meeting first at the Institute, then in the vestry of the Congregational Church, finally in the Town Hall. When the High Street School was occupied in 1899, space became available for classes in the Centre School.

By 1903, Sharon parents became dissatisfied with the lack of a well at the South School, the shabby condition of the North School, and the closing of the

West School for six days when no substitute could be secured for a sick teacher. Parents of the Districts renewed their demand for a central school with transportation provided. By 1907, all the District Schools were closed and classes were consolidated at the Centre School.

In March, 1909, voters appropriated $3,400 for the site on Pleasant Street and $20,000 to build and equip a new High School. The imposing wooden structure delighted the Committee as "commodious, well-heated, well-lighted . . . a magnificent proof of the confidence of the citizens in the schools." Sharon High School was then certified by the College Entrance Examination Board of New England, and secondary education had been permanently established.

In 1915 the School Committee sold the East, West, and North properties. Superintendent Fitts was serving only one day a week at $360 a year, but the following year, at his recommendation, a full-time Superintendent was employed.

Participation of our country in World War I brought many changes to Sharon. The cost of the schools had increased 98.5% in ten years. The town was employing Mr. Vernon Ames as Superintendent and Principal of the High School. School enrollment increased 25.6% to 475 children and costs were up. Transportation alone — divided among the barges, the first auto, and the trolley line — cost $2,996.20. Again the Committee faced a demand for space. The Grammar School was still poorly ventilated, poorly lighted, lacking in sanitary facilities, and overcrowded. It seemed best to build a new school on South Main Street, with ample space for playgrounds, an athletic field, and victory gardens, one of the popular civilian war efforts.

In 1921, there were four hundred ninety children in school and the congestion was so great that forty children in the first and second grades were meeting in the lower Town Hall, while thirty-two others were attending school in rooms over Pettee's Store. Previously there had been double sessions for several weeks for Grades One and Two.

The Class A rating given to the high school by the State Board of Education was jeopardized when some elementary classes were enrolled there, causing grave problems.

After many special town meetings, the money was finally appropriated, and the Grammar School, later called the Charles R. Wilber School, was opened in 1922.

Once again all Sharon's building problems had been settled for the moment, but only two years later a committee was appointed to make recommendations for a new high school, the Pleasant Street building having exceeded its capacity at 100 students. Again, many town meetings were necessary before citizens finally voted to add the high school to the Wilber School.

Moving day was made a memorable event when on Friday, March 22, 1929, each student carried his books and personal belongings from the Pleasant Street building to a previously assigned locker in the new high school.

By 1932, a separate principal had been engaged for the high school, and the new superintendent, Mr. Page, was able to devote his energies to his theories of education. He believed that school rooms should be homelike. Creative work was encouraged everywhere, and classroom libraries were established for all elementary grades.

At this time a "tutoring" class was established under law, for retarded children. In 1945, Kindergarten was re-established after a lapse of many, many years. In 1947, money was appropriated for the education of the physically handicapped. Reading tests showed Sharon scoring above average, and the town felt great pride in the school system.

The 1950's saw an increase of 100% in total population and a 200% increase in school enrollment! The post-war boom was on, and the town grew dramatically. During the fifties Sharon built more than twice as many classrooms as had been in existence at the beginning of this period. In spite of the tremendous effort on the part of the town to keep abreast of surging enrollment, in six of the ten years, part or all of our elementary school pupils were on double sessions.

The Cottage Street Elementary School was opened in December of 1951 and an addition in 1954. The Heights Elementary School was opened in 1955 and the East Elementary School in 1958.

In September 1957, Senior High pupils moved into their new building on Pond Street, the third new high school building in Sharon's history. Extensive changes were then made in the South Main Street building to make it better suited for both junior high and elementary use.

The year 1958 was a memorable one in the field of education in the United States. Spurred by Russia's Sputnik, there was a growing and genuine desire nationally to strengthen and improve all aspects of the educational system.

The Sharon staff and school committee assessed its system and inaugurated the following major changes:

1. The introduction of advanced classes at Grades V and VI.
2. Educational television for enrichment purposes in Grades II to VI.
3. The introduction of an accelerated program in mathematics at the junior high school.
4. The revision of programs in mathematics, science, and English at the high school.

In 1961, for the first time, the school budget exceeded one million dollars. A voluntary summer program was introduced. The summer school courses were designed to strengthen or enrich learning.

The next step in the building program called for an addition to the High School; this was completed in 1963. Then Sharon built a new Junior High School on Mountain Street and it was ready in 1966. Now for the first time in over a decade, Sharon had sufficient classrooms for its pupils at all levels.

Sharon citizens also voted to become a part of the Southeastern Regional Vocational Technical High School, and in 1967, Sharon became one of nine towns sending pupils to this new school. Southeastern programs are designed for students who have a particular interest in mechanical, vocational or technical education.

In 1967, a three-year federal grant was received to be used in cooperation with seven other towns at the Blue Hills Center located in the High Street Building. The purpose of the Center was to generate new ideas and methods in:

1. Special education classes for emotionally disturbed children.
2. The development of in-service courses for teachers.
3. The use of television as an educational tool.

The Metco program was first implemented in Sharon in 1967. Under this program, black students from the city of Boston are brought by bus to the

Sharon schools. Sharon receives reimbursement from state funds for each child's tuition, transportation costs, and for staff salaries.

In the seventies, many citizens were volunteering their time for the benefit of the school. Citizens were serving on a study committee appointed by the School Committee, working with the P.T.A. and volunteering their services within the school.

From 1971 to 1976, intensive work went on in curriculum study designed to meet the needs of today's youngsters. In-service courses in mathematics, science, and learning disabilities have been offered.

At the Intermediate School, the staff has implemented a new Human Adjustment Program.

In 1973, after a year of study, a group of interested parents sought to establish two alternative education programs and an elementary alternative school was housed at East Elementary School and a high school alternative program was begun in a wing of the Sharon High School.

The year of 1973 brought budget problems to the school system. For the first time in many years Sharon citizens did not approve the school budget, but voted a reduced budget. Later in the year a special town meeting was called to restore part of the money to the budget.

It may be coincidental that the needs of Sharon, the laws of Massachusetts, and the goals of our democracy coincide in this, our country's bicentennial year. Sharon's population has stabilized, the growth of the fifties and sixties has slowed down so that the historical effort to provide classrooms has been realized — now Sharon has to determine the degree of educational opportunity it wants for all its children.

Public Law 766 has provided the impetus for meeting the needs of children with learning disabilities. There have always been sincere efforts to educate Sharon students, but until now, Sharon's greatest success has been in preparing a suburban student body to enter college, for which success it is justly proud. But now that school rooms have been built and the academically talented are succeeding at quality colleges, are we ready to make a reality of our goals?

Will class size be such that children will receive the individual attention they need for reaching their academic potential while learning to get along with each other?

Will children with disabilities, whatever their cause, know our genuine concern and receive our concrete support so that they may more fully participate in our democracy?

Will the Sharon Public Schools continue to expand programs and pupil placements so that our nation's goal of "one nation under God, indivisible, with liberty and justice for all" becomes a reality?

We have the questions; the writers of the tri-centennial history of the Sharon Public Schools will know and judge our responses.[2]

Footnotes

1. "School Days," reprinted from *The Sharon Advocate*, December 25, 1975, was based partly upon an article by Harry George Higbee in the Advocate, June 29, 1935.
2. Dorothy M. Chase, *The Development of the Sharon Public School System* . . . presented as part of the National Education Association Centennial, 1957. Sharon Town Reports, Parts I and II

An Early View of the Center School on School Street

The School Administration Building, Formerly the Center School above   *Photo by: J. K. Harris*

The Charles R. Wilber School - 1919   *Courtesy: W. B. Roach*

The High Street School   *Boyden Collection*

The Pleasant Street School   *Photo by: J. K. Harris*

The Middle School   *Photo by: J. K. Harris*

The Cottage Street School   *Photo by: J. K. Harris*

The Heights Elementary School   *Photo by: J. K. Harris*

The High School   *Photo by: J. K. Harris*

The East Elementary School   *Photo by: J. K. Harris*

201

The Junior High School, Mountain Street   *Photo by: J. K. Harris*

Sacred Heart College

Stoughtonham Institute
and Its Founder,
Sanford Waters Billings

Courtesy: K. Cartwright

The Public Library, 1976

Photo by: J. K. Harris

HISTORY OF THE SHARON PUBLIC LIBRARY

By Esther S. Chase, Elizabeth Farrar, and June H. Pharmakis

CHAPTER 21

The Town Record for 1877 provides the first written information regarding the founding of a free public library for Sharon. It is evident that the citizens recognized a need for this service, and sought support for it by inserting in the Warrant of April 2, 1877, Article 15: "To see if the Town will vote to appropriate the money received for Dog License the present year for the foundation of a fund to be used for a free public library or act any thing relating thereto."

It was so voted, and the sum of $234.17 was listed in the auditor's report of the Receipts and Expenditures of the Town of Sharon for the year ending March 1, 1878.

Again in 1878, the Dog License was added to the Library Fund, and the Town Treasurer was authorized to act as Trustee . . . "and when the Fund shall amount to One Thousand Dollars it shall be used for the purchase of books for the Foundation of a Free Public Library for the Inhabitants of this Town."

This clearly would not permit the actual opening of the library for several years, as the sum of money provided by the County Dog License continued to be approximately $250.00. Therefore, the 1879 Warrant included Article 14: "To see if the Town will reconsider the vote passed at the Annual Meetings of 1877 and 1878 . . . and authorize the amount already accumulated for a Library to be expended for the same purpose. . . ."

The Town Meeting of March 3, 1879 voted to draw and appropriate the money, and appointed a committee of seven (G. M. Gay, C. T. Howard, J. M. Bullard, C. D. Hixon, H. A. Lothrop, L. H. Monk, and H. V. Butler) to act as Trustees until the next Annual Meeting. They were given full power to provide for the Library, which was opened to the public on June 7, 1879 with Mrs. Adeline Wood as librarian, and a collection of 524 books, 93 of which were a private agricultural library donated for public use.

The first publication of the new library was the "Catalogue of 1879," printed in Boston by Meliam Beuse, 35 Congress Street, in which the hours of opening were given as "Tuesday & Saturday evenings, 6 to 9 o'clock; Saturday afternoons from 3 to 5 o'clock." A complete listing of the book titles followed under the classifications of Agriculture, Biography, Fiction (117 books), History, Juveniles, Miscellaneous, Poetry and Travel.

During the following five years, the library was enlarged both by gifts and further town appropriations. The first written report of the Trustees of the Library appeared in the Town Record of 1881, listing a book collection of 1,277 and a total circulation of 8,809. A local Fair was held that year for the benefit of the library, which raised $321.89. Insurance coverage in the amount of $1,000 was taken out by the Town for the library, now valued at $1,200. The first published report of the library appeared in the Annual Report of Receipts and Expenditures of 1886, prepared by the librarian, G. M. Cooledge.

Legislation reorganizing the Board of Trustees to consist of six persons to hold office for a term of 3 years, two members to be elected annually was passed in 1887, and has endured to the present day.

Periodicals were added on a regular subscription basis to the collection of 2,743 books in 1887, and the librarian recommended publication of a second catalog at the earliest opportunity. That good use was being made of the collection, there is no doubt; however, the Trustees indicated their concern that so many of the books borrowed were from classes "Fiction" and "Juvenile" (ages 14 up).

Two substantial bequests were made to the Trustees of the Library in 1889, the Russel Drake Fund of $300.00 and the Eliza G. Perkins Fund of $500.00. Both were established to provide income to be used for the purchase of books for the library.

Emma A. Baker was appointed librarian in 1889, and after some delay, a new supplementary catalog of books was published. Further supplements appeared as needed, until 1903, when the library, with 6,400 volumes on its shelves, closed for two months for the purpose of reclassifying books and writing cards for a permanent card catalog index.

The Twenty-fifth Annual Report of the Library Trustees to the Town of Sharon was submitted in 1904, and contained the news that a portion of the bequest made by Mrs. Olive E. Hayden would be used to purchase "of Dr. George A. Dennett, the building lot, corner North Main and High Streets, 100 x 105 ft. with the intention of offering the same to the voters to be used as a site for a library building." "Dr. Dennett generously returned $100.00 of the purchase money, desiring it to be used as the nucleus of a building fund."

This was indeed good news, as housing the library had presented perplexing problems for some time. The two rooms of the Town Building which had been equipped for a smaller book collection were quite inadequate now, since there was no remaining space for study or reading within the building. At a special Town Meeting held October 24, 1911, the sum of $325.00 was voted to move the library to a vacant store in the Dennett Block, at a rental of $250.00 per annum. This move was considered temporary, as Trustees and residents alike were looking forward now to having a new building with a separate children's room, reading room and reference collection.

The library re-opened in its new quarters on November 11, 1911, with a collection of 6,000 to 7,000 books. The original hours of opening were maintained, even though greater use was being made of the library each year. In 1911 afternoon hours were added and the library was opened on Thursdays as well as Tuesdays and Saturdays. Juvenile books were issued only on Tuesday evenings and Saturday afternoons.

The new location with the additional space caused a jump in circulation to nearly 15,000 in 1912. A telephone became part of the business equipment, and a rental collection of fiction titles was added, so that popular fiction could be purchased and paid for by the rental fees, rather than from the regular book budget, all of which was needed for non-fiction titles if the library was to meet American Library Standards.

Miss Isadora Bennett Paine became the third librarian in Sharon in 1913, and was assisted by Mrs. Edith S. Hodsdon. The age limit for children was lowered to nine years, and two books of non-fiction were issued on one library card. Previously, one had been the limit at any one time. "A joint meeting of the School Board, School teachers, Library Trustees and Librarians was held . . . to hear Miss Zaidee Brown from the office of the State Free Library Commission talk on the subject of 'Cooperation between the Public Library and the Schools.' " Subsequently, "an arrangement is effected by which from 20 to 30 volumes selected from lists made out by teachers are to be sent to each grade once a month the coming year." The school program was very successful and was maintained until 1969 when Sharon added an Elementary School Librarian.

The years 1911-1915 were extremely active for the Board of Trustees and various civic committees, for the townspeople were determined to obtain their new building without delay. In the summer of 1911, the Center School Association, composed of many of the older residents and former residents who had attended the old Center School, started a building fund in the amount of $753.94. At the September meeting of the Sharon Improvement Association, a committee was appointed by the president to formulate a plan for securing a public library. This committee recommended the incorporating under Massachusetts statutes of the Sharon Public Library Association with an eighteen-member Board of Directors, presided over by President J. Eveleth Griffith.

The total membership of the Association, 535 citizens, raised largely by contribution the sum of $1,800, but the difficulties of obtaining sufficient monies within a reasonable length of time became apparent, and the Directors decided to apply to Mr. Andrew Carnegie for assistance. The sum of $10,000 was offered and accepted, and the building was constructed for that amount, plus incidentals of approximately $1,000 paid from the Treasury of the Association. The architect was Mr. C. Howard Walker of Boston.

Thus the first Sharon Public Library building was secured without expense to the Town. So successful were the plans that they were extensively distributed to other towns in Massachusetts through the Division of Public Libraries. Several years later they were recommended in a pamphlet prepared by the American Library Association for nationwide distribution, and appeared in *The Brickbuilder*, an Architectural Monthly, the issue of January 1915, and were included in the *Encyclopedia Britannica* article on Library Architecture (14th edition, 1929).

By 1923, the popularity of the new library had been thoroughly established, and the annual circulation was something over 20,000. Mrs. Edith Hodsdon, assistant librarian since 1909, was appointed librarian to fill the vacancy left by the resignation of Miss Paine, and continued to serve the town in this capacity until 1949.

In this same year, the Trustees accepted the gift of the Historical Collection from the Sharon Historical Society, and cases were installed in the library auditorium to properly house it. The gift also included $1,000, the income of which was to be used for the preservation and maintenance of its collection and for the purchase of historical books.

Other donations and gifts were noted frequently, and the Fortnightly Club indicated its interest in the library by devoting one of its meetings to the subject. It was shortly after this that memorial donations of books were made by the Club each year honoring deceased members in this thoughtful and much appreciated manner.

A weekly story hour for children from ages four to ten was held on Saturday afternoons in the summer of 1928. Regular exhibits of children's books were prepared for Children's Book Week, and there was considerable interest in the work of the elementary schools begun in 1913. It was not until 1948, however, that the downstairs auditorium was converted into a separate library and reading room for children. Mrs. Marion Steensen was appointed children's librarian when the room opened on November 30. During the following year, 475 children registered for library cards, and a total of 7,569 books were loaned. By 1951, both registration and circulation had doubled.

Mrs. Mildred Bolan became the fifth librarian of the Sharon Public Library in 1949 and continued to serve as adult librarian until 1970, when she retired from full-time employment. Mrs. Mary Bell was appointed children's librarian in 1950, and served until her retirement, also in 1970. Both of these women served the library well and faithfully during these years.

Expansion of the book collection and services continued during the early fifties. Hours of opening were increased to meet the ever-growing demands on the facilities by the public. New lighting was provided, and a machine system of charging was installed in the new custom-made circulation desk.

In 1957 the Board of Trustees took a long look at the future. Two major surveys were made, one by Miss Alice Cahill of the Division of Library Extension, the other by Mr. Joseph L. Wheeler, an outstanding authority on library building. As a result, additional staff was added to assume regular duties, a systematic weeding of the collection was recommended, and plans were made to engage a professional librarian.

A Building Study Committee was formed to investigate the matter of space which was acutely needed. The original building could no longer contain the book collection now estimated to be 20,000, and it soon became apparent that no amount of alteration could improve the existing conditions. Therefore, in 1959 the sum of $4,400 was requested and obtained from the Town Meeting for plans for a new addition. The architectural firm of Korslund, Lenormand & Quann, Inc., were engaged, their plans approved, and the sum of $72,000 provided for construction, which was completed in December of 1960.

Mrs. Juanita Blakely, the first administrative librarian, engaged in 1959, resigned in 1960. Mrs. Esther Chase filled the vacancy the following September. She remained until 1967 when she resigned to accept another position. During Mrs. Chase's tenure, many changes were accomplished. The card catalogs were revised, the collection was updated, the staff was expanded, and many programs of interest to all citizens were conducted.

Until the appointment of Mrs. Patricia Iseman in September of 1968, Mrs. Mary Chase served as acting librarian. Mrs. Iseman resigned in February 1970 and, until the appointment of Miss Elizabeth Farrar in August 1970, Mrs. Laura M. Hayes served as acting librarian.

During these years the library was fortunate in having an active Friends of the Library group. This group sponsored Story Hours for children, as well as a number of cultural programs of interest to adults. In addition, they spent long hours doing many mundane things of great value to the library — painting chairs, processing and mending books, filing, etc.

During these years the Eastern Massachusetts Regional Library System was established with monthly visits from its Bookmobile, which enabled the library to augment its collection with books it might not otherwise have been able to provide.

In 1973, the Regional Library System dropped its Bookmobile service. Instead it established daily delivery of requested materials from the Thomas Crane Public Library in Quincy. In 1974 more than 750 items were borrowed in this manner.

The Town of Sharon participates in the State Aid for Public Libraries program. In 1972 the portion of the law requiring free service for all residents of Massachusetts was implemented, and the Board of Trustees voted to provide this service. Sharon has a number of out-of-town borrowers, and many residents of Sharon avail themselves of the opportunity to use other libraries.

As the town has grown, so has the library, and it is time once again to plan for expansion not only of the facilities, but of services. The history of the Sharon Public Library has been a richly rewarding study of an alert and devoted group of citizens working together toward a most important goal — the best possible education for all.

TRUST FUNDS OF THE SHARON PUBLIC LIBRARY

Over the years a number of Trust Funds have been set up for the benefit of the Sharon Public Library and to augment its collection.

In 1929 the Trustees received one hundred dollars from the estate of *Cynthia Bates*. This money was invested by the Town Treasurer, the income to be used for the purchase of books of non-fiction, or for the upkeep of the building.

In 1964 at the March Town Meeting, the Town voted to accept the gift of one share in the Sharon Co-operative Bank from Mrs. Lizzie M. Burke, to be known as the *Lizzie M. Burke Fund*, to be administered as a Trust Fund by the Trustees of the Sharon Public Library and used to purchase books relating to homemaking and home economics.

In 1909, *Lucius Clapp* of Randolph left the sum of three thousand dollars to the Public Library of Sharon, to be invested and kept as safely as may be by the Trustees. The income is to be used for the purchase of books and papers for the library.

In 1950 the Town voted to accept as a Trust Fund of the Public Library a bequest of five hundred dollars from Joseph A. Cushman. The terms of the bequest stated that the fund was to be known as the *Joseph A. Cushman Fund*, and the income only was to be used for the purchase of books on Natural History or Geology. By accepting this bequest, the Town acknowledged a generous gift and a fitting memorial to a distinguished resident of Sharon.

The 1915 report of the Trustees states, "The late Elizabeth C. Estey of Dorchester bequeathed to our library a fund amounting to $1,468.74, the income from which is to be expended in the purchase of books in the memory of her father, George S. Estey, and her aunt, Elizabeth W. Hinckley, both of whom were born in Sharon." The income from this fund, known as the *Estey-Hinckley Fund,* is to be used for the purchase of books on Nature and Science and for the purchase of the best books of fiction.

In 1930 *Georgiana W. Hampton* bequeathed her house and land on Bradford Avenue and her bank accounts to the Congregational Church and the Sharon Public Library. Her mother and another individual were given life tenancy, after which the property was to be sold and the profits divided between the library and the church. In 1946 the Town accepted $694.60 as the library's share. The use of the Hampton Fund is unrestricted.

Probably the three oldest funds, now lumped together, are known as the *Perkins-Hayden-Drake* Fund.

Russell Drake	1881	$300.00
Olive Hayden	1898	553.75
Eliza A. Perkins	1900	500.00

The income from these funds is unrestricted.

In 1923 the *Sharon Historical Society* disbanded, and their materials were given to the library along with a treasury balance of $1,011.00. Some of this money was used for display cabinets, and the rest has been invested with the intention of using the income to maintain the collection or to buy historical materials.

In 1965 the Town authorized the Trustees to set up a fund to be known as the *Library Trust Fund* in order to accept gifts and bequests of money for specific purposes. Portions of the principal and the interest may be used at any time for the purchase of books and other materials as suggested by the donors.

Interior of the Former Library, 1914

The Square in 1911 Showing the Former Library at the Far Right in the Dennett Block

Nineteenth Century Figurehead from the Whaler "Pocahontas"   *Courtesy: Kendall Whaling Museum*

THE KENDALL WHALING MUSEUM

By Nancy Lang Hays

CHAPTER 22

Landlocked in Sharon, Mass., the Kendall Museum doesn't have the salty flavor of the museums at New Bedford and Mystic, but then it doesn't seek that atmosphere.

The museum is an outgrowth of Henry Plimpton Kendall's lifelong fascination with whaling. As a young man, he watched the ships leaving and returning to New Bedford.

Henry Kendall, the son of a country preacher, was a self-made man, who founded a large international firm which bears his name. As his business became more profitable, he was able to allot more and more time to amassing his collection. Paintings, prints, scrimshaw and all the tools of the whaling trade were stored in various places.

When the museum was opened it contained the largest and most universal collection solely on whaling in the world. Other museums, such as the Peabody in Salem, the Bourne in New Bedford, and the Mystic Seaport have fine collections, but are not exclusively devoted to whaling.

The purpose of the museum is to aid those people who are interested in paintings, scrimshaw, models, and harpoons. Many states from Hawaii eastward are represented in the visitor's log book. The curator of the Rei-jksmuseum came to see the Dutch material and said it was more comprehensive than their collection. Several British museum curators have been visitors.

When a visitor enters the museum, he will find an Oriental rug warming the floor of the entry hall. Two large panbones from a whale's jaw flank the front door. The bones have been scrimshawed by a French-born artist, Leonard Harnois, who now lives in New Bedford. Two framed lithographs, which were the artist's inspiration, hang directly below each bone drawing.

Since scrimshaw is in great vogue today, the first room to be viewed is the decorative scrimshaw room containing part of the museum's 1400-piece collection. Brightly lighted glass cabinets form walls, with glass shelves holding the collection. In this way, each piece is illuminated and viewable from every angle.

Scrimshaw, the art of etching on sperm whale teeth, or any other material readily available, was practiced by the crews of whaling ships in the 19th century. While an ordinary merchant ship could function with a crew of only eight, a whale ship needed a crew of 25 to man its three or four whale boats.

Because on an average, only one whale a month was caught, time hung heavy for the extra men. Scrimshawing became a means to while away the long, lonely hours on voyages that sometimes lasted three and four years. The farm boys who often made up the crews were not skilled as artists, but were able to trace pictures from books such as *Godey's Lady's Book*.

The glass shelves also hold ornate watch stands, pie crimpers or jagging wheels as they are sometimes called, collapsible swifts used for winding yarn; toys, canes, napkin rings, thimbles, whale bone busks which were used to stiffen the corsets of the fashionable ladies of the time, knitting needles, and jewelry. In addition there were numerous engraved sperm whale teeth with a small wooden stand for display purposes, which often found their way to a place of honor on many New England mantles. The human fist is often seen on cane heads. The artist had only to use his own fist for a model.

More long Oriental runners cover the floor of the hall leading to the small Japanese and Eskimo rooms, as well as to the much larger American and Dutch-English rooms.

The Japanese scrolls are favorite exhibits. One scroll, dated 1798, depicts 23 whales and other useful great fish. A model of an ornately painted whale boat, propelled by eight paddle-shaped oars is significantly different from the very utilitarian, unadorned American whale boats.

Seals and walrus were food and oil for the Eskimo, who used walrus tusks for scrimshawing. Two tusks in the exhibit show real artistic talent — one is a drawing of a caribou, the other shows an archer chasing birds and an Eskimo in a kayak on a walrus hunt. Several intricately carved miniature totem poles are outstanding for their skill on a very small scale.

After the intimate scale and feeling of the Japanese and Eskimo rooms, the American room is big, bright, bold and brash. A woman's eye would immediately note the throne-room sized red Oriental rug and the gracefully proportioned Chippendale and Adams sofas. Glass-topped shadow box tables display more of the museum's scrimshaw treasures. The walls of the vast room are hung with paintings and prints showing whale boats and men, tossed about in every conceivable way, by the awesome tails of whales.

Two figureheads command one end of the room. One is a larger than life, brilliantly painted figure, probably that of Pocahontas. Her head is encircled with red, green and blue carved feathers. Her dress is painted to match, with the addition of lots of gold braid. The other figurehead is an Indian warrior, equally gaudy, as was the fashion.

A gigantic carving from the sterncastle of a ship completely fills the upper half of the wall behind the figureheads. A large model of the "Alice Mandell" rests in a rectangular glass case, looking as if she were riding at anchor in some faraway place.

A twenty-eight foot whale boat from the schooner "John R. Manta," the last active whaler out of New Bedford, completely fills one side of a room packed with shops belonging to all the trades connected to whaling, such as cooper, rigger, sailmaker and instrument maker. Two harpoons, bent into a loop, are grim reminders of the massive power faced by whalers. Lances, harpoons and other gear used in the chase are displayed on a wall. They look rather fragile when compared to the size of a whale.

The Dutch-English room is equally divided between the two nations. Paintings graphically show the rigors withstood during the ice-bound Arctic trips. Despite the comfort and warmth of the room, the chill of the polar region persists. An oil painting by Claes Van Wieringen, dated 1637, is one of four in the world signed by the artist. (Reprinted by permission of *The Providence Journal.*)

The Kendall Whaling Museum   *Courtesy: Kendall Whaling Museum*

Eugene Fisher - Teacher, Illustrator, Horticulturist

THE ARTS IN SHARON

Chapter 23

SHARON CIVIC ORCHESTRA

By Babbie Brittain Erkelens

The Sharon Civic Orchestra, founded in 1948 by Esther Klein, has contributed much to the cultural life of Sharon and attracted many professional people to the town. Outstanding soloists have performed with the orchestra.

From its early beginnings with a personnel of eleven, the Orchestra grew both in size and musical competence. The program in 1965 lists more than forty members, and the last three years saw the performance of two serious concerts, a children's concert, and the Pops each season. As an added cultural attraction during this period over 1100 paintings by local artists have been exhibited at the mid-winter concerts.

The founder, Esther Klein, retired after thirteen years as conductor, handing the baton to Philip Hoffman, assistant conductor of the Orchestra and Director of the Sharon public school music program. During the early years of the program, the Orchestra had loaned instruments to the school and had encouraged music students through the granting of scholarships to talented school children. One of the main objectives of the Orchestra, the Scholarship Fund has given out over $6,000 in awards through the years.

Thanks to the hard work of members and the two conductors, the Orchestra in the summer of 1963 had reached the stage where it could benefit from the conductorship of John Bavicchi, composer-conductor-teacher, who strove to improve the quality and standards of the Orchestra's performances.

The seventeen years of the Orchestra's life saw joint concerts with the Sharon Civic Chorus; the introduction of the Orchestra's music school which attempted to continue where the public school music program left off; the continued availability of fine music; and an increase in musical scholarships.

The Sharon Civic Orchestra presented Mid-Winter Classical Concerts and Summertime Pops Concerts annually from 1948 through 1965. At its height the orchestra contained 16 voilins, 5 violas, 6 violoncellos, 2 double bass, 2 flutes, 1 piccolo, 2 oboes, 1 English horn, 5 clarinets, 1 base clarinet, 2 bassoons, 5 french horns, 4 trumpets, 3 trombones, 1 tuba, 2 percussion and 1 tympani players, and 1 harp, always accompanied by Marion Healy on the piano. Jeannette Chase served as concert mistress in the early years, followed by Philip Hoffman and Arnold Levine as concertmasters.

THE SUNSET-4

By Donald Webber

Since the early 1960's The Sunset-4 have been blending their voices in barbershop singing, an uniquely American style of a cappella four-part harmony.

Starting very humbly, as a bit of impromptu entertainment, at a public supper on behalf of one of our local churches, this approach to music caught the interest and desire of several men. Very shortly they were getting together on occasion, to see what kind of sound they might get with a little hard work. In a few months they made another church appearance, and Wednesdays quickly became "quartet rehearsal night."

Over the years, some ten different voices have harmonized in and out of the group, its present complement having been together a little over two years. Under the basic musical guidance of Jack Schultz, who sings the baritone part, lead Don Webber, bass John Colaneri, and tenor Ernie Blake, have lent their harmony and light humor to make many a club, lodge, or church function a night to remember.

Novelty tunes, turn-of-the-century numbers, standards, and present-day ballads are all part of the repertoire of The Sunset-4 Barbershop Quartet.

SHARON COMMUNITY CHORUS

By Anna L. Hughes

The Sharon Community Chorus is now in its tenth season. The group is directed by Anna Hughes and accompanied by Carolyn Falby. Members, now numbered forty-two, rehearse every Thursday at the Community Center.

Over the years, the chorus has built a wide, varied repertoire with music ranging from folk to Broadway, to serious classics and religious music.

Each spring the chorus performs at a Friday-night service at Temple Sinai. This service is sung entirely in Hebrew. The group has sung at a Sunday service in the Unitarian Church and presented a program of ecumenical music at the Congregational Church. It has also sung at installation ceremonies in the Masonic Temple in Boston; at the Art Festivals of the Sharon Creative Arts Association and in local Senior Citizens' shows; and during Deborah Sampson Week in Sharon in December 1975.

Performing in nursing homes is among the other activities of this lively, enthusiastic group in which membership is open to all who love music.

OUR CHORUS HERITAGE

By Babbie Brittain Erkelens

Without music in a home, a church, and a community? Incredible! Yet such was the case in the New England of those stern and rock-bound Plymouth Pilgrims and Boston Puritans — no singing, no playing, no dancing, no Christmas! (But oh, fie, did mothers at spinning and in lullabys, and fathers on the convivial hearth surreptitiously evoke the ancient heritage?)

218

Well, at least the Pilgrims had brought over "Ainsworth's Version of the Psalms", — just in case. In twenty years they produced "The Bay Psalm Book", the words intoned by the congregation, each in his own pitch and rhythm — no instruments — they were "of the devil".

It got so grim in Boston with this and all other prohibitions, that the hermit (1625) Blackstone (who had given the 1630 arrivals some of his land) took off and drove cattel and chattel to Rhode Island, bewailing, "I left England because of the Lord Bishops, and I now leave New England because of the Lord Brethren."

It was pleasanter in Dorchester in 1630, and the first hundred years thawed a little faster, for about 1730 we find — oh, horrors — a bass viol, from the nearby Milton factory! By this time Dorchester was the largest town in New England.

Now we had best get our geography straight. In the maze of changing names and places, here's how our Sharon fared:

1630   Dorchester
1665   Pole Plain (a continuation of the Poles' land, founders of Taunton)
1684   The New Grant "South of the Blew Hills"
1707   Second Precinct of Dorchester
1726   Old Stoughton (not to be Canton until 1797)
1740   Second Precinct of Old Stoughton
1765   District of Stoughtonham
1775   Town of Stoughtonham
1783   Town of Sharon

Boston's hardest hundred years finally produced, of all things, a choir director, Chief Justice Samuel Sewall of the Old South Church. Furthermore, he dispensed singing along with judging through the Stoughtons, even unto the tavern of Ebenezer Billings at Pole Plain. North of Boston in Newbury, Reverend John Tufts in 1712 compiled "Easy Instruction of Psalms, Contrived".

Something unique was cooking in Stoughton, First Precinct (Canton). Elijah Dunbar, just out of Harvard, started a singing school. It was so popular that in 1762 fifteen young men decided to form a Glee Club, with Elijah conducting them, and in such wise

The Music Society in Stoughton (MSIS) had its inception as an amateur, volunteer, secular singing group — the first in America, or anywhere else. They held sings in homes and taverns for the next 24 years, always on tap for church services, commemorative events, weddings, funerals and other occasions of mixed emotions. But all was not roses on February 11, 1761 when "there was prodidgious jangling" over religion with the Braintree boys — but they "made it up" much later on August 4th, and on the 24th there was even "fine fidling". (sic.) In 1764 there was small-pox.

About 1770 William Billings from Boston came to the house-cumtavern of Robert Capen in Stoughton, Third Precinct "over the Mount Hunger Fields" (present Stoughton) to continue Elijah's singing school. This lad was to become the great progenitor of American music, a man for all seasons of the heart, and kissin' cousin to our founding Billingses. William Billings was born October 7, 1746, son of William, a Cornhill Shopkeeper, and Elizabeth Clark, an aristocrat. At 14 he lost his father, and had to use the knowledge gained from common schools plus John Barry's instruction in the New South Choir. Sam Adams was there, and so was the Brattle organ (well!) — first one in Boston, second in America, 1713. Bill had his own tannery on Boylston Street, often chalking inspired music on the hides. At a safe distance from this smelly business, in Newbury Place, he set up a printing shop — Paul Revere did the engravings. So radical, innovative and daring was he, that something dreadful was scrawled across "Billings Music" sign:

"*2 furious cats, suspended by the tail*
    Were swinging cheek by jale;
Not man could bear, nor demons sustain
    The fiendish caterwaul of rage and pain",

author unknown, whereas, William turned out six textbooks, many original and some "lifted" compositions, and "Chester", the rallying song in home and field of the Revolution, promoted by Samuel Adams.

Still, poor William had problems! His poverty, his deformed, wizened frame and blind eye made him the butt of many a bully. However, there was nothing wrong with his charisma, for he became Conductor Emeritus of the two Stoughton Societies and friend and mentor of masters and aspiring musicians around him. Though himself untrained, William Billings let nature dictate his harmony and style. He despised foreign music (especially English); he organized choirs, singing schools, chorales, and instituted the pitch pipe and bass viol; and with friends like Sam and Paul, how could he lose? All this didn't get him a decent living, but it got him Lucy Swan of Stoughton (Canton) — a pupil. Major Swan père was opposed, but they married on July 26, 1774, and the singing must have been something wonderful. (Wouldn't Swan have been surprised had he known that in 1785, as a Colonel, he would lose the competition for leader of the budding OSMS to Elijah Dunbar?)

Billings' last work in 1792 found him in dire monetary distress, and in 1800 he died. He was interred at the foot of Boston Common, leaving $1500 to Lucy and six surviving of their nine children, and a Legacy of Music which spread up, down, and across our fair land. During the Bicentennial the music of William Billings was sung by many societies, in churches, clubs, choruses, and groups of all kinds to honor him.

REVOLUTION STOPS THE MUSIC

On November 7, 1786, the singers gathered again at the home of Robert Capen and organized the Old Stoughton Music Society (OSMS) embracing the MSIS and admitting many other members. Elijah Dunbar was their conductor, to remain so for the next 23 years. Sharon's lone and charter member was Jesse Billings descended from our Ebenezer's and Roger's lines. His great grandson, the Reverend Osmond Jesse Billings, was born at 40 Billings Street and is a courtly gentleman of 98 years and total recall. He lives on Maskwonicut Street with his daughter Carolyn, her husband Clifford Falby and their sons Verne, Bruce, and Wayne, a very musically talented family.

Supply Belcher fondly dubbed Uncle Ply, left Stoughton for Maine in 1785, and later wrote the "harmony of Maine" for which he was known as "the Handel of Maine". Too bad he had to go even before the OSMS could get the credit. But we had Swan, Ingalls, Jaziniah, Sumner, Jacob French, his brother Edward (Sharon), Edson, Wittermore, Read, and other composers on the native heath.

LOG OF YE FLAGSHIP OSMS

From the perspective of the Sharon Connection:

1787   June 5, Purchase the *Worcester Collection*, plus a record book, and resolve to establish a lasting foundation . . . the president shall beat ye time.

1787   The Old First Meeting House town down. Second begun, 10 rods south. "Boys up to 16 to set in the 3 hindseets in the side Galary."

1790   Jan. 4, Dues raised from 2 shillings to nine and fourpence. Dismiss any member not paying . . the poll. Three leave meeting.

Interlude. And then it happened: Our reputation for superior singing got around, and Dorchester, stung and skeptical, challenged us to a contest duly held in a great hall. Their mixed chorus plus a viol did nobly, but they lost when the OSMS, without books, instruments or ladies, rendered Handel's "Halleluiah Chorus". A frantic ovation proclaimed our prowess.

1797   Feb. 23, Old Stoughton becomes Canton, Third Precinct gets the name and fame of Stoughton.

1797   Nov. 22, This day the Rev. Philip Curtis of Sharon dies, after having served 56 years.

1799   Edward French composes "New Bethlehem" for ordination of controversial minister Jonathan Whitaker.

1800   A new century, this day January 1.

1802   Feb. 15, The OSMS comes to Sharon for the first time; rehearse at Williams' Hall (gone, site of Hixson's on King's Grant 1727, opposite Cobb's land).

1802   March 20, 24, 27, 29 Our Revolutionary Soldier heroine Deborah Sampson Gannett lectures at the Federal Street Theater in Boston; at the conclusion all stand and sing "God Save the 16 States" (words set to "God Save the King")!

1802   April 15, House (gone) of John Savel, Saw-Mill Hill near pond.

1802   June 7, John Savel's Hall, (upstairs Pettee's old store in center, moved to 32 Station Street). Downstairs Jeremiah Gould serves rum flips to the gentlemen around his fireplace.

1803   Feb. 28, Savel's.

1803   Oct. 31, Upham's Hall, Canton, James Beaumont (builder of great stone viaduct) introduces the flute. Several walk out.

1804   Jan. 23 and 26, Savel's.

1804   Nov. 12, Jonathan Cobb's tavern (1740, beautifully preserved, an historic landmark).

1805   Feb. 11, Nov. 18, Dec. 2, Cobb's.

1807   Feb. 12 and June 6, Cobb's.

1808 - 1818 Our Edward French Sr. elected and serves as 1st and 2nd Vice Chorister (gone are his house and saw-mill on Maskwonicut Street).

1809   Jan. 2, Thomas and Barney Richards' tavern (gone), Bay Road (now Parrish Farm).

1810   Oct. 15, Supper at Cobb's; cost two shillings thruppence, spirits one shilling thruppence.

1813   Baptists leave Second Meeting House. Trinitarians using Watt's books, Unitarians using Belknap's.

WAR OF 1812 STOPS THE MUSIC

1818 - 1824 Edward French president.

1820   First Christmas Day meeting and sing, Samuel Johnson's in center of town (now on High Street). (These Christmas sings plus often a sermon, held in area towns for next 60 years.)

1821   Calvinists (Congregationalists) leave second meeting house, take communion silver ("1 flaggod, 2 tankards and ye littel cupps") and baptismal font along with them.

1822   Jan. 1, Johnson's New Year's Sing.

1825   June 6, Johnson's.

1826   Dec. 25, second meeting house, public worship and sing. Over to Johnson's sing from Collection of Handel and Haydn Society, our juniors by 28 years.

1826   Publish The Stoughton Collection.

1828   June 2, Capt. Charles Ide's "Quaker Inn" (Cooperative Bank 1934-1948 until new building 1963).

1829   Johnson's tavern "with spirits".

1830   Tension over Whitaker causes Tom Richards to nail up his pew with a horseshoe, and go out singing the anti-tryant Sumner "Ode On Science".

1836   First Sharon Singing School, vestry new Calvinist Church.

1837   "no more spirits" — temperance has won (though some sneak out a bottle or two in their tall beever hatts from Hixon's).

1838   Calvinist Church burns down — young Jonathan Cobb has to be baptised from a pudding dish in the second church.

1842   Third Church (Unitarian) built.

1844   Red letter day for the tribbles (ladies) — invite them to sing (at last).

1845   Practice session at Unitarian Vestry; Albert Hewins 1st violin, John Hewins 2nd violin, Joseph Hewins octave flute, George Dunbar trombone, Joel Pettee double bass viol, Theophilus Dunbar post horn, (all Sharon boys).

1847   Singing School of Leonard Marshall (from Boston).

1857 - 1860 Addison Johnson, Vice Chorister.

1864   Dec. 25, Braintree — William and Lucy Billings' grandson Perez Cushing gives eulogy on Civil War Veterans.

1884   April 24, Sharon Lower Town Hall, Soirée of Louise (Thayer) Bryant's pupils.

1886   Celebration Publication. June 9, the OSMS "Centennial Collection of Sacred Music", (American and European compositions) — the ladies guiding us.

1893   Aug. 14, 15, World's Columbian (yep, Christopher) Exposition, Chicago. Sharon's Sanford Waters Billings, president OSMS, conducts at the fair (his dream to have them represent Mass. and they do). Several go from Sharon. Sanford's son, 15-year old Osmond Jesse sings and has a marvelous time.

1897   Sharon Fortnightly Club is founded, and Federated in 1898.

1900   Another new century, this day January 1.

1901   Sharon musicians hold practice session in Old Town Hall, built 1883 (torn down for new one by 1964).

1902   President and leader of OSMS orchestra Edwin A. Jones writes to ten countries and confirms MSIS and OSMS oldest in world.

1903   Oct. 29, Lower Town Hall, Sharon Historical Society first meeting, 100 members, John G. Phillips president.

1904   Phillips returns from year in Europe. Sharon singers render "Ode on Science" (Sumner) and Keller's "American Hymn" and present him with gavel of wood from his birthplace, the Congregational parsonage which was torn down for a new one that year.

1904   Sewing Circle and sing at Parsonage.

1905   Feb. 27, 28, *The Incognitos*, Dadmun and Rider; Town Hall Sharon, Memorial Hall Canton.

1905   Oct. 4, Osmond Jesse Billings' ordination at Congregational Church.

1905 - 07 Historical Society "Rambles" visits Sharon landmarks, and sings at each: Ole Roebuck tavern site, and Mrs. Addison Johnson serves her Election Cake; Poor Farm (Everett Street); Plimpton Pines; Devil's Brook and Mann's Pond; Rock Ridge Cemetery; site of old Belcher Farm off Bay road; and many others.

1906   Jan. 25, the Fortnightly Club, very musically oriented, presents Robert Burns Festival on his birthday, wearing tartans. Always close their meetings, as does Historical Society with his "Aulde Lang Syne."

1907   Old Home Week Concert given at old Town Hall, Sharon by OSMS.

1908   Jan. 1, OSMS incorporated.

1908   June 3, Sharon Choral Society first public concert, Town Hall, William R. Lang conducts.

1909   May 14, Spring Concert, Charles P. Scott conducts.

1909 - 1914 Series of Spring and Mid-Winter Concerts, Fred Wodell conducts.

WORLD WAR I STOPS THE MUSIC

1921   Fortnightly presents Elgar's *Banner of St. George*, Marion Hosmer conducts.

1928   Polyphonic Society forms and presents following:

1928   May 3, 4, Gilbert & Sullivan's *Pinafore*, Norman Strauss conducts in old Town Hall.

1930   March, Gilbert & Sullivan's *Pirates of Penzance*, W. Herrick Brown conducts in new High School Auditorium on Main Street (built 1929). Following performances were all given in this high school accompanied by small orchestra or piano.

1931   May, Gilbert & Sullivan's *The Mikado*, W. Herrick Brown conducts.

1932   May 12 & 13, Balfe's *Bohemian Girl*, Ruth Hall conducts.

1934   March, Victor Herbert's *Sweethearts*, Ruth Hall conducts.

1938   Oct. 27 & 28, Gilbert & Sullivan's *Gondolier's*, Sally McMahon conducts.

1939   March, Mendelssohn's *Elijah*, Russell Cook conducts.

1940   March 31, Concert of selections from the Classics, Russell Cook conducts.

1940   Nov. 1, Gilbert & Sullivan's *Ruddigore*, Sally McMahon conducts sponsored by Sharon Fortnightly Club, perfect for Hallowe'en!

WORLD WAR II STOPS THE MUSIC

1947   Oct. 24, Cadman's *The Sunset Trail*, Dorothy Richardson conducts.

1949   March, Annual Mid-winter Concert, Marion Hosmer conducts.

1950   Jan. 20, Annual Mid-winter Concert, Marion Hosmer conducts.

1951   May 8, Choral Selections at Pops Concert with Sharon Civic Orchestra.

1951   Nov. 17, Annual Concert, Hetty Archer conducts through 1955.

1952   April 6, Brahm's *Requiem*.

1952   Dec. 7, Handel's *Messiah*.

1953   April 18, Spring Concert.

1954   March 7, Verdi's *Requiem*.

1955   March 13, Dvorak's *Stabat Mater*.

1956   April 8, Bach's *Peasant Cantata* and Boito's *Prologue in Heaven*, Fred Teuber conducts.

1957   April 6, Spring Concert, Louis Pichierri conducts.

1958   March 15, Faure's *Requiem*, Louis Pichierri conducts.

1958   Sept. 6, Gilbert & Sullivan's *The Mikado*, Joseph Klein conducts.

1958   Nov. 2, Haydn's *Creation*, Arnold Johnstad conducts at the new High School on Pond Street.

1959   Sept. 5 & 6, Gilbert & Sullivan's *Pinafore*, Joseph Klein conducts at Canton new High School.

1960   May, *Judas Maccabaeus* with Brockton Festival Chorus and a large children's chorus, Arnold Johnstad conducts at Temple Israel Reformed, West Elm Street, Brockton.

1964   April 4, Schubert's *Mass No. 6, E Flat Major*, John Bavicchi conducts assisting the Belmont Community Chorus, also presented in Belmont.

1965 - 1975 *Each year* on Friday preceeding Christmas, on the steps of Sharon Unitarian Church, site of the First Parish, we meet and sing.

1966   Dec. 11, *Pettee's second store* in the square burns down.

And so all ends . . .

Sharon Personnel of Old Stoughton Musical Society up to 1929

Jesse Billings Sr., 1786	William C. Myrick, 1879
Edward French Sr., 1801	Joseph W. Perry, 1879
Joseph Hewins, 1801	Warren S. Skinner, 1879
Benjamin Richards, 1801	Mary L. Stone, 1879
Nathaniel Morse, 1802	J. M. Watson, 1884
Frances Curtis, 1803	Mrs. J. M. Watson, 1884
Elijah Hewins, 1804	A. H. Pickering, 1859
Edward French Jr., 1808	L. R. Pickering, 1859
Joel Hewins, 1819	E. R. Wilson, 1859
Jesse Billings Jr., 1820	A. G. Hixon, 1859
Nathaniel Gould, Esq., 1820	C. D. Hixon, 1859
Charles Ide, 1820	Mrs. H. C. Billings, 1874
Sanford Billings, 1822	Mrs. P. A. Perry, 1874
Amasa Hewins, 1822	Miss Ella Mann, 1875
Obed Johnson Jr., 1822	Sanford Water Billings, 1879
Jeremy Gould, 1823	Arthur D. Colburn, 1879
Jedediah Morse, 1825	Mrs. Edmund Hewins, 1879
Moses Richards Jr., 1829	Laura V. Hewins, 1879
Seth Hewins, 1829	Mrs. S. A. Stone, 1886
Russell C. Benson, 1841	Mrs. Mary C. Piquet, 1889
Allen C. Weld, 1852	Osmond J. Billings, 1891
* Addison H. Johnson, 1854	Charles S. Curtis, 1893
Josiah Perry, 1854	Benjamin G. Boles, 1895
George N. Richards	Eugene Tappan, 1900

    * Civil war casualty

Bibliography

Currier, John. *Sketch of the History of Newbury, Newburyport and West Newbury, Mass. 1635-1902*. Boston: 1902.

Erkelens, Babbie Brittain. *Cherish the Past, an Historical Playlet in One Act*. Mimeographed copies, 1967, 1972.

_____ . *The Massapoag Story, an Historical Pageant*. Mimeographed copies, 1965.

Griffith, J. Eveleth. *Sharon the Beautiful*. Issued under the Direction of the Publicity Committee of the Sharon Improvement Association. Boston: Griffith-Stillings Press, 1912.

Huntoon, Daniel T. V. *History of the Town of Canton, Norfolk County, Massachusetts*, Vol. 1. Vol. 2: Index — *Who Was Who and What Was What in the History of Canton*, by Alice Reynolds. Published by the Town. Cambridge: John Wilson & Son, University Press, 1893. Republished April, 1975. Bicentennial Limited Edition, by Friends of the Little Red House, Inc.

Moody, Pauline. *Massachusetts' Deborah Sampson*. Privately published 1975.

Osgood, Herbert. *The American Colonies in the 17th Century*. 3 Vols. New York: 1904-7.

Phillips, John Goddard, ed. *A Memorial of Eugene Tappan*. Publication No. 6. Sharon Historical Society, Jan. 1910.

Pratt, Amy Morgan Rafter. *The History of Sharon, Massachusetts to 1965*. One Section of Thesis for Master of Arts, Boston University Graduate School, 1936. Revised 1941. Privately Published by Frieda Billings Cushman. Bridgewater, Mass.: Dorr's Print Shop, 1966.

Sharon Co-operative Bank, Sharon, Mass. *Sharon . . . on the Old Post Road*. Boston: A. W. Ellis Co., 1965.

Sharon Historical Society, Sharon, Mass. Publications, April 1904-April 1908. Various publishers, 1904-08.

Talbot, Solomon. "Sharon," *History of Norfolk County, Massachusetts*. Philadelphia: J. W. Lewis & Co., 1884.

The Tercentenary of Massachusetts Bay 1630-1930, a Pamphlet. Massachusetts Department of Education, 1930.

Winslow, Elizabeth. *Samuel Sewall of Boston*. New York: Macmillan, 1964.

THE SHARON ART GROUP

By Virginia Chase Earle

The Sharon Art Group, the first art club of its kind in Sharon, was formed in 1930 when the population of the town was 3,351. It functioned for 19 years, terminating with an exhibition of members' work at the Twentieth-Century Club, Joy Street, Boston, in 1949. The membership included Art School graduates and students, and self-taught, disciplined artists.

The organizers were Bertha Remick, Albert Seibert, Esther Odiorne, Ethel Armstrong, Jeannette Chase, and May Sartori Brown.

A simple charter was drawn up. Its purpose was to bring together all persons in town interested in art; to foster and encourage appreciation of good art here; to have qualified, outside artists come to speak; and to get constructive criticism.

As the Group grew, the members became very ambitious, acquiring many outstanding speakers, or demonstrators, in all fields of art. Among the remembered speakers who willingly gave of their time to the Sharon Art Group were Stanley Woodward, prominent seascape painter, and Royal B. Farnam and Dana Vaughn of the Rhode Island School of Design. A president of Massachusetts College of Art spoke at a meeting sponsored jointly by the PTA and the Art Group at the High School.

Meetings were held once a month, some being work nights, with a model sitting. Landscape artists made many field trips together in Sharon or elsewhere during this decade, providing us with artistic records of scenes and buildings in Sharon, some of which have changed, or no longer exist.

The first exhibition was held in the Highland Street homes of Mrs. Edwin A. Simpson and Mrs. William G. Darrow. Afterwards exhibits were given each spring in either the Congregational or Unitarian vestry.

This small organization of about 30 members contributed to the cultural climate of Sharon for two decades. It drew together people surprisingly diverse, and congenial, who might never have met but for this common interest. Some became life-long friends.

Over the years, the membership included Eugene Fisher, a prominent zoological illustrator affiliated with Harvard College Museum and Wood's Hole Oceanographic Institute for many years. Fisher was also a horticulturist known for his experiments in cross pollination of gladioli in which he created more than 200 new species. A graduate of the Normal Art School in Boston and a capable landscape and flower painter, he was a helpful and beloved teacher on field trips.

Fay Hoffman Church, known as Peggy, was an adept portrait, flower, and landscape artist who worked in a bold and colorful technique. Peggy held classes in her home (site of the Baptist Church parking lot) and later in the Fleming barn across the street.

Little is known about the background of Patricia Barnard who produced programs regularly on Channel 2 from the Boston Museum of Fine Arts, taking viewers on tour through various galleries and current exhibitions.

Nora O'Leary, of the golfing family, became Home Sewing Editor for the *Ladies' Home Journal*, a post she held for many years until 1975 when she became Fashion and Home Sewing Editor for *Family Circle*.

Bob Hare, a co-owner of Hare Advertising Agency in Boston, painted landscapes as a recreation.

Dr. Joseph A. Cushman held honors in the field of micropaleontology, including the coveted Hayden Medal, and an honorary degree from Harvard. His analysis and classification of foraminifera, the study of minute fossils, required extensive research and original documentation. He was a very humble man, working and teaching quietly in his laboratory on Brook Road in Sharon. After his death, his work was transferred to the Smithsonian Institution in Washington, D. C. and is still being actively carried on there. For recreation Dr. Cushman painted in oil and water color the landscapes he dearly loved around his home, and in New Hampshire. His membership in the Sharon Art Group was a joy to him and he contributed to its exhibits. Having a great sense of humor, he drew delightful pen and ink cartoons.

Ann Shepard and Margaret Moore, scientific illustrators for Dr. Cushman in his Sharon laboratory, were active contributing members of the Group.

May S. Brown, a teacher in the Sharon school system for many years, was a very active and devoted force within and for the organization from start to finish. Self-taught, she was an excellent draftsman and strong oil painter of flowers and landscapes.

Bertha Remick was an experimentalist with color whose work was reminiscent of the impressionists.

Helen Glines' hooked rugs and their designs were creations of unusual beauty. Later she studied portraiture, enjoying this art until recently when eye operations were necessary.

Charter member Jeannette Chase was a capable draftsman, painter, and pastelist of landscapes and portraits of animals, people, and flowers. As a young woman she was a professional violinist and later served as concert mistress with the Sharon Civic Orchestra for several years.

Ethel Armstrong, an enthusiastic charter member and still an active artist, became an adept water colorist, painting flowers and landscapes.

Rev. Norman Cawley, a former minister of the First Congregational Church in Sharon, painted as a hobby. His plaques of churches became popular and are still in demand.

Louise Parker was an Art School student.

Another Art School student was Virginia Chase. Now, as Mrs. Robert K. Earle, she is a professional oil and pastel portrait painter, and teacher.

Leanna Hansen and Esther Odiorne worked in various media. Henry Hansen painted and was a capable woodcarver. John Beach operated his own printing business in Boston, painting in his leisure time. A Mrs. McDonald held pottery classes for adults and children in her barn on Glendale Road. Albert Seibert, Sibble Fiske, Joan Kidd, Virginia MacMechan, Winifred Ballantine, Taidia Kaler, Isabelle Simpson, Walter Fairfield, and Katherine Savage painted and exhibited with the Group.

Two Sharon artists who have had an influence on the arts in Sharon are the late Henry Klein and Ann Dann.

Henry Klein, a commercial artist in the advertising field with some Art School training behind him, exerted an influence on the Sunday painters for several years here in Sharon. Some people went on to become more than amateurs. From the time that the Sharon Civic Orchestra functioned, Henry became involved in the planning and hanging of the art exhibits which were shown in conjunction with the concerts.

It was common practice for the enthusiastic Henry, prior to an exhibit, to call the artists for the titles of their paintings for the program. From those who gave a negative response he demanded titles which left the artist with no alternative but to create — sometimes in a hurry! It could be quite a stimulating experience, particularly if you were going through one of those unproductive periods we all hit one time or another.

Ann Dann, head of the Art Department of Sharon High School for many years, also taught privately. She capably created backgrounds for many school performances and stimulated interest in animal painting.

ART IN SHARON 1967-1972

By Marilyn Z. Kahn

When people speak of art, i.e., "Art in Sharon," too often they think of the visual arts — painting and sculpture. The founders of the Sharon Creative Arts Association had a broader viewpoint. Its basic aim was to bring to the people in Sharon an opportunity for a creative experience and to encourage an appreciation of all the arts: music, drama, and dance as well as the visual arts.

The Sharon Creative Arts Association consisted of an Art Group, a Choral Group, a Modern Dance Group, a Drama Group known as the "Masquers," and a Photography Group. Each group had its own activities as well as joint ventures and culminated in an exciting Art Festival each year.

THE ART GROUP

Concentrating in the areas of painting, sculpture, and graphics, the Art Group had a lively and varied program designed to educate and inspire artists and the members of the community.

Workshops were held at the Community Center on a regular basis, giving experienced artists and Sunday painters alike an opportunity to explore such mediums as pen and ink, oil, and charcoal as well as different subject matter, i.e., drawing from live models, still life, and landscape. These workshops found experienced artists and novices sitting side by side, each benefiting from "cross pollination." Such artists as Dorothy Appel, Gloria Bubly, Vera Cross, Lori Durocher, Jan Ehrenworth, Marilyn Z. Kahn, Phyllis Sheehan, Louise Wentworth, and Winnie Westlake taught at these workshops.

In the spring of 1970 the workshops went outdoors. Most of the sessions were on the Community Center grounds. On occasion we took off, however, as when a group ranging in age from 21 to 78 piled into a Volkswagon bus and went to Mrs. Deeg's property on Mountain Street to sketch her leaning barn. These outdoor work sessions were most productive as some of these sketches inspired two of the winning note-paper designs submitted by Phyllis Sheehan in the SCAA note-paper design contest. (The other winning design submitted by Marilyn Z. Kahn did not use a Sharon scene.)

The Art Group's evening program included films and demonstrations by some fine New England artists. Davis Carroll and Helen Pierce demonstrated water color; Margaret Agner, silk-screen; Roz Farbush, expressionist painting; Lu Stubbs, sculpture; Sol Levenson, an overview of art; and Gary Rickson demonstrated surrealism and symbolism in painting.

One of the most exciting programs consisted of a film workshop where the people attended watching a film on creating collage paintings. Then with the materials provided by the S.C.A.A., they were able to experiment in this fascinating technique. A number of other fine films were shown — too many to list here.

Exhibits serve multi-purposes giving inspiration to the artist as well as bringing pleasure to many. The Art Group had many exhibits throughout the community. Paintings were hung in the Library, the Town Hall, the Needham National Bank at Cobb's Corner, and in some of the larger exhibits held at the Community Center.

In one exhibit in 1970, S.C.A.A. honored five Sharon recipients of overseas scholarships given by the Boston Museum School: Elaine and John Avakian, Nicholas and Paulette Edmonds, and Lu Stubbs. This was a varied and interesting show of paintings and sculpture.

Some exhibits brought to Sharon well-known New England artists like Mo Com of Brookline (mentioned in *Who's Who in Art*) and Roz Farbush of Scituate, a winner of many awards and teacher at the Boston Museum School. S.C.A.A.'s Art Group exhibited in South Shore Art Shows at the Brockton Art Center.

The Art Group worked with other S.C.A.A. groups such as the "Masquers" by designing posters and programs. For the production of Shaw's *Arms and the Man* the Art Group took an active part by painting the scenery. It was completed just in time for the dress rehearsal. We all stood back to admire our work only to be notified by the fire chief that the scenery could not be used unless it was fire-proofed.

These large pieces of the set had to be lowered through the windows of the Community Center to the parking lot where we hastily sloshed flame retardant solution onto sets, parking lot, and ourselves. The play went on as planned.

One of the highlights of the Art Group's final active year, 1972, was an Art Studio Tour. Seven Sharon artists opened up their studios to the community and demonstrated their craft.

Jan Ehrenworth demonstrated the very difficult process of collagraphy in her large downstairs studio with a wall-to-wall picture window facing Briggs Pond. Gordon Morrison demonstrated and exhibited his fascinating nature and animal paintings in his upstairs studio in Post Office Square. Dorothy Appel was working in oils in her delightful impressionistic style in her home studio.

Nicholas Edmonds showed his methods of creating his large wooden sculptures, and his wife Paulette showed her paintings and etchings in their barn studio on South Main Street. Lu Stubbs demonstrated and talked about her sculpture techniques in her lovely studio behind her home. Miriam Gourley demonstrated sand sculpture masks and exhibited her paintings in her home studio. Marilyn Z. Kahn demonstrated oil painting in her razor blade technique, and the woodcut process as well. Refreshments were served in her charming old home.

ART IN SHARON TODAY
By Lu Stubbs

Artists of all persuasions have found their niche here in the town that's "a better place to live because it's naturally beautiful." They include painters, sculptors, portraitists, printmakers, commercial artists, free lance artists, art teachers, art students of various ages, art directors, illustrators, designers, interior decorators, weavers, potters, jewelers, and also art historians. Questionnaires sent to the artists in town have revealed statistics corroborating what we suspected all along that Sharon really has attracted and nurtured a large number of very talented, creative people. Certainly the future will show that they will have contributed further to the town's artistic heritage, which is already rich and full.

The educational backgrounds of Sharon's artists are as varied as their skills. They include not only the fine schools in this area — Boston Museum School, Massachusetts College of Art, New England School of Art, Vesper George, Butera, School of Practical Art, Rhode Island School of Design — but also Yale University and the outstanding art schools in New York City: The Art Students' League, Pratt Institute, Traphagen, and Brooklyn Museum School. Some have studied under excellent artists not affiliated with schools, and others have pursued their education in other parts of the country such as southern California, Houston, Texas, and Washington, D.C., as well as abroad, in France, England, Holland, and Italy.

In turn, Sharon artists have taught, or do currently teach, at Boston University, Boston College, Butera, Pine Manor, Milton Academy, Art Institute of Boston, Boston Museum School, and in several area high schools. Some offer adult classes in their own Sharon studios or at places such as the Attleboro Museum, Brockton Art Center, Boston Center for Adult Education, or Oakes Ames Memorial Hall, North Easton. They have given art demonstrations and lectures, they have juried shows, written articles (poetry too), and have appeared on TV.

One teacher has expressed the thought that "creativity is a gift, and so in turn should be shared in some way with others." Another has said, "Part of the joy of teaching is the students' increased awareness, and their perception of nature. Their comments on how they see nature differently . . . what sunlight does on leaves or on the side of a building . . . seeing color and form around them and beginning to express them verbally or in their work." Another: "Sometimes you wonder at the worth of teaching weekly adult education classes. Then you feel the enthusiasm of your students who say they couldn't wait for class time to come — or who don't want to leave at the end of the evening — or you accept the small gifts they sometimes bring you, or the intangible gift of seeing what they produce under your guidance. Then you cease to wonder."

The work of Sharon artists has been very widely exhibited in New England and elsewhere. Near Sharon, the beautiful Brockton Art Center and the intimate Attleboro Museum have hosted one-man and group shows. In Boston, their work has been exhibited at City Hall, Prudential Center, Boston Arts Festival, Jordan Marsh Company, Symphony Hall, Boston Cyclorama, and at numerous galleries. It has also been seen at area colleges: Boston University, Brown, and Wheaton; at schools: Milton and Phillips Andover Academy; at museums: the DeCordova and the Worcester Museum; and at art festivals in Cohasset, Scituate, and Providence. This is only a small fraction of a long, impressive, and far-reaching list.

Our artists can boast inclusion in numerous important collections. One outstanding member of the Sharon art community, Virginia Chase Earle, has done hundreds of oil and pastel portraits which are in public buildings and private collections, including two oils of John F. Kennedy, eleven World War II heroes, and our own Deborah Sampson. Shirley Pransky did skillful portraits of interesting foreign students at Boston University who later became important members of their own governments. Consequently, her work is in the collections of the Kenyan ambassador to Zaire, Africa, and of the chief information officer in the government of Guyana, South America. A third portraitist and present director of the Attleboro Museum, Vera Cross, has her delicate pastel portraits in many appreciative homes, both in and out of Sharon. Gordon Morrison, portrayer of nature's wonders, has done many sensitive wildlife paintings for the Massachusetts Audubon Society, as well as illustrations in *Fortune, New York Times Magazine, Playboy*, and *Seventeen*. Currently he is working on 1300 illustrations for a wildflower book by Sharon's Lawrence Newcomb, to be published in 1977. John Baker, painter, sculptor, and art historian, has created about three dozen imaginative sculptures consisting almost totally of articles found at the Sharon Town Dump. A dozen of these are in private collections. Jan Ehrenworth, talented printmaker, has her work in the collections of many Boston and local banks, hospitals and firms, as well as in numerous homes. Sculptor Lu Stubbs has recently unveiled an over-life-size bronze sculpture of three women at Hearthstone Plaza, Brookline. Other artists, too numerous to mention, have their work in collections from New England to California, as well as in Canada, England, Switzerland, and Holland.

Awards abound among Sharon's talented artists: Phi Beta Kappa and Highest Honors as art school graduates, gold, silver and bronze medals, monetary awards, ribbons, popular awards and fellowships. Jack Rothschild, commercial artist, has been awarded numerous medals as an outstanding art director. Sculptor Nick Edmonds has won four fellowships, two from the Boston Museum School for travel and study in France, Spain, and the Scandinavian countries; the third, a Colman Award of funds for improvement to his studio; and the most recent, a Fulbright, for living in Japan and studying the Japanese wood-carving techniques. In addition, he was recently the subject of a short film showing him at work in his studio.

Our artists are not only involved in their own work, but also in professional organizations, art associations, and other related groups. Eleven Sharonites belong to the Boston Visual Artists' Union. Others are members of WEB (Women Exhibiting in Boston), the New England Sculptors' Association, New England Woodcarvers, Inc., National Woodcarvers Association, Boston Art Directors Club, Advertising Club of Boston, the Copley Society, the Cambridge Art Association, and the Canton Art Association. Many were active in the Sharon Creative Arts Association and were also charter members of the Brockton Art Center, as well as at the Attleboro Museum, whose former director, Betty Dunlop, is another fine multifaceted Sharon artist.

THE DANCE GROUP
By Marilyn Z. Kann

Dance was part of the Sharon Creative Arts Association from its inception in 1967. The goal was to have people participate creatively in dance and aim for a workshop setting where people interested in dance could become involved at two levels. One level would be purely workshop, consisting of a group interested in a movement experience both as exercise and a creative stimulant. The second level would consist of people with previous dance experience who were more advanced and would be interested in developing their skills, exploring creative dance ideas through choreography. The people at ths level would then put these skills to use and become part of a performing group. Dance classes would be formed as the first step towards this desired goal.

In January of 1968, classes were offered at a minimum fee. Over 50 women and teens responded to the first advertisement. Three evening classes a week were held at the Junior High gym for four months. This culminated in the most skilled of the group participating in an original piece of choreography under the direction of their multi-talented director-teacher, Jan Ehrenworth. The piece was performed at the SCAA Springfest, our first art festival held at the Junior High School in the Spring of 1968.

The following fall classes continued at the Junior High until we were invited to utilize the new Community Center facilities. That year creative dance was offered to children from kindergarten to sixth grade in addition to the adult group.

In the spring of 1969, the SCAA Arts Festival was held at the Community Center and again the dancers, who were developing more skills in both movement and choreography through participation in class, performed several dance pieces.

Classes continued successfully in 1970. Also participating, separately, were children who were developing along parallel lines. In the Arts Festival of 1971, the established group performed beautifully. That year the director also had a happening on the front lawn of the Community Center where everyone was invited to join in the fun.

The following year, the performing group was invited to perform at various civic functions and with the money received was able to purchase costumes. The dancers in the group became a very cohesive unit, going together to dance performances and taking Master Dance Classes in Boston and New York.

The dance groups chose names. The adult group appropriately called themselves "Danceworx"; the children's group became "Young Movers." The efforts of these groups were rewarded in a fine concert given by them at the Junior High School in the spring of 1972. Fourteen dances were performed with good lighting, effecting costuming, and several original scores. We had come a long way from 1967 and our then-stated goals.

The performing group disbanded at the end of that year. However, dance, and interest in dance, thrives unabated in Sharon. Several adult members of the former group teach numerous successful dance classes in the Sharon Community to adults and children, sharing past and present experiences and love of dance with all who participate.

THE SHARON PLAYERS

By Pearl Schiff

The Sharon Players have had a somewhat disjointed history. Founded in the mid-1920's under the impetus of Mr. and Mrs. Beardsley Lawrence, the group began life largely as a social club, meeting in the basement of the library. For several years its theatrical activities were confined to book-in-hand readings and the performance of short playlets for the membership only. Beginning in the '30's one play a year was put on in Town Hall, until the more serious demands of World War II years put a halt to such frivolous pursuits.

After the war a few of the members started the Players afresh, this time putting on their plays in the basement of the Congregational Church. Actively involved during those years were, among others, the Max Tetlows, the Clayton Harveys, the Donald Brookfields, Edward and Ann Hall, Edward and Helen Chiten, Evelyn Glover, Evelyn Lechter, Phyllis Borr, Richard Forsythe, Jr., and Nancy and Richard Witherell. One remembered production was *The Littlest Angel*, an original puppet show by John Bradford. The year 1954 saw the last production of the Players in the Congregational Church. *Born Yesterday* was so morally offensive to the governing body of the church that the Players were forced to seek new quarters.

With the Unitarian Church providing a haven for meetings, the Players again went through a reorganizational crisis. Rehearsing in playrooms and living rooms, they readied *Blythe Spirit*, under the direction of Richard Witherell, for production in the auditorium of the then High School on South Main Street, now an elementary school. With Dick Forsythe, Jr. as the harried husband, Joan Bloom as the materializing spirit of his dead wife, and Pearl Schiff as the spirit-banishing Madame Arcti, rehearsals went well.

It was not until dress rehearsals that the deficiencies of the old High School as a theater became apparent. There were other problems, too, one being that community support had dissipated as interests became more diversified. The Sharon Civic Chorus was experiencing similar difficulties. Only the Sharon Civic Orchestra was on a solid foundation. This led to the formation of a loose alliance of the three cultural activities under the name of the Sharon Civic Music Association, for the purpose of mutual support in scheduling events and promoting ticket sales.

Scheduled for promotion in November 1955 was *My Three Angels.* Two weeks before performance date the play was in a crisis stage. The cast was inadequately rehearsed, the set had not been constructed, there was no backstage crew. In a last-ditch effort to salvage the production, Pearl Schiff, with no prior experience, was asked to step in as director. The rehearsal schedule was drastically stepped up, old and new members rallied to get a set onstage. Props were assembled — including a live chicken — and suddenly they were ready for opening night. But a half hour before curtain time a new crisis arose. A small Christmas tree essential to the action — complete with cherished ornaments loaned by the Cliff Myatts — had disappeared from the stage. In a hurried raid on town property, a suitable tree was located and chopped down, a few ornaments were scrounged up, and the curtain was opened. Despite the last-minute frenzy, the play went on without a hitch, with Louis Schiff, Arnold Bartlett (then principal of the High School), and William Mulligan playing the three escaped convicts who solved the problems of the couple whose home they invaded (played by Pearl Cartoof and Carl Feldman). The next night the mystery of the missing Christmas tree was solved. An overzealous teacher, fearing the delicate ornaments would be broken by her students using the stage, had locked the tree in a closet.

In regular succession the Players put on *The Heiress,* April 1956, Nancy Witherell director, starring Claire Kravetz and Arnold Bartlett; *Sabrina Fair,* in the fall of that year, Pearl Schiff director, with Helen Chiten in the title role; *All My Sons,* November 1957, Arnold Bartlett director, with Richard Clark, Fred Van Veen, and Pearl Schiff in major roles, proceeds for the benefit of the PTA scholarship fund; and *The Late George Apley,* Chappy Bengen director, with Dick Clark in the title role.

By this time the Players had an experienced backstage crew. Set construction was organized under Bob Levy, assisted by Bernie Hammer; Sid Kier was the efficient stage manager, with Abbie Norman and Natalie Shapiro on props; and Pearl Cartoof was in charge of makeup.

In 1959 came the bold decision to undertake Arthur Miller's *The Crucible,* to be staged in the new High School, with Pearl Schiff directing, assisted by Bob Robert. Casting alone was a challenge, and new members were recruited to fill the many parts, including, by fortuitous chance, Alice Brown, a gentle, soft-spoken, white-haired grandmother who played the role of her own true-life great-great-great-great-aunt, Rebecca Nurse who was cried out and hanged as a witch in Salem. Because of this relationship the *Boston Globe* ran a full page of pictures with scenes from the play in its Sunday magazine supplement.

Detective Story followed in December of that year, directed by Kay Brookfield and starring Nat Shulman and Charlotte Chester, with a large and competent supporting cast.

In May 1960 the Players presented a program of three one-act plays: *Portrait of a Madonna,* directed by Bob Robert; *Ways and Means,* with Kay Brookfield directing; and *Aria Da Capo,* under the direction of Pearl Schiff. *Aria,* by Edna St. Vincent Millay, was entered later in the year in the one-act play competition of the New England Theatre Conference, with a fine performance by Charlotte Chester, Davis Hamer, Ray Blakely, Richard Bolan, and Fima Haimson.

In October the offering was again an Arthur Miller play, the powerful *A View from the Bridge*, with Pearl Schiff directing.

In 1961 the Players offered a subscription series of three plays for the year. The first, in February, was *Philadelphia Story*, directed by Ann Hall and starring Lucille Bailey.

This was followed in April by another dramatic triumph, *Come Back Little Sheba*, under the direction of Pearl Schiff. Pearl Cartoof as the slovenly Lola and Nat Shulman as the alcoholic Doc were masterful in their portrayals, ably backed by Lois Klickstein and Morris Klickstein in the two other major parts.

The fall offering was *Witness for the Prosecution*, directed by George Quenzel, with Zelda Batt and Morris Klickstein in the lead roles.

After *The Shrike*, in May 1962, directed by Pearl Schiff and starring George Quenzel and Charlotte Chester with a very large supporting cast, there was a hiatus until November 1963, when the players, again under Pearl Schiff, presented *Rose Tatoo*, starring Fran Rafkin and introducing Joseph Sangiolo, who was recruited from an out-of-town theater group not only because of his fine acting but because of his facility with Italian idiom, a must for the play. Roberta Cartoof, in her role of the young daughter, represented the second generation in the Sharon Players.

Despite the quality of the plays, community interest and attendance were falling off, while at the same time more and more requests were coming in for the Players to lend their talents to other organizations within the community for special programs. Under the presidency of Frank Cohen, the Players embarked on a number of such cooperative undertakings, doing cuttings, condensations, and book-in-hand performances for other groups. A whole series of one-act plays and condensations were done for a Temple Israel study group, each play followed by general discussion. Through the years such community activity included a cutting of *Glass Menagerie* for Sharon Interfaith Council, and a series of book-in-hand readings for Temple Israel. These were from *Death of a Salesman* and *Suddenly Last Summer* and the short plays *Offshore Island* and *Cat in the Ghetto*, the latter being a "world premiere" performance of an original play.

Notable among the offerings was "an evening of Brecht," a program of readings, songs, poems, and excerpts from Bertolt Brecht, which was performed several times, including a performance for the New England Theatre Conference, of which Sharon Players was a member. Directed by Sherman Rafkin, the cast consisted of Fran Rafkin, Bob Robert, Frank and Helen Cohen, Norton and Ruth Werksman, and Lou and Pearl Schiff.

An excerpted version of *Raisin in the Sun* inspired the Players in 1965 to undertake a full-scale production with the proceeds to go to the Sharon Interfaith Council and the Sharon Fair Housing Committee to help finance their joint undertaking "Operation Discovery," a project to bring fifty black children from segregated schools in Boston into Sharon daily by bus for a six-week summer program of playground and lakefront activities with Sharon youngsters, with lunch, play clothes, and other necessities provided.

The Sharon Players were anxious to have the play a truly interracial undertaking and actively sought out both old and new black residents for tryouts.

234

The result was an amazing discovery of new talent. With no prior stage experience, Jo-Ann and George White, a husband and wife playing the husband-and-wife roles of Ruth and Walter Younger, were naturals, as were newcomers Andrew Rodrigues, Eugene Ellis, and Charles Banks in supporting roles. Young Wendy Richardson, a native-born Sharonite, was a delightful Beneatha Younger. Subtle makeup artistically applied by Pearl Cartoof transformed Fran Rafkin into the black mother, while Pat Smith changed not only color but also her sex to play the young son. Sherman Rafkin was a convincing "liberal" racist, and Morris Klickstein and Frank Cohen added their bits.

With this artistic and financial success the Sharon Players came to an end. Job pressures and family pressures had taken their toll. At intervals since, new theater groups have formed in Sharon and dissolved. But the magic of theater is such that someday, no doubt, there will be a new Sharon Players ready to raise the opening curtain.

THE DRAMA GROUP
By Marilyn Z. Kahn

In the fall of 1967, Bob Robert and Charlotte Chester, who had been leading performers with the then defunct Sharon Players, became co-chairmen of a new group. This drama company of the Sharon Creative Arts Association was called "The Masquers."

Their first play *Mary, Mary!* directed by Bob Shepard was the first full scale performance at Sharon's newly acquired Community Center. This performance was a sell-out. The Masquers went on to produce a second success *Come Blow Your Horn* with Mike Belise directing.

Bob and Joan Shephard became co-chairmen and put on a few mini-productions. During this time a group of the Masquers under the leadership of Gwynne Jamieson created a delightful puppet show, playing to crowds of Sharon children.

Then Jennifer Parkinson took the helm, and with Paul Wessel directing, they produced *Arms and the Man* to mixed reviews, and *Exit the King*, an artistic triumph.

In 1970 Bill Appel entered the picture. He produced a traveling company with a condensed one-act version of *Dear Me the Sky is Falling*, along with several book-in-hand performances. Then in 1971 the Masquers presented their last and perhaps finest production. This was Edward Albee's *Everything in the Garden*. It starred one of this area's finest actors, George Guild, and co-starred a new-comer, Janet Abrahamson. This presentation was produced and directed by William Appel, who also served as President of the Sharon Creative Arts Association at that time.

Editor's note: A new drama group, the Sharon Community Theatre, was formed in the summer of 1976. Interest in local theater was renewed by the success of William Appel's *She Was There*, performed during Deborah Sampson Week the previous December.

ARTS FESTIVALS
By Marilyn Z. Kahn

A truly exciting time it was each spring when all the groups worked together to put on a Fine-Arts Festival, with choral music, modern dance, drama performance, painting exhibits, and craft demonstrations in the beautiful setting of the grounds of the Community Center.

Children were encouraged to submit original works of art to an art contest with prizes given out during the festival. Our fine High School Band, under the direction of Mr. Fleishman, played on the steps of the building.

The Sharon Creative Arts Association, a registered non-profit organization, is still with us fulfilling the goal of encouraging an appreciation of the arts in Sharon. Having invested its funds, the interest is used to purchase art books for the library.

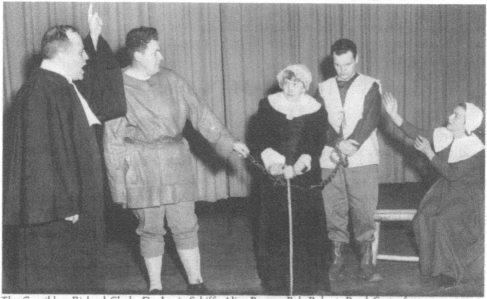

The Crucible - Richard Clark, Dr. Louis Schiff, Alice Brown, Bob Robert, Pearl Cartoof
Photo by: Boston Globe

The Crucible - Richard Forsythe Jr., Sol Krasney, Lucile Bailey, Frances Rafkin, Fred Van Veen
Photo by: Boston Globe

Choral Groups - 1971 SCAA Art Festival   *Courtesy: M. Z. Kahn*

Weaving Demonstration - 1971 SCAA Art Festival   *Courtesy: M. Z. Kahn*

Dance Happening - 1971 SCAA Art Festival   *Courtesy: M. Z. Kahn*

The Unitarian Church   *Photo by: J. K. Harris*

UNITARIAN CHURCH

By Phyllis Brookfield

CHAPTER 24

Sharon's Unitarian Church owes its birth to a small group of settlers who landed at Nantasket May 30, 1630, having departed from Dorchester, England, some time earlier. Accompanying this group were two ministers, a Mr. Warham and a Mr. Maverick, who together established the First Church and Parish of Dorchester. With the exception of the already-founded religious society at Plymouth, the Dorchester Society was the oldest religious Society in Massachusetts.

In 1637, the Dorchester proprietors opened up a new grant extending southerly which included Pole Plain, Sharon's earliest designation as early as 1661, some of the settlers in Pole Plain appealed to the Dorchester proprietors to found a village. Eventually, the small group of settlers multiplied so that in 1727 they petitioned to form a parish separate from the distant parish in Stoughton. In the year 1737, the First Meeting House was erected. Having constructed this meeting house, the inhabitants of Pole Plain directed their energies to the task of acquiring a minister. Mr. Philip Curtis who had preached among the group for three months was offered an inducement, in addition to his salary of 150 pounds, of a gratuity of 200 pounds. He accepted the call and became the first minister of the First Meeting House on November 30, 1741.

Going to church on the Lord's Day in years past was an all-day affair. Services were so long that it was customary for families to bring food which was eaten during an intermission. The length of the intermission was established by a vote of the board. The Reverend Mr. Curtis served the Parish for fifty-five years during which time he officiated at 1,926 baptisms, 313 marriages and 403 burials.

In 1765, Pole Plain which had been renamed Stoughtonham as a separate part of Stoughton, finally acquired its own identity and formally became a town. In 1787, the second Meeting House was begun on land given by the Reverend Mr. Curtis along with one quarter of his salary.

In addition to this amount contributed by Mr. Curtis, other funds were obtained through the auctioning off of pews which belonged to the purchasers and their heirs for life. Those not auctioned off remained the property of the Town and were sold as bidders became available. This meeting house on the present site in Sharon's square was completed by late October, 1787, with the exception of the bell. Subscribers were solicited and on May 3, 1790, a committee reported that more than enough money had been collected to go ahead with the purchase of a bell. Although a bell was purchased, it cracked within ten years and in 1811 another bell cast by Paul Revere and Son was purchased for $205.19. This Revere bell still hangs in the belfry.

After the death of Rev. Philip Curtis, Rev. Jonathan Whitaker was called as the Pastor of the Parish. He had graduated from Harvard in 1797 and the Rev. Abiel Holmes, father of the poet, Oliver Wendell Holmes, delivered his ordination sermon on February 27, 1799. Mr. Whitaker was a man of strong religious and political convictions and was frequently outspoken about them. So much so that he developed much antipathy within the parish. Matters became so strained that in 1813 a small group of people withdrew from the church to form the nucleus of the present First Baptist Church. Eight years later, in 1821, another group departed to establish the Christian Society, later to become the Congregational Church. They took all the communion silver and parish records with them which were lost in a fire in 1836. The new Parish Minister from 1821 - 1826 bought a new communion set for the church at this time.

Although town meetings had always been held at the Old Meeting House, in 1830 because the building was too large for the remaining members to maintain, it was decided to tear it down and build the present smaller structure. This was accomplished in 1842 at a cost of $2,548. Although the town claimed to own the Meeting House and land, it was found there was no legal claim to either one. In March, 1876, the present fence around the front of the church grounds, otherwise the Common, was erected at the cost of $520.75. From 1893 - 1899, a woman minister, Rev. Eliza Hickok, served the church which was a rarity at that time.

From 1900 - 1904, the congregation dwindled to six faithful souls, under Rev. John C. Kimball's ministry. After his resignation, there was no resident minister for twenty-two years. Ministers during this period held services in the afternoon, serving their regular churches in the morning. Rev. Walter C. Pierce came to the church in 1926. During his pastorate, the church was redecorated and when the church was rededicated, a little child was presented for baptism. The years had erased the previous bitterness and an era of friendliness ensued between the various churches in Sharon which has strengthened over the years. Through the 1930's, 40's, 50's and 60's many changes took place in the church. Rev. Rowland Gray Smith followed the Reverend Mr. Pierce as minister. Then Rev. A. R. Shelander became the pastor. During his ministry, the congregation dwindled until there was discussion about possibly letting the Congregational Church take over the meeting house. A number of interested Unitarians decided to try to stimulate interest in the church by getting a young theology student from Harvard and were fortunate in acquiring John Baker, who was ordained in the church following his graduation from Harvard. During his ministry the church made considerable progress and gained strength significantly so that a Parsonage was bought on Glendale Road which is still used by resident ministers.

After four years of service John Baker was selected by the Rockefeller Foundation to become the Director of the Salzberg Seminars in Austria (where he stayed for three years) and Rev. Herbert Vetter became the parish minister for one year, followed by Rev. John Kolbjornsen, also ordained in our church, for five years. During his ministry the church flourished, space under the front steps was converted into a minister's study, and the Vestry was made more open and roomy by installing a replacement furnace in a new location outside the Vestry, an addition built just for the purpose. When he left because of a call to a much bigger church, Rev. Ray Blakely became minister for a year. Rev. Robert D. Richardson, although not a resident of Sharon, was our next minister. He came each week from Concord and was instrumental in promoting the building of a six-room Sunday School wing. He also established and endowed a scholarship fund for deserving church school children. Mrs. Dorothy Richardson, a well known singer and choir director, gave much spiritual inspiration and enjoyment to the congregation for over twelve years, retiring because of illness. After Rev. Robert D. Richardson left because of illness, Rev. Gregg Carter was the minister for a year. Rev. Donald Wassman was the minister for about four years. At the present time, Rev. Richard Glessner serves as the minister for both the Unitarian-Universalist Church in Foxboro and the Unitarian Church in Sharon. At this time, in 1976, the church is still active, although small compared to the other churches in town. The annual Bean Supper, held every September on the church grounds for over 23 years, is a colorful welcome town affair and reminds townspeople that the Meeting House on the church square is still the Welcome Center for many town activities.

An Early view of the Unitarian Church and Surroundings

The First Baptist Church   *Photo by: J. K. Harris*

FIRST BAPTIST CHURCH

By Ardeth L. Parrish

CHAPTER 25

Thirty-eight years after the American Revolution, in 1813, when there were only twenty states composing the Union and the population was less than eight million, the Baptist Society in Sharon was formed with twenty-six members (ten men and sixteen women). Their names are perpetuated in the history of the Town's leading families through these many years. Joshua Whittemore, Levitt Hewins, Jeremiah Richards, Ezekiel Capen, and Benjamin Gannett, Jr., husband of Deborah Sampson Gannett, were among the band which planned and served as officers of the Society.

Prior to this, the only church in Sharon was that of the Standing order and everyone was compelled to support this church, regardless of his religious beliefs. There were some who believed in the divinity of Christ and were not in accord with the philosophy of the pastor of the church at that time as they felt his views were largely unitarian. However, as no preacher could be obtained with evangelical views, the group finally invited the pastor of the Baptist Church in Medfield, Rev. William Gammell. He was a fluent speaker and "preached the truth with great plainness and eloquence." As a result of his preaching, several were converted to Baptist views. Joshua Whittemore and Levitt Hewins, two of the leading men in Town, were baptized in Billings Pond in 1812. They were considered the first Sharon Baptists. Crowds came even from neighboring towns and the baptism made a deep impression on all who viewed it.

The following year, after the Baptist Society was formed, Rev. Henry Kendall of China, Maine, was secured to preach by Mrs. Nancy Low, May, 1814. Rev. Kendall may be considered the founder of the Sharon Baptist Church. He was a man of great piety and devotion and of more than usual ability.

In 1816 the Female Charitable Society of Sharon was organized to assist in the "support of gospel preaching," and in 1818 the Sunday School was started under the pastorate of Rev. Samuel Wait. The Reverend Mr. Wait secured the confidence and respect of the entire community.

From 1824 to 1831 the church was unable to support a pastor. However, the members met every month and "occasionally had preaching." Up to this time the church had no separate house of worship, but had purchased a house on South Main Street as a parsonage, and services were held in the second story, the pastor's quarters being on the main floor.

With large accessions to the membership in the winter of 1831 to 1832, under the pastorate of Rev. Caleb Greene, it was deemed necessary to build a new sanctuary. It was dedicated July 4, 1833 — the same year in which the Massachusetts Bill of Rights was amended to allow entire freedom of religion for all.

Several changes have taken place in the edifice since 1833. In 1852, thirteen and one-half feet were added to the length of the church and the pew doors taken off. In 1854, the pipe organ was installed by funds raised by the Ladies' Society and a large contribution from Mr. and Mrs. Samuel D. Hitchcock. "It was an instrument of unusual sweetness and tone" and after years of long and admired service, it was replaced with our present organ.

In 1873, the church spire was added and the following year improvements were made in the sanctuary.

The parsonage, in dire need of repairs, was sold in 1886, and a new one built at 28 South Main Street. This was sold in 1913 and a house was leased on Summit Avenue. The present parsonage, on the corner of North Main Street and Glendale Road, was purchased in 1920.

In 1897, the present stained-glass windows were installed, and it was noted that there was a great need for more adequate Sunday School accommodations. However, no plans were finalized until 1903 when a fire, caused by a falling oil lamp chandelier, made it necessary to remodel.

The title to the land was cleared, the church turned around to Main Street, and the vestry added on the south side. A choir loft was also built and the present organ installed, a gift of Andrew Carnegie and E. S. Stockwell. At the same time a baptistry was installed in back of the pulpit.

On Easter Sunday, March 27, 1910, the Sharon First Baptist Church was re-dedicated. One of the five young women baptized on that special occasion was Phyllis Matthews who has belonged to the church longer than any other living member.

In the following years improvements were made to the church grounds, and in 1950 the basement of the sanctuary was excavated and a room constructed, chiefly from the "time and talents" of the church family. Now called the Pine Room, this area serves the need for Sunday School space.

In 1956, one portion of the church agreed to separate from the membership and decided to become a part of the General Conference, taking up another location in town.

Vital repairs were made to the organ in 1957, and at that time the console was moved from the choir loft to the sanctuary floor.

In 1962, the electronic chimes system was installed, a gift of Mrs. Augustus E. Weller. In April of that same year, it was voted to purchase the Griffin property at 27 South Main Street for additional Sunday School area, and in 1967 when another addition was added to the vestry on the south side, the house was torn down to provide a parking lot. This new section, contracted for $75,063, provides the church with the Hunnewell Hall, the Friendship Room, the Sunday School Superintendent's office, lavatories, and a new church kitchen. At the same time, the former kitchen was remodeled for the pastor's study and office.

In the summer of 1972, approximately 160 years after the first baptisms at Billings Pond, at two separate services, a total of eleven of the church family accepted Christ as their personal Lord and Saviour and were joined in the ordinance of baptism by Rev. Everette St. Clair Nickerson at the Lake Massapoag home of Mr. and Mrs. Roland Hodge. It was a spiritual revitalization to all those who attended.

October 15, 1974, saw the Fiftieth Anniversary celebration of the Bethany Class. Fifty to sixty members from Maine to Florida were present. Recognition letters were received from New York, Connecticut, and the State of Washington. The highlight of the evening was a greeting from their former teacher, Mrs. Harriet Tuttle, of East Winthrop, Maine.

Five days later another testimony of faith was witnessed when eight Spanish-speaking Americans from newly formed Baptist churches in this area were baptized in the church.

Now as we celebrate our nation's 200th anniversary, we ponder and reminisce over our church's past, and pray strongly and deeply for its future. This country was founded on religious freedom for all. The Lord blessed the first members of this church — may He continue to offer His abundant blessings.

Turning the First Baptist Church   *Boyden Collection*

The First Congregational Church   *Photo by: J. K. Harris*

HISTORY OF
THE FIRST CONGREGATIONAL CHURCH

By Sydney S. Morgan

CHAPTER 26

Eleven people, on June 16, 1821, signed the instrument that constituted them the "Christian Society in Sharon." This was the culmination of years of dissension and controversy that had waged, not only in Sharon, but throughout Massachusetts.

Since 1740, the First Congregational Church had served as the Parish Church for the residents of the second precinct in Stoughton, called Stoughtonham. The Reverend Philip Curtis ministered to them for fifty-five years. Following his death, the parish called Rev. Jonathan Whitaker as pastor and he was ordained February 17, 1799. Mr. Whitaker, who had graduated from Harvard in 1797, was a very fluent speaker though somewhat tactless. A man of strong religious beliefs, he espoused the anti-Calvinistic theology which became recognized by the Unitarian name in 1815. He entered wholeheartedly into politics. He was a Federalist, while most of his congregation were Democrats. There was nothing undecided about his views, and he did not hesitate to state them. Needless to say he created a great many enemies.

These differences were insignificant compared to the religious differences which arose among his parishioners. As early as November 1812, an article at Town Meeting requesting Mr. Whitaker's dismissal was proposed, but voted down. This matter came up again a number of times in the next few years.

In 1815 matters finally came to a head. The church records for November 8, 1815, state: "The Church met. On account of some serious difficulties, which had lately arisen among the people, and an alarming opposition made to the Pastor, the Church voted to concur with the Pastor in calling an ex parte Council."

The "ex parte" Council confirmed the action of the Church and Town in dismissing Rev. Whitaker.

It may have taken four years to get rid of Rev. Mr. Whitaker, but it took more than that to find a new minister upon whom all would agree. Indeed, that proved to be an impossibility. The rift had become too great between the Unitarians and Congregationalists. First one man would be called to the ministry and found wanting, then another would be found just as unsatisfactory to the opposing faction.

Finally the inevitable break came. On June 9, 1821, at a church meeting held at the house of Philip Curtis, a committee consisting of Deacon Benjamin

Fairbanks, Deacon Joel Hewins, and Brother Lemuel D. Hewins was named to prepare rules and regulations necessary for the formation and government of a religious society. The church meeting of June 16, 1821, accepted the committee report and the Christian Society in Sharon became a reality.

While the reason for separation in the report was failure to agree upon a minister, the real trouble was the differences between the Unitarian and Trinitarian doctrines.

The original eleven, whose orthodox or Trinitarian views impelled them to separate, were joined by thirty-two others before the month was out. On November 7, 1821, a committee of five was named to consider the building of a meeting house and on January 15, 1822, it was voted to go ahead with construction. The spot chosen was across the street from the church they had left, between Mr. Samuel Johnson's house and the school house.

At a meeting of the Christian Society held at the Center School on the fifth of November, 1822, it was "Voted to purchase of Mr. Lewis Billings a piece of land joining the new Meeting house lot of 56 rods as contracted for on 29 Jan. for 25 dollars; for 140 dollars 50 cents the whole containing 2 Acres 2 quarters and 34 rods at 165 dollars to cents."

The precedent for what happened in Sharon was set in the First Parish of Dedham. There also, a violent and bitter dispute took place between the orthodox church majority and the liberal society majority. In all Colonial towns the parish society was responsible for the support of the religious services, while the Church was concerned with the promotion of spiritual life. In 1820, the matter was carried to the Supreme Court which ruled that the society held the property title, regardless of its agreement with church doctrines.

Thus the Sharon Congregationalists moved to their new church across the street, taking with them the communion service. They called as their first pastor Rev. Joseph B. Felt.

The Reverend Mr. Felt had been one of those filling the pulpit during the long period that the church was searching for a pastor. Coming from the Tabernacle Church of Salem, Mr. Felt, in his letter of acceptance, was not overjoyed with the offer of four hundred and fifty dollars salary plus ten cords of wood delivered to his house. He said, "The terms you offer are as favorable as we would expect while in your embarrassed situation. Still, when viewing them in connection with the trials which result not only from the ministry in general, but from your particular state, I must say, did not duty weigh more with me than pecuniary compensation, I should decline conforming to them."

On January 25, 1824, Mr. Felt requested dismissal from the church. The Society appointed a committee fo "inquire of Mr. Felt his principal reason for leaving the Society." Mr. Felt replied, ". . . 1st The uncertain method of raising the salary. 2ndly The supposed inability of the church to fulfill their present contract with me."

After appeals to neighboring churches for aid, a proposal to unite with the Baptists, an offer to share ministerial services with a Stoughton church, none of which were successful, the Reverend Mr. Felt was granted his dismissal on May 7, 1824.

To provide a more viable organization, the Church and Society adopted a new constitution in July 1824, which gave the church members more power in the affairs of the Society, and provided for taxation of the members to support religious services.

On September 20, 1825, the church voted to call Rev. Jonathan Curtis, who had been preaching to them on a weekly basis. Rev. Jonathan Curtis was installed as pastor on October 12, 1825, by an Ecclesiastical Council of neighboring churches called for that purpose.

In June of 1826, fifty-four women of the church formed the Dorcas Society. Their pledge, "We, the undersigned, desirous of doing something in the cause of benevolence and promoting Christ's Kingdom associate ourselves together for this purpose. . . ."

Almost immediately their contributions included money "for the support of the Gospel in this place," the Norfolk County Education Society, and boxes of articles sent to missionaries in the west.

The Reverend Mr. Curtis served the church for nine years, performing the normal ministerial duties. It was necessary on only two occasions to appoint a committee to admonish backsliders who insisted on attending Universalist meetings, and in both cases they promised to repent.

The Revere bell which hangs in the belfry was purchased in 1833 for $170, and the inscription "Revere Boston" on it signifies it was the work of Joseph Warren Revere and the Revere Copper Company. At the annual meeting of the Christian Society in March 1833 it was voted "to pay Joel Hewins Three Dollars to take care of the Meeting House and ring the Bell for the use of said House one year."

In July, 1834, Mr. Curtis asked to be dismissed having received a call from a church in Pittsfield, New Hampshire.

Prayer meetings were held at the interval of public worship until the arrival of Rev. Jacob Cummins from a church in Stratham, New Hampshire. In addition to salary, the society had agreed that under certain conditions the Reverend Mr. Cummins could have a new house. The site selected for the parsonage was opposite the meeting house on a portion of the land left to the church by Nancy Gould, who had died in 1832.

The Sabbath School was organized in July of 1835.

Suddenly, the meeting of February 21, 1837, voted that "it is of the opinion of this meeting that the usefulness of Rev. Jacob Cummins as our minister is greatly diminished."

Whether or not this had to do with the financial situation the church found itself in because of Rev. Jacob Cummins' demands is not known. The Ecclesiastical Council, which was hastily convened from surrounding churches, recommended that "under existing circumstances it is expedient that the pastoral and ministerial relations of Rev. Jacob Cummins with the church and society in Sharon be dissolved after next Lord's Day."

In August of 1837, the church called Mr. Lucius Root Eastman to be their minister. On November 25, 1838, tragedy struck. In the words of the Reverend Mr. Eastman: "The Church and Society met as usual to engage in the morning services. Scarcely had they commenced when there was the cry of fire. The partition had taken fire from the stovepipe and there being many shavings between the floor of the gallery and the plastering beneath, the flames spread so rapidly that all attempts at saving the house were useless. A stormy west wind hastened the work of destruction. At 1/4 past eleven, the spire fell, at once the beautiful edifice was in ashes save a few pieces of charred timber, a few window sashes and blinds and the cushions and trimmings of the house and pulpit. The communion furniture was lost. The bible and two psalm books were saved. Loss $3,000. No blame can be attached to anyone. It was the Lord that did it. It is right. May it be overruled for the good of this Church, Society and Town. . . ."

The Unitarian Church immediately offered their facilities, which were accepted.

Plans were made to rebuild. A contract was signed with Fales and Peck of Milford to construct the Meeting House in the style and design of the "Medway Village House" for $3,550. The original color scheme was white with "Paris Green" blinds. The records state, "Raised the Meeting House June 13, 1839." The society had incorporated and sold stock to obtain the money for construction.

On April 5, 1840, the Men's Club was formed as a "gentlemen's association . . . to aid the American Board of Foreign Missions."

In February, the Reverend Mr. Eastman had requested to be dismissed from the church in accordance with the terms of his contract, and was dismissed September 3, 1840, with "best wishes and fervent prayers."

In May of 1841, the Rev. Lebbeus R. Phillips was called to be pastor. He was ordained on July 29, 1841.

In 1843, it was voted to charge the Town of Sharon thirty dollars per year rent for holding the Town Meetings in the church vestry, the money to be used for the furnishing of the vestry.

The Rev. Lebbeus Phillips had been in continuous ill health for several years. In 1859 he had been given a three months vacation for this reason, but in February 1861 he requested, and was granted, dismissal from the church.

Perley B. Davis of New Ipswich, New Hampshire, was given a call to settle with the church in the gospel ministry, and was ordained by the church in Sharon on January 29, 1862. Reverend Davis requested a six weeks leave of absence to serve with the Christian Commission, who were supplying ministers to work as chaplains in the Army of the Republic during the Civil War.

On March 4, 1865, the church met from twelve to one o'clock to pray for Abraham Lincoln, at the time when he was receiving the oath of office for the second time as President of the United States.

On April 2, 1867, the Reverend Mr. Davis was dismissed from the church at his request. He had received a call from a church in Hyde Park. The call from the Hyde Park church which had been an insistent one, was interpreted by Mr. Davis as being "the finger of Providence" pointing him in this direction. As a going away gift, the Reverend Mr. Davis presented the church with a new communion service.

After a year of hearing candidates, the church called S. Ingersoll Briant of Beverly to be their pastor. He was ordained in the church on April 22, 1868. Mr. Briant resigned his pastorate in November of 1873 because he felt unequal to the task, and was dismissed on March 25, 1874.

Henry C. Weston of North Bennington, Vermont, was called by the church with the society concurring, in June 1874.

About this time, with no official notice of change, the church records begin referring to itself as the Orthodox Congregational Church in Sharon.

During the spring of 1881 the Reverend Mr. Weston was seriously ill, and in June he tendered his resignation because he felt he could no longer carry on. The church first accepted the resignation and then, at the behest of the society, reversed their vote. They elected instead to release Mr. Weston from his pastoral duties, conferring on him the title of Pastor Emeritus effective August 1, 1881. He never recovered from his affliction and died on February 24, 1883.

The church next called Edward G. Smith of North Leominster to be its Pastor, and he was installed on December 7, 1881.

When the Sharon Hydraulic Company first started to deliver water to the townspeople, the church was a major stockholder allowing the use of the land on which the pumping station was located, and paying regularly for upkeep of the equipment and for pipe laid to new subscribers.

In November 1885, the church voted . . . "to sell to the Sharon Water Company all their interest in the flume, pump house, pumps and all other property on the premised conveyed; also the right and title we have in the reservoir situated northwest of the Unitarian common . . . ; also all rights to take water from Beaver Meadow Brook with adjacent springs; all rights to supply the inhabitants of Sharon village with water. . . ." There is no record in either the church or society annals of any money being paid.

The Reverend Mr. Smith was dismissed from his pastorate on July 1, 1887. The church did not call a new minister right away. They left the supply of the pulpit up to the Prudential Committee, who prevailed upon Reverend George F. Stanton of Lowell to fill the post as "Acting Pastor" for one year or less. This temporary arrangement lasted for ten years. The society voted in 1896 to "procure a Pastor who is willing to reside in Sharon."

Church membership had been increasing steadily and more space was needed. Membership of 128 answered the roll call at the annual meeting, either by proxy letter or in person. In 1898 the church building was raised four feet, two courses of the stone foundation taken away, and a seven foot high "first story" built of wood underneath the building. Stairs were added in the vestibule for access to the second story level sanctuary, and the church made "comfortable for winter."

Ushers were used to seat worshipers for the first time in 1902. Prior to this the pew owners had their seats reserved.

In 1904 electric lights were installed in the church and vestry. In this year also, it was voted to tear down the old parsonage because of the high cost of repairs. The old cellar hole was used and a new foundation constructed with stones left over from the raising of the church. A public reception celebrated completion of the new parsonage in July 1905.

On January 14, 1915, the church reorganized by incorporating under the name of "The First Congregational Church of Sharon." Accordingly, the Christian Society at its meeting of April 5, 1915, voted to transfer all property and rights in its name to the church, and to dissolve after necessary papers and acts were completed and passed.

On November 24, 1918, the letter of resignation of Rev. Almon J. Dyer as pastor of the church was read, to take effect on December 22, 1918. He had served the parish for twenty-one years.

In February 1919 the church voted to call Joseph B. Lyman of Orono, Maine, as their pastor. He was installed on June 4, 1919.

The early 1920's were prosperous years for Sharon and for the church. Missionary giving reached an all time high as the church members shared their good fortune with those throughout the world.

In 1921 they petitioned Warren G. Harding, President of the United States, to immediately call a conference of nations to see if an "Association of

Nations" could be formed to overcome the obstacles to the peace of the world still existing.

Mr. Lyman resigned to accept the position of Minister-at-large for Southeastern Massachusetts on March 11, 1928. He was dismissed on May 6, 1928, with resolves engrossed upon the records commending him for his faithful service and for his work in the church and community. In December 1929, Norman B. Cawley accepted the pulpit. He was installed on February 19, 1929.

The depression years hit Sharon hard, and the church also felt the financial pinch. Deficits in the budget, borrowing to pay bills, appeals to the congregation to save fuel and lights, and the reduction of the Pastor's salary are noted.

In spite of this, membership continued to rise. On May 26, 1932, "modern" Dorcas was formed. Originally founded in 1826 as the Dorcas Society, it had changed its name in 1914 to the Women's Union, and in 1915 to the Women's Society. It together with the Harriet D. Lyman League, an organization of the younger church women, voted to disband both organizations and to unite all women of the church into one society, under the original name.

The Rev. Mr. Cawley resigned on October 9, 1938, after ten years as pastor. The church granted him six months leave of absence with the resignation to become effective on June 1, 1939.

On June 28, 1939, the Pastoral Selection Committee recommended the call to the Pastorate of Otto Karl Jonas of Springfield, Massachusetts. He preached his first sermon in the church on September 10, 1939, and was installed officially as Pastor on April 3, 1940.

In November of 1940, a committee studying the need for a Parish House reported that additional facilities were urgently required. An analysis of the town and the make-up of its 3,656 population indicated top priority for an assembly hall, not only for church, but also to fill community needs.

Then came Pearl Harbor and World War II. Otto Jonas was called to active duty as a chaplain in the Army, and ordered to report for duty at Fort Sheridan, Illinois, on July 25, 1942. The church granted him a leave of absence for the duration of the war. In October 1942 Rev. Harry W. Foot was called to be Acting Pastor of the church.

By necessity, construction of the Parish House was postponed. The annual meeting of 1943 saw the unveiling of an honor roll of those from the church now serving in the armed forces, with forty-nine names inscribed to date. It was to number one hundred and twenty-one by October of 1945.

With the war over, Mr. Foot resigned his interim pastorate, and Otto Jonas came home on June 2, 1946. The Parish House again commanded everyone's attention. A meeting was called for January 28, 1948, and the church voted to proceed with construction. Ground-breaking ceremonies were held on May 12, 1948, with Dr. Walter Griffin as Parish House chairman turning the first shovelful of earth. After many problems with escalating costs and unforeseen additions, the Parish House was declared complete at the annual meeting of May 4, 1949. It was dedicated on September 25, 1949.

The enlarged facilities were put to full use. Sharon was enmeshed in the postwar building boom and as the newcomers sought a place to worship, the church was ready.

Then on December 2, 1952, Rev. Otto Jonas resigned effective January 31, 1952. Rev. Harold S. Hannum of St. Johnsbury, Vermont, was called to the pastorate by the special meeting held September 30, 1953. He was installed on January 17, 1954.

By 1957 expansion of facilities were again necessary, and the church voted to undertake another major expansion. The plans called for raising the Parish Hall up six feet in the air and moving it thirty-two feet to the north; building a new first story underneath for classrooms; building a new kitchen and entryway in the space between it and the church. The sanctuary was to be remodeled and completed by the addition of a divided chancel and a new ceiling. The present pipe organ was to be rehabilitated and located within the new chancel area with a new console. During the summer months of 1960, members of the congregation and townspeople watched with interest as the Parish Hall was separated from the church and jacked to its new second floor location. The church was rededicated on September 10, 1961.

In May 1961 the church voted to affiliate itself with the United Church of Christ.

In June 1962, Rev. Harold Hannum resigned to accept the pastorate of Phillips Congregational Church in Watertown, Massachusetts, effective August 31, 1962.

Rev. James G. Pirie of Billerica, Massachusetts, was called to the church on May 19, 1963. Installation as pastor took place on February 23, 1964. Mr. Pirie resigned as minister on March 4, 1973, effective May 1, 1973, to take the position of Director of Elderly Affairs for the city of Marlborough, Massachusetts.

Rev. Richard E. Leidberg of Dayton, Ohio, was called to be pastor on January 6, 1974. Mr. Leidberg had served as Student Minister for the church from 1954 through 1956, while studying at Andover Newton Theological School.

In 1975, the church was notified that it had been selected to be placed on the National Register of Historic Places.

The Morse House, Congregational Church and Library   *Photo by: J. K. Harris*

Our Lady of Sorrows Catholic Church   *Photo by: J. K. Harris*

THE HISTORY OF THE CATHOLIC CHURCH IN SHARON

By Mary Ann Boulet

CHAPTER 27

Before the American Revolution the Catholics in the original colonies had been under the jurisdiction of the Vicar Apostolic of London. In 1784 the American clergy petitioned the Holy See in Rome for the appointment of a superior from their own country — and Father John Carroll was named "perfect apostolic." Five years later, in 1789, he was designated Bishop of Baltimore. The diocese of Baltimore originally included all land east of the Mississippi, from the Ohio River, except Florida, and numbered approximately 25,000 members with about 30 priests. In 1808 four new dioceses were established within these same boundaries. New England, one of the four named dioceses, included 8 churches: two in Boston, one in Salem, one in New Hampshire and four in Maine. Within a short time the number of Catholic immigrants and the leadership of Bishops Cheverus and Fenwick brought about the development of many parishes throughout New England.

Some of the immigrants from Ireland came directly to Sharon and worked on the railroad, in the knife factory, and on farms. In 1846 they requested that a priest be assigned from the Boston Archdiocese to celebrate Mass in Sharon. A parish priest of St. Peter's and Paul's Parish in South Boston was delegated to come to Sharon on Sundays and holy days. These masses apparently were celebrated in private homes since there was no chapel until 1866.

In 1861, when a parish was established in Canton with Father Flatley as pastor, jurisdiction of the Sharon parish was transferred from South Boston to Canton. During this time a chapel was built and named "The Tiny Chapel of Saint Aloysius." The lumber used was wood that remained after the Catholic Church in Canton was completed in 1866. The framing was assembled on the ground in Canton by their Sexton who was also a carpenter and it was then carted to Sharon. The chapel served the needs of the Catholic community for about 25 years. Although it has been remodeled and no longer resembles a chapel, it can be seen at its original location at 176 Pond Street.

In 1872 when Stoughton was established as an independent parish, Sharon became a mission church of the Stoughton parish and was served by Fathers Norris, Kiely and Curtin.

Father Kiely began collecting funds in 1889 from the Catholic families in Sharon in order to build a larger church to accommodate the parish which was growing at an ever-increasing pace. The site chosen for the new church was the

Kempton farm on Cottage Street. The owners were reluctant to have their land used for a Catholic church, so the land was purchased by Mr. and Mrs. William Roche (Mrs. Roche was the former Katherine O'Leary) and a few years later purchased from them by Father Kiely for the Boston Archdiocese. Members of the parish built the foundation which is made of fieldstone. Work was started in 1891 and in 1893 the building was completed and named "Our Lady of Sorrows," a title which refers to the Blessed Mother and the seven sorrows of her life. It continued as a mission church until June 27, 1906, when it was named an independent parish with a resident pastor — Father George A. Costello.

Father Costello remained until 1916 and during that time the rectory was built by his parents and eventually its ownership was transferred to the Boston Archdiocese. One of the rooms in the rectory (now the office) was often used on cold winter mornings as a chapel for weekday masses. A long pew in the office is a reminder of the days of wood and coal burning furnaces that required constant tending. The building which is now used as the Parish Hall was originally used as a barn for the pastor's horses. When he acquired a Stanley Steamer, a small garage was built next to the barn. The area that is now a parking lot on the south side of the church was a beautiful rose garden and the site of May Processions. The church originally had plain glass windows. During Father Costello's stay they were converted to stained glass windows which were donated by some of the parishioners as memorials for their relatives — as indicated on each window. A large stained glass window in the sanctuary was donated by Father Costello in memory of his parents.

First families of the parish included:

Callan	Gibbons	Lynch	Poirier
Cole	Griffin	Maguire	Prue
Conley	Hagan	Markt	Quinn
Daler	Harrington	McDonald	Rau
Daley	Holland	McNair	Reagan
Downey	Hurley	O'Brien	Roche
Gavin	Leary	O'Leary	White

Father John T. O'Brien served as pastor from 1916 to 1925 and Father William F. Lyons served from 1925 to 1926. During these years an extra Sunday mass, in addition to the two regular masses, was added each summer in order to accommodate the people who vacationed in Sharon and the children who came to the summer camps near the lake. Members of the parish assisted in the transportation of the campers to and from church.

Father Michael Madden was pastor in the years 1926 to 1929. In December, 1928, the Esty pipe organ, which had been donated by Mrs. P. J. Hurley, was dedicated. This organ is still being used by the present organist and choir director, M. Eloise Horn. Other women who have served as organists and choir directors include Lillian Griffin, Mary Flood, Margaret Hagan Nugent, Alice Gavin, Suzie Callan, and Rose Hand.

In January, 1929, extensive repair work was begun on the church. Four large pillars were placed along each side of the church to support the roof and the original steeple was removed. An impressive life-size crucifix, which had formerly been located in a shrine at the rear of the church, was hung high above the sanctuary and it remains there today. The cost of these renovations was $15,163.

As Sharon's population increased, the Catholic parish continued to add new parishioners. The number of Sunday masses gradually increased to five and, beginning in 1936, an assistant priest was assigned to the parish.

The following men were pastors between 1929 and 1950:

Rev. James A. Donnelly	1929 - 1931
Rev. Jeremiah J. Herlihy	1931 - 1942
Rev. Patrick J. Dawson	1942 - 1945
Rev. Lyman F. Merrill	1945 - 1949
Rev. Cornelius P. Murray	1949 - 1950

Groups that provided social, religious and educational activities during these years included: the Holy Name Society (for the men of the parish); the Women's Club; the Women's Sodality; the Confraternity of Christian Doctrine (for the religious education of the children); Youth Council; Boy Scouts and Cub Scouts.

An elaborate ceremony was planned in 1956 to commemorate the fiftieth anniversary of the parish. Father Richard McShane, a greatly loved priest who was popular with non-Catholic as well as Catholic Sharonites, was pastor at this time. At a solemn Pontifical Mass on June 30, 1956, the celebrant and preacher was Archbishop Richard J. Cushing (who later became Cardinal Cushing).

Father Daniel O'Connell became pastor in 1962. Assisting him at this time was Father John O'Donnell, a newly ordained priest. Father O'Donnell played an instrumental role in conveying the teachings of Vatican II to the members of the parish. Vatican II called for a number of significant changes in the style of Catholic worship — such as the use of English rather than Latin in all parts of the Mass, the priest facing the people and inviting their participation in the Sacrifice of the Mass, congregational singing, and the elimination of gestures and actions which had lost their sacramental usefulness through the centuries. Unfortunately some Catholics, in Sharon and throughout the world, were upset and confused by these and future changes.

Vatican II also called for greater involvement of all Catholics in the life of their Church. This led to the establishment of Parish Councils in the Boston Archdiocese. Our Lady of Sorrows was among the first parishes in the area to form a Council. The entire parish was invited to attend the first meetings — which began in February 1969. After a few meetings a Steering Committee was formed of volunteers to study the needs of the parish and the ways that the Parish Council could meet these needs. Following a year of study and planning, the first elections were held in March 1970.

Father Richard Butler replaced Father O'Donnell in 1970. He provided continuing support for Father O'Connell and the Parish Council.

The objectives of the Parish Assembly and Council, as stated in their Constitution, are "primarily to increase our sensitivity to the voice of our Creator, as manifested in these times and our circumstances, so that we may lead more meaningful and satisfactory lives, individually and as a community, by experiencing more fully, love of God and of our neighbor." The Parish Council functions as the Executive Board for the Assembly. The Assembly includes "all persons, lay or clerical, who reside in the Parish, or serve the Parish or attend Parish functions and support the Parish." The Council consists of the Pastor, six Representatives-at-large, and a representative of each of the six Commissions.

The function of the Spiritual Development Commission is to maintain and improve the spiritual life of parishioners.

The Religious Education Commission has the responsibility of planning and implementing religious education programs for the children and adults of the parish.

The Parish Activities Commission plans and carries out social events and has reinstated the annual Christmas Bazaar.

The Youth Commission, which may include teenagers and/or adults, plans activities for the youth of the parish and has recently formed a CYO.

The Christian Service Commission serves those who are in need of assistance due to physical, emotional, sociological, or economic concerns.

The Administration Commission assists the pastor in carrying out the financial, maintenance, and communication responsibilities of the parish.

Changes which have come about in the last decade include the Sanctuary renovation (the decision to remove the old altar and the statues caused some displeasure since these were of sentimental value to a number of parishioners), the introduction of lay lectors (male and female), and of Extraordinary Ministers of Communion (also male and female).

There are five masses each weekend. The 5 o'clock Mass on Saturday afternoon is a Folk Mass with music provided by a group of teenagers who sing, with guitar accompaniment, new as well as traditional hymns. The 7:30 A.M. Mass on Sunday is the only mass without music. The 9:30 Mass has become a Family Mass which is planned to appeal to families with young children. The girls' choir sings at this mass. The 10:45 Mass has a boys' choir. At the Noon Mass music is led by an adult choir, and, once a month, there is a baptismal service during the mass.

In the reception of sacraments, a great effort is made to educate the parents as well as the children, so that the sacraments become an important part of the family's life rather than a once-in-a-lifetime ritual with very little meaning.

One project that is now awaiting approval by the Archdiocese is the building of a new Parish Hall. Parishioners have contributed to a fund for this building which will be located on the former Holbrook property on the north side of the church.

Architect's Plan of Proposed Parish Hall at Our Lady of Sorrows   *Plan by: J. A. Newell*

The number of parishioners has grown from 350 in 1906 to 1,628 in 1975. With this increase in membership it is interesting to note that the church has returned to being a one-priest parish — mainly because of a shortage of priests. However, with the involvement of parishioners in all phases of parish life, the burden of the pastor is lightened and shared by the Catholic community. The present pastor, Father J. Richard Quinn, came to Sharon in the summer of 1975. He is assisted on weekends by Father John T. Burke, in residence, and Father Timothy O'Leary, a member of the faculty at St. John's Seminary.

Bibliography

Birkhaeuser, J. A. *History of the Church.* Frederick Pustet and Co., 1888.

Canton Historical Society, Canton, Mass. Minutes of a Fast Day Walk.

Lord, Robert H., John E. Sexton, and Edward T. Harrington. *History of the Archdiocese of Boston, 1604 - 1943*, Vol. III. Boston: Pilot Publishing Co.

McShane, Richard S. Golden Anniversary Program. Sharon, Mass.: Our Lady of Sorrows Parish, 1956.

Parishioners of Our Lady of Sorrows, 1893- 1976.

Records of Our Lady of Sorrows Church, June 15, 1925 to August 31, 1930. Weekly announcements.

Sullivan, James S. *The Catholic Church of New England.*

Williams, John Joseph. *Episcopal Register, 1889 - 1907.* Archdiocese of Boston.

St. John's Episcopal Church   Photo by: J. K. Harris

SAINT JOHN'S EPISCOPAL CHURCH

By Helen D. Lawrence

CHAPTER 28

At the close of the nineteenth century, Sharon was emerging from a farming community and taking on the aspect of a residential town. A permanent population of a thousand was augmented by a growing colony of city people during the summer months. It was the summer of 1892 when George hewins, a native of Sharon living in Boston, and William W. Doherty, both Episcopalians, felt the need of an Episcopal Church.

During the following year contact was made with the Diocese and in August 1893 at 3:30 P.M. the first Episcopal service was held in the Unitarian Church. The service was conducted by Rev. Charles J. Ketchum, on that and succeeding Sunday afternoons during the summer months.

In 1894 regular services were established and conducted by Rev. George Walker from Canton and the Reverend Mr. Jones from Walpole. These services were held regularly throughout the year, first at the home of Mrs. Mabel Copeland, 40 Pleasant Street, and later over Pettee's store in Post Office Square.

In 1899, due to the indefatigable work of Mrs. Copeland (in whose memory the baptismal font was given), $414.15 was raised toward a church. Money was borrowed from the Diocese and 19,848 square feet of land on High Street purchased. Ralph Adams Cram, a distinguished Boston architect, was hired, and in 1902 the first small part of St. John's Church was built of native fieldstone at a cost of $3,000. It was deeded to the Trustees of Donations and so recorded in Dedham October 1, 1905.

The first regular minister was Rev. George Walker. Mr. Walker travelled with horse and buggy serving Foxboro, Canton, and Stoughton as well as Sharon. Sharon's share of the expense was $4.00 a week. In 1911 Mr. Walker was unable to carry the burden, and Rev. Frank Rathbone conducted the services until 1915. .

The church was gaining in membership now and it was felt that one who could give more of his time to Sharon was needed. Rev. Willard Roots, who lived in Mansfield and was rector of the Episcopal Church there, shared his duties with Sharon until 1921, when ill health necessitated his retirement. He was followed by the Reverend Mr. Partridge, two theological students John Lyte and Robert McAvoy, and Professor John Scammel of Boston University.

During this time the Sacrament was administered once a month by Rev. John Love from Joy Street, Boston.

The years 1940-42 were shared with Canton by Rev. John Dallinger and Rev. Frederick Hicks, respectively.

In 1940 the membership had increased and we were able to pay the diocesan debt. October 6 the building was consecrated by the Rt. Rev. Raymond A. Heron, Suffragan Bishop of the Diocese of Massachusetts.

Then in 1942 the Mission had grown enough and had maintained sufficient strength to call its first full-time, resident clergyman. Rev. George W. R. McCray came to Sharon at that time and remained for nine years. In 1948, six years after Mr. McCray's arrival in Sharon, St. John's Mission accomplished what it had set out to do in 1892. It became a self-supporting Parish, i.e., it supported its building and its clergy. The church was no longer a Mission, but a Parish — its clergyman was no longer a Vicar, but a Rector.

A contributing factor in the fulfillment of the church's status in the Diocese was the acquisition of a rectory at 51 Summit Avenue. This was a bequest from Miss Amelia Schwartz who had been a member of St. John's.

Much had been accomplished in this period. The narthex was added; the Sacristy was enlarged; a small kitchen and toilet facilities added to an enlarged undercroft. The beautiful carved altar, pulpit, lectern, dossal, altar rail, pews and frontals, and stained-glass windows were contributed as memorial gifts (all listed in Memory Book).

In 1955 facilities were expanded including an addition to the undercroft, to accommodate the growing Sunday School, and a new kitchen.

In 1959 the house at 19 High Street was purchased for additional space and for Church School classes.

The Reverend Mr. McCray left in 1951 and was succeeded by Rev. David McA. Pyle of Concord, New Hampshire until 1957. Rev. John W. Schaefer from the Church of the Redeemer in Brookline was our next Rector until 1965. He went to New York and Rev. Dwight Fortune from Beverly served until 1974. At the present time, 1976, the Rector is Rev. Donald A. Milligan.

A word should be added about the women of the church from Mrs. Copeland's day to this, for their never failing effort and hard work has helped the church over many a financial hump.

There have been many changes since 1892. Many staunch supporters are no longer with us but many new ones help to fill their places.

1950 View of St. John's Altar

Early View of St. John's

First Church of Christ, Scientist   *Photo by: J. K. Harris*

264

FIRST CHURCH OF CHRIST, SCIENTIST

By Phyllis Sheehan and Nancy Cushman

CHAPTER 29

The Christian Science Church in Sharon began with ten students who had been holding informal "Sunday Afternoon Gatherings" for those interested in the study of the Christian Science Lesson Sermons. On September 18, 1905 they met to organize the Christian Science Society in Sharon which, like all of their churches and societies, was "designed to commemorate the word and works of our Master, which should reinstate primitive Christianity and its lost element of healing" — as stated in their Church Manual. On October 1, 1905 they began holding Sunday services in the Lower Town Hall.

About a year later they also began holding Wednesday Evening Meetings which, in addition to brief readings from the Bible and the Christian Science textbook, included time for members of the congregation to spontaneously tell of their healings brought about through reliance on God as taught in Christian Science.

Within a year after that, they had also established the Sunday School for students up to the age of twenty, which teaches the Scriptures and how they can be applied to daily life.

The Lower Town Hall continued to be their church home for four years until 1909 when they rented the Unitarian Church Sunday mornings and Wednesday evenings. Unitarian services were held in the afternoon.

They continued there until 1918 when "owing to scarcity of fuel for heating purposes during World War I the Baptist Church and the Christian Science Society associated with the Congregational Church in holding all their services in the Congregational Church Edifice."

After the war ended, services were again held in the Unitarian Church. Later when the Unitarian Church was damaged by fire they were again kindly allowed to use the Congregational Church. Except for this brief period they continued to use the Unitarian Church until their own church was built in the late 1920's.

In January 1927 the status of the organization was changed from a Society to a Church and the name was changed to First Church of Christ, Scientist, Sharon. In November of that same year the cornerstone was laid for the present church edifice on the corner of Highland and Main Streets.

In photos showing the construction of the church may be seen a sign pointing up Highland Street which reads, "Christian Science Reading Room." This room had been established in 1926 in a room rented in the home of one of the members at 9 Highland Street. The purpose of Christian Science Reading Rooms is to provide a quiet place open to the public where all who wish may study and borrow or purchase the Bible and all authorized Christian Science literature.

Later a room was maintained for this purpose in the church edifice until in the 1960's one was established in Sharon Square where it would be more accessible to the general public. The Christian Science Reading Room in Sharon Square still continues to welcome students and visitors today.

It is the custom of all Christian Science Churches to have their buildings completely free of debt before being dedicated. The Christian Scientists in Sharon accomplished this in about two years after the first services were held in the new edifice on July 1, 1928. The church building was then dedicated on October 19, 1930.

From the beginning the church services have been conducted by two readers elected every three years by the church members in accordance with the Church Manual which requires that each branch church or society be strictly democratic in its government. The Sunday Lesson Sermons read in all Christian Science churches throughout the world are prepared by The Mother Church, The First Church of Christ, Scientist, Boston. They are comprised of references from the King James version of the Bible and the correlative passages from the Christian Science textbook, *Science and Health with Key to the Scriptures* by Mary Baker Eddy, the discoverer and founder of Christian Science. The Bible and the Christian Science textbook are their only preachers.

Everyone is cordially welcome to attend all Christian Science Sunday services and Wednesday evening meetings, as well as the Reading Room which is open daily.

Interior of First Church of Christ, Scientist   *Photo by William Grant*

Christian Science Reading Room in Post Office Square   *Photo by William Grant*

Temple Israel, 1976   *Photo by: Kennan*

JEWISH COMMUNITY CENTER OF SHARON TEMPLE ISRAEL

By Rabbi Shamai Kanter and Marilyn F. Kogos

CHAPTER 30

In previous publications it has been stated that the congregation was organized in 1936, but in recent research of the Jewish Community in Sharon, it was discovered to have begun in the early 20's. At that time a small group of Jewish families (some summer residents, others year-round) worshipped at the small Temple on Harding Street — the only place for worship at the time. Those families who lived "up-town" walked (or drove) down to Harding Street until the "up-town" group started meeting at the small white building in the rear of the Rosenstein Mansion House on Pond Street. These were the humble beginnings of the now Temple Israel.

The ladies of this small group of Jewish families would gather at the Shapiro home on South Main Street to socialize and organize in 1925 the Sharon Hebrew Ladies Aid, Inc., which is now the Sisterhood of Temple Israel. Recently the Sisterhood now numbering 500 Jewish women met and celebrated their 50th anniversary. The goals and ideals of this pioneer group were to do worthwhile charitable work and to help out those who were less fortunate with financial aid. Their first project was taking a child from Dorchester and moving him to Sharon to help cure his asthma. From this charitable act they moved on to others, driving to Stoughton and Foxboro in the one car that was available.

It was back in 1936 that the first concerted effort was made to establish a Temple, or as it was known then, a "Jewish Community Center of Sharon." There were 32 members that first year, and it was the very next year that the present land was purchased.

There was not yet any building. Meetings of the members were held in any home which had enough chairs! Saturday and High Holy Day services were soon held in the small building in the rear of the Mansion House, the old hotel for vacationers which was only recently razed.

The wise founders realized that a religious education is the cornerstone of a religion, and one of the first steps was the obtaining of a teacher of Jewish History and Hebrew. Classes were held for the children wherever there was space available: in the Legion room of the old Town Hall, in rented space above the stores at Post Office Square, in a classroom of the original High School.

In 1949, the first structure of Temple Israel was established. What is now the present Sanctuary and small meeting room were combined with an office for the Rabbi to make up this first facility. A few short years later, the Hebrew School was built, and in 1962, the structures were joined and expanded to create the present building.

Needless to say, this did not "just happen." The establishment and growth of any religious center comes about as a result of the dedication and effort of those who recognize the need for worship and study, and so it was here in Sharon.

Temple Israel today is a handsome physical structure which fronts on Pond Street. Its facilities include a Sanctuary, for worship, a large and impressive auditorium for religious and social functions, two additional meeting areas for adult and youth programs, and other meaningful facilities. It serves over 500 Jewish families of the area. It is one of the largest Temples of Conservative Judaism in the region.

The Temple has a very active Youth Program, a most interesting and intensive Adult Education Program, and provides a "home for the spiritual, educational and social needs of its Community."

And to bridge the present and the past, it is equally fitting to quote the words of one of the founding fathers of the Temple who was asked for the background information: "I remember the past whenever I enter our Sanctuary, for it was here that we saw the future."

Founders, 1937

President	Frank Einis
Vice-president	Morris Jacobson
Treasurer	Max Berger
Clerk	Joseph Charnas
Financial secretary	Maurice Friedman

Members

Phillip Aranson	Harry Gross	Sidney Paul
Morris Bell, Jr.	Paul Kerstein	Benjamin Rosenstein
Abraham Berenson	Hyman Kouris	Barney Shapiro
Jacob Bock	Hyman Leventhal	Carl Singer
Max Carvin	Myer Meltzer	Harry Stern
Louis Dubinsky	Morris Morrison	Isadore Ulman
Hyman Fishman	Charles Paul	Morris Ulman
Gustov Goldberg	Henry Paul	Morris Winer
William Gordon	Robert Paul	Louis Young

The Sharon Hebrew Ladies Aid, Organized 1925, Incorporated 1937
Members

Rae Bock	Minnie Meltzer
Rose Shapiro	Sarah Gordon
Rose Fishman	Rachel Shapiro
Eva Stern	Clara Young
Jennie Miller	

An Early View of Temple Israel

Rosenstein's Mansion House used as a Youth Center and Hebrew School   *Photo by: Kennan*

Congregation Adath Sharon   *Photo by: J. K. Harris*

CONGREGATION ADATH SHARON

By Samuel N. Cedar

CHAPTER 31

In the summer of 1932, a small group of Jewish people formed the nucleus from which the Congregation Adath Sharon became a reality. After many years of worship in private homes, they started the Congregation and decided to build a synagogue.

The land on Harding Street was donated by Mr. and Mrs. I. M. Kaplan. Sisterhood Adath Sharon was formed to assist the Congregation in any way it could.

On Sunday, August 2, 1942, the formal dedication of the Temple, the first Jewish house of worship in Sharon, took place with many town and other dignitaries present. A few years later the burning of the mortgage on the Temple was held.

The Temple itself is a small colonial building, with a capacity of about 175. The majority of the members were also affiliated with other Temples in their winter home towns, but the love they have felt for this small Temple still persists. Rabbi Isaac Hochman became the first Rabbi. Rabbi Sidney Pataschnick served from 1972 until Rabbi Arnold M. Fine came in 1976.

In the beginning, the Temple was used only during the summer months because of the majority of its members were here at that time. But gradually members stayed later in the year and services for the High Holidays were being observed here also.

A Hebrew School has now been added, and many new and young worshippers have also joined. The Temple is open for services all year. Recently a very successful nursery school has been operating weekly on the premises. Mrs. Roz Rosenthal has charge of it.

The president was Jack Glassman until he was succeeded in 1976 by Joel Lehrer.

Temple Sinai   *Photo by: J. K. Harris*

First President of Temple Sinai   Joseph Sacks
First President of the Sisterhood   Mrs. Alice Michaels
First President of the Brotherhood   Theodore H. Shamitz

TEMPLE SINAI

By Eleanor Shamitz

CHAPTER 32

During the year of 1956, several Jewish parents met and founded The Sharon School of Jewish Education. This small but vigorous group successfully conducted this institution for two years. About 40 children attended grades two through five on Sunday mornings. Four local teachers, under the supervision of some of the parents, comprised the teaching staff. The facilities of Temple Adath Sharon were made available to the school by the trustees of the Temple.

It soon became evident that a school for children only had limitations in that there was not a companion facility for the adults with the same orientation. During this same period, most of the people associated with The Sharon School of Jewish Education, and others, had been discussing the possibility of founding a Reform congregation in Sharon.

The outcome of these discussions led to the chartering of a new Reform congregation known as Temple Sinai of Sharon on February 12, 1958. The first president of Temple Sinai was Dr. Joseph M. Sacks. The Sharon School of Jewish Education then voted to dissolve and become part of Temple Sinai.

The new congregation initially had about 60 families which soon grew to 100 families. Religious services were conducted at the Bell House as were activities of the school. The school grew to encompass the first through the tenth grade, and expanded its curriculum to include instruction in Modern and Biblical Hebrew. During the spring and autumn of 1958 and the winter and spring of 1959, services were conducted by visiting Rabbis made available by the New England Region of The Union of American Hebrew Congregations.

The year 1959 also saw the start of a building fund campaign. The abilities and energies of the young congregation were thoroughly employed from the granting of the charter on February 12, 1958 until the new home of the congregation on Ames Street was dedicated on May 27, 1961, a span of but 40 months.

Temple Sinai now numbers close to 300 families.

In Bicentennial year 1976, Temple Sinai elected its first woman president, Mrs. Eleanor Shamitz, who was a founding member. The same year 17 women participated in a Bat Mitzvah after a year of study with Rabbi Daniel L. Kaplan. On September 18, 1976, the Temple celebrated its 18th year at a gala occasion. This constituted a special time in Jewish life as the number 18 stands for "Life" in the Hebrew language.

Evangelical Baptist Church   *Photo by: J. K. Harris*

THE EVANGELICAL BAPTIST CHURCH

By Rev. Robert Butler

CHAPTER 33

The Evangelical Baptist Church was begun on April 15, 1956, with services held in a private home. The group was small, but there was an uncommon spirit of fellowship and unity of purpose. From the beginning this body of Christians sought to involve themselves in the work of evangelism and Christian education through a weekly Sunday School, Vacation Bible School, and boys' and girls' clubs.

Five months later, on September 16, 1956, services were moved to the old frame building on Main Street that was Sharon's Town Hall. The Church is very grateful to the town administrators for making this facility available. Services were held there for four years. On October 28, 1956, the Evangelical Baptist Church was incorporated under the laws of the Commonwealth of Massachusetts.

Several months later, April 15, 1957, the first full-time pastor was called, Rev. C. Alan Olsson. Mr. Olsson served the Church for five and one-half years. Under his guidance, the Church became affiliated with the Baptist General Conference, a nationwide fellowship of over 600 Baptist churches. It was also during this period that the Church's building program was begun. A choice parcel of land on the corner of South Main Street and Ames Street was purchased in December of 1958. Construction was begun immediately on a large split-level parsonage, and the dedication of that building took place April 19, 1959.

In the fall of 1962, Pastor Olsson was called elsewhere, and the Church's second pastor replaced him, Rev. George A. Van Alstine. Pastor Van Alstine began his ministry on February 3, 1963 and remained as the Church's spiritual leader until June 18, 1972.

Late in 1965 there arose among the people a strong desire to complete the church building. Work progressed rapidly under the guidance of contractor Rufus R. Purdy, a member of the church. The building was dedicated on June 5, 1966.

On June 1, 1973, the Church extended a call to their pastorate to Rev. Robert Butler. He remains in that position at the present. Mr. Jonathan Swedberg is the youth pastor.

YOUNG ISRAEL OF SHARON

By Sidney Nicoll

CHAPTER 34

The Orthodox branch of Judaism is represented in Sharon by the Young Israel of Sharon. Only a little over four years old, it is also the newest and smallest congregation in Sharon.

Located at 12 Oakland Road, just a few steps from South Main Street, the synagogue's building is a two-family house with the congregation occupying the first floor, and a tenant the apartment on the floor above. The location near the center of town is necessary, as is the type of building. The location is important as Orthodox Jews do not ride on the Sabbath or holidays, and a location within walking distance from the various sections of Sharon is necessary. Because of the small size of the congregation (16 members), it would not be possible for the congregation to own its own building unless it had an income property to help carry the costs.

Despite its modest size and accommodations, the congregation has taken giant strides in its short history. The original founding members first met in members' homes when the group was formed as the Sharon Orthodox Minyon early in 1972.

The first major impetus was given when the group was provided both the facilities of Temple Israel and the participation of its members in the services of the new congregation. This was vital as there must be ten men present in order for Jewish services to be held, and there were only a few members at that time.

During 1973 and early 1974, the next impetus came with new members moving into Sharon and joining the congregation. The added membership made independence possible.

In October 1973, the congregation moved to its present location as a tenant, with an option to purchase. This option was exercised in October of 1974 when adequate financing was obtained.

Another milestone was reached in the summer of 1974 when the congregation was formally admitted as a member of the National Council of Young Israel and officially known as the Young Israel of Sharon, Inc.

Utilizing items such as pews, prayerbooks, Torahs, and various furnishings from congregations in the greater Boston area, as well as gifts from individual donors, the congregation is established and growing each year.

Despite its short existence, it has already overcome a major disaster. In January 1976, a fire broke out in the apartment of the tenant above the synagogue causing major damage to both the apartment and the synagogue. However, the congregation continued to hold services for over three months at the residence of its president, Sidney Nicoll, since his home is centrally located. Following the completion of the repairs, the congregation moved back into its newly redecorated sanctuary for Passover. The Young Israel of Sharon plans to be a part of the religious life of Sharon for a long time to come.

Young Israel of Sharon   *Photo by Kennan*

Sharon Town Offices   *Photo by: J. K. Harris*

SHARON TOWN GOVERNMENT

By Wilfred H. Howe

CHAPTER 35

INTRODUCTION

The history of Town Government in Sharon portrays successful Democracy in Action. Sharon has enjoyed honest and effective local government well served by many officers, employees, and dedicated citizens.

It is obviously beyond the scope of this discussion to cover past and present detail. The Sharon Public Library has a considerable collection of material on Town History, from the earliest days to the present. Annual Town Reports and other documents are on file at the Library and the Town Hall. There is an excellent 52-page *Town Government Handbook* compiled by the League of Women Voters.

In the following pages, an attempt is made to present a broad overview, indicating how local government was established and how it has grown and has been modified to cope with the problems and the increasing complexity as the Town developed from a tiny settlement, through the stages of a small rural community, then a period with active small industry, to its present status as a very up-to-date and modern suburban "bedroom" town.

"Open town meeting" is a time honored feature of local government in many Massachusetts towns, including Sharon. Every registered voter is entitled to attend, to stand up and be heard, and to vote on every item on the agenda of the meeting. Town meeting vote is required on every town expenditure, on all town by-laws, and on many other town functions. The open town meeting is frequently cited as an outstanding example of successful "pure" democracy.

In outward form, the open town meeting is little changed since the early days. In this section on local government, there is considerable emphasis on tracing the development of this unique form of democratic government to meet the needs of the town as the town has grown and the character of the population has changed.

BACKGROUND

The Puritans who settled Boston came to the New World motivated to worship in accordance with their own religious beliefs. However, this did not mean freedom of religion as this is now understood. The Puritans set up their own "established" church with church and government closely linked. There was little tolerance for any form of dissension. Every inhabitant belonged within one or another church parish; all the land was a part of some parish, and a corresponding township. This contrasts with the practice in many other states, where land area was divided into counties, and, as settlements developed, the settled areas were incorporated as townships, leaving considerable "county" areas not in any township. Services such as schools in these areas are the responsibility of the county. In Massachusetts, counties do not have these responsibilities, a significant factor in town-county relationships.

Town and parish were almost one and the same. Church membership was a prerequisite for voting and office holding. There were property-income requirements. Church attendance was mandatory, with fines for non-attendance. The expenses of the church, including the salary of the minister, were paid by the Town. The minister was in charge of the schooling, serving as both administrator and teacher. He was generally the best educated man in the community, and was much respected.

There was a large degree of "home rule" in each town, in both religious and temporal matters. This was an inevitable consequence of the difficulties of travel and the lack of communications. However, it was also a matter of policy as well as expedience, and was definitely part and parcel of the colonial government in this area.

There was of course a Royal Governor for the Colony, and trade and commerce outside the colony were closely regulated for the benefit of the mother country, but in most matters affecting day-to-day living, control was almost completely in the hands of the colonists and their local government. While the "General Court," subject to limitations from the Royal Government had full authority respecting the towns, this control was sparingly exercised with "home rule" and self reliance predominant in the towns and corresponding parishes, especially in outlying areas.

EARLY DEVELOPMENTS — PRIOR TO 1765

Sharon received its charter as a separate township in 1765. However, settlement began much earlier, with a couple dozen families in the area as early as 1660. A large area south and east of Boston, extending to the border of the Plymouth colony, was a grant to the Dorchester Proprietors. To provide for an expanding population, the Proprietors opened a considerable area as the "new grant" — the "second precinct" of Dorchester. An area including what are now Stoughton, Canton, Sharon and Foxboro was set off and incorporated as the Town of Stoughton in 1726.

Settlements developed along the roads, such as they were. There were two through roads in what is now Sharon. The Bay Road, now the eastern boundary of Sharon, was a direct route to Taunton, and thence by water to Narragansett Bay and beyond. The Post Road meandered from Boston through what are now Dedham, Norwood, Walpole, Sharon and Foxboro on to Providence. Some sections of the Post Road in Sharon are still in use — most is abandoned and overgrown. Billings Tavern, née Wainman's Ordinary, was on the Post Road at what is now South Main Street, northeast of the cranberry bog at the Foxboro town line.

The original settlement of what is now Sharon centered around the Billings Tavern. Ebenezer Billings, the proprietor, was a strong and effective leader in this tiny community. It is reported that he established honest, kindly relationships with the local Indians. While there was little that would be regarded as local self-government in the area, the friendly relationships with King Philip, the Indian leader, spared the community from devastation in 1675 and 1676 during "King Philip's War."

The center of what was originally incorporated as Stoughton developed around Cobb's Tavern, located where Sharon, Canton and Stoughton now adjoin. This was the location of the Church of the Stoughton parish. Attendance at this church by the people in the community around Billings Tavern was difficult. The trip over the full length of what is now North and South Main Street, the all day church service, with an hour or so of time out for a noon meal, and the trip back in late afternoon was just too much. In 1739, the residents of what is now Sharon petitioned the General Court to be set off as a separate parish and precinct. Stoughton opposed, and the petition was denied that year, but was allowed when the petition was again submitted the next year. The first meeting of the "second precinct" of the Town of Stoughton was held on July 18th, 1740. A moderator, clerk and assessors were elected. A church for the precinct was organized with a membership of 24. At a precinct meeting in August, 100 pounds was appropriated "for preaching." Initially, services were conducted in Billings Tavern. A young man, Philip Curtis, preached to the community on June 7th in 1741, and was "called" to the ministry of the second parish. After some negotiation, he agreed to come at a salary of 150 pounds a year "plus firewood." He commenced his ministry on September 30th, was ordained on January 13th of the following year, and served the town for 55 years. He was an outstanding individual. As minister, he was in charge of the schools, and served as administrator and teacher.

With a separate parish and a new minister, a "meeting house" was next. During the early 1700's, the town had grown along what are now North and South Main Streets, and between what is now the center, and Lake Massapoag. The people from the Billings Tavern area favored locating the Church in that area. However, the majority of the populace preferred a location near the center of the parish. The site finally chosen was at the present center, where the Unitarian-Universalist Church now stands. Building was started in 1743, and completed the following year. By 1747, there were 36 new members, in addition to the original 24.

During this period, the second parish shared in the local government as a part of the Town of Stoughton. It was responsible for its church, school, and poor, and for the roads within its boundaries. There was a single representative to the General Court from the entire Town. Town meetings for the town as a whole were held at the center near Cobb's Corner. Partly because of the inconvenience of attending the meetings at Cobb's Corner, and for other reasons, there was considerable pressure to become a separate township, and in 1765, the community received a charter from the General Court, becoming the Town of Stoughtonham. In 1775, an enabling act by the General Court gave the Town its own representative. Finally, in 1783, the name of the Town was changed to Sharon. The Town initially petitioned to take the name of Washington, but when it was discovered there was already a Town of Washington in the Berkshires, the Biblical name of Sharon (Isaiah 35:2 and 65:10) was selected.

EARLY DAYS OF THE TOWN OF SHARON — 1765 to 1835

The first Town Meeting of the Town of Stoughtonham was held July 8, 1765. Elected were a moderator, three selectmen who were also the asessors and the overseers of the poor, a clerk, a treasurer and a constable. In addition there were 10 surveyors, a fence viewer, a warden, a tythingman, a measurer of leather sealer, 2 field drivers, a deer reave and 6 hog reaves. We still have fence viewers, field drivers and a measurer of leather, but their duties are nominal. Notable by its absence is any school official – schools were the responsibility of the minister. The selectmen were responsible for the roads in addition to their other duties.

The Town meeting was of course basic. Meetings were frequent. In this early and simple society, with a small and stable population, Town Meeting was very effective. The franchise was limited to church membership, with also property-income qualifications. Those who were eligible to vote were responsible men, with a clear understanding of town problems.

Records show that money was the major problem. Town Meetings discussed money for the minister, for schools, for the surveys of Town boundaries, for preservation of fishing rights, and for the poor. The town was frequently in arrears on the salary for the minister and for the teachers. Many of the citizens "worked out" their taxes on the roads. Money problems were exacerbated by wild currency inflation, starting with the Revolutionary War and continuing until years later to complete devaluation of paper money.

From the beginning, there was predominant revolutionary enthusiasm. Spirits ran high in the early days of the Revolutionary War, but was difficult to maintain as the war dragged on, with hardships and defeats. Early in 1775, Town Meeting voted to raise, train and equip a group of "minute men," to serve under the direction of the Massachusetts Committee of Correspondence. Twenty-eight men and 2 officers were enlisted. The Town paid for training and equipment. Later 25 men were hired for the "U.S. Army," with a bounty paid by the Town of 17 pounds for three years' service, later increased to 13 pounds, 6 shillings per year.

Times were hard. There was no effective central government during and for some time after the war. The strong "home rule" tradition stood the Town in good stead. There was much hardship — paper money was becoming worthless, and "hard" money was very scarce. But in those early days, hardship was accepted; the homogeneous, pioneer stock was accustomed to "make do"; the people and their Town managed to cope with problems as they came along.

The population of Sharon stayed at about 1000 from 1765 to 1835. What is now Foxboro was originally a part of Stoughton and became a part of Stoughtonham when this became a separate Town in 1765. In 1778, Foxboro was set off and itself became an independent Town. A number of other changes in the boundaries between Sharon and surrounding towns since that time have produced "artificial" changes in stated population, not the result of births and deaths, nor of people moving in or out.

Church-State and corresponding Town-Parish controversy in the early 1800's added problems. Philip Curtis, a pillar of strength and unity, resigned in 1797 and passed on a year later. He was succeeded by Jonathan Whitaker, an able, well-educated, even brilliant man. He proved to be a divisive force in the community at a critical time, and was finally dismissed in 1816. Meanwhile the Christian Society, which later became the First Congregational Church in Sharon, had left the fold. The Baptist congregation was active, and by 1835, there were three churches, including Baptist, in the center, as well as three stores and a one-room school. In 1822, the General Court formally dissolved the bonds between the towns and the church parishes. Schools were taken over by the Town. In our increasingly ecumenical culture, it is difficult to comprehend the importance, the distress and bitterness caused by this religious controversy.

The separation of Church and State was the principal change in town government during this period. Membership in the established church or any other religious body was no longer a requirement for voting and holding office, with a considerable broadening in the franchise. However, the character of the Town and its government remained about the same. Sharon was very much a small town, with a stable, rural population, and a strong home rule. It was still a day's journey from Boston. The Town Meeting was a strong working operation. Meetings were frequent, being called whenever a major problem affecting the Town occurred. The general store at the center was a political as well as a social center. The voters had a full understanding of how the government really worked, and knew personally the men involved. With the broadening of the franchise, there was close approach to a real, working "pure democracy".

GROWTH IN SHARON — 1835 to 1900

Population of Sharon doubled from 1000 in 1835 to 2000 in 1900. The Boston and Providence Railroad started operation in 1835, bringing Sharon much closer to Boston and Providence, and a little later, to New York and the whole outside world. With goods transport no longer limited to ox carts over miserable roads, small industry flourished. Water power was developed, with dams and ponds on the streams. The coming of industry brought other changes as well as the increase of the population. Mill workers, many of whom were brought in from outside the town, tended to be different from Sharon's rural population.

Town government adapted to the needs and wants of this different and larger population. The form of government remained about the same with additions to cope with the growing functions of Town Government. There were Water Commissioners and a water department for the public water system. There were Trustees of the Public Library. A Highway Surveyor took over construction and maintenance of the roads from the Selectmen; there was a Tree Warden, and so on. All these offices came along quite naturally as the needs arose. The earlier offices continued, with the selectmen continuing to serve as assessors and as overseers of the poor.

The School Committee had already been set up, when schools were transferred from the Church to the Town. There is a separate section in this volume on Sharon Schools. However, as a matter of interest in Town Government, from an early date women voted for and served on the School Committee, although not for other Town offices. It appears that this franchise was not widely exercised. The Town Report for the year 1900, when the Town population was 2000, shows 110 women registered to vote and 36 actually voting for School Committee in that year.

Sharon again demonstrated its patriotism in the Civil War. Sharon furnished 146 men, 8 over quota; 18 died in service. The town provided $12.00 per month for each man in the service. A committee was established and empowered to grant additional funds to needy service families. However, in contrast to the Revolutionary War, there was a strong federal government; although conditions were simply awful by any modern standards, personal hardships in this area were significantly less in the Civil War than during the Revolution.

During this period, the procedure of contracting the care of the poor to the lowest bidder was supplanted by a Town Almshouse (poor farm). This was a quite extensive farm. Most of the food for the inmates was raised on the premises, with inmates providing labor within the limits of their capabilities. Surplus produce, including milk, chickens and eggs, potatoes, and other farm products were sold, to a considerable extent to the Sharon Sanitorium. (The final action in this Almshouse operation came in 1919, with a Town meeting vote to sell the property). Before, during, and long after this period, the selectmen continued to be the overseers of the poor.

Gradually town government became more formal. Town Meeting became an annual affair, authorizing annual budgets, and conducting routine business. There were occasional "special" meetings as needs arose. The Warrant for the town meeting for the year 1900 shows 23 articles. There was the usual blanket article for appropriations for Town operations. There was an article regarding wage rate for labor on the highways; another article proposed authorization to purchase land for a dumping ground; there were the usual routine articles. All pretty much cut and dried. However, in 1900, there were only 385 registered male voters eligible to vote in Town Meeting. A good many of these had been born and brought up in Sharon. There was still a high degree of personal communication both ways between the majority of voters and the government of the town.

This development of formal procedures was in part the result of increase in regulation of local affairs by the State legislature. Laws covering all kinds of Town operations were passed; boards and commissions were established which promulgated rules and regulations. This was a significant trend, particularly toward the end of the nineteenth century. It is still increasing. Many of the regulations are desirable, and often necessary for the protection and safety of the citizens. A number provide for standard practices, for dealing with all kinds of situations. They are, generally, well intended. However, particularly in recent times, there has been considerable criticism of the bureaucracy inevitably involved in centralization of control. Rules, once established, are difficult to erase, even though outmoded. In many instances, judgements made locally with a knowledge of local situations are superior to more or less arbitrary rules intended to cover a whole gamut of conditions. Regardless of the pros and cons, the very effective "home rule" practised in the Towns in Massachusetts in earlier days has been wiped out to a very considerable extent. And one of the results is a much more formal, less flexible Town Government.

SHARON TOWN GOVERNMENT IN THE 20TH CENTURY

By the turn of the Century, promotion of Sharon as the healthiest town in Massachusetts was well under way. Sharon was assuming its present character as a suburban residential community. There was excellent rail service to Boston, and a street railway with connections all over the area. Population growth, already increasing, has continued right up to the present, more than doubling in the past 25 years. Small industry in town has almost completely disappeared. The recent revival of industrial development has been entirely out on Route 1, along the boundary of Walpole. Relatively few of the employees live in Sharon.

Sharon Town Government has lost most of its personal flavor, in the sense of loss of personal contact between most of the citizens and the Town officers and employees. This is of course inevitable with a Town population of over 13,000. It is augmented by the increasingly transient character of the population. Many of the new people in Town come from Boston or other large cities, with a background of impersonal, political city government. Nowadays people come and go at a rapid pace. Even though Sharon is predominantly a town of single residences, owned by their occupants, it has been estimated that on the average, families stay in one place less than ten years. Except for the people who become involved in Town Government in one way or another, most people do not really understand the working of their Town Government.

The Town Government has adapted well to the growth and change in character of the population, and the increasing demands and complexity. Sharon, as a very inviting suburban community, increasingly attracts able and successful business and professional men and their families. Sharon has been most fortunate in the people who are able and willing to contribute their skills and abilities on the various Town committees.

For convenience and brevity in what follows, the word committees will be used in a generic sense to cover all the boards, commissions, authorities, trustees and the like in the Town.

Committees have always been basic in Town Government. When Sharon received its charter in 1765, the first Town Meeting elected a Board of Selectmen, who also served as assessors and overseers of the poor, and, in addition were responsible for the roads and other Town functions. When the Town took over the schools from the Church, a School Committee was elected. Other Committees were established as need arose. By 1900, there were ten.

As the town has grown, and government has become more complex, new committees have proliferated. *The Town Government Handbook*, compiled by the League of Women Voters, has a list of 18 permanent (standing) committees. And there are a lot more. Some, not on the list, are mentioned in the Handbook. There are the "ad hoc" committees set up with specific tasks, and dismissed when the task is completed. There are still others, including those set up since the Handbook was compiled.

In the early days, when the Town was small and the government was simple, Town policies were worked out in the Town Meeting. This function has now passed almost entirely to the system of Town committees. Under present conditions, attempts to develop policy on the Town Meeting floor almost inevitably result in confusion and frustration. In the present set up, the Warrant Committee works with those concerned, especially with the concerned Town Committees, and as required by statute, presents a recommendation on every article which can come before the Town Meeting. The motions on the articles, as presented by the Warrant committee to the meeting represent well thought out and carefully prepared proposals.

Unless convinced of the validity of these motions as presented, the Town Meeting can vote them down, or can vote to amend. Town Meeting can express its desires, loud and clear, and is heard by everyone involved in Town Government. But experience in Sharon and in other towns shows that real trouble is likely if the Warrant Committee does not get the supporting vote from the Meeting on any significant proportion of its recommendations.

Town committee functions permeate the entire structure of Town Government. Some groups, like the Board of Selectmen and the School Committee operate through full-time executives (the Executive Secretary and the Superintendent of Schools) who operate within the authority delegated to them. Other committees, for instance, the Nominating Committee for the Warrant Committee, operate entirely on their own. The Planning Board makes extensive use of outside consultants for some of the more technical phases of its work. Committee procedures vary, but without exception, results depend on the competence, dedication and plain hard work of their members. With the exception of the Assessors, and the nominal salaries of the Selectmen, none of the Town Committee Members are paid for their services. Sharon has been most fortunate in the calibre and dedication of the members of Town Committees who have contributed so importantly to the Town.

The close cooperation between the Committee system and the full-time elected officers is a major factor in the effectiveness of Sharon Town Government. All part- and full-time Town employees, with the exception of the Town Clerk and the Town Treasurer-Tax Collector, are appointed, in many instances under State rules prescribing appointment procedures. Financial procedures are subject to State Audit. The Town has been fortunate in the choice of its employees. They form a very competent, cooperative group who have served the Town well. The system of voluntary committees and full-time employees has worked well, individually and collectively.

Reverting to the subject of the traditional "open" Town Meeting, there is no question of the effectiveness of this truly democratic procedure when Sharon was a small, stable, rural community. For Sharon in 1976, with over 13,000 population, and for the larger town projected for the years to come, there is a question as to its practicality. Many towns the size of Sharon have turned to "representative town meeting" with a limited number of elected "Town Meeting Members". The really large towns in the state have all turned to this representative form as a matter of necessity.

As recently as the 1940's when Sharon was about half its present size, town meetings were pretty routine. Business was usually completed in a single session, with adjournment before 10:00 o'clock not unusual. There were exceptions, as when a meeting was held in a circus tent rented by the town to accommodate the crowd which voted for the (then) High School (South Main Street between Station and Chestnut Streets). This building provided an auditorium which accommodated the town meetings for many years, until the present High School auditorium was completed. In a few instances there was an overflow, with the excess seated in the gymnasium. This was very slow and cumbersome, and, fortunately infrequent.

Nowadays, Town Meetings tend to drag out, with a great many people wishing to be heard, running to two and three sessions, each lasting till after eleven. Many people feel frustrated; many are simply bored. They attend only when a major issue is at stake, and leave as soon as the issue is decided. Particularly when a third session is required, there are seldom three hundred people present at the final adjournment. This is hardly a valid representation of the body of registered voters as a whole.

The apparent lack of specific accomplishment does not necessarily mean that these meetings are ineffective. As was mentioned earlier, the townspeople express their feelings loud and clear, and are heard by everyone in the Town Government. There is nothing like open Town Meeting in its opportunity for the citizens of the Town to communicate with their Town Government. It is just unfortunate that Town Meeting is now so limited as a channel for communication from the town officials to the people. Taken as a whole, it does perform a useful function. It is an important tradition, and a popular institution with a number of people. Unless and until it becomes unmanageable, it will almost certainly continue in Sharon.

The Old Town Hall   *Boyden Collection*

The Board of Selectmen: Colleen Tuck, Robert L. Currie-Chairman, Norman Katz,
Photo by: Kennan

Town Clerk and Accountant, Arthur E. Collins 30 Years of Service
Photo by: Kennan

The Police Department, 1976   *Photo by: Kennan*

The Fire Station, 1976   *Photo by: Kennan*

Fire Chief Walter B. Roach - 41 Years of Service   *Photo by: Kennan*

The Fire Dept., 1976   *Photo by Kennan*

THE SHARON FIRE DEPARTMENT

By Walter B. Roach

CHAPTER 36

Sharon's Fire Department had its beginning on the night of November 9, 1885, when a group of residents appointed by the Selectmen as engineers met at the home of A. D. Colburn for the purpose of appointing a chief, first assistant, and second assistant. C. A. Hixon was chosen second assistant and clerk.

On January 2, 1886, C. F. Bryant of the Hook and Ladder Committee turned over to the engineers of the fire department the first piece of apparatus purchased for the town.

On May 1, 1886, another organization meeting was held and in addition to reappointing the chief and assistants, 19 men were named as members of Hook and Ladder Company No. 1 for one year. Twelve men were appointed to Hose Company No. 1 and eight to Hose Company No. 2, bringing the total number of members of the Fire Department to 42.

On May 24, 1886, Samuel Leonard and Charles S. Curtis were appointed members of the Fire Department and assigned the duty of ringing in fire alarms. The bell of the First Congregational Church was rung to sound the alarm. At this meeting it was also voted to buy one 44-foot extension ladder and one 21-foot ladder from the Combination Ladder Company of Providence, Rhode Island.

It is interesting to note that April 30, 1887, was pay day for the members of the department, with the pay ranging from fifty cents to two dollars for the year.

The records show that on April 17, 1887, an alarm of fire was sounded at 3:15 A.M. The members of the department responded without apparatus since the location of the fire was outside the water district. The fire was in the lower shop of the Lothrop Manufacturing Co. The shop with office and separate building were completely destroyed.

The first Hose House was built in the year 1887 at a cost of $887. The plans cost $8.

The first report of the engineers of the fire department recorded in the Annual Town Report was made in the year 1888. It goes into detail as to the valuation of all property destroyed or partially so, and whether insured or not and amount of insurance paid. It also states that the water tank was kept full all that year. Also that the hydrants were painted and carefully looked after by engineer E. E. Farnam. The equipment consisted of 1,500 feet of good reliable hose. The Hook and Ladder Truck was improved by having two new "Babcock Extinguishers" added, making it better equipment than ever before. Also, there were three hose carriages in good condition.

The department moved into their new quarters the first of the year, and in consequence of having a convenient and proper place for the apparatus, the members showed renewed interest. A suitable building was secured in the "Knife Shop" village at a small cost, and a new hose carriage with 500 feet of hose was installed. A donation of $25 was made by L. H. Shepard towards a fund to purchase rubber coats for the members of the department. Through the efforts of the engineers enough money was raised to purchase 24 coats.

In the year 1891, a new Hose House was built at the "Knife Village" at a cost of $900 and a bell tower was built on Center Hose House. Later the same year a bell was placed in each of the Hose Houses. The bells were given to the Town by J. B. and Dexter Packard.

At the March Town Meeting of 1895 it was voted to purchase a supply wagon to displace two hose carriages of the Center Hose House. By so doing it gave the Town better fire protection and reduced the number of men necessary in the fire department by eight, thus saving the Town considerable money. It was also voted at the same meeting to purchase a fire alarm system, which included three boxes, one gong, and a striker. The striker was connected with the bell in the tower of the Congregational Church. [Pettee's store received the calls and relayed them to the Church where the bell was rung as an alarm. Immediately horses on ice carts in summer and coal carts in winter were driven to the fire station to be hitched to fire-fighting apparatus.]

The first Fire Department Muster held by the Sharon Company was in 1911, when the departments of North Attleboro, Plainville, Wrentham, Foxboro, Walpole, Mansfield, North Easton, and Canton were entered in Sharon. There were games for prizes and a parade, with the apparatus of all the towns represented taking part.

In 1935, the fire alarm system was extended approximately 5½ miles and four new alarm boxes were added. The total number of miles of fire alarm system wires was approximately 30. The system was renumbered and a number of new locations established.

Today's equipment includes two 100-gallon per minute, two 500-gallon per minute, one 750-gallon per minute pumpers, one 75-foot aerial ladder truck, one 250-gallon per minute forestry truck, and one fire alarm truck with boom. Lake rescue equipment includes a 16-foot aluminum boat with five horsepower motor and trailer, a resuscitator, three skin-diving units, a porta-power unit for automobile rescue work, a vacuum cleaner for water removal from basements, a gas explosion meter, ten gas masks for entering buildings, and complete radio communications between station and equipment and all Norfolk County fire departments.

Walter B. Roach was made permanent chief in 1956, and the department today has 12 permanent and 15 call firemen.

In conjunction with the construction of the new Municipal Office Building the Central Station was enlarged to house all the equipment in 1964, barracks added for the men, and the fire alarm system was modernized for the first time since 1894.

In 1965 we had seven permanent men on duty, and by 1975 we increased to chief and twelve, with four shifts and three men per shift, with a workweek of 42 hours.

In 1964 collective bargaining for fire fighters was permitted by law. In 1969 the permanent members of the department joined the International Association of Fire Fighters, Local 1880.

Around this time we had some members with long years of service retire, or move out of town. Allen R. Littlefield, 19 years and 10 months, moved out of town in 1966; Albert J. Murphy, 25 years, retired in 1966; Arthur A. Lindberg, 26 years, retired in 1968; and Linwood Fifield, 22 years, retired in 1975.

The chief's family has around 155 years of service in just the Fire Department. Seven served as call and permanent members. Chief W. B. Roach was the first man ever to be appointed as a permanent man to the department in Sharon, and he was also the first permanent chief.

Fire Alarm has had 103,000 feet of wire added, with replacement of new alarm boxes — old interfering type was taken out to stop the possible chance for getting wrong numbers. We have all schools, the Catholic and Congregational Churches, Temples Israel and Sinai, Sharon Manor, elderly housing, the Recreation Center, Salvation Army Camp, and shopping centers covered with master alarm boxes. A total of 110 fire alarm boxes covers the Town.

Large Fires in Sharon

Lothrop Manufacturing Company	April 17, 1887	3:15 A.M.
Boston Icehouse, first fire	Dec. 20, 1903	
last fire	1925 or 1926	
Tom Pru Boarding House, first fire	1909	
last fire	ca. 1928	
Morse Block on So. Main and Chestnut Sts.	Jan. 19, 1904	1:45 A.M.
Burkhart Icehouse	July, 1907	
Mann's Mill	1919	
Boys' Home		
Sunset Lodge	Dec. 31, 1931	12:30 A.M.
Singer's Inn — Salvation Army dormitory	Nov. 30, 1953	4:56 A.M.
Pancake House	May 13, 1961	11:09 P.M.
Pettee Block	Dec. 14, 1966	1:59 A.M.
Brush fires, Bay Road — Mountain St.	April 26, 1942	1400 acres
Bay Road — Mountain St.	July 26, 1972	1860 acres

Editor's note: Chief Walter B. Roach plans to retire in 1977 and at that time will have given the Town of Sharon 41 years of loyal service — a remarkable record.

Years of Fire Department Service: a 1906 photo of William H., Walter J., and George V. Roach
Courtesy: W. B. Roach

Fireman's Muster Parade   *Boyden Collection*

The Early Fire Department The Horses' Were From Brymer's Stable   *Courtesy: W. B. Roach*

SHARON'S WEEKLY NEWSPAPERS

By Walter L. Reeve

CHAPTER 37

The first news item that appeared in any paper about the area now known as Sharon was a detailed account, printed in *The Boston News Letter*, in 1717, of the death of Ebenezer Billings. Billings was owner of the famous Billings Tavern that was located near the present cranberry bogs on South Main Street.

The Boston News Letter, a weekly, America's first regular newspaper, was started April 24, 1704, by John Campbell, postmaster of Boston. Because it backed the Tory cause, publication ceased in 1766.

Other weekly newspapers, such as *The Norfolk County Gazette*, printed news of this area in the later 1700's or early 1800's. Most of the real news, however, was transmitted around the countryside by mail coach drivers, horseback riders, and travelers who stopped in the small towns. People, of course, were hungry for news and it wasn't long before the first of what were to be several weekly newspapers began printing news of Sharon. These are presented in chronological order and every effort has been made to authenticate dates of publication through actual authentic copies on hand.

THE MASSAPOAG JOURNAL

This was the first weekly in the area. Though named after Lake Massapoag in Sharon, it was printed in Canton. Edited by William Bense, this paper, which carried news of Sharon, was a four-pager; subscription price was $1.00, 2¢ per copy. The last authentic copy on file bears the date of 1857, and from the volume number, it appears the paper was started in the early 1850's.

THE CANTON JOURNAL

The Canton Journal took over some years after *The Massapoag Journal*. Its supposed first publication date was 1867, but volume numbers of papers on hand seem to indicate 1876 as the starting date. N. T. Merritt was the publisher in 1876 followed by E. B. Thorndike in 1878. Sharon news was printed and information from several sources indicates the forerunner of *The Sharon Advocate* was printed on the back pages of the *Journal*. Authentic copies of the *Journal* of that period are very scarce, one 1876 copy is on file in the office of the Canton Publishing Co., and one at the Canton Public Library.

THE SHARON ADVOCATE

This was the first weekly under its own banner devoted to Sharon. It was printed in Canton by E. B. Thorndike and its editor was William B. Wickes, under the banner of *The Sharon Advocate*. New volume numbers were started and a copy of Vol. 1, No. 1, dated January 6, 1883 is on file in the Sharon Publishing Company's office.

The paper was not quite separated from *The Canton Journal*, as Canton news was still printed in the paper. During the 1890's the *Advocate* and the *Journal* were printed together as combined issues. One such paper dated July 26, 1895, Vol. 19, No. 33, is on file in the Advocate office. Before building its own printing plant in 1956 at 66 South Main St., Sharon, the paper had been printed in Canton for nearly 75 years. *The Sharon Advocate* since it became Sharon's weekly newspaper in 1883 till 1976, a period of 93 years, has never missed a single issue. Its present-day circulation is about 3200 copies per week;

it comes out Thursdays, and as in 1883, sells for 5 cents per copy. It is believed to be the only weekly in the United States that still sells for 5 cents.

The Sharon Advocate is printed by the Sharon Publishing Co. Inc., of Sharon Mass., and is edited by Walter L. and Esther M. Reeve.

THE SHARON OZONE

This was published in Foxboro by Alden and Barron. Volume numbers and copies on hand indicate a starting date of 1884. It sold for 4¢ a copy (at one time, 3¢) and carried, besides news of Sharon, news of Mansfield, Foxboro, Wrentham, and Walpole. It was later purchased by F. W. Marshall, who changed its name to *The Sharon Enterprise*.

THE SHARON ENTERPRISE

This began publication in 1895. Vol. 1, No. 21, is on file. Harry M. Hight was the editor, having bought it from Marshall. He merged it with *The Sharon Advocate*, which he acquired after the death of W. B. Wickes. Copy of Vol. 4, No. 25, is on file.

THE SHARON NEWS

A short-lived paper, started by Sanford Waters Billings in 1901. It ceased after appearing a few times. An authentic copy, dated September 6, 1901, is on file. It sold for 3¢ a copy.

THE SHARON ITEM

Appearing in 1909, *The Item* was published by William Wheeler and sold for 3¢ a copy. In 1910 when the Sharon Publishing Co. was formed *The Item* was purchased and incorporated into *The Sharon Advocate*.

THE SHARON TRANSCRIPT

This weekly started publication in 1946. It merged with the Advocate in 1956.

There were other weeklies in the area that printed news of Sharon, the foremost being *The Foxboro Times* (started in 1871) which gave good coverage to Sharon. Pratt and Clarke were the publishers and E. W. Clarke was the editor. There is an authentic copy on file of this paper, dated January 30, 1874 — Vol. III, No. 45, old series.

Thus, by the records covering a long period of time, from about 1850 when *The Massapoag Journal* appeared, to the present-day *Sharon Advocate* there has always been a weekly newspaper to print the news of Sharon.

Weekly newspapers have certainly had a long and glorious past in the history of our country, and it is hoped they will continue into a brighter future.

SPORTS AND RECREATION

By Richard Hosmer

CHAPTER 38

During the early days of our town, as in other country villages throughout the nation, the tasks of livelihood did not leave time for the sports and recreational activities we enjoy today. Fishing and hunting provided enjoyable diversions but were primarily a means of adding to the food supply. Individual competitive sports included such activities as running, throwing, riding, wrestling, and shooting, but not until the middle of the 19th century did organized athletic events gain popularity. From that time to the present, Sharon citizens of all ages have participated with varying degrees of skill and enthusiasm in various activities; most unorganized, many highly organized.

The earliest recorded attempt at any organized sports activity was the formation of a baseball team in the mid-1800's. Known as the Massapoag Club, the Sharon team became unofficial state champions in 1857 by winning three straight games from the Boston Olympics before 2000 spectators on the Boston Common Parade Ground.

The contest received considerable publicity in the Boston and Providence papers. One account declared it to be the "best game ever played in Boston." It is not known if this distinction endured until Game Six of the 1975 World Series!

Successors to the notably successful Massapoags were sponsored by the Sharon Baseball Association, one bearing the name "The Ozones" in honor of the alleged health-giving properties of Sharon air.

Home games were first played on fields located at the corner of High Street and Summit Avenue, later on the Hewins property south of the Town Hall. Both these fields, particularly the latter, provided interesting obstacles such as stone walls, ditches and the fire house. One report of a game with the South Walpole team describes the stone wall and fence jumping antics of the Sharon players in pursuit of the visitors' triples and home runs.

As civilization, in the form of house building, encroached upon the earlier playing areas, the teams moved to an improved surface in the rear of the present location of the Pleasant Street School where games were played for several years until further building forced another move to O'Brien's field across the street from the former Sacred Heart building.

The town team which played in the period just before World War I had a few highly talented players, one or two of whom attracted the serious attention of a major league manager. The war took its toll of many of the town teams in the area and Sharon's, too, faded into obscurity. In more recent years men's softball teams have played regularly in local leagues on the Ames Street playground diamond.

Baseball continued to be played by the High School and by boys of all ages on numerous makeshift fields throughout the town. This period of unorganized but intense action in turn was succeeded by the highly organized Little League, Babe Ruth, and American Legion Leagues we have today.

The availability of numerous ponds and lakes in the area contributed to the popularity of skating and ice hockey. The Lake, Mann's Pond, and the Sanitorium flooded bog were the most popular sites. Hockey games were always in progress, intermingling with skaters, fancy and ordinary.

The inlets to the smaller ponds provided interesting ice paths to explore and thin ice areas for games of "tiddly" which involved skating gingerly over spots which gave way — not quite to the breaking point — under the weight of the skater.

A large flat rock at the south end of Mann's Pond provided a base for a sunset bonfire to warm the hockey players unable to continue their game in the darkness.

There were few attempts to organize hockey until the advent of indoor rinks, although the grammar school had a team for a brief period in the mid-1920's and played teams from Sacred Heart School. It was organized and coached by a female teacher who also formed a school baseball team and who, incidently, effectively maintained classroom discipline with a wooden paddle made for her in the "manual training" class.

Other winter activities included coasting on the various hills throughout the town, Pettee's then as now being one of the best. Excellent coasting was also provided by streets packed slick with hooves and pung and sleigh tracks. Saw Mill Hill on North Main Street, Billings Street and Depot Street were among the fastest until plows, sand, salt, and automobiles forced the Flexible Flyers to the open hills.

Skiing was enjoyed without today's sophisticated equipment. Wooden skis with leather straps were slipped on over ordinary boots or overshoes. Usually skiers shared a hill with coasters and, in the absence of even the most rudimentary tow, spent more time dodging sleds and laboriously walking up the slope than they did gliding down.

When sleighs and pungs were common, they too provided do-it-yourself recreation for the young. The trailing edge of the runners provided convenient platforms for hitching rides. Most drivers paid no attention though some used their whips to dislodge unwelcome riders.

Basketball was first played in a gymnasium located on Stone Street and later in the Town Hall.

The completion of the then new High School — now the Intermediate School — provided much improved facilities and Sharon High School began to establish its long and enviable record as a basketball powerhouse with many teams advancing to the much-sought former Tech Tourney and now Eastern Massachusetts tournament play-offs at Boston Garden. Girls' teams too had many successful seasons — during one noteworthy span in the 1930's they lost just one game in three years.

During this period "shooting baskets" became a popular pastime at hundreds of backyard and front-of-garage hoops at all times of the year.

Soccer was introduced at the High School upon the completion of the present building in the mid-fifties and for several years Sharon was the leader in its league.

Demand for football as a High School varsity sport accelerated soon after the soccer program was firmly established. Contrary to popular legend, until its formal establishment in the 1960's Sharon had never had a varsity football team. In the early 1900's a Canton team challenged a group of students from Sharon High who responded with eleven men, no equipment, and no practice. A 9-0 pasting by Canton cooled their ardor. A few informal intra-mural games were played by High School youngsters in the early fifties, but were discontinued because of lack of equipment and time for practice.

As with hockey and baseball, pick-up sandlot games were played on fall afternoons on the same lots used for baseball in the spring.

The adoption of football as a Sharon High School varsity sport was preceded by organized Pony League and Pop Warner teams for younger players who, completely equipped, were coached by interested adults.

Other organized school athletic teams included track and field, cross country, field hockey, gymnastics, softball, golf and tennis.

Unorganized individual-type recreation encompassed many different activities, much of it centered on the Lake which provided fishing from the shore and from row boats rented from Desmond's on the north beach. There were picnic groves around its rim and, during the very early years of this century, an excursion boat attracted groups from as far away as suburban Boston who rode the trolleys right to the lakeshore. Autumn brought duck and goose blinds for water fowling.

Swimming was centered on the north side of the lake with a raft and diving tower available. In the twenties swimming instruction and life saving classes were begun. Youngsters growing up in Sharon during this period considered swimming across the lake the final test of their effectiveness — and the first step toward proving their adulthood. In at least one instance a girl outdid the boys in a group by swimming over and back.

For some who sought swimming closer to the center, the great black iron standpipe located at the rear of the Unitarian Church property provided a challenge. The climb to the top was easily accomplished via the metal ladder attached to the outside. The ladder on the inside had gradually rusted away hence a rope tied to the top of the tank and thrown inside was necessary for retrieval after a dive from the top into the depths of the fresh, cool spring water for which Sharon was famous before the days of chlorination.

The standpipe also provided a convenient target for rifle practice for some living a few hundred yards away. The delayed, resounding "plunk" of a 500-grain bullet from a low velocity 45-70 rifle fired safely over the intervening houses and yards provided entertainment for the riflemen and didn't seem to bother anyone else. The lead bullet would drop harmlessly to the base of the tank after contact. The effect of missing was never a concern because such an eventuality was never even considered! The swimmers were never endangered because they were generally the same ones who did the shooting.

Firearms were common. Most boys had a .22 rifle for "plinking." Usually they were single shot models such as the old Stevens "Favorite." Sand pits were used for target practice and the town dump for shooting rats.

In the late twenties, a group of adults with young ideas set up a 200-yard range in a field in the woods east of the Sharon Country Club and called themselves the "Massapoag Rum & Rifle Club." They fired heavy caliber standard and reload ammunition and were rigorous about restricting the "rumming" until after the "rifling." The plot of ground later became the site of a daytime nudist colony and then a training area for the local state guard unit during World War II.

The Sharon Fish and Game Club was established at its present site off East Street in the early 1900's and provided a more organized setting for pistol, rifle, and skeet shooting. The Massapoag Sportsmen's Club was formed later at facilities off Belcher Street.

The Sharon Country Club started as a 9-hole golf course on the O'Leary farm on East Street. The first clubhouse was a small rustic building near the center of the property — a structure now used for storage. The present clubhouse was originally the O'Leary dairy barn. Cows roamed freely on the course and were kept off the greens by black pipe fences. In the twenties the land was purchased by the club, "improved" from a cow pasture to a more conventional type course and the barn conversion was completed.

Two clay tennis courts were located near the "old" clubhouse and for a while were quite active. Tennis gradually faded out when, as so often happens with tennis as part of a golf club, conflicting interests competed for available funds and support.

The principal tennis activity in the town was centered at the courts between the railroad station and Beaver Brook. Now organized as the Sharon Tennis Club this was originally started shortly after the turn of the century by a few individuals who were interested in playing tennis regularly. They received permission to construct two courts on Water Department land. It is alleged that this site in the woods was selected because its seclusion permitted Sunday tennis without encountering the objections of those who frowned upon such activities on the Sabbath. It was reasoned that what people couldn't see, they couldn't object to.

Originally there was a small clubhouse and a water tower which was filled with water pumped from the brook and used to moisten the courts.

Horses served many utilitarian needs of our early settlers. As the gasoline engine replaced them in such roles as plowing and hauling, many were retained for "hacking," racing, and jumping. Numerous woods roads on Moose Hill and surrounding areas provided miles of soft footing and occasional gates for jumping. For shoeing, the horse was ridden to the farrier on Ames or Tolman Street; for ailments the vet visited the horse. Now it is the other way around — the vet does not make house calls but the horse-shoer does.

Sailboats were used on the lake from the earliest days. In recent years, however, their numbers have multiplied. The Massapoag Yacht Club was originally located near the site of the Boston Icehouse which dominated the south side of the lake for many years.

The club, whose present site is next to Kiddie Camp, is host to several classes of sailboats and conducts weekly races throughout the summer as well as a fall regatta which attracts visitors from other clubs as distant as New Jersey. The shifting winds and dead spots of lake racing provide visitors with an experience of exquisite frustration not frequently encountered in their ocean racing.

In the winter when the ice is thick enough and the snow is light enough and the winds are strong enough, iceboating conditions prevail and provide a not too dangerous thrill for those with sufficient alertness to avoid the crevices and open water which are common even in the coldest weather.

Children growing up in Sharon have enjoyed other geographical advantages in addition to the Lake: Beaver Brook for trout fishing and exploring; Devil's (really Massapoag) Brook for falling into after climbing Devil's Rock and enjoying the numerous moist paths in the area; Moose Hill with its fire tower to climb, sometimes by shinnying up the girders; the Bird Sanctuary with its museum and summer nature courses; the sand pits behind Norwood Street, remnants of the days when the Boston-Providence Railway was built, for building huts and playing games.

Those activities such as baseball and "scrub" football which required reasonably open and cleared land were well accommodated by numerous privately owned tracts such as White's field on Billings Street, Hastings' on Cottage, Stressenger's on High Street Extension, Hewin's on South Main, to list a few, and public areas behind schools on High Street, School Street and Pleasant Street.

As civilization inexorably encroached upon these cherished acres, various civic-minded individuals initiated action to provide replacement facilities which would be forever protected from such mundane interference as human habitation.

Drake's field at the foot of Pettee's Hill was one of the first attempts to combine private and public support for such an enterprise. The enthusiasm of the proponents exceeded the realities of the magnitude of the problems involved in converting rocky, uneven, damp ground into a playground. The construction of a bridge over the original grade crossing at the railroad station and its attendant road widening finally tipped the scales against the project.

Another group, headed by Dr. Walter A. Griffin, having investigated various possibilities for a dedicated play area, selected a site on Ames Street. The fields were not originally the cleared, grassed area of today. The property was rocky, uneven, poorly drained and covered with saplings. After a few discouraging setbacks in the attempt to convert the land into a playground, persistence prevailed and the Walter Griffin Playground administered by the Sharon Civic Foundation evolved.

The High School, which had moved from Pleasant Street to South Main Street in the late 1920's, lacked space for any outside athletic activities and quickly responded to the availability of the playground facilities to expand their athletic program.

In the early thirties the Civic Foundation, utilizing the physical contributions of its members and monetary assistance from interested townspeople and organizations, initiated a summer playground program for the youth of Sharon. Swimming instruction at the nearby lake and adjacent Hammershop Pond, arts, crafts, games, cookouts, athletic events, archery and others were included in the program which attracted hundreds each summer.

A sailing program was later introduced, originally with two Sprite Class sailboats (now grown to a fleet of eight) and the loan of a couple of larger privately owned boats. This somewhat unique opportunity provided by the

Civic Foundation invariably attracted more young people than could be accommodated each year. The enthusiasm of the students converted numerous local families to the pleasures of sailing.

With the town's acquisition of the St. Francis Retreat Lodge, facilities for professionally supervised recreation programs became feasible. In 1969 the Civic Foundation turned over to the newly organized Recreation Department all its playground equipment and made available the use of its buildings and land at the Dr. Griffin Playground. With the additional facilities of the schools, the beaches, and the newly acquired property overlooking the lake, the new department soon expanded the original playground and swimming programs to those of the present which encompass nearly every possible recreational activity. The success of this undertaking is attested by the large participation by Sharon citizens young and old and the tributes extended by other communities in using Sharon as the model of possibilities.

Throughout the entire period of the known recreational history of our town, an unusual amount of initiative and self-reliance has been evident — not only in the case of individual unorganized pursuits but in group functions as well. The Tennis Club was built by those who wanted a place to play. It was until fairly recently maintained by the do-it-yourself efforts of its members — caring for the courts, constructing fencing, building a storage house. No frills; the objective is "tennis."

So also with the Massapoag Yacht Club. It is for sailing and racing. There is no clubhouse for social activities; members care for the docks and the grounds.

The Fish and Game Club relies on members' labors for much of their needs. A badminton group which started in the Intermediate School gymnasium originally laid out and marked the courts themselves each fall; installed and removed the nets each night. Even the present-day Recreation Department programs include the volunteer support of many talented and interested individuals.

May this resourcefulness be retained for the next 200 years.

The Tennis Club   *Boyden Collection*

Sailing on Lake Massapoag   *Photo by: S. S. Morgan*

307

The Recreation Center   *Photo by: J. K. Harris*

Swimming Lessons at the Recreation Center

HISTORY OF THE SHARON RECREATION DEPARTMENT

By David I. Clifton

CHAPTER 39

The Town's first full-time professional Recreation Director was hired in October 1968. Planning, programming, and organizing with the Recreation Committee expanded the Recreation Department over an eight-year period producing added strength and participation with each succeeding year.

Without a doubt, the single biggest reason for any success or growth by the Recreation Department has to be the Sharon Center facility as a town recreation building. The Community Center not only houses many of the town recreational programs but also provides a home for fifty local organizations. The former Retreat Lodge property (20 acres) was purchased by the Town in 1967 through state and federal funds. It was one of the best investments ever made because this Community Center building has brought many local people of all ages together to enjoy leisure time activities.

The spirit of working together to promote the Center was almost contagious from the start. Organizations, individuals, and many volunteers alike contributed materials, equipment, time, and energy to help the Community Center succeed. It would take a large section to write the names of all those who lent the needed hand during the early days of the Center. History well knows that achievement is best accomplished by the many.

The ups and downs of that first year of the new Community Center were apparent. First, would residents use the facility? Second, would the Town provide a budget? Third, would the programs grow and improve? Eight years of growth and change has shown the answer to all three questions to be "Yes!" It has always been the philosophy of the Town officials from the very beginning that "if one young person in the community is influenced for the good, it is money well spent."

The following is a list of some of the activities sponsored by the Recreation Department during the past eight years at one time or another:

Marathon	Fishing Derby	Senior Ball
Swimming	Sailing	Cheerleading
Tennis	Arts & Crafts	Tiny Tot Recreation
Gymnastics	Playgrounds	Magic
Chess	Karate	Women's Fitness
Golf	Yoga	Basketball
Baseball	Drama	Baton Twirling

Chorus	Social Activities	Photography
Volleyball	Ballroom Dance	Cooking
Art	Jazz, Tap, Ballet	Dance with Physical Fitness
Archery	Ping Pong	Plays
Special Events	Parties	Afro-American Dance
Dog Obedience	Movies	Acrobatics
Skating	Square Dancing	Tumbling
Dancing	Teen Drop-In Center	Teen Center
Calesthenics	Judo	Softball
Coffee House	Trips	Contests
Music Appreciation	First Aid	Smoking Clinics
Lifesaving	Baby-sitting Course	Track and Field
Pass, Punt, & Kick	Ceramics	Fourth of July
Street Hockey	Bowling	Concerts
Jogging	Handicapped Program	Senior Citizens' Drop-In
Intramurals	Annual Events	Animal Shows
Camping	Family Night	Cookouts
Mystery Ride	Holiday Celebrations	Creative dance
Ham Radio Operators	Bicycle Club	Art Festival
Ski Trips	"Seniors on the Go"	Hiking

Sailing at the Recreation Center   Photo by: Kennan

Playground Special Event   Photo by: Kennan

HISTORY OF THE SHARON CONSERVATION COMMISSION

By Lawrence Newcomb

CHAPTER 40

When the Sharon Conservation Commission was created in 1959, it was one of the first six in the state, and consequently in the nation, since Massachusetts pioneered the conservation commission idea. On the recommendation of the Planning Board, which had recognized the need for planned open space in the Town, an article was included in the town warrant and at the March 1959 town meeting approval was voted.

The first members of the Conservation Commission were Mrs. Henrietta F. Becker, Albert W. Bussewitz, Robert I. Kalis, James J. McGoff, Willard Rhodes, Mrs. Ardys F. Whitcomb, Secretary, and Frank A. Chase, Chairman.

The new commission under Frank Chase's able chairmanship immediately sprang into action, and before long it became well-known throughout the state as a leader in the town conservation movement. One of the first tasks was to prepare a large-scale map of the Town showing the present land uses and providing a picture of the long-term acquisition program planned by the Commission.

The main feature of the plan was a greenbelt of conservation land extending through the Town along the course of Massapoag Brook. In the next few years this plan became a reality with the securing of 100 acres along the designated strip, half of it donated by public-spirited citizens. One of the important pieces needed to complete the greenbelt was Mann's Pond, which was very generously given to the Town by Robert and Nancy Cushman. Just recently the integrity of this scenic spot was assured by the purchase by the Commission of the wooded slope on the east side of the pond. Other donors of important sections of land along Massapoag Brook were Gardner Gaines, Mrs. Frieda Cushman, Mr. and Mrs. Martin White, Rev. Osmond Billings, Robert Bachman, and the Massapoag Sportmen's Club.

As land was acquired it was opened to the townspeople by the construction of a trail network, the backbone of which is the Massapoag Trail running three miles from Massapoag Lake to North Main Street. Six rustic bridges were built, the trails were marked with orange or blue paint, and an attractive trail guide was prepared and distributed to 3,000 home owners. In June 1966 the Trail was formally opened by a Conservation Day celebration which included guided hikes, talks, and a photography contest, as well as the dedication ceremony in which town and state officials took part. More than 300 schoolchildren joined in the event by hiking the trails.

Besides the greenbelt, the Commission has been concerned with preserving other open areas in the Town, particularly those involving the protection of wetlands. These lands which were once thought of as worthless swamps are now recognized as vitally important to our present and future water supply. Extensive holdings have been acquired in three sections of Sharon — Great Cedar Swamp in southern Sharon, and marshes bordering the Neponset River and along Massapoag Brook in North Sharon — to keep them from being developed. Much of this land was donated or purchased at a nominal price.

In 1971 a concerted effort was made to alert the voters to the importance of spending money for wetlands, especially those surrounding Lake Massapoag, the Town's greatest natural resource. A brochure was developed and mailed just before town meeting supporting an appropriation of $50,000 for this purpose. The article was passed without a dissenting vote, and the fund has since been restored to this level at all subsequent town meetings. As a continuous control over the loss of wetlands, the state requires that anyone who proposes to fill such an area must first have his plan reviewed by the Commission at a public hearing.

One of the measures adopted by the state to foster land acquisition by the cities and towns is the Self-Help program, by which the state can reimburse the community for 50% of all land purchases which qualify for the program. Sharon's Commission was the first in the state to qualify for and receive this aid, and the Town has benefitted from it on a number of occasions since. A good example is the purchase in 1968 of the Recreation Center land and bathing beach at the southern end of Lake Massapoag, with three-quarters of the purchase price being reimbursed to the Town by Self-Help and federal funds.

Conservation easements are another way in which open space is being protected in Sharon. These are instances in which the landowner makes an agreement with the Town not to develop his property and to grant access to the public. A section of the Massapoag Trail is protected by an easement from Lawrence Arguimbau, and an easement on a tract of rocky woodland off Wolomolopoag Street was donated by Lawrence Peck.

Other activities that the Commission has sponsored over the years are tree planting, a two-day town-wide program stressing environmental needs, litter clean-up campaigns, and conservation camperships for young people. In fact, any cause which concerns conservation can count on the Commission for complete support.

The present members of the Commission are Mrs. Janice Adler, Eugene P. Flynn, Walter L. Reeve, Theodore A. Waldron, Edward A. Welch, Lawrence Newcomb, Secretary, and Mrs. Henrietta F. Becker, Chairman. Other Commission members not previously mentioned who have given valuable service in the past are Bryce C. Moulton, Dr. John G. Read, Mrs. Emily Parcher, Theodore G. Scott, Jr., and Joseph P. Murphy.

No history of the Commission would be complete without emphasizing the strong influence that Frank Chase, the first chairman, had on its development and later accomplishment. Through his intimate knowledge of Sharon and its government, his engineering know-how, and his deep interest in the land, he was the ideal person to set the Commission in motion and to build up the high regard and support that it presently enjoys with the townspeople. Not only was he the guiding force for conservation in Sharon, but he was also instrumental in setting a number of commissions in other towns on their feet. He has inspired others to carry on the work he so well began.

With over 500 acres of woods, ponds and streams under its protection, the Conservation Commission has done much to help keep Sharon green and a better place to live.

Devil's Rock   *Boyden Collection*

Devil's or Massapoag Brook   *Boyden Collection*

MOOSE HILL WILDLIFE SANCTUARY
AND NATURE CENTER

By David E. Clapp

CHAPTER 41

The accumulation of land for a "Bird Sanctuary" began in Sharon in 1918. With the passage of time and the changing of ownership, the Massachusetts Audubon Society now has over 230 acres of land on the rise called Moose Hill. In the first days of the movement to protect endangered species and create hunting laws, the Massachusetts Audubon Society was formed. As membership grew and time went by, the society determined a need for a reserve. Sharon was on the train lines and had available land that was owned by George W. Field, then Commissioner of Fisheries and Game. The Field property and the land that was slowly accumulated by the Society soon came under the guidance of MAS staff centered on Moose Hill.

The area was quite unlike the present condition. The house that Dr. Field used is the first house on the left after the S-curve. The first MAS residence/ museum is the house opposite. The existing MAS residence/program center has been in use since 1922. The most noticeable change in the area has been the continual disappearance of farm land. In the early 1900's the area was quite heavily farmed and fields were common. Today, the area is almost totally wooded and harbors fewer and different species of animal life.

The activities of the Moose Hill Wildlife Sanctuary are evidenced in many areas: wildlife management, educational programs, and the exhibition of a land ethic. The sanctuary staff is involved in land management that will provide as great a variety in habitat as is possible.

We live in an area that has a tendency to fill in rapidly with oak trees. The wildlife management plan for Moose Hill suggests the maintenance of open space and field areas. This management is followed by a variation in plant and animal forms.

The educational aspects of the sanctuary are best seen in the tours available for school groups and the classes we offer on a variety of natural history topics. Wildflowers, birds, trees, and many other topics are explored with both children and adults. The Moose Hill Day Camp is an opportunity for children from the first grade to the eighth grade to participate in outdoor exploration and discovery.

The land ethic concept is something that is rarely taught, but is rather a respect and affinity that is acquired from sensitive and knowledgeable people. The respect for the ability of land, the uniqueness of land and the importance of land-use planning and management is a feature that is rarely fully present in anyone. Moose Hill offers a stable area where people can return over and over again to reinforce the basic tenets of life and its cycles.

The Moose Hill Sanctuary serves its role as an educational facility through the expertise of the entire MAS staff. The role of wildlife sanctuary and its efforts to provide variation in habitat are activities that could not go on without the consent, willingness, and energies of our neighbors. The Kendall Trust and the Gagnon Family have been extremely important in the formulation and implementation of trends and activities on Moose Hill. A debt of gratitude that is immeasurable is owed to the neighbors.

The sanctuary is presently serving 35,000 people per year in some manner. Visitors, students, hikers, birders, and people out relaxing all contribute to the Moose Hill population. There is a parking area where Moose Hill Street and Moose Hill Parkway join, and trail maps are available here. We welcome you during the daytime and hope that you will lend your support to both your local sanctuary and the Massachusetts Audubon Society.

"Farm Fair" Games For Kids at the Moose Hill Sanctuary   *Courtesy: D. E. Clapp*

THE FLORA OF SHARON

By Lawrence Newcomb

CHAPTER 42

For those who like to explore the countryside, Sharon has a rich diversity of plant life in its woods, fields and swamps and along its roadsides. For every kind of locality there is a different group of plants which like the conditions they find there, be it dry or wet, shaded or sunny, rich earth or barren hillside. As the seasons change, new flowers and fruits appear, so that there is always something interesting to discover about plants whenever or wherever you roam.

Fortunately, there is still a large part of Sharon which is still undeveloped and explorable, even though, like all of our suburbs, open space is disappearing all too fast for those of us who enjoy the country. Several large tracts that are being preserved in their natural state are the Borderland State Park in the southern end of town, and the Moose Hill Audubon Sanctuary and the Kendall property around Moose Hill. Another place to visit is the Massapoag Trail maintained by the Conservation Commission. The Trail passes through three miles of unspoiled scenery from Massapoag Lake to North Main Street with many wild flowers and ferns all along its route.

Sharon, as well as the rest of Massachusetts, lies in the Transition Zone of plant life, where plants from the north intermingle with those from the south. In this zone the woodlands are mostly made up of a mixture of deciduous trees, such as maples, oaks and hickories, with an occasional pure stand of white pine or beech and, in a few places, hemlock. However, because of its relatively high average elevation compared to the surrounding towns, Sharon has more species that you would expect to find farther north. For example, white and yellow birches are quite frequent in our woods, but are rare in neighboring Stoughton.

Once one becomes familiar with the distribution of plants, you will note that many plants are fussy about where they grow; they like a particular type of home or habitat. Wherever you find an unusual habitat, you are apt to find unusual plants there. A good example is the quaking bog north of Wolomolopoag Pond where the mat of vegetation has grown out from the edge of the bog and is actually floating on water, giving a quaking sensation when you step on it. Here insectivorous plants and other bog plants make their home since they have been able to adapt to the very acid soil conditions of a true bog. Although the town has designs on this area for a reserve water supply, it is hoped that the only quaking bog in Sharon can be preserved.

Another geological feature in Sharon with unusual plant species is the steep ledges left by the glacier on the southern facing slopes of our higher hills, such as Moose Hill, which provide the rocky, well-drained site that some wild flowers seem to prefer. There are other less conspicuous spots where special growing conditions have attracted a group of plants that are found there and nowhere else in town. It is always a pleasure to discover these unusual species, as it was for me last year when on the rocky slope of Bluff Hill I came across a colony of bladdernut, a shrub that has only been recorded once before east of the Connecticut River.

The yearly parade of wild flowers begins in the early spring when in the swamps the skunk cabbage thrusts its mottled hood out of the frozen muck. In late April the same swamps are yellow with the flowers of the marsh marigold or cowslips. In the woods in spring will be found jack-in-the-pulpits, true and false Solomon's seals, bellworts, blue and white violets, and in a few places the yellow variety. Goldthread, clintonia and bunchberry like the deepest woods where rarely the painted trillium is also found. Later on in May, the pink lady's slipper or moccasin flower is luckily still quite common in our oak and pine woods. The flowering dogwood show masses of white under the trees, while the Canada mayflower or wild lily-of-the-valley carpets the ground beneath. Yellow buttercups and bluets brighten the meadows and wild geraniums grow along the borders of the woods.

Once the leaves have come out on all the trees, most of the woodland plants cease to flower. However, in acid open woods the shinleafs, the pipsissewa and its relative, the striped wintergreen, bloom; also the saprophytes which obtain their food from decaying matter like the mushrooms — Indian pipe, pinesap and, rarely, the spotted coralroot. In the summer, though, the fields and roadsides are full of flowers. There are daisies, clovers, black-eyed susans, yellow and orange hawkweeds, and Queen Anne's lace, to name a few. In the swamps you will find blue flags, turtleheads and the elusive large and small purple fringed orchids. White and yellow water lilies, arrowheads and pickerel weed line the margins of ponds and streams. Finally, in the fall, asters and goldenrods and the cardinal flower add their touches of color. These are only a few of the 400 or 500 species of wild flowers found in Sharon. In addition, 27 species of ferns occur within its borders. For those who seek them out, the plants of Sharon offer endless possibilities.

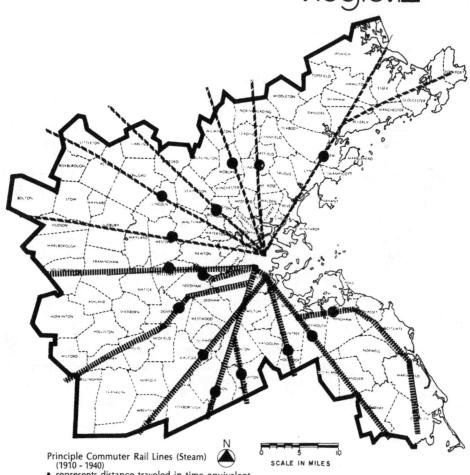

the Cities and Towns of the MAPC Region

Principle Commuter Rail Lines (Steam)
(1910 - 1940)
• represents distance traveled in time equivalent
to that needed to reach Sharon

N

SCALE IN MILES

Metropolitan Area Planning Council
44 School Street
Boston, Mass. 02108
1-(617)-523-2454

REFERENCE DATA
1970 Massachusetts population: 5,689,170
1970 MAPC population: 3,013,687 (52.98% of
total)
Square miles in region: 1,422.90 (910,656 acres)
MAPC membership: 101 cities and towns
19 cities: 1,651,368
82 towns: 1,362,318

PLANNING, GROWTH AND TRANSPORTATION

By George B. Bailey

CHAPTER 43

The growth of most New England towns occurred so gradually that few residents would call their town's evolution "planned." Occasionally, a residential or industrial development corporation created a town[1] but more often towns were formed by a combination of economic forces, governmental actions, and the ability of man to subdue or adjust to natural features. The form towns take is closely related to transportation which in turn is related to land uses. A use like a millsite can create a need for a road. The road then gives new accessibility to land through which it passes, creating new uses. To this day, these private or public investments benefit some, create costs to others.

The Early Town Plan

Sharon grew in the 17th century in part because war taxes on Dorchester residents were considered excessive[2] and emigration resulted, an early instance of "urban flight."

Sharon's first street pattern seems to have followed Indian trails. Bay Road was an easily travelled path to Narragansett Bay via the Taunton River. Another route led to Providence and followed what is now Main Street along a ridge east of the deep valley overlooking the Beaver Brook. The early post road route west of Moose Hill was joined by the Main Street route from Milton around 1700. A 1726 map[3] of the town showed 102 acres of "common" close to the present town center. It was here that the first meeting house was located, at the high point of the road like most New England town centers, safe, dry, and clearly visible from afar. The locational decision was a political one. The vote of the parish meeting chose the site of the present Unitarian Church in preference to the west edge of Moose Hill.[4] Apparently, Billings, Pond, and Depot Streets all converged at the center as a result of this decision.

Town Growth in The Late 1700's

The 18th century population was largely dispersed by farming and clustered at mill dams. Roads joined these areas to the center.

Public roads were created when private ways were surveyed and built, with land contours suitable for wagon travel, on well-drained soil with moderate grades. The way became an official town street when selectmen would "lay out the street" and seek town meeting acceptance, "taking" the street, compensating landowners when necessary, a procedure still required today. Man-made obstacles existed. The occasional abrupt turn in today's street may be the result of an uncooperative landowner in Colonial times, who successfully persuaded the town meeting to refuse to take.

Well into the 19th century, the pattern changed little as growth was slow. But everywhere in the Western world steam was replacing water power, permitting concentration of manufacturing enterprises near large populations and harbors where coal was cheap. Sharon's industries diminished. For those that remained after the 1840's, however, the new railroad's proximity meant transport to principal markets was fast and direct.

Tourists Enter The Economy

Middle-class city dwellers' interest in vacations and day trips in the country brought Sharon into its next role: haven for city dwellers seeking altitude, water, and repose. While the Old Colony Railroad and the Eastern Railroad had shore and sea with which to entice Bostonians, the Boston & Providence Railroad had only inland communities, Great Blue Hill and Lake Massapoag. The lake was particularly accessible from the railroad, about a mile from Sharon Station and only one-third mile from the Sharon Heights area where a small platform and stop soon were established at Garden Street. By 1879 there were several hotels in Sharon; the grandest of them, Massapoag House (on the site of today's Community Center), was described in *Scribners Magazine* in an article "Wheel Around the Hub."[5] The Boston Bicycle Club, to celebrate the first 35 miles of their 100 mile two-day trek on high wheelers, had gathered at Massapoag House on September 17, 1879, with their ladies who, having arrived earlier by steam train, greeted them from piazzas overlooking the lake. Other hotels around the lake were at Cedar and along Beach Street, and at the school site on South Main. The clean air and altitude attracted lung patients who recuperated at the Tuberculosis Sanatorium on Upland Road, also close to the station.

Commuters Come To Town

The vacationer soon discovered Sharon as a year-around home. Steam train commuting was changing the shape of American cities in the 1880's. Rates were being reduced to encourage city-dwellers to move to the suburbs.[6] Josiah Quincy, Boston railroad financier then reformer, induced the legislature to pass a law requiring that on petition of 200 people, a railroad would run trains reaching and leaving Boston at 6 A.M. and P.M., which would cost on a yearly basis 0.5¢ a mile for distances not exceeding 15 miles. The idea was to "mitigate the distressful living conditions of workers by enabling them to live in houses built on cheap land in the suburbs."[7] Whether this move benefited the workers is not clear but real estate speculators in the vicinity of railroad stations certainly must have found a benefactor in Quincy. The towns within 15 miles found houses of the upper middle class lining streets near railroad stations from 1880 on through the 1920's.

Sharon was beyond the 15-mile point but some of the additional runs serving Canton had to pass through Sharon. Because nature had interrupted the land masses in the southwest region with Great Blue Hill and the thousands

320

of acres of the Fowl Meadow of the Neponset River — portions of the former becoming part of the Metropolitan Park System in 1893 — a discerning housebuyer could find a trip to and from Sharon no more time-consuming than a much closer suburb on most other lines, there were so few stops for the Boston & Providence trains. From 1890 on, rail fares plummeted and housing within walking distance of the station filled almost every available acre. Streets near the station were quickly built up: Chestnut, Walnut, Oakland, Pine Road, Edgewood, Ridge, Valley, Forest, and South Pleasant along with Highland, High, Glendale, Summit, and Maple were carved out and by 1910 all had much of their present character as did Pine Grove Avenue, Upland Road, and nearby Norwood Street on the west side of the tracks.

Sharon's growth rates were dramatic in the 90's, leading all other communities in the eastern part of the state.[8] The west banks of Beaver Brook remained undeveloped, an exception to the rule. It appears that if landowners in the area that became Moose Hill Parkway had been receptive to land sales in the 90's Sharon's growth in that period could have been even greater. One other small railroad-related area in town is the Mansfield Street enclave, built with wells and four-acre lots in the 1920's close to the East Foxboro railroad station.

Pedestrianism: Great Leveler

Only the commuters' ability to walk in all weather limited housing locations. Town growth was constrained little by terrain and not at all by lack of water. Extensions of the water system far outpaced development, signalling a cozy relationship between land developers and the Town Hall.[9] Carriages must have been used by some but walking was considered healthy, comfortable, and safe. No autos were bothersome until after 1910. Walking had another subtle benefit, that of bringing youth into early equality with adults. No license was needed to travel the streets by foot or bicycle and Sharon commuters met each other and their children on the streets as they traveled to and from their homes and the station.

The City, The Streetcar and Sharon

The urban problems of the 19th century, as seen by the urban philosopher-statistician Adna Weber[10] could be mitigated by reducing the concentration of people in the cities. For middle-sized cities, "the trolly car and bicycle may serve the purpose." In larger cities, "surface cars whose maximum speed was 9 or 10 mph; or elevated systems (12 mph max.) could not serve this purpose adequately." Only steam railroad or elevated or underground four-track systems permitting express trains averaging more than 25 mph would suffice, he said. Boston was well on its way toward this goal by 1890. A few years later the orderly growth of cities and enlightened public policies would be ended by the proliferation of the auto and its usurpation of the once safe streets of 19th century suburbia.

This future was not obvious to the early 20th century transit entrepreneur. In Sharon a single track trolley line was laid from Cobb's Corner to the "Grove" off East Foxboro Street in 1901, giving residents of built-up areas of Dorchester and Mattapan a chance to visit the lake at low cost. Harding, Beach Road, Lake Avenue, Grove Street were built up in this period and a new community of Irish middle class on Beach Road and Jewish middle class on Harding and Lake Avenue began to move to Sharon in the summer. The pleasant little trolley car was not to last, however, and in the early 20's stopped operations. Its effect on development was slight because of its seasonal character; North Main Street had too many farms, swamps, and ponds to permit much more development, and Cobb's Corner did not experience commercialization until the 1950's, despite its transit transfer function during the streetcar period.

Growth Since 1920

Sharon's present population is spread over areas far from public transportation. Two autos per dwelling became a necessary cost of living. From the 20's on, the auto released the last restraint to continuous development although there remained public lands, private organization open space, or an occasional speculator or conservation-minded landowner to limit development opportunities. In Sharon, the Kendall and Ames Estates, Conservation lands, the Massachusetts Audubon Sanctuary along with Griffin-donated and controlled lands have prevented continuous strip development of every available acre. Sharon's 1890 railroad suburban character gradually blended with auto-dependent homes and decentralized school facilities.

Speculative builders appeared in town on several occasions, records show. The area between South Main, Oakland, Station Street and the railroad was platted for 361 5,000 square-foot lots in 1888, where only 78 exist today after 87 years of development pressure. The proposed grid-iron layout ignored the terrain and did not prove feasible, fortunately for the town's middle-class image. Chestnut Street, Ridge, and Oakland Roads all were constructed in a curvilinear pattern to accomodate the gracious exurban homes of the 1900's that still dominate the area. Sharon adopted zoning, a concept first introduced nationally in the 20's, under Article 25 of the Town Meeting of March 13, 1933, at the recommendation of the Planning Board, which had been formed several years earlier. Use regulations and sign restraints were very detailed and to a large extent remain in effect today. Lot area regulations, however, were set at a level far below the typical residence then in town (10,000 square feet per dwelling) and it was not until the post World War II boom that lot area minimums were increased to 40,000 square feet. Sharon's extensive frontage on U.S. 1 constructed along town borders in the early 30's was not zoned for commercial use, unlike that in nearby towns. No doubt among the restraining influence was one of the principal landowners, H. P. Kendall, himself a Planning Board member in the 1940's.

Today the town's growth continues to be controlled by exogenous factors: regional population and work centers, the relative tax rate and relative attractiveness to both speculative builder and potential new resident, transportation costs, and availability.

However, the town's own attention to quality of services; schools, libraries, recreational facilities, and preservation of Lake Massapoag are likely to continue growth pressures. New land use plans, controls on water extensions, acquisition of open space, and limitations on growth at the edges of town may be used to contain the demand and protect our environment for coming generations.

Footnotes

1. Beacon Street, Brookline, was largely planned, developed and controlled by West End Street Railway Co., who introduced the first electric streetcar to Boston. Lowell was chosen as the site for a large manufacturing center because its location on the Merrimack River made it ideal. The Lowell Canal & Power Co. designed houses and factories and maintained the canal system.
2. Amy Morgan Rafter Pratt, *The History of Sharon, Massachusetts to 1865*. Thesis submitted in partial fulfillment of the requirement for the Degree of Master of Arts 1935, Boston University Graduate School. Rev. 1941. (Privately Published by Frieda Billings Cushman, 1966), p. 2.
3. Pratt, flyleaf.
4. Pratt, p. 9.
5. *Scribner's Monthly*, February, 1880.
6. Edward C. Kirkland, *Men, Cities and Transportation, a Study in New England History.* (Harvard Univ. Pr., 1948), p. 292.
7. Kirkland, p. 295.
8. *Sharon Enterprise*, Oct. 14, 1894, reported that of 23 cities and towns, Sharon had the fastest growth both of real and personal property in 1893 and 1894.
9. Sharon's water system began in 1885 and by 1890 extended to Ashcroft Road on the north, Walnut Street on the south, Ames Street on Pond, and past Cottage Street on Billings to the west. Subsequent extensions were made out Massapoag Avenue to Capen Hill by 1895, South Main and Gunhouse by 1905, Maskwonicut and North Main by 1903, Upland Road (then Depot Street) and Moose Hill Parkway by 1909. Extensions of the water system far eclipsed the growth area of the 90's which was concentrated in the area near the station.
10. Adna Weber, *The Growth of Cities in the 19th Century.* (Cornell Univ. Pr., 1899).

The Boston Bicycle Club Stops at Cobb's Tavern

An Early View of the Square

A View of the Square - 1976   *Photo by: J. K. Harris*

THE YEARS OF GROWTH — 1945 to 1976

By Stanley T. Dingman

CHAPTER 44

In 1965, eleven years before the nation's Bicentennial Anniversary, Sharon celebrated its own 200th birthday in a three-day observance that featured a block dance, a bean supper, and a parade. Though little mention was made of it then, the twenty years preceding that birthday celebration had been momentous ones for the town.

For the nation, 1945 was to become an historic year for it was to see the end of the second global war. Germany surrendered on May 7, and Japan capitulated some three months later on August 17.

There was no such dramatic indication that it was to be an historic year for Sharon. Yet forces that would eventually change the character of the town were then at work.

The post-war baby boom then was nothing more than a whisper in the night. There was little intimation that the nation was soon to experience a dramatic increase in population and even less intimation of the influence that increase would have on Sharon.

In 1945, Sharon was a small town, quietly shedding the aura of the mountain lake resort which it had been for several years. It had a population of 4,073 and an annual meeting appropriation of $284,488.10. No doubt, the per capita obligation of $69.84 seemed an outrageous burden to the residents, but it was a modest sum compared to what it was to become some thirty years later.

Activity in those days centered around Post Office Square where a storefront bank, a small post office, a stationery store, a hardware store, and five small food stores met the modest demands of the residents. The police force consisted of Chief Egitto T. Lavezzo and Officers William F. Cornell and Robert G. Feist. Their duties could not have been too onerous for the record shows that there were but 73 arrests and prosecutions for the year. Of those, thirty were for auto violations. Bob Feist, with his intimate knowledge of the comings and goings of the residents, found time to write for the Advocate, a chit-chat column that was later to become the work of Tess the Tatler (Dorothy Dennen).

Breaking and entering was practically unheard of and residents had no qualms about leaving doors and windows unlatched as they went up town or "to the Square," to do their errands. The amount budgeted for Protection in 1945 was $26,059.49 and that was for both the police department and the fire department.

Education was a rather modest activity. Forty-four seniors graduated from the high school and went on to greater accomplishments. The school population was 699 students, including 26 who were resident patients of the Sharon Sanatorium on Upland Road. There were 22 teachers and seven persons with special assignments. The total salary budget was $53,068.70.

Most of the residents were seemingly content with their unhurried pace of life. Their families were established, their society was fixed. They had no desire to be engulfed by a horde of strangers. There were few homes available and those who bought them found it difficult to penetrate the fixed patterns of their neighbors. The attitude was expressed sometime earlier in this letter to the editor:

> . . . it will be a mistake for the newer comers, if they would accomplish the most good, to antagonize their elders by assuming too much of the know-it-all attitude while trying to institute reforms or to establish what may appear to them, more modern methods. They should bear in mind that Sharon is a conservative old town, and its native inhabitants feel a loyalty to its past history not fully appreciated. Let them therefore be gracefully considerate of this honorable spirit of loyalty even though accompanied, as it often is, by a seeming lack of progressiveness. It is only through harmony and good will that much progress can result.[1]

A lack of homes was by no means limited to Sharon. The war years had brought the housing industry to a standstill. But with labor and materials once more available, developers sought to meet the insistently growing demand for homes. Sharon, with its tiny population centered in its 25 square miles of farms and forest, had lots of land on which to build. Its natural beauty and excellent transportation made it doubly desirable.

That Sharon was to be a target for developers must have been evident by 1946. In that year, the Planning Board recommended that a zoning by-law be adopted requiring that house lots in the single residence and trunk highway districts be of at least 10,000 square feet while those in the general residence district be of at least 8,000 square feet. It was a by-law that soon proved inadequate.

By 1950, large developments had gone in at Sharon Heights and at what had been the Hare Farm on North Main Street.* Sewerage and drainage problems were so pronounced that the need for by-law changes was self-evident. It was not long before mimimum lot sizes were increased to 20,000 square feet for Single Residence Area B and to 40,000 square feet for Single Residence Area A.

While sewerage and drainage conditions were significant reasons for requiring large lot sizes, they were not the only reasons. An added factor was the desire to decelerate and control growth. But the lot size requirements were to affect the character of the town. To maximize their returns, builders built big houses on big lots. Big houses cost more money. Thus, Sharon zoned itself into an upper middle-class community.

*The Planning Board approved additional sections of two subdivisions on South Main Street and one on North Main Street and also has approved an entirely new subdivision off Massapoag Avenue. These subdivisions add up to 237 buildings. Planning Board report, 1950.

This was to become evident as the years went by. According to a 1969 report[2], Sharon's housing is high priced in comparison to the rest of Boston's south suburban area. "Homes in new subdivisions are priced anywhere from $30,000 to $80,000, although most are in the $35,000 to $45,000 range . . . the greatest demand will lie in the $18,000 to $21,000 range (24 percent of the demand). No new housing is available in this range in Sharon."

It is interesting to note that in 1969 more than half the housing that existed in Sharon had been built since 1959.[3] The community, which had been settled for more than 300 years, doubled its number of dwellings in twenty years.

There are, no doubt, many reasons why Sharon has proved so attractive during these years since the last world war. But industry has not been one of them. During its years, Sharon has seen several bustling industries that turned out cannon and cannon balls, knives, cotton cloth, hoes, plow shares, leather, trowels, tools, and paint. However, by 1945, only one remained: the Sharon Box Company and this offered little employment activity. It was not jobs that brought people to Sharon.

That industry should slip away from Sharon during the years when it was being best served by the railroad seems anomalous. Yet that is what happened. By 1835, the Boston and Providence Railroad had completed the Canton viaduct and was providing through service with connections to New York and Washington. Despite this, Sharon's industries disappeared one by one and it was not until 1949 that the town expressed any concern. It was then voted "That it is the sense of the meeting that the town desires the establishment of a Light Industrial District." The moderator was instructed to appoint a committee of three to look into the matter.

As a result, a Light Industrial District was finally established in 1960. The intervening years had been spent in argument over how and where this was to be accomplished. To help maintain the residential character of the town, the district was set up along the western boundary where Interstate Route 95 effectively segregated it from the rest of Sharon. At present there are a motel, a restaurant, and nine manufacturing or warehousing firms in the industrial district. In total, they are assessed at $3,830,000 and contribute $1,953,402 to the annual revenue of the town.

Though the railroad did nothing to stimulate or maintain industry in Sharon, it undoubtedly was influential in the growth of the town. (It has often been said that the whistle of the night train disturbed the slumber of the residents.) During the latter part of the 19th century, and the early part of the 20th century, it provided transportation for the hundreds of visitors who came from the crowded city to enjoy the clear air and the amenities of the many resort hotels and inns that had become Sharon's major industry. Train service was excellent and remained that way until the mid-1950's. Even in 1952, it was still possible for a traveler to board, in Sharon, the midnight sleeper to New York and Washington. Commuter service was frequent and fast, and usually dependable. During the late 40's and early 50's, the morning trains took hundreds of Sharonites to their businesses in Boston.

But in a way, the railroad was to be an agent of its own doom. With the advent of the railroad, the town had quickly developed up the slope east of the station and toward the square. All of this was within easy walking distance of the trains. Enticed, in part by the good commuting service, more and more people saw Sharon as the ideal community in which to live and raise a family. But by this time, available buildable land was at some distance from the station. Thus, people needed autos to get back and forth to the station. Since they had to drive part way, many elected to drive the whole way. As industry dispersed itself along Boston's circumferential Route 128, the railroad provided a direct route for fewer and fewer Sharon residents. Inflation pushed commuting fares higher and higher even as the quality of service diminished.

Like the alligator that started eating its tail, the railroad seemed to be devouring itself. It might have by this time completed the process had not the Massachusetts Bay Transportation Authority provided other nutriment. In 1965, the MBTA assumed operation of the commuter trains, aided in part by a subsidy from the town itself. In 1976, Sharon paid $115,287.37 to the MBTA so that railroad service would continue to be available to residents who wished to commute to Boston.

If the railroad can be said to have been an influence in the growth of Sharon, then it probably can be said to have helped to bring a new industry to Sharon: education. That education was to become Sharon's prime industry was foreshadowed in 1945, when Roger K. Poole, Superintendent of Schools, stated in his annual report:

> Forward looking citizens have been aware that sooner or later the Town would have to face the problem of building a modern elementary school to replace the three frame buildings now in use.

The three frame buildings have never been replaced. Two of them continue to serve the school system; one as the administrative office, the other as an adjunct to the so-called Middle School. The third, the future of which is in doubt, now houses some social service agencies.

There were additional intimations of an educational crisis. John B. Chaffee, who replaced Roger Poole as Superintendent of Schools, wrote in 1946, "Sharon must eventually face the problem of adequate housing for a growing school population." By that time, the school enrollment had climbed to 727. Probably much of that was due to the fact that the kindergarten had been established under the direction of Emma Harris.

Evidently convinced by Mr. Chaffee's warning, the town, in 1946, voted for a committee to consider a site for a new elementary school. At the same time, recognizing the inadequacy of salary schedules, the school committee voted a temporary increase of $400 per year for teachers. And the town, that year, voted to increase the school committee from three members to six, a process that was to take some time as one new member was to be elected each year.

In the twenty years following Mr. Poole's warning, Sharon's school population increased dramatically. In that period, three new elementary schools with a total of 45 classrooms were built. A new high school went up in 1957, accommodating 700 students. Five years later, the town voted $742,000 for constructing and equipping an addition to the high school to provide space and facilities for another 500 students. In the meantime, the town had already moved to acquire land on Mountain Street for a badly needed junior high school. This was completed in 1966, and, at last, the burgeoning school population seemed to have been contained.

In those twenty years, the school enrollment rose from 699 to 3,549, a figure not much lower than the entire population had been in 1945. The cost of schooling had jumped to $1,607,863.11. Dramatic as that twenty-year increase might have been, the next four years showed an increase of another $1,000,000.

In the years from 1965 to 1975, the school budget again almost doubled itself, and the Bicentennial Year budget is estimated at $5,694,664.

To provide these new schools, the town, over the years, borrowed $7,180,000. Such a figure, of course, is not the actual cost of providing the needed school buildings and facilities. The Wilber School needed alterations and repairs to fit it for its new role as a Middle School. And each year, the town paid about as much in interest as it paid on its bonds.

Naturally, as more children filled more classrooms, more teachers were needed to instruct them. "The school year 1975-1976 was begun with 205 members of the teaching staff." The pupil-teacher ratio had dropped from 31.7 in 1945 to 17.1. The apparent discrepancy is probably due to expanded curriculum choices in the junior and senior high schools designed to improve the quality of education. And quality education had long been the goal.

In 1950, Herman H. Richardson, Superintendent of Schools, said, "I think I judge correctly when I say the people of Sharon will not be satisfied with 'average' or 'a little better-than-average' schools." That sentiment was echoed in 1953 in the Selectmen's report signed by Clarence I. Peterson, Dwight P. Coburn and John T. Andrews:

> . . . inferior education embodies the threat of mediocrity to the children of the community, who, in the last analysis, are the only priceless assets we possess.

Quality education was the goal, and over the years, the townspeople seemed resigned to, if not content with the increasing costs. That is, until 1973 when it was voted to accept the Warrant Committee's recommendation that $325,000 be taken from the proposed $6,513,075 budget. That was an 18-month's budget, for 1974 was the year in which the state mandated a change from a calendar fiscal year to a July-June fiscal year.

Though the amount was later reinstated by court action, the town had indicated its concern that more than 60 per cent of the annual budget was needed for the operation of the schools at a time when the school enrollment was beginning to decline. By 1975, the enrollment had dropped to 3,498 from the high of 3,777 in 1968.

There was to be little hope for relief, however, for the next year (1974), the Special Education Act (Chapter 766) was to become effective. This legislation requires each community to identify the specialized needs of all children and to provide appropriate educational programs. Though the intent seemed to be for the Commonwealth to fund the added programs, there has been considerable confusion. Superintendent of Schools, James J. Dowd, wrote in his report for 1975:

> The impact of compliance with Chapter 71B of the General Laws (better known as Chapter 766) continues to be one of great concern in the budget deliberations. Not only are we concerned with the growth in this area, but we are also concerned that the whole area of reimbursement from the Commonwealth is not clear . . .

The history of education, however, is not the whole history of Sharon. It has been subjected to the vagaries of economics and weather as well as those of legislation. While there were no major disasters in the years from 1945 to 1976, the town did experience considerable inconvenience from four hurricanes within a period of six years from 1945 to 1960.

For 1954, the Selectmen wrote:

> No report would be complete . . . without some mention of hurricanes Carol and Edna, which visited their unwelcome and devastating havoc upon the Town on August 31 and September 11. We have only to be thankful that, notwithstanding the very heavy damage both wrought, neither caused any loss of life or serious personal injury . . . special commendation is . . . deserved . . . by Highway Surveyor Lawrence Peck, Fire Chief Philip Whitney, Police Chief Jim Lavezzo, C. D. Director Raymond Barley, and their respective departments . . . To date, the cost of the two hurricanes to the Town treasury has been approximately $22,000.

The following year, hurricane Diane struck. Heavy flood damage resulted and the newly established Public Works department had its hands full repairing roads and culverts, a job that was "costly in terms of both money and time . . ." In 1960, "The Town was also fortunate in escaping as lightly as it did from hurricane Donna."

Long-time efforts to preserve the appearance of the Square went up in smoke and flame on December 11, 1966, when the Pettee building burned. Things were never to be the same again. Some of the disappointment and despair was evident in this 1967 comment by the Selectmen:

> Since then the deterioration has been more rapid and the appearance of the center of our Town is truly deplorable. Although we had a traffic problem before the fire, this has now been eased to the point where there is not enough traffic to support the merchants . . . and some of them are leaving with every indication that either their stores will be left vacant, or will be tenanted with less desirable activities in a constantly downgrading spiral.

Much as this altered the appearance of the Square, changes had been taking place over the years. As early as 1952, Norfolk County Trust Company opened its branch at 15 Post Office Square. By 1963, the Sharon Cooperative Bank had outgrown its quarters in the 130-year old Quaker Inn. As no buyer could be found for the structure, it was torn down and the present building erected. Three years before that, an addition had been made to the public library. Similarly, the post office had outgrown two or three homes in the Square and in 1960 moved to its new building on South Main Street.

The area around the Square was changing too. A parish hall was added to the Congregational Church in 1949. Eleven years later, this was raised and a lower floor built beneath it. Zoning changes permitted shops and businesses to move into what had been residences on South Main Street between Depot and East Chestnut. In 1948, the Town voted $30,000 for the construction of a fire and police station at their present location. And the same year, $45,000 was appropriated for the construction of the highway garage on South Main Street. The Town continued to grow and "One of the highlights of 1963 was the beginning of construction of the new town hall and the additions to the fire and police stations." Multiple residences (apartments) which heretofore had been limited to the Sharon Garden Apartments near Cobb's Corner began to move into the center of town in 1973, culminating with Watson Plaza in 1975.

All the while new buildings were going up, Sharon was endeavoring to maintain its residential and recreational character. The Town acquired Hammershop Pond and the land around it in 1955, though the Conservation Commission was not set up until 1959.

Two years later, the Commission was given 14,000 to purchase land along Massapoag Brook from Billings Street to the Canton town line. In 1962, Mr. and Mrs. Robert Cushman gave Mann's Pond to the Conservation Commission. Land acquisitions continued over the years, and by 1975, the Conservation Commission had more than 500 acres of woods, ponds, and streams under its protection.

Massapoag Lake continued to hold its summer resort attraction, but as the population grew, so did concern for maintaining the recreational value of the lake. In 1954, some 330 youngsters were enrolled in various swimming programs. The number jumped to 456 in 1955 and in 1956 reached 628. By 1974, the enrollment was 1,000. The Park Department report in 1956 stated:

> There is no accurate measure of the number of people who made use of the beach . . . However, 1,002 car stickers were sold, 2,566 resident tags and 1,475 guest tags. A total of 1,541 non-resident parking tickets were sold on weekends and holidays.

By 1965, however, study techniques were somewhat more efficient. The Lakefront Study Committee reported:

> Maximum attendance was found on Saturday, July 17, 1965, when 1,875 people used the beach and 204 cars were parked. Peak usage during that day showed over 1,000 people and 130 cars on the beach between 2 and 3 P.M.

That committee had been created in 1961 and as a result of its recommendations, Beach Street was relocated to eliminate traffic hazards and to provide a much wider beach area to accommodate the ever-growing number of residents who wished to use the beach. In 1967, the Town voted $35,000 for the construction of an administration building at the beach.

At a special meeting in September, 1967, the Town voted to purchase the St. Francis Retreat Lodge which the large hotel at the south end of the lake was then called. With this $335,000 acquisition the Town really went into the recreation business. The Selectmen in their 1968 report wrote:

> One of the major achievements of the year was the town's response to the need and interest in recreation for Sharon youth and adults. At the Special Town Meeting in June, it was voted to use the former St. Francis Retreat Lodge, purchased by the town in 1967, as a recreation center. . . . In accordance with the recommen-

dations of the Recreation Study Committee, the March Town Meeting approved the appointment of a Recreation Committee to advise the Selectmen on a broad range of year-round recreation activities. A Recreation Director was appointed in October and a wide variety of recreation programs immediately made available to residents of all ages. The youth of the town worked hard to build a "teenage center." Volunteer aides assisted the Recreation Director as instructors. As of year end, over 1,500 individuals and 17 organizations were utilizing the facilities of the newly named "Community Center . . ."

By 1975, the playground program and special events had attracted almost 5,000 children and young people, while a host of other activities, including baseball, swimming, sailing, and dancing among others, brought out close to 4,000 participants.

In December, 1974, the Town acquired the Sacred Heart School property, renamed it Deborah Sampson Park and greatly increased recreational opportunities and facilities.

Though recreation is becoming a major concern, and education has been Sharon's biggest industry for many years, the Town has felt the impact of other, and sometimes more frightening events during these later years. There was a time, 1962, when nuclear attack was considered possible, if not imminent. To be prepared, the Town Meeting voted the following resolution be adopted:

> WHEREAS, there is the possibility of an occurence of disasters of unprecendented size and destructiveness resulting from enemy thermonuclear attack;

> NOW, THEREFORE BE IT RESOLVED that in absence of statutory authority and guidance from the federal and state governments, and until such authority or guidance is made known or martial law is declared, it is the sense of this meeting:

> 1. That during the period between any air-raid warning and the following "all clear" signal or during the period between any air-raid warning and the time when all possible danger (including danger from fall-out) from any attack following such warning shall have subsided, the then holders of the following town offices, if within the bounds of the town and willing and able to act and then only in the order hereinafter designated, *shall have and may exercise, in addition to any other authority vested in them by law, any and all authority over persons and property, necessary or expedient for meeting such state of emergency.*

National politics were also a concern, and that year the town was voting Republican. Senatorial candidate George C. Lodge got 2,336 votes to Edward M. Kennedy's 1,735. John A. Volpe polled 2,404 votes to Endicott Peabody's 1,960 for governor, and Edward W. Brooke got 3,320 votes as candidate for attorney general. Sharonites, however, seem to resist political patterning. In the 1960 Presidential election, two years earlier, the Kennedy-Johnson slate outpolled the Nixon-Lodge ticket 2,535 to 2291. In 1966, Sharonites gave majority votes to the Republican candidates for senator and governor and to the Democratic candidate for representative.

In 1968, Humphrey and Muskie outdrew Nixon and Agnew, but Margaret Heckler outdrew her Democratic opponent. Democratic candidates again came out ahead in the 1972 Presidential race, but Republican Senator Edward W. Brooke far out-distanced his Democratic rival.

Practical, administrative matters also occupied the attention of the selectmen and the citizens during these years of growth. Zoning and gravel removal, water mains and water supplies, garbage collection and rubbish disposal, all demanded attention. Compounding these problems was inflation. In 1968 the Selectmen wrote:

> The economic growth of the town brought many problems. Increased costs in all municipal functions, along with increased population, housing, and the demand for services, brought a staggering increase in the tax rate, imposing an increased burden on the residential property owner. . . . More industrial activity of the kind permitted by the Zoning By-Law will be necessary, however, in order to bring significant financial assistance to the town.

And in 1974, the new board reported:

> In the operation of Town government during 1974, the Selectmen have tried to deal realistically with the economic problems presented by the continued upward trend of inflation. In many areas, such as labor negotiations and purchased services and commodities, this has proved to be not only difficult, but has once again forced re-evaluation of priority lists to determine the most essential items as opposed to items which can be postponed to another year.

But there were problems other than those of economics. Population increases seem to bring social problems which are reflected in the number of infractions of the law. The number of arrests and prosecutions had grown to 416 in 1975 from 73 in 1945. Not only did the total number increase, but also did the rate per thousand of population. In 1945 the rate was 18 per thousand. In 1975 it was over 30.

Improved enforcement techniques undoubtedly had some influence on the statistics, especially in motor vehicle violations. The use of a radar timer to detect speeders was initiated in 1961. Of it the Selectmen wrote, "coincidental with its use, there has been a substantial drop in the number of accidents occurring in Sharon."

Motor vehicle violations, however, were by no means the major concern, as the Selectmen pointed out in their report for 1967:

> The Police and Fire Departments continue to provide a most satisfactory level of performance . . . Although we are not pleased with some of the notoriety which has befallen the Town during the past year, we can take pride in the efficient and effective manner in which our POLICE Department has solved the murder at

the Sacred Heart School, apprehended housebreakers and effectively dealt with the serious problem of drug usage by our youth. The Plans and Objectives Committee has recommended the establishment of a Detective Bureau within the Police Department to cope with the rising crime rate.

The Selectmen that year were Francis I. Sullivan, Milton O. Corey, and George L. Greenfield.

These problems had not abated by 1975, for the report lists armed robbery, assault and battery, breaking and entering, illegal possession of alcohol, barbiturates, LSD and marijuana, as well as willful injury to property.

Despite its problems, however, Sharon has been and continues to be a congenial community. In 1945, it still strongly reflected its Protestant Christian heritage, with the Congregational, Unitarian, and Baptist churches dominating the religious scene. At that time, there also existed the Episcopal, Christian Science, and Catholic churches. A small synagogue, Adath Sharon, had been established on Harding Street, and members of what was to become Temple Israel were meeting in the old Mansion House on Pond Street.

The first structure of Temple Israel was built in 1949. As of 1957, there were an estimated 1,000 Jewish families in Sharon. Temple Sinai on Ames Street was dedicated in 1961. The Evangelical Baptist Church was established in 1956, and in 1959 built its own church on the corner of South Main and Ames Streets.

Racially, Sharon seems to have proved much more appealing to blacks than any of the neighboring communities. "At the time of the 1970 census, Sharon which has one-seventh of Quincy's population . . . had twice as many black residents at 258." The Norfolk County census of that year showed:

	Canton	Norwood	Sharon	Walpole	Westwood
Population	17,100	30,815	12,367	18,149	12,750
Blacks	66	38	258	124	16

As might be expected of any community, Sharon has always endeavored to "maintain the character" of the town. But all efforts to preserve the past bring something new. Some of the changes have been highly visible. Others have been much less so, but perhaps, more highly pervasive. Certainly, any former resident, returning after a thirty year absence would find that the town had changed dramatically. Yet for all the changes, there remain some basic characteristics. Sharon residents take an active interest in their town and its affairs. Perhaps more than in most towns, the citizens are the government, a fact recognized by the Selectmen who wrote in their 1975 report:

> As in the past years, many citizens gave freely of their time and expertise to contribute such a great amount to the efficient and able execution of our town government. Sharon continues to stand out in services administered and general good government. This is, in large part, due to the unselfish giving by those individuals who lend support to various committees which are concerned with planning and administration of many areas of community matters. The Board wishes to acknowledge the extent of their endeavors to

the smooth and orderly operation of our town, and to sincerely thank the persons involved for all they have contributed.

Footnotes

Unless otherwise noted, fact, figures, and quotations are from Sharon Town Reports of the years indicated.

1. Phillips, John G. *Historical Scrapbook*, Volume II, 1910.
2. *Reconnaissance Report: Initial Housing Element, November, 1969; Sharon, Massachusetts.* Prepared by Bureau of Planning Programs, Sharon Town Officials, Massachusetts Department of Community Affairs.
3. Ibid.
4. Gordon, Albert J. *Jews in Suburbia*. Boston: Beacon Press, 1959.
5. Susan Scheible, *Quincy Patriot Ledger*, March, 1974. (No date given. Clipping in Sharon Public Library).

Post Offices of 1976 and of Yesteryear

Photo by: J. K. Harris
Boyden Collection

Dwight P. Colburn proclaims the 200th (1965) Anniversary Underway   *Photo by: K. F. McLean*

The Sharon Bicentennial Committee Members Gentlemen Standing Left to Right: V. Mirabile; W. L. Reeve, Chairman; S. S. Morgan
        Ladies Seated Left to Right: Mrs. Arnold P. Clough; Mrs. Charles H. Newcombe Jr.;
Mrs. Donald W. Brookfield; Mrs. Babbie Brittain Erkelens

SHARON BICENTENNIAL 1765-1965

By Ardell Newcombe

CHAPTER 45

The Town of Sharon celebrated its 200th birthday eleven years before the nation's Bicentennial celebration. A bronze plaque erected permanently in the Sharon Town Hall commemorates that historical observance.

A proclamation officially opening the series of events was signed by the Board of Selectmen of that year, Milton O. Corey, George L. Greenfield, and Francis X. Mahoney, on June 10, 1965, and the opening celebration of the anniversary started Friday, July 2, 1965. Religious, educational, civic, fraternal, and patriotic organizations, as well as industrial and business establishments supported the official Town of Sharon Bicentennial Committee in planning and activating the events.

Friday, July 2nd, a supper at the First Baptist Church and the pealing of church bells throughout the town preceded opening ceremonies on the steps of the Unitarian Church. Many state and, of course, local dignitaries attended. Afterward, a block dance was held in Post Office Square.

On July 3rd, a bean supper was held at the Unitarian Church grounds, followed by a jazz and pop concert.

The Sharon Bicentennial Parade, including marching town officials, police force, marching bands, antique autos, colorful floats, equestrian units, and fire department equipment from surrounding towns and Sharon, was the highlight of the Fourth of July, with prizes awarded to various divisions of the parade. Following the parade, many respectable residents and visitors were unsuspectingly caught for ignoring the posted warnings for "Breeches of Decency, Decorum, and Upright Conduct" and found themselves in the stocks or pillory provided by Sturbridge Village, all good-naturedly accepting their "punishment". A beautiful display of fireworks climaxed the events of this day.

Sites of historical significance were marked throughout the town and guides were stationed at each one for the tour which took place on October 2nd and 3rd, 1965. Included in the tour were Unitarian Church, Morse Residence, Lothrop-Seville House, Cobb's Tavern, Deborah Sampson Gannett Home, Mann's Cotton Mill, Rock Ridge Cemetery, the Job Swift House, Lake Massapoag, the Holmes Homestead, Site of Billings Tavern and grave of Ebenezer Billings, and site of Old Post Road.

"Wheel Around the Hub" Bicycle Tour on Tuesday, Oct. 12, 1965 was followed by the Sharon Bicentennial Dinner at St. Francis Retreat Lodge on the shores of Lake Massapoag (now the Sharon Community Center). Selectmen, former selectmen, town moderator, the official town Bicentennial Committee, the Bicycle Trek Chairman were introduced and a presentation of Historic Family Certificates made to descendants of the town's early settlers. Entertainment and dancing followed the excellent dinner and concluded what everyone declared a happy conclusion to Sharon's birthday party.

A commemorative booklet described Sharon's development and progress over the two hundred years was compiled and sold along with commemorative coins, seals, banners, and spirit of 1765 bonnets and tricorns.

The police department, department of public works, the civil defense department, R. W. Jones Electrical Co., Clifford Jerauld, and Paul Ares donated their services, and the following people were responsible for the outstanding success of the events and projects of the Town of Sharon Bicentennial, 1965:

Central Committee
Walter L. Reeve, *Chairman*

Sydney Morgan, *Co-Chairman*
Mrs. Arnold P. Clough, *Secretary*

Mrs. Donald W. Brookfield, *Treasurer*
Mrs. Charles H. Newcombe, Jr.,
Public Relations

Friends of the Sharon Bicentennial Committee
Dr. Arnold Barton, *Chairman*

Mrs. Marilyn Goldberg, *Treasurer*
Rev. James G. Pirie
Rev. Donald Wassman

Mrs. Dolly Rabinovitz,
Souvenir Sales Chairman
Mrs. Mary McMahon,
Assist. Souvenir Sales Chairman

Parade Committee
Vincent Mirabile, *Chairman*

Mrs. Lillian A. Clough, *Secretary*
Mrs. Vincent Mirabile, *Tel. Secretary*
Eugene Brady, *Parade Marshal*
Charles Amorosino, *Master of Ceremonies*
Chief Walter B. Roach, *Fire Trucks Div.*

William Statham, *Antique Autos Div.*
Tammy Blood, *Equestrian Div.*
Richard Wright, *Communications*
Bernard Rosenberg, *Communications*
Walter O'Neill, *First Aid Stations*

Parade Line-up
H. Murray Armstrong, *Chairman*

Nancy Taylor, *Clerk*
Donald Atkinson
Herbert Shosteck
Bernard Delman
John Howe

Town Criers

Sherman Palan
Richard Bushlow

Publicity Committee
Mrs. Charles H. Newcombe, Jr., *Chairman*

Paul Ares, *Merchants Coordinator
and Sound Engineer*
Harold Levitan, *Photographer*

Mrs. John Colenari, *Secretary*
Walter O'Neill

Wheel-Around-The-Hub Committee
George Bailey, *Chairman*
Lucy Bailey, *Secretary*   Mrs. Sherwood Steere
Vera Cross, *Art Work*   Davis Hamer
Bernard Delman

Banquet Committee
Vincent Mirabile, *Chairman*
Marilyn Goldberg, *Tickets*   Mrs. Emily Parcher, *Centerpieces*
Dr. Arnold Barton, *Tickets*

Pageant Committee
Mrs. Babbie Brittain Erkelens, *Author*

Historical Tour & Exhibitions Committee
Sydney Morgan, *General Chairman*

Historical Family Committee
Frank K. Cross, *Chairman*   Mary Nelson
Otis Tolman   John Forrest

Historical Site Committee
Richard Chase, *Chairman*
Theodore Waldron   Ruth Wilson
Gardner Derry   Katharine Cartwright
Mary Nelson   Donald Webber, *Art Work*

Historic Site Guides Committee
Barbara Burns   Robert Carlson

Historic Costumes Committee
Mrs. Robert Wood
Mrs. Robert Schofield

Historic Exhibits Committee
Mrs. Helen Harriman   Rev. Donald Wassman
Walter Roach   Rev. Daniel Tuttle
Rev. James Pirie   Mr. and Mrs. Chandler Jones

Commemorative Booklet
Stanley Dingman, *Chairman*
Donald Webber, *Art Work*

Advertising Committee
H. Murray Armstrong, *Chairman*
Frank Lucas, *Art Work*

The enthusiastic participation of so many dedicated Sharon towns-people demonstrates the pride residents of this town feel for their beautiful and historical community.

Landowners to Accompany Sharon Map of 1794-95

1. John Savels
2. Obed Johnson
3. Mathew Harlow
4. Sylvanus Clark
5. Joshua Whittemore
6. Benjamin Hewins
7. David Hewins
8. Nath. Bradshaw
9. Enoch Hewins
10. Ebenezer Fuller
11. North Branch Schoolhouse
12. William Withington
13. Ezra Gould
14. David Lawrence
15. Thomas Coney
16. Rev. Philip Curtis
17. Joseph Hewins
18. John Savels
19. Johnson's Brook
16a. Schoolhouse
20. Oliver Curtis
21. Capt. Savels
22. Dr. Elijah Hewins
23. Samuel Esta
24. Road to Sharon by Widow Holmes
25. Col. Gridley's
26. Gridley's Mill
27. Road by Mr. Cummins'
28. Stones on the great hill
29. Stones on the knoll
30. Cummins' land
31. Stephen Wentworth
32. Isaac Johnson
33. Benjamin Johnson
34. Javan Morse
35. Dr. Samuel Capen
36. Ezekiel Capen
37. Joseph Morse
37a. Capt. Lemuel Capen
37b. Gilead Morse
38. South Branch Schoolhouse
39. William Tolman
40. Solomon Gay
41. Solomon Gay, Jr.
42. Widow Sarah White
43. Nathan Drake
44. Abiel Drake
45. David Drake
46. Joseph Drake
47. Spencer Drake's Store
48. Job Swift
49. Joseph White
50. Capt. Edward Tisdale
51. Solomon Willis
52. Double Oak
53. Joseph Randall
54. Nathaniel Gould
55. Benjamin Raynolds
55a. Benjamin Randall's Tavern
56. James Billing
57. Capt. Elijah Billing
58. Royal Kollock
59. Josiah Talbot
59a. Jona. Sholly's Shop
60. John Smith
61. Billing's Branch Schoolhouse
62. Jonathan Billing, Jr. house and shop
63. Jonathan Billing
64. Elijah Fisher
64a. William Holmes
65. Shop
66. Ebenezer Holmes
67. Elijah Baker
68. William Savage
69. John Drake
70. John Drake, Jr.
71. Seth Allen
72. Archippus Drake
73. Joseph Jordan
74. Smith
75. Zebulon Holmes
76. Benjamin Holmes
77. Aaron Fisher
78. Jacob Fisher
79. Col. Ezra Morse
80. Benjamin Fairbanks, Jr.
81. Jeremiah Fairbanks
82. "Dea." Benj. Fairbanks
83. T. Holmes
84. David White
85. Benjamin Hodges
86. Benjamin Hodges, Jr.
87. John G. Ruepeke
88. Sawmill bridge
88a. John Hewins
88b. Deacon Jacob Hewins
89. Joshua Johnson
90. Joseph Gannett
91. Benjamin Gannett, Jr.
92. Samuel Lovett
93. East Branch Schoolhouse
94. Simeon Rhoades
95. Daniel Rhoades
96. Simon Gould
97. Levi Morse
98. Elijah Morse
99. Isaac Felch
100. Parker Billings
101. Jeremiah Rhoads

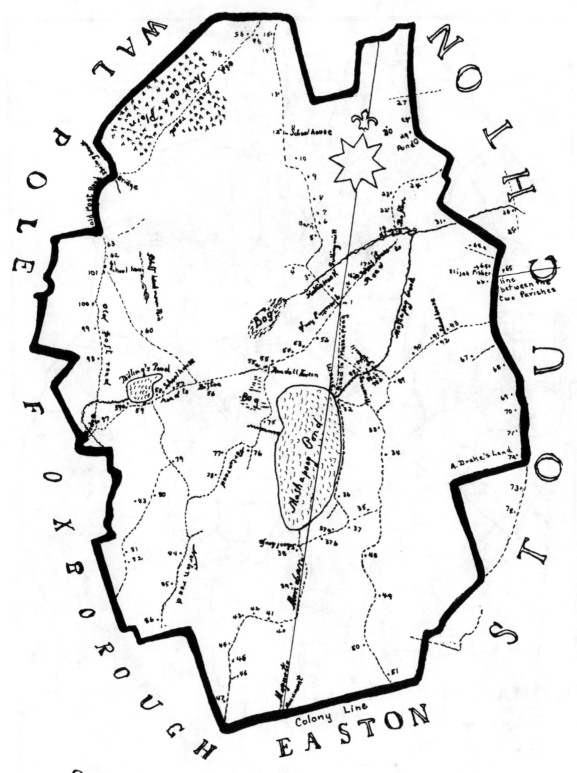

WALPOLE

STOUGHTON

FOXBOROUGH

EASTON

Colony Line

School House

Pond

line
between the
two Parishes

Elijah Fisher

Bog

Billing's Pond

Bog

Massapoag Pond

A. Drake's Land

Randall Eaton

Plan of the Town of Sharon according to an actual survey made in the year
1794 & 1795 and laid down by a scale of fifty chains to an inch or two hundred rods to an inch
pursuant to an order of Court dated June 18, 1794

341

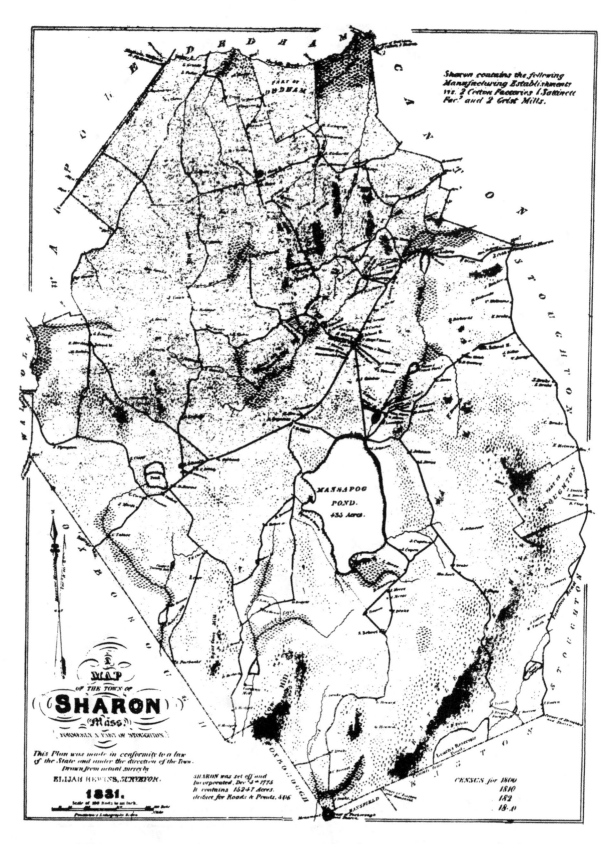

Sharon contains the following
Manufacturing Establishments
viz. 2 Cotton Factories 1 Sattinett
Fac.y and 2 Grist Mills.

MASSAPOG
POND.
435 Acres.

MAP
OF THE TOWN OF
SHARON
(Mass.)
FORMERLY A PART OF STOUGHTON.

This Plan was made in conformity to a law
of the State and under the direction of the Town.
Drawn from actual survey by
ELIJAH HEWINS, SURVEYOR.
1831.
Scale of 100 Rods to an Inch.
Pendleton's Lithographic Scale.

SHARON was set off and
Incorporated, Dec.r 4th 1775.
It contains 15247 Acres.
deduct for Roads & Ponds, 406.

CENSUS for 1800
1810
1820
18.0

342

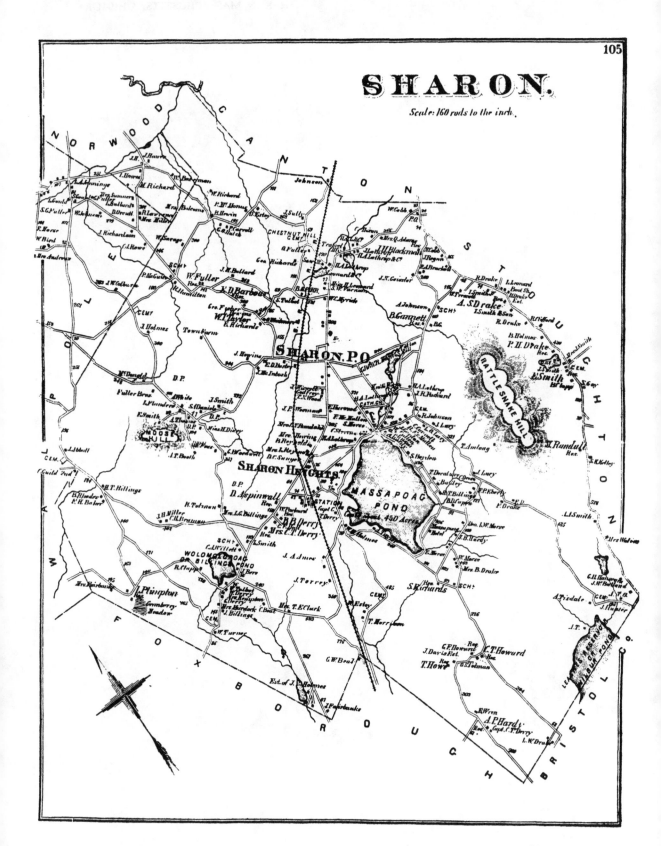

SHARON.

Scale: 160 rods to the inch.

INDEX

Hobbs, Matthew, 9, 118
Hobbs family, 40
Hodsdon, Mrs. Edith S., 207
Hoffman, Philip, 217, 218
Holland family, 256
Holmes, Anna, 86
Holmes, Arnold, 101
Holmes, Donald, 101
Holmes, Merilyn, 101
Holmes, Merrill, 101
Holmes, Warren M., 55
Holmes family, 42
Horn, M. Eloise, 256
Hosmer, Richard, 301 - 306
House family, 42
Howard, C. T., 205
Howe, Wilfred, 281 - 289
Hubbard, Dr. John P., 173
Hughes, Anna L., 218
Hughes, Cindy, 100
Hughes, Gordon, 100
Huntley, Bill, 135
Hurley, Mrs. P. J. 256
Hurley family, 256
Hurricanes, 330
Husselbee, Shirley, 193 - 196

Ide, Charles, 125
Indians: Chiefs, 1, 2, 3, 4, 6, 7, 9, 16;
    tribes 1, 2, 3, 4, 5, 8, 9; evidences in
    Sharon, 8; graves 8, 44; hospitality 7;
    land deeds, 2, 4, 7, 8, 83; language
    (Algonquin) 1, 8, 9; ownership 113;
    physical appearance, 7 - 8; political
    organization, 4; population, 3, 9;
    religion, 5, 6, 7; residences, 3
Industry, 130, 327; industries 109 - 132,
    327; modern Industrial Park, 130
Iseman, Mrs. Patricia, 208

Jacobs, Dr. Philip, 174
Jacobson, Morris, 270
Jamieson, Gwynne, 235
Jerauld, Al, 159
Jerauld, Clifford L., 61 - 62, 135 - 137,
    157 - 162, illus. C. Jerauld's first de-
    livery truck, 156
Johnson, Addison, 127, 222, 224
Johnson, Benjamin, vii, 118
Johnson, Edith (Leonard), 84
Johnson, Isaac, 111, 118, 186
Johnson, Josiah, 119
Johnson, Obed, 186
Johnson, Otis, 55
Johnson, Samuel, 248
Johnson family, 40, 43, 179
Jones, Ebenezer, 57
Jones, Chandler, W., i, 183 - 187
Jones, Frederick, 100

Kahn, Marilyn Z., 227 - 229, 231 - 232,
    235 - 236
Kaler, Taida, 227
Kalis, Robert I., 311
Kanter, Rabbi Shamai, 269 - 270
Kaplan, Mr. and Mrs. I. M., 273

Katz, Norman, 99, port. 290
Keating, William B., i
Keeling, John L., i
Kellogg, A. Clinton, 140
Kempton, Mrs. George, 38, 179
Kendall, Henry Plympton, 173, 213, 322
Kendall Trust, 315
Kendall Whaling Museum, 173, 213 -
    215, illus. 215, illus. figurehead from
    the whaler Pocahontas, 212
Kerstein, Paul, 270
Kidd, Joan, 227
Kiddie Camp, 58, 304
Kier, Sid, 233
Kilkus, John, 100
King, Herb, 160
King, J. G., 147
King Philip's Rock, 9, illus. xiv
Kingsbury, Archie, 139
Kingsbury family, 42
Kitson, Mrs. Theo Alice Ruggles, 46
Klein, Esther, 217
Klein, Henry, 227
Klickstein, Morris and Lois, 234
The Knife Shop, illus. 133
Knife Works Pond, 111 - 112, 113
Knight, Sarah Kemble, 18 - 19, 181
Kogos, Marilyn, 269 - 270
Kollock, Royall, 31, 65
Kollock family, 42
Kouris Hyman, 270
Krasney, Sol, port. 236
Kravetz, Claire, 233
Krovitsky, Eli, 140

Lavezzo, Egitto T., 325, 330
Lawrence, Beardsley, 232
Lawrence, Helen D., 261 - 262
Leach Pond, 124
League of Women Voters, 287
Leary family, 256
Leavitt, Louise P., i
Lechter, Evelyn, 232
Lehrer, Joel, 273
Leonard, Benjamin, S., 128
Leonard, Emmon , 120
Leonard, George F., 120
Leonard, Nathaniel, 57, 109, 111
Leonard, Nathaniel, Jr., 113
Leonard, Sally, 70, 123
Leonard, Samuel, 293
Leonard family, 42, 43
Levenson, Sol, 228
Leventhal, Hyman, 270
Levine, Arnold, 218
Levy, Robert, i, 233
Lindberg, Arthur A., 295
Library Trust Funds (Sharon Public)
Lightbody, Homer, 135
Littlefield, Allen R., 295
Loring, J. P., 147
Lothrop, Darius, 117
Lothrop, Gilbert, 117
Lothrop, H. A., 84, 125, 205
Lothrop, H. A. and Co., 112, 113,
    117

176, 177

"Sharon Spring," Haskel, 180

Sharon Street Railway, 152

Sharon the Beautiful, Griffith, 53, 54, 58

Sharon town government vi, 281 - 289, 326, 330 - 334; ports. of town clerk Arthur Collins, 270, selectmen; Robert L. Currie, Norman Katz, Colleen Tuck, 290; Fire department 293, 331, 333, ills. 291, 297, Fire department muster, 296; ports. of Chief Walter B. Roach, 292 and of William H., Walter J. and George V. Roach, 296; Police department, 331, 333, illus. 291; poor farm, 31, 286; Public Works department, vi, 144; old Town Hall (Town House) 179, 180, illus. 289; illus. Sharon Town offices, 280

She Was There, Appel, ii, 87, 235

Sheehan, Bo, 159

Sheehan, Phyllis, 228, 265 - 266

Sheldon, Robert T., 140

Shepard, Ann, 226

Shepard, Bo and Joan, 235

Shepard, L. H., 294

Shoemaker Valley, 127; "Shoemaker Valley," Phillips, 180

Shulman, Nat, 233

Shurtlieff, 44, 77, 80

Simpson, Mrs. Edwin A., 226

Simpson, Isabelle, 227

Smith, Carl L., i, 150

Smith, Charles F., 121

Smith, Captain Israel, 95

Smith, Pat, 235

Smith family, 42

Snow family, 55

"Sources of Sharon History", Phillips, John G., 180

South Station (Boston), 149

Spaulding, George, 152

Sports and recreation: baseball, 303, 305, 309, American Legion league, 302; Babe Ruth league, 302; Boston Olympics, 301; Little League, 302; Massapoags, 96, 301, Ozones, 301; basketball, 302, Tech tourney, 302; fishing, 58 - 59; football, 303, 305, Pop Warner teams, 303, Pony league, 303; hockey, 303; iceboating, 59; sailing, 59, illus. sailing on Lake Massapoag, 307 and at Recreation Center 310; skating, 59, 302, tiddly, 302; skiing, 302; soccer, 303; swimming, 303, 307, illus. swimming at Recreation Center, 308; tennis, 304, 309; Massapoag Fish and Game Club, 59; Massapoag Rum and Rifle Club, 304; Massapoag Sportsmen's Club, 304, 311; Massapoag Yacht Club, 59, 304, 306; Sharon Baseball Assoc., 301; Sharon Country Club, 304; Sharon Fish and Game Club, 59, 304, 305; Sharon Road Runners' Club, ii; Sharon Tennis Club, 304, 306,

illus. 307; Recreation Department, 309 - 310, 332, illus. Recreation Center 308.

Stage coaches, 23, 24, 30, 145

Stanton, Edward M., 95

Stern, Eva, 270

Stern, Harry, 270

Steensen, Mrs. Marion, 208

Stockwell, E. S., 244

Stolar, Philip, i

Stone, Henry, 148

Stoughton, Mass., vii, x, 1, 7, 9, 22, 23, 77, 79, 81, 86, 124

Stoughton Branch Railroad Co., 145

Stoughton Trust Co., 140

Stoughtonham, District of, viii, ix, xii, 9, 22, 23, 29, 56, 63, 123, 219

Stoughtonham, Town, 9, 219, 293

Stoughtonham Institute, 46, 191, 193, illus. 203; port. of its founder, Sanford Waters Billings, 203

Stratton, Robert, 158

Streets, numbering system, 33

Stuart, Kincaid and Long Bros., 158

Stubbs, Lu, 228, 229 - 231

Sturtevant, Manson, 43

Sucker Brook, 54

Suffolk Co-operative Bank of Boston, 141

Suffolk Resolves, 23, 40

Sullivan, Frances I., 334

Surr, Nikki Erkelens, iii

Sweet, Lou, 140

Swift, Job, 32, 38, 44, 92, 93, illus. of Swift house, 187

Swift family, 43

Talbot, Edmund, H., 47, 123

Talbot, Solomon, 14, 58, 67, 84, 113, 118, 119, 179, 180

Talbot family, 42

Tappan, Eugene, 38, 53, 59, 86, 179, 180; port. 178

Tappan, Robert, 14

Taverns, hotels and inns in Sharon, 103 - 105: Billings Tavern, viii, 16 - 22, 28, 103, 122, 181, 282 - 283, 299; Caledonian, 104; Carvin's Hotel, 105; Cobb's Tavern, 23 - 27, 28, 103, 283, illus. 102; Crescent Ridge Farm, 104; Elm Lawn, 104; Glendale, 105, illus. 107; Green Manor, 105; Ingleside, 104; Johnson's Tavern, 103; Samuel Johnson's Tavern, 29; Lake View Hotel, 104; Lawn Crest Inn, 105; illus. 106; Mansion House, 105; Massapoag Hotel, 58; Massapoag Lake House, 104, 320; Noyes Tavern, 23; Pancake Inn, 295; Quaker Inn, 104, 120, 330; Randall's Tavern, 29, 104, 191; Roebuck Tavern, 13, 181; Rosenstein Mansion House, 269, illus. 271; Savage Tavern, 104; Seven Gables Inn, 105; Sharon Inn, 104, illus. 105; Singer's Inn, 105, 295; Stoneholm, 103, illus. 106; Sunset